DON'T BLAME
THE PEOPLE

DON'T BLAME
THE PEOPLE

Robert Cirino

Vintage Books
A Division of
Random House, New York

to my parents

Acknowledgments

Many thanks to my brother Don Cirino who read and helped edit the manuscript, offered encouragement and suggestions, and helped with some of the research that provided information for the tables included in this book. Many thanks also to George Simpson for the many hours he spent editing and making suggestions for the final manuscript. I am grateful to Mrs. Sally Seitter Jones who read the preliminary manuscript and made grammatical corrections and suggestions, and to Joan Edmunds for her comments on the manuscript. Thanks to Eleanor Riley, Sharon Lee and Mrs. Pat Lago for their part in typing the manuscript. The book would have been impossible without the use of the UCLA, El Camino College, Los Angeles Public and Redondo Beach Public Libraries. Thanks also to the many dedicated American journalists who have painstakenly criticized and analyzed the products of American mass media. I have noted their contributions wherever possible either in the text or in the notes. I am very much indebted to what I have learned from the frankness and sincerity of the students at Huntington Park High School and Fulda Jr. High School. Many of the ideas contained in the book were developed while attending courses in anthropology taught by Dr. Edmund Carpenter at San Fernando Valley State College.

Robert Cirino

Contents

Tables

DON'T BLAME
THE PEOPLE

Introduction

A renewal of faith in common human nature, in its potentialities in general, and in its power in particular to respond to reason and truth, is a surer bulwark against totalitarianism than a demonstration of material success or a devout worship of special legal and political forms.

John Dewey*

As a high school and junior high school teacher I have come to have ever-increasing confidence in the reasoning ability, the sense of justice and the humanitarian concern of the vast majority of Americans. This has caused me to disagree emphatically with those communication spokesmen, politicians, intellectuals and educators who display contempt for the ability of the common people to make intelligent decisions on issues confronting our nation. These are the leaders who consider it their patriotic duty to make secret decisions or to guard the public from being exposed to "alarming" information or "dangerous" views—views that may attack or embarrass those maintaining the status quo.

In a classroom situation, where I was able to take pains to provide a forum for conflicting viewpoints, I found that most students came to support what I took to be sensible, practical, just and humanitarian views. Whether superior, average or below average in classroom performance, most students want to eliminate poverty. They are appalled that many of the rich can avoid paying their fair share of taxes. They feel that racial injustice is an evil and that everything possible should be undertaken to eliminate it. They think that population control and pollution control should have a much greater priority than they have. Many feel that sending a man to the moon for political reasons isn't worth the enormous cost required, that United States intervention in Vietnam is wrong, and that present-day tax laws are unfair.

Assume that Americans in general, like my students, would make

* sources for chapter quotes are listed in the back of the book following notes for Chapter 22

what I take to be sensible decisions if they were exposed to many views, with each view having an equal opportunity to be heard. Why then do Americans seem to support a status quo which has sponsored or condoned racism, launched the intervention in Vietnam, ignored starving people here in America, fashioned an unjust draft and tax, and done little about pollution and birth control? Distorted views and priorities have been accepted because of the difficulty—on the part of the citizenry at large—of recognizing propaganda techniques used by the establishment to preserve the status quo.

My students, I found, had a hard time spotting these techniques as they existed and exist in the mass media until they were pointed out to them. And, I find, this is not a shortcoming peculiar to students. History affords many examples of high-echelon scientists and scholars who have been persuaded by propaganda to accept racism, unequal opportunity and exploitation.

Techniques of persuasion are successful when those who oppose establishment policies do not have access to the media. Such techniques can be offset only when opposing views have an equal opportunity for media use. Could America have ignored the hungry if the poor had had their own ABC, NBC or CBS? Could Americans have ignored racism if the blacks had had at their disposal communication technology and techniques equal to those of the Establishment? Did the white newspaper, newsmagazine, radio or television audience receive the black man's viewpoint in an arena where all ideas had an equal chance to be presented?

The establishment has prevented real public participation by not allowing all ideas to compete fairly for public acceptance. They have allowed free speech, but rendered it worthless by not allowing anti-establishment voices to have *equal* access to the technology of persuasion. The right to speak is of little value if no one is listening. A person speaking to eighty million people has quite an advantage over someone with a conflicting view talking to a thousand people in an auditorium or ten people on a street corner. The idea that gets amplification and extension through the media—not necessarily the most reasonable idea—is the one which wins the endorsement of the people.

Those who are in positions controlling access to media can take advantage of this fact to gain public support for ideas and policies which would not be accepted by the majority of people if they had to compete fairly in the open market place of ideas. Supreme Court Justice Hugo Black stated the importance of having ideas compete fairly when he stated in 1945 that the right of free speech "rests on the assumption that the widest possible dissemination of information from diverse and antagonistic sources is essential to the welfare of the public."[1] Indeed, the right of the people to hear competing ideas fairly presented is more vital to protecting America than any strong military could be. For what decides where and why our great military force will be used is the information given us by our communication system. To mistakenly commit our military power could mean disaster for the United States.

I think the military intervention in Vietnam is just such a misuse of our military resources, our manpower and our national wealth. Almost all politicians and scholars—doves and hawks—now think that our involvement in Vietnam was a mistake. Polls show that more than half of all Americans agree. In this case our communication system failed to alert us in time to avoid this mistake.

Had those opposing our involvement had an equal use of communications technology, United States involvement could not have been initiated or carried out in the first place; it would have been revealed as unwise and unjust. But the millions of American adults who opposed the war on principle and who advocated an immediate and orderly withdrawal of all U.S. troops owned no television stations, daily newspapers or mass-circulation magazines.

Some may claim that the price of affording all viewpoints equal access to mass media would be so expensive as to be impossible. But should price determine or be allowed to determine the picture we get of what's happening in the world any more than a profit system should determine who gets justice or what kind of strategic defense system best protects the country? Information is the basis upon which decisions of life and death are made for nations as well as for people. Our communication system is to our country what the radar is to a jet plane landing in a dense fog. Would anyone suggest the airline economize on its radar? What is the price of a better radar compared to the cost of the plane crashing because its faulty radar communicated the wrong information? And what is the cost of a few billion dollars—to give the American people a more complete picture of the world—compared to the $30 billion yearly cost of the mistaken war in Vietnam or the $19 billion extra needed for politically motivated manned spectaculars to the moon (compared to unmanned exploration)?[2] Like a plane poorly guided, our nation has been off course because the picture of the world presented by our communication system has pre-vented the ordinary citizen from being exposed to messages that for many years have told us that the war is a mistake, that sending a man to the moon is not an intelligent space program, that starvation in America exists, and that racism is wrong and that it will exact a terri-ble price some day.

This country will assuredly be off course in the future as long as the most vital element of our society— the communication system—is for sale and is primarily in the hands of those with special interests to promote. America can no longer survive if it continues to allow media owners to communicate to its citizens a distorted and limited view of what's happening in the world.

Besides producing a distorted view of the world, the shackling of dissent produces other undesirable consequences. The lack of real competition in ideas prevents people from actively considering all available viewpoints. The result is a lack of intellectual participation and boredom, the same type of boredom that students feel in the classroom when they are not given the chance to speak and decide for themselves. Textbooks and lectures bore them because, like the mes-sages in mass media, they are one sided attempts to sell a point of view. They do not allow the student the chance to present his view-point and to decide for himself which among many ideas is the best. At best he may be given a choice of deciding between or presenting two or three establishment ideas, but students seem to spot that for what it is—a sham battle—and look outside the realm of politics for real participation, excitement and decision making.

The shackling of anti-establishment ideas by the mass media leaves only one avenue in which to capture a public hearing—the path of violence or demonstration. Would the blacks in Watts have had to burn the ghetto to bring attention to their plight if they had been the publishers of the *Los Angeles Times* or had control of NBC radio and television? Would there be so many anti-war demonstrations if there were mass media owners who allowed anti-war journalists to use the techniques of persuasion to urge an immediate and orderly with-drawal of all troops from Vietnam? One reason that pro-administra-tion demonstrations have been so poorly attended is because the entire commercial communication system, by using their bias to support or condone the basic United States presence in Vietnam has already done the demonstrating for the supporters. The "silent majority" is silent because they have no need to demonstrate to make their voice heard.

From the beginning of the American involvement in Vietnam the establishment media have been doing the cheerleading for them. An open and fair market place of ideas in the mass media would eliminate the need for most demonstrations, many of which end in violence. Twenty-three years ago, the Commission for a Free and Responsible Press tried to tell the media representatives this:

> Freedom of expression can never be made a costless immunity by shackling hostile response, for response is also expression. Free expression is destined not to repress social conflict but to liberate it. But its intention is that the level of social conflict shall be lifted from the plane of violence to the plane of discussion.[3]

Since this expert advice the mass media have continued to suppress expressions of hostile social conflict. It is now evident that only a non commercial communication system that allows all viewpoints equal control of access to mass media can decrease the level of violence and produce an open market place of ideas that will allow the average citizen to use his reason and sense of justice to make the intelligent choices the present communication system has prevented him from making in the past.

1   The Story of Hunger: Anyone Interested?

> The modern press itself is a new phenomenon. Its typical unit is the great agency of mass communication. These agencies can facilitate thought and discussion. They can stifle it. They can advance the progress of civilization or they can thwart it. They can endanger the peace of the world; they can do so accidentally, in a fit of absence of mind. They can play up or down the news and its significance, foster and feed emotions, create complacent fictions and blind spots, misuse the great words, and uphold empty slogans. Their scope and power are increasing every day as new instruments become available to them. These instruments can spread lies faster and farther than our forefathers dreamed when they enshrined the freedom of the press in the First Amendment to our Constitution.
>
> The Commission on Freedom of the Press, 1947

In May, 1968, CBS News presented the hard-hitting documentary "Hunger in America." This was CBS News at its best. Although a few reports and articles about hunger in America had been appearing in the press since early 1967, this program brought home to every American the fact that millions of their fellow countrymen were suffering from hunger and malnutrition. The program made hunger a national issue overnight. Politicians who for years had been able to hide their criminal neglect or outright opposition to feeding the starving stood exposed by CBS. Embarrassed, the Department of Agriculture immediately expanded its food program to forty-two more counties, increased the monthly surplus of food going to the poor, and called for expansion of the food stamp program.[1] CBS earned well deserved praise from almost every quarter and received an Emmy award for outstanding news documentary program achievement.[2] However, all this deserved credit and praise could not erase the fact that for thirty years CBS and the rest of mass media have censored or played down starvation in America.

Back in 1938, *Fortune* magazine sent a press release of its quarterly survey of public opinion to six New York City dailies. The survey showed 54 percent of the people backed Roosevelt as against 34 percent who disapproved of him. Accompanying the survey was a *Fortune* editorial also for release. It stated: "It is neither possible nor desirable for a democratic government to sit by while a third of its citizens starve and almost as many fear for its jobs."[3] The editorial went on to criticize the social conscience of business. The *New York Post,* which featured the survey and editorial on Page One, revealed that four out of the six dailies, including the *New York Times,* completely ignored this significant press release about starvation.[4]

Senator La Follette speaking on the floor of the Senate in 1941 said:

> Forty-five million people . . . are reported to be below the safety line in diet. A good many of them are actually hungry. All of them are failing to obtain the food elements which are necessary to prevent chronic fatigue, digestive disorders, and lowered resistance to disease. . . . Twenty million families must live on not more than 8 or 9¢ per person per meal. About 14% of all American families must live on an average of 5 cents per person per meal.[5]

Not a word of this appeared the next day in the *New York Times.*

In 1948 the Federal Security Agency released a report that stated: "Thousands of dependent children are undernourished to an extent bordering on starvation. Many lack shoes and clothing needed to enable them to attend school."[6] The *New York Times* apparently felt this was not newsworthy, for not a word of it was printed.

The sort of hunger article that the establishment media did allow is exemplified in a February 9, 1950 Associated Press story which no doubt left its readers with the impression that if there were any hungry people in the United States, they were being fed by a responsive government. The headline on Page One of the *Times* proclaimed:

HUGE STOCKS OF SURPLUS EGGS, MILK OFFERED TO NEEDY BY GOVERNMENT

The article made no mention of hunger or starvation. The government, the article reported, was solving the problem of having too much food.

The *New York Times* did cover a 1950 story on starvation. On Page 7 it reported that President H.L. Mitchell of the National Farm Labor Union "complained to President Truman today that thousands of farm children were starving in the Southwestern and Southern states." Mitchell "told of 100 children found starving at a migratory workers' camp near Phoenix, Arizona and said it wasn't an isolated case. He claimed 100,000 or more children could be found the victims of similar conditions."[7] The then Representative Richard Nixon was one of a group of Congressmen who investigated a similar charge made in a film shown to the House Labor Committee a year earlier. Nixon, denying Mitchell's claims, said the film misrepresented conditions at the Di Giorgio farms. Mitchell said the film was meant to depict corporate farming in general, not specifically Di Giorgio farms. Nevertheless, it appears Nixon and his colleagues had no enthusiasm for investigating further. But in this case the *New York Times* did. It published a series about California migrants by Gladwin Hill. If others had chosen to investigate they would have found evidence to back up the Union president's claims. Hill said the "recent episode of the hundred starving migrant children in Arizona was only a tiny symptom of a widespread regional condition of which this valley is a focal point."[8] He revealed in a Page One story:

> In Tulare County last November the deaths of eleven children in such surroundings were officially ascribed to malnutrition. One-hundred and fifteen deaths of infants under one year old in the county last year were flatly attributed by Dr. R. Lepen Knight, county health officer, to inadequate housing, sanitation and clothing.[9]

The only shortcoming in Hill's reports was the optimistic ending which depicted local officials as having the intention of doing something about the situation.[10] This type of conclusion helped continue the apathy that has characterized America's concern with its starving.

Despite these gruesome facts, starvation in America didn't interest the media. Few Americans were aware of such facts when the news again emerged from beneath the covers of the press. Near the end of a 1956 article headlined

KEFAUVER AND BENSON
CLASH ON FOOD PROGRAM,

a significant paragraph appeared. Senator Kefauver claimed that an unpublished report "showed that one of ten families in the nation, or a 'conservative' estimate of 15,000,000 persons was inadequately fed according to officially accepted standards." Kefauver charged that the Eisenhower administration was suppressing a report that indicated a food stamp plan would solve the problem of farm surpluses. Secretary of Agriculture Benson accused Kefauver of breaking normal procedure by disclosing parts of the report.[11]

It seems the press didn't bother to investigate Kefauver's charge. And hunger in America would probably have been completely ignored by the press if Senator John Kennedy campaigning in 1960 had not made a speech in which he said:

> The facts are that 17,000,000 Americans go to bed hungry every night. Fifteen million families live in substandard housing. Seven million families are struggling to survive on an income of less than $2000 a year.[12]

A truly sensational claim, this was worth putting on the front page and investigating. But that wasn't done. The *New York Times* placed it in the middle of Page 16 with a small headline, and Richard Nixon was later to say as he had to a similar claim ten years earlier—that it wasn't true. The press seemed glad to let the issue die; no investigations were initiated, no TV documentaries produced.

Kennedy's claim again became an issue in September when Richard Nixon demanded a retraction, thereby causing Kennedy to qualify his claim by substituting "undernourished" for hungry. However the three network television newscasts did not mention anything about this conflict.[13] Of the three network radio newscasts checked by the author—Peter Hackes on NBC, Lowell Thomas on CBS and Edward P. Morgan on ABC—only the latter mentioned it.[14]

One of the first things President Kennedy did when he entered office was expand the food stamp program. This apparently led the press and therefore the public to think that the problem was essentially solved. It wasn't. Millions in America were still hungry, many starving. The nation was still assimilating in its educational system the mentally and physically retarded children from past years of hunger. This could be discovered not by reading any front page headlines but by reading the text of a 1964 AP dispatch printed on Page 25 of the *New York Times*. Headlined

POOR DIETS HELD PERIL TO SOCIETY,

the article reported a news conference which summed up the conclusion of an international conference on the prevention of malnutrition in pre-school children. An American scientist said that: "Severe malnutrition among children in underdeveloped countries threatened to lead to a society crippled in body and mind in those countries by 1984." Dr. Paul Gyorgy said: "Even minor malnutrition can bring on certain physical defects (and possibly) retardation of mental development." At this same news conference another scientist "said the situation and prospect were not greatly different as regards children in slum and sub standard socio-economic areas of the United States. . . . "[15] A truly sensational claim predicting that America may be producing millions of mentally and physically retarded people because children are not getting enough to eat. Such a claim from so responsible a source was certainly very newsworthy, but somehow the media was able to keep the cover on the hunger story for another three years.

A story in the back pages of the *New York Times* in 1965 revealed an alarming and ominous situation, one begging for media exposure. An article reporting the Southern Christian Leadership Conference (SCLC) attack on the Department of Agriculture and local officials for holding up food distribution, set forth this fact: "57% of the South's 1,107 counties and parishes do not participate in either of the U.S. Department of Agriculture's two distribution programs for low income families."[16] To anyone even slightly familiar with poverty in the South, that fact meant hunger and starvation in the majority of counties.

In April of 1967 the word "starvation" made it into a headline on Page 28 of the *New York Times:*

SLOW STARVATION SEEN IN MISSISSIPPI[17]

A few days later the words *hunger* and *malnutrition* made their way into a subhead in an article detailing the complaints of nine senators concerning the lack of congressional action in making funds available to feed the hungry. The senators reported they "heard testimony and observed, first hand, conditions of malnutrition and widespread hunger in delta counties of Mississippi that can only be described as shocking, and which we believe constitute an emergency." They also warned that "the emergencies in Mississippi should not blind us to the emergencies elsewhere in America. . . . "[18] The *New York Times* found room for this article on Page 51 while the same day on Page One they featured a sports item and two articles that were closer to public relations releases than news releases. One article, with the headline

NON-RED NATIONS IN ASIA TAKE HOPE,

applauded U.S. foreign policy. The other told of how Ford and Mobil were seeking a fume-free car. Also on Page One was a photograph of a veteran's parade.

Urgent and continuing problems deserve to make the front page and to be reported in newscasts at repeated intervals lest the public forget about them and assume the problems are solved, thus enabling politicians to continue doing nothing. The *New York Times* during February and March 1950, and April and May 1960, had no articles about hunger in America on the front page. During June and July 1969 one such article appeared. The *Los Angeles Times* during the same six months had no articles on hunger in America on the front page. The *Honolulu Star-Bulletin* had no items on hunger in America on its front page from January 12 to May 31, 1969. The following Table demonstrates that besides space, other topics, some of them totally insignificant, have a far higher news priority than hunger in America. [see TABLE I]

The broadcasting industry performed no better. During a six-week period in 1960 none of the three evening network television newscasts mentioned hunger in America even once.[19] Of the three fifteen-minute network radio newscasts studied, E. P. Morgan had 2 items, Peter Hackes and Lowell Thomas had none.

From July 10 to September 10, 1969, *Huntley-Brinkley* newscast failed to mention hunger once. *Walter Cronkite* newscast had a few items on hunger included in its coverage of space. In contrast to this neglect, both newscasts together had 82 items using 18:57 minutes on the stock market, 36 items using 71:07 minutes on trivia, 22 items using 54:54 minutes on sports, and 134 items using 269:34 minutes on space.[20]

Mutual and ABC news-on-the-hour newscasts from August 22 to October 22, 1969 (weekdays) had no items about hunger in America. Taken together they had 20 items using 2:16 minutes on the stock market, 11 items using 2:46 on trivia, 64 items using 21:44 minutes on the Arab-Israeli conflict, and 24 items using 4:34 on space.

The news media's habit of not giving priority coverage to hunger in America as an urgent and continuing emergency of crisis proportion may account for the fact that thirty years after widespread starvation

TABLE I

FREQUENCY OF NEWS ITEMS ABOUT HUNGER IN AMERICA:
FEBRUARY AND MARCH 1950, APRIL AND MAY 1960, JUNE AND JULY 1969

Newspaper	Hunger in America		The Entertainment World		Other Trivia	
	items p.1	photos pp.1,2,3	items p.1	photos pp.1,2,3	items p.1	photos pp.1,2,3
Los Angeles Times	0	0	33	10	73	13
New York Times	1	0	10	0	19	7
Honolulu Star-Bulletin (January 12 to May 31, 1969 only)	0	0	Included In Trivia		91	26

	Religious Events		Crime		Accidents		Space	
	items p.1	photos pp.1,2,3	items p.1	photos pp.1,2,3	items p.1	photos pp.1,2,3	items p.1	photos pp.1,2,3
Los Angeles Times	25	2	37	7	283	46	75	24
New York Times	35	5	41	0	44	19	65	38
Honolulu Star-Bulletin	42	33	29	0	N.A.	—	49	41

*Stories of national significance only, other categories include stories of both local and national distribution or interest was revealed, and three years after nine senators claimed it was an emergency condition, and one year after taking office, President Nixon still hadn't declared an emergency in order to immediately try to put an end to what he himself finally admitted to be a "deplorable and embarassing" problem. It may explain why politicians can still look respectable when they allocated $1.5 billion to feed the hungry when all agreed in 1969 that at least an annual 3 to 4 billion dollars was needed to feed the 12 to 15 million Americans who go hungry in a country whose government easily finds in its coffers the billions supposedly needed for building supersonic planes, subsidizing farmers not to grow food, and building new weapons for the arms race.

2 Auto Safety: A Deadly, Crippling, Disfiguring Silence

> There is an instrument of devastating effectiveness
> which we have only superficially, often hypocritically,
> employed. It is called the power of the press.
>
> Let's face it. We in the trade use this power more fre-
> quently to fix a traffic ticket or get a ticket to a ball
> game than to keep the doors of an open society open
> and swinging, by encouraging honest controversy, or, if
> you'll pardon the term, crusading for truth and justice.
>
> Edward P. Morgan, ABC News

Hunger was allowed to exist because the media, through deliberate neglect and apathy, kept it from being a national issue of prime importance until 1968. Hunger in America isn't the only deplorable situation the media have allowed to go on almost unnoticed for years. Ralph Nader, in his book *Unsafe At Any Speed,* claimed that the auto industry,

> by dominating the channels of communications through which the
> customer receives his information about automobiles, has obscured
> the relation of vehicle design to life and limb and has kept quiet its
> technical capability of building crash-worthy vehicles.

Noting that pressure can be applied by advertising money and other subtle forms of pressure, Nader continued: "It is more than coinciden-tal that radio, television, newspapers and magazines have so long ig-nored the role of vehicle design in producing . . . collisions."[1] Ironically, as if to prove Nader correct, not even one out of over 700 newspapers accepted the offer to run a serialization of his book.[2]

An analysis of how the media treated car design as a possible cause of accidents and injuries shows Nader correct in blaming media for failing to inform the people about this issue. This can be seen by noting how America's best news medium, the *New York Times,* han-dled the problem over the years. We can assume, and my research indicates, that the other 99.9 percent of the press did even worse than the *Times*.

Writing in the *American Medical Association Journal* in January 1937, Dr. Clair Straith, plastic surgeon and nationally recognized specialist in the treatment of facial injuries caused by automobile accidents, pointed out that the majority of "severe, crushing, facial injuries" were sustained by young women sitting in the seat next to the driver. With an eye to reducing such injuries and personal tragedies that followed disfiguration, he made a few suggestions to automobile manufacturers:

> . . . projecting objects on the instrument panel (handles, knobs and cranks) add to the hazard. Elimination of such objects from the passenger's side of the instrument panel should be attempted by motor car engineers. The use of 'crash padding' might do much to minimize the seriousness and extent of these injuries.[3]

The Associated Press sent out a short news release on the article. It was printed on Page 2 of the *New York Times*. It reported that Dr. Straith "called facial disfigurement an even more tragic product of auto accidents than sudden death."[4] But the article contained not even a hint that Straith felt that many cases of disfigurement could be prevented by a better designed car. The press didn't bother to pursue the matter and as a result the people heard nothing about it.

Later in 1937, Dr. Straith wrote another article which appeared in the AMA *Journal*. Lamenting injuries caused by machinery, he said: "Man's ingenuity has enabled him to perfect 'Frankenstein's' monster which now turns about to destroy. Mechanical progress has become a double edged sword."[5] He then wrote specifically about automobile injuries he knew about from first hand experience. He said that when the

> guest passenger is thrown violently forward against windshield or instrument panel . . . crushing of the nose, cheek bones and marillae, facial lacerations and rupture of the eyeballs results. The seriousness of many of these injuries could be greatly minimized if projecting handles, knobs, cranks and other features on the instrument panel and doors could be eliminated entirely in construction. It seems possible that many if not most of these projecting features could be recessed or made flush with the body of the car. . . .
>
> For several years I have had crash padding installed in my own cars to cover prominent portions of the instrument panels for the

protection of children and other guest passengers. Designers of automobiles should, I believe, make further efforts to eliminate these
hazards by some such means.[6]

To emphasize his point, Dr. Straith even included a photograph of
the interior of his own car showing the padding that he had installed.

Both the article and the photograph were completely ignored by the
New York Times and the rest of the media.

Ten years later Dr. Fletcher Woodward, who had treated many
disfigurements resulting from auto accidents, declared at the 1948
annual session of the AMA that "automobiles should be redesigned to
stress safety rather than speed and appearance." He recommended
padded dashboards, safety belts, safer windows, and the elimination
of projecting handles and knobs. The *Times* reported this but hid it in
a few paragraphs under a large article on Page 20 headlined

RADAR BEAMS HELD AID IN DIATHERMY[7]

Later in 1948, Dr. Woodward wrote an article in the *American
Medical Association Journal* criticizing automotive engineering. He
noted that 15 percent of all accidents involved defects of a mechanical
nature and that automobiles could be redesigned to prevent many
accidents. Using medical diagnoses of injuries sustained in auto accidents, he described car features which caused the injuries and illustrated in detail the corrections that could be made. He concluded that
there was an "abundance of evidence to render it at present possible
to build motor cars capable of withstanding collisions at high speed
with greatly reduced likelihood of injury to occupants."[8] Not a word
of this potentially controversial article was printed in the *Times*.

There were others who criticized the auto industry. Arthur Stevens,
president of the Automobile Safety Association, spoke out many times
in an effort to inform the people how the auto industry for years had
been disregarding pleas to redesign their cars.[9] He never made priority news in the media. The *Times* did publish one of his letters to the
editor,[10] but every newspaperman knows that the editorial page is the
least read part of a newspaper.

Dr. Horace Campbell, speaking before a meeting of the American
College of Surgeons in 1955, claimed that for about $30 per car man-
ufacturers could install four safety features that would substantially
reduce injuries and deaths. This claim, like those of Dr. Straith and
Woodward, was certainly a priority news item—worthy, one might

think, of waking up the media from its long slumber on the issue. But nothing happened. The speech was entirely ignored by the *Times*. Later the *Times* made a reference to the speech on its editorial page. In this editorial the *Times* came out with a respectable plea that: "safety, not color and power, should be the outstanding feature of the 1956 automobile." But in the editorial were statements that revealed the *Times* as an instrument of the auto industry. Noting safety improvements made by the industry, the *Times* stated: "Certainly American car makers have not been indifferent to the importance of building safety factors into their products." The *Times* suggested no government or legislative action; instead, it suggested leaving the problem in the hands of those who for twenty years had been the least enthusiastic about safety engineering: "It would seem that the auto manufacturer is in the best position to give such protection."[11]

Not all politicians agreed with leaving the people's safety in the hands of such protectors. A few felt the auto manufacturers would never make the needed changes unless forced to by legislative and court actions. A few days after the *Times* editorial, Senator Frank Barrett introduced legislation requiring safety belts on all cars sold for interstate travel. To put some teeth in his law, he provided for a $1000 fine or imprisonment for a year, or both, for any person selling a car not equipped with belts. This was one of the first serious congressional attempts to force the auto industry to take safety engineering seriously. Evidently the *Times* didn't think the proposal worthy of bringing to public attention in any big way. The item was given one inch of space at the bottom of Page 18.[12]

Was legislation really needed or had the auto industry as the *Times* claimed, "not been indifferent to the importance of building safety factors into their product?" The record shows some improvements as having been made, but safety features that could easily have been installed and which would have saved thousands of lives were ignored by the industry. The industry's record on this issue, detailed in the 1966 book *Safety Last,* reveals that Dr. Straith, "as early as 1934 had numerous conferences with the automobile makers, begging them to design and construct the car interior so as to inflict as little injury as possible upon the occupants should crash occur."[13] Dr. Woodward's detailed suggestions of 1948 were also ignored and ridiculed.[14] Two and a half years after Senator Barrett's 1955 attempt to force the industry to adopt seat belts, General Motors, Chrysler, Ford, Studebaker and Packard opposed seat belts as standard equipment.[15] Henry

Wakeland, Nash automobile engineer for five years, put most of the blame on General Motors:

> The automobile companies are tightly organized against the rest of the country. They will not compete in safety. But GM is the real foot dragger. If it were not for GM, the rest of the industry would have moved before this.[16]

The Automobile Manufacturers Association in 1961 opposed a bill that would have required car makers to install safety padding on all motor vehicles, saying the requirement was "impractical and unnecessary."[17] The same year, the head of General Motors ridiculed what he termed were self-styled experts and amateur engineers by describing their safety suggestions as "radical and ill conceived."[18] Despite the manufacturers' record of apathy and opposition to most features, Henry Ford II in opposing safety legislation in 1966 said: "If these critics who don't really know anything about safety of an automobile, will get out of our way, we can go ahead with our job . . . ."[19] The *Times* in a special report found room to *objectively* report Ford's claim at the top of Page One. The industry often explained that they were giving the public what it wanted—that public education was needed first. This was true. But a major reason why the people didn't demand safety features is that the instruments of communication were cooperating with the automobile industry in keeping the problem from becoming the national issue of importance that it deserved to be, and that it later became as the result of Ralph Nader's book. The media kept the people from knowing about unsafe cars just as it had kept them from knowing about hunger in America.

Representative Kenneth Roberts, chairman of the House Subcommittee on Traffic Safety, heard testimony in 1956 from some of the people the head of General Motors had ridiculed as being radical, ill-conceived amateur engineers and self-styled safety experts—the same ones that Henry Ford II claimed didn't know anything about the safety of an automobile. They included spokesmen for the American Public Health Association, the American College of Surgeons, The American Medical Association and several experienced automotive engineers. All emphasized the capability of the automobile industry to make a safer car. These were the same people whose complaints had been ignored or deprecated for years by the media.

It seems reasonable to ask the following: After these critics were finally heard by Congress, why did it take ten more years before Congress passed its first legislation requiring mandatory safety standards? The answer rests with the media's use of bias. Unable to ignore completely the congressional investigation and the increasing clamor of the critics for urgently needed legislation, the press dutifully reported some of what the critics had to say, but in a biased way that did not arouse great public interest or indignation. This is evident in the press treatment which the *Times* gave to a dedicated priest who spent five years building a car he hoped would demonstrate the fact that safer cars could be built. Completing his car in 1957, Father Juliano drove it to New York City in order to put it on display. The car had many mechanical breakdowns on its way. This is the aspect the *Times* jumped on. The story was headlined:

DREAM CAR HERE AFTER 15 MISHAPS, RADICALLY DESIGNED SAFETY AUTO NEEDS 7 TOWS

A photograph of the car appears above the caption:

DREAM CAR IS A NIGHTMARE ON ROAD

The article went on to say that the car taxed the patience of the policemen and, "Ironically, the car, which was designed to emphasize safety features, almost became involved in a number of accidents."[20] The article made no mention whatsoever of the safety features and their purpose, nor did it even hint at why Juliano had bothered to go to all the trouble to demonstrate safety design features in the first place. No statements by Juliano were mentioned or quoted. Readers are left with the impression that Juliano is some kind of a clown with a preposterous idea. Evidently Juliano hadn't considered that whatever he had to communicate to the people about auto safety would have to go through the digestive apparatus of the media.

The American Medical Association made the alarming claim that "10,000 people killed in auto accidents in 1960 would be alive today if they had been wearing seat belts" (based on the conservative estimate that safety belts would have decreased fatalities 25 percent).[21] This made no headlines. It was included in an article in Section III, Page 11, of the *New York Times,* in an article that heralded the Ford Motor Company as a great auto safety crusader. Another similar claim made in 1962 was placed in Section X without a headline to call attention to it. John O. Moore, a pioneer researcher in seat belt safety, stated that seat belts could make the "difference between permanent disability and minor hurts for 200,000 people each year."[22] A 1965 story serves as example of the type of automobile news which the *Times* felt deserved a Page-One display. The two-column headline read:

66 AUTO TO STRESS POWER AND A SPORTS LOOK[23]

In its general tone, this article seems more of an advertisement for the auto industry than a news story. It could well have been written by a public relations firm.

An analysis of the frequency in which the safety engineering issue received priority news treatment also confirms Nader's claim that the communication industry did its best for the auto manufacturers. Neither the *New York Times* nor the *Los Angeles Times* had even one mention of the issue on their front pages in February and March of 1950 or in April and May of 1960. The three network television newscasts, along with the three network radio newscasts mentioned in the previous Chapter, completely ignored the issue for the six-week period preceding the 1960 election.

As we shall see, this record of suppression of news about a life-and-death issue is not an isolated case by any means. Our society is dependent on a communication system dominated by those who have the power and the determination to deny divergent viewpoints an equal chance to be heard. Many are more concerned with money than with saving lives. The result is always the same: The people suffer.

3 Smoking: How to Protect the Advertiser

> I really look with commiseration over the great body
> of my fellow citizens, who, reading newspapers, live
> and die in the belief that they have known something
> of what has been passing in the world in their time.
>
> Thomas Jefferson

Two million Americans quit smoking in 1968 alone, and more than 13 million have quit since 1966.[1] By 1970 32.6 percent of all adult male smokers and 11.8 percent of women smokers had given up the habit.[2] More than 100,000 doctors have stopped smoking.[3] There is little doubt that the decrease in smoking is prompted by the belief that smoking causes lung cancer. A recent Gallup Poll found that 71 percent of Americans shared this belief.[4] Not everyone who believes smoking is a cause of cancer quits smoking, but many do. Unknown millions never begin smoking because of concern for their health; the drop in the percent of college freshmen who smoke is one indication of this. As a result of quitting the habit or never beginning in the first place, millions of Americans will have added years to the most precious gift of all—life. I wonder how many millions of Americans would have quit or never begun smoking in the 1940's and 1950's had they been fully aware that cigarettes could take away eight or more years of their life. Consider, now, the fact that information that would have convinced many to quit smoking was available beginning in 1938, but for years such information was censored or played down by the media—to such an extent that even as late as 1958 only 44 percent of the people thought smoking a cause of lung cancer.[5] Those who would never have begun smoking, or would have quit had they known the health hazards earlier, have cause to blame the media of robbing them of life itself.

The most reliable media, such as the *New York Times,* didn't censor all the information outright. This newspaper merely placed it inconspicuously in the middle or back pages so that it never became the urgent life-and-death matter or the front-page controversy it deserved to be. Outright censorship was often used by the majority of the press and, unfortunately, most Americans got their news from the less reliable media then as they do now. An indication of the extent to which smoking news was censored is seen in the way New York City dailies covered two different stories. An AP story in early 1938 presented the findings of Dr. Raymond Pearl of John Hopkins University. Dr. Pearl presented life tables showing the relationship between smoking and longevity. The tables showed that 66,564 non-smokers survived to sixty years of age compared to 61,911 moderate smokers and 46,726 heavy smokers.[6] He pointed out that: "smoking is associated with a definite impairment of longevity."[7] He noted that the shortening of life was proportional to the amount of tobacco smoked, and that it affects even moderate smokers enough "to be measurable and significant." George Seldes checked the New York dailies and discovered that six out of eight of them censored the story completely.[8] Ten years later the media wasn't performing any better. In 1948 an AP story sent out on the wires said: "The cigarette companies won't like this, but a man who ought to know thinks a lot of citizens are digging their graves with their own lungs." It added that the man, Dr. Alton Ochsner: "takes a dim view of the cheery, four-color cigarette advertisements." Soon after sending this out on its wire, the AP sent out a bulletin eliminating the above comments from the story because they were too "controversial."[9] Nevertheless the trimmed-down story was still available to the nine New York dailies for their use if they thought it newsworthy. They didn't—eight out of nine declined to print it, including the *New York Times*. The *Times* also neglected to review two books detailing the effect of smoking on life expectancy.[10]

The *New York Times* dutifully printed most stories. I discovered that of the 27 possible news items during the period 1938-1953 that related to smoking, the *Times* suppressed only the one AP story mentioned above. Unlike many of the papers that repeatedly censored such news, the *Times* was content to keep the stories on the back pages. An examination of these apparently low priority news items in the *Times* reveals there were facts here that might have convinced all but the tobacco industry that smoking was definitely linked to lung cancer and a shortened life span. The 1938 article on Dr. Pearl was placed on Page 19, taking only two inches of a sixteen-inch story on science and longevity. And although Dr. Pearl's tables on longevity were available then, the *Times* did not print them until a year later.[11]

In the two and one half years after the initial article on smoking there were 5 more articles, none of them being placed any further forward than Page 15. From October 1940 to July 1944 there were no items at all listed in the *Times* yearly *Indexes*.

Buried in the back of the newspaper next to the marriage announcements, a four-inch article appeared in 1944 describing some surprising actuary statistics made public by the Northwestern Mutual Life Insurance Company. "Long-term studies of large groups of policy holders," the article related, "had shown 26 to 100 percent rises in death rates among heavy smokers in the 30 to 50 age brackets as compared with non-smokers."[12]

In 1948 the *Times* placed on Page 11 an AP story which summarized the findings of tests made at the Mayo clinic. Tests on a thousand patients revealed that "on the average, smokers were found to get coronary thromboses 10 years earlier than non-smokers."[13]

In 1949 a Dr. E. A. Graham was described as having discovered that "it has been very rare" to find a man with lung cancer "who had not been an excessive smoker for years, or at least who had not formerly smoked cigarettes excessively."[14] This AP story was placed on Page 24 of the *Times,* and was so small as to be inconspicuous.

In 1950 many cancer experts assembled in Paris to compare and discuss their findings. Three different groups investigating independently all found that the "lungs of smokers show far higher incidence of cancer than pipe or cigar smokers," and that "more women who smoked cigarettes had lung cancer than did women who did not." The article reporting on this important conference also noted that Dr. Morton Levin had found that 14 of 1000 cigarette smokers developed lung cancer as compared to 6 of 1000 non-smokers. This significant news item was placed on Page 27.[15]

In 1952 a United Nations group reported a rise in cancer deaths all over the world. The UN group cited the findings of the Medical Research Council of England and Wales which showed that for men above the age of 45 the risk of developing lung cancer "may be fifty times as great among those who smoke twenty-five or more cigarettes daily as among non-smokers." The Council flatly stated: "Smoking is an important factor in the cause of cancer of the lung." This information was set forth in one paragraph of a fifteen-inch article placed on Page 26.[16]

Writing in the *British Medical Journal* in 1952, Dr. Richard Doll and Professor Bradford Hill stated unequivocally that the association between lung cancer and smoking was "real." Supporting this was the statement: "Similar studies in the United States revealed the same."[17] This was relegated to Page 22.

For anyone in 1953 still entertaining doubts about smoking, it should have been cleared up by an article which summarized various reports presented by medical specialists. Four different medical reports "stated in strong terms" and "without qualification" the link between cigarette smoking and lung diseases. Dr. Ernest Wynder presented a report of thirteen independent studies which showed that "the prolonged and heavy use of cigarettes increased up to 20 times the risk of developing cancer of the lung." One report warned that the "use of tobacco may mean the difference between life and death for persons with disease of circulation." The article concluded by taking notice of the fact that "all speakers agreed that smoking was a causative factor in lung cancer."[18] This news was placed on Page 16 of the *Times*. The *Times* did put one smoking article on Page One during this fifteen-year period. It was a December 1953 article implying that there was still a great deal of uncertainty about the link between smoking and disease, and that the government was actively concerned about guarding the people's health.[19]

Even more significant than the playing down of this issue by burying it on the back pages was the scarcity of stories on it that appeared from 1938 to 1953. No articles at all were listed in the *Times' Indexes* for the years 1941, 1942, 1943, 1945 and 1947. Even more noteworthy is that except for the *Reader's Digest* and a few other media agencies, none went out of their way to alert the public. The best media performance seemed merely a dutiful reporting, in an inconspicuous manner, of those stories it might have found difficult to ignore entirely. There were no newspaper crusades to arouse the politicians to pass legislation requiring equal time and space to combat the persuasive power of cigarette commercials. There were no stories of the tragic deaths that were now known to be associated with cigarette smoking. More than 99 percent of the media have continued to accept advertising without demanding a warning. The media in effect have joined with the tobacco industry in opposing legislation controlling ads. There were no crusades to gradually eliminate the billions of dollars of tax payer money being spent to subsidize tobacco growers. There were no crusades against our government spending tax payers' money to send billions of packs of disease-causing cigarettes to Europeans that were starving in the late 40's.

Scholars have noted the poor performance of the news media in the area of smoking and health. Writing in the *Columbia Journalism Review*, Arthur E. Rowse analyzed the media performance in covering smoking news from 1954 to 1962. He chose twelve major stories and examined how they were covered by twelve highly regarded newspapers including the *New York Times, Baltimore Sun, Washington Post* and *Des Moines Register*.[20] His study revealed that smoking news, finally after fifteen years, began to make the front page. In the first 4 stories, he found that about half the newspapers put them on Page One. About 10 percent of the papers censored the items. The papers did a poor job of covering the congressional hearings on smoking in 1957. Of a total of 72 possible stories in 12 papers (6 possible stories for each paper), only a total of 5 articles made Page One, 48 appeared elsewhere and 24 were omitted. Rowse noted that "nearly every story between 1950 and 1954 contained a Tobacco Institute statement dismissing the evidence as inconclusive." This tended to mislead the readers into thinking that there was really a genuine difference of opinion among medical experts. This was not true. With few exceptions, the only differences of opinion were between those doctors paid by the cigarette companies and those who had no special interest to serve.

Supported in part by millions of dollars of cigarette advertising money, the broadcasting industry understandably never became a crusader against smoking during these years. For example, from 1938 to 1955 there were no documentaries on the problem. CBS had a program in 1955. NBC waited until 1962 and ABC waited even longer.[21] News coverage was dutiful but never comprehensive or enterprising. A survey of the three network radio newscasts analyzed earlier shows no coverage at all of three events involving smoking and health that occurred during the six-week period preceding the 1960 election. One story reported on the International Cancer Conference held in Tokyo where there was "considerable agreement that the incident of lung cancer was high among persons who had smoked steadily for 20 years or longer."[22] Another story announced the American Cancer Society's nationwide campaign to woo teenagers away from smoking. The Society was distributing a chart showing that smoking one half pack a day increased a person's chance of getting lung cancer 8 times, and two packs, 20 times compared with a non-smoker.[23] The third story ignored by all six major newscasts was an AP release in which Dr. Daniel Horn of the American Cancer Society predicted that the then rate of 100 people dying each day from lung cancer would double in ten years. Dr. Horn was quoted as saying: "An attack on teenage smoking is the only way to reduce deaths from lung cancer."[24] The broadcasters' ignoring of Dr. Horn's gruesome prediction certainly didn't help inform teenagers. Nonetheless the broadcasters carried ample smoking news in the form of advertisements—all good news, without a warning, about the wonderful rewards of smoking. At the same time Dr. Horn was carrying on his campaign against teenage smoking, four out of the ten favorite programs of 6–10 year-olds carried cigarette ads and five of the ten most favored by teenagers were interrupted by a Madison Avenue attempt to sell the smoking habit.[25] It's hardly surprising that Dr. Horn failed in his efforts to discourage teenagers from smoking. Today teenage smoking is on the increase[26] and even many grammar school children are smoking.

Here we see how our advanced technology of communication has been put to the service of elements whose interests are diametric to those of the public. A technology that as early as 1938 could have brought home to all Americans the truth about smoking has been used instead to bury this truth for as long as possible. No one can now argue that informing the public wouldn't have made any difference; the thirteen million Americans who have quit smoking since 1966 are testimony enough to refute this. The media has failed in two important respects on the smoking story: first, in failing to give the people adequate and fair information on the priority basis that the problem deserved, second, in failing to expose through creative reporting the politicians and powers who fought to prevent the government from requiring warnings on advertisements and equal time and space for anti-cigarette ads—requirements that were justified by scientific findings as early as 1938. It is now clear that had the media done its job in informing the public on the danger of smoking when it should have, countless thousands of Americans who died an early death would still be alive today.

4   The Role of Mass Media

Current confusion over the respective roles of the new media comes largely from a misconception of their function. They are art-forms, not substitutes for human contact. Insofar as they attempt to usurp speech and personal, living relations, they harm.

Edmund Carpenter

In a primitive village where men depend on direct access to their environment rather than on mass communication technology for a picture of what is important in their world, it would be impossible for society to neglect matters as important as hunger, hazardous automotive engineering and the effects of smoking. In such a village, conditions or events which constituted a dangerous threat to the people's or society's health, once revealed, would not be ignored. They would be priority news items. Only people completely dependent on modern technology of communication could be left ignorant or misinformed about concerns vital to the life or death of individuals and society. When we compare modern man with primitive man we see the extent to which modern man is dependent upon the mass media for his information and very existence and therefore susceptible to being so totally deceived about what is important to society.

More than ninety-five percent of man's time on earth has been spent as a hunter and gatherer. By necessity he lived in small groups. He dealt with his world through direct individual experience—in religious rites, dancing, story-telling and just plain talk. He did not get all his information first hand, but messages, no matter where originated, ultimately had to be communicated to him by another person in a face-to-face situation. His feelings of sadness, joy, hostility or approval were to a very large extent affected through interactions among people he knew face-to-face. In contrast, modern man can hate a person he has never talked to or seen face-to-face. He can experience joy over the victory of a football team whose members he doesn't know or whose gridiron performance he has never seen. He can become sad because of a tragedy which happened to someone he has never met in a place he has never seen. He can approve of a person he has never talked to or seen. He can be persuaded by leaders he's never talked to to kill someone he has never seen, or to give up his life for reasons he's never really considered. He has not talked face-to-face with more than a fraction of one percent of the people he knows as his countrymen.

Still, this modern man is surrounded by people; he often sees more people in one minute than the hunter and gatherer would see in his whole lifetime. Theodora Kroeber tells of Ishi, a California Yana Indian, who, when brought to a large city and taken to a movie theater, was so taken by the number of people in the theater that he paid no attention at all to the moving picture on the screen. Modern man has become accustomed to such crowds. It would be hard to convince a person jammed into a commuter train in Tokyo or a shopper in a Los Angeles discount house during Christmas that man needs more company. But large cities are called lonely by their occupants, who know crowds are not company. Such people may seek companionship in a book, or a magazine, a movie or a TV show.

For many a housewife, the TV set runs through the entire day. She may find comfort and a sort of companionship through the set's simply being *on*—and when it breaks down she finds herself suddenly alone, as if actual human company has left.

In a primitive village a man could survey his entire village at a glance. Out of the total landscape he could see the setting and place occupied by his village, his people, and himself. He could be pretty sure that his single view at that time encompassed in space almost everybody and everything that would concern him. He experienced it all directly. He knew by walking and running where his home and companions fit into the background of plains or mountains. Through eating, hunting and digging he knew the physical characteristics of plants and animals. As a result, his sense of where he was in the physical world was tactile and physical. What happened outside his direct experience was not part of his world.

For modern man, the entire world is his village, though he cannot at a glance see even a millionth of this global village, the people in it, or the activities going on. And, just as primitive man's world was synonomous with his means of experiencing it, so modern man's idea of the world's landscape and his place in it is determined by the information that the communications media bring to him. For him, these media must in large part act as substitutes for direct physical experience in giving him a sense of orientation to his world.

Such events as the hunt provided great adventure for primitive man. The dividing up of the meat gave an opportunity for much human interaction and conversation. And the hunt itself served as a conversation piece for days. With great style and mimicry hunters would relate even the smallest details of their adventure to a fascinated audience. The movements of the deer, its stools, how it reacted when shot by the arrow, the hunters' every move—all these were of great interest to the village at large.

There were other things to talk about too: since privacy as modern man knows it did not exist, everything someone did, said or felt became public. It was impossible to keep economic transactions, arguments, laughter or the expressions of hate, jealousy or love from becoming the subject of gossip. Everyone lived within hearing or seeing distance; there were no sound-proof walls. There was not the anonymity offered by great numbers of people. Gossip about all these intimate human interactions constituted a big part of everyday life.

Compared to the hunter, modern man has little that is of a personal nature to talk about. His job may be boring and of little interest to others. A person who talks about all the little happenings at the factory or office is the bore of the party. Intimate gossip makes for better listening, but modern man zealously guards his privacy. He knows little of the money transactions, problems or the intimate life of his friends. And more often than not he knows nothing of the life of those who live next door, across the street or in the adjacent apartment. He will know next to nothing about the private life of people he works next to eight hours a day. There is little direct experience that provides substance for conversation—topics that might substitute for the fascination of the hunt or the chance to witness the human interactions going on in the village.

The mass media fill this void each day by offering such diverse excitement as adventures on the battlefield, divorces, rapes, space spectaculars, demonstrations, marriages, noteworthy political statements, solo sailings around the world and heart transplants. The man who has nothing to talk about is the man that has not been turned on by mass media.

The vicarious pleasures a man of today may experience through exposure to the media do satisfy at least to a degree his need to feel a part of his community—the world. He knows no other life, so it makes little difference to him that his neighbors and his community become people he has never talked to and cannot reply to.

These contrasting ways of experiencing communication—the face-to-face versus the technological—are responsible for a significant difference between so-called primitive man and mass media man. Primitive man participated directly in society; modern man is mainly an observer of his society. To the hunter and gatherer the world was his small band of people and the environment that he knew intimately. From a modern perspective this life seems extremely narrow and limited. But the fundamental essence of human life can more reasonably be described as a process of being and participation than simply a process of receiving information and observing. Primitive man had to individually participate in the ordering and editing of all incoming communications. There was no intermediate technology to do it for him. As an in-person witness to battles, births, deaths, dances or music, he is a part of them too. Being in the vicinity of the event and knowing personally those involved precluded for him a passive observational role. In contrast to primitive man's interaction with the source and subject matter of communication messages, mass media man is by necessity passive. He cannot edit the real event he is hearing about; it has already been edited. He cannot decide what is important; this has already been done for him. He cannot personally interact with the event or people he "meets" through the media as they "visit" his livingroom or apartment. He may become very *involved* with what he sees, hears or reads about via the mass media, but no actual *participation* occurs. He may get so involved that he calls a senator a bastard, but the senator does not hear him and thus does not interact with him.

Mass media man is primarily an observer, a receptor of the images, sounds and print projected to him. He responds now and then within the narrow limits of acceptability as defined in the mass media, but he is basically a receptor as he allows mass media to fill the voids of participation with the fill of pre-edited news and entertainment. And just as it is impossible to think of the primitive hunter and gatherer apart from what he saw, heard and participated in, so it is impossible to conceive of modern man apart from what he reads, sees, hears and is involved in through mass media. *Man, in extending his eye and ear*

*through technology, has had to hand over to those who operate his elec-
tronically extended eyes and ears the major organizing and editing decisions that he used to make for himself.*

This fact has ominous implications. It means that no one can be
free from the effects of bias that exist in the mass media. Even more
significant, no one can escape the hidden bias that is purposely implanted in mass media by those who control and manage it. Since
modern man needs mass media to survive he must absorb the bias. He
is like a prisoner faced with the choice of no food at all or food with
a bit of tasteless accumulating poison. If the bias in media forms
attitudes and views of the world which are hostile to new measures
that may be needed to save man from destroying himself through
overpopulation, pollution of war, the result can only be disaster. We
shall see that this problem is real—the bias is there, subtle or overt.
Whether it's your local newspaper, your television news, *Life, Time,
Reader's Digest* or the *New York Times,* you will see that bias is there,
and it is consistently a one-sided bias that favors the status quo and
the establishment that it sustains. We shall see that our means of
communication have been prostituted for profit and monopolized by
wealthy moderates and conservatives with varied special interests. To
make matters worse, people of average and below average reading
ability are the ones least able to find and read the competing anti-
establishment views which are hidden away in books and journals
outside the mainstream of society's communication system.

America is now being forced to pay for the past and present prostitution of its means of communication. Decisions based on distorted
views of the world resulting from the bias in mass media have resulted in tragically mistaken priorities, death and suffering. Hunger,
automobile design and the effects of smoking were not the only problems intentionally ignored for decades by mass media; there were
others even more significant which were and are extracting an even
higher price from society.

5   Pollution and Overpopulation: They Weren't Always Newsworthy

> Letting a maximum number of views be heard regularly is not just a nice philosophical notion. It is the best way any society has yet discovered to detect maladjustments quickly, to correct injustices, and to discover new ways to meet the continuing stream of novel problems that rise in a changing environment.
>
> Ben Bagdikian

In his book *The Population Bomb,* Dr. Paul Ehrlich states that mass famines will plague the world within twenty years, "and it is now too late to take action to save many of those people."[1] Even today, with no mass famines, 416 people die every hour from starvation or malnutrition.[2] There just isn't enough food now, and there never can be enough food to keep pace with man's present rate of increase, an increase that in 900 years would allow one square yard for each 100 people.[3]

To avoid catastrophe worse than that already being caused by overpopulation, man must curb his birth rate. Both Dr. Lee A. Du Bridge, President Nixon's top science adviser, and Dr. Roger Egeberg, Assistant Secretary for health and scientific affairs in the Department of Health, Education and Welfare, have claimed that curbing world and United States population growth should be our government's first priority.[4]

This problem of increasing numbers of people contributes to another ecological problem—pollution of the environment. Our once beautiful lakes, rivers and oceans have become sewers. Our air is poison; the earth is contaminated. The health of every American is attacked daily by these silent forms of violence and death. Two hundred experts from fifty countries found pollution increasing at such an accelerated pace that it would eventually cause the end of man's life on earth.[5]

These are not problems that occurred overnight. Experts have been making urgent pleas for controlling population and pollution for the last twenty-five years. But did the news media alert us in time? A study of news media reveals that these problems seldom if ever were featured as important news items until the Nixon Administration jumped on the anti-pollution bandwagon in late 1969. Then, all of a sudden, pollution, environment and population increase became high priority news.

Television and radio call attention to important problems by repeatedly featuring various news items dealing with the matter. By placing a news item on the front page with big headlines and accompanying photographs, newspapers can make any subject the conversation topic of the day for almost every American.

The following are figures of the frequency and priority which television, radio and newspapers gave to the topic of ecology. I chose to study network newscasts because they are in my view the best the broadcasting industry can offer. Similarly, the *New York Times* was chosen because it is consistently ranked as the best newspaper in the United States. The *Los Angeles Times* serves as a comparison. It has changed from an inferior newspaper to one that now ranks among the best out of the more than 1700 dailies.[6] The following newspaper analysis considers only news stories on the front page and photographs on the first three pages—places where the most important news items and photographs of the day are featured. A newscast is roughly equivalent to a newspaper front page in the number of items and amount of news featured. Network newscasts deal almost exclusively with stories of national interest; thus to provide a fair comparison between the two media, newspaper articles of purely local distribution or interest were excluded from some categories. Both national and local stories of accidents, the entertainment world and what I term trivia (beauty contests, kite flying, sporting events, animals at the zoo, etc.) were included to illustrate the extent to which insignificant news is featured by the news media in comparison to population and pollution news.[7] [see TABLE II]

As can be seen by Table II, both newspapers showed equal neglect of population, world hunger, and pollution. The fact that unimportant items were featured by the *Los Angeles Times* in 190 articles with 235

TABLE II

THE FREQUENCY OF POPULATION AND POLLUTION NEWS: NEWSPAPERS, FEBRUARY AND MARCH 1950, FRONT PAGE

Newspaper	Population, Birth Control		World Hunger		Pollution	
	items p.1	photos pp.1,2,3	items p.1	photos pp.1,2,3	items p.1	photos pp.1,2,3
Los Angeles Times	1	0	0	0	0	0
New York Times	1	0	0	0	0	0

Newspaper	Accidents*		The Entertainment World*		Other Trivia*	
	items p.1	photos pp.1,2,3	items p.1	photos pp.1,2,3	items p.1	photos pp.1,2,3
Los Angeles Times	146	104	13	66	31	65
New York Times	16	6	2	0	5	3

*Includes stories of both local and national distribution or interest

photographs compared to the *New York Times'* 23 articles and 9 photographs does not mean that the *New York Times* neglected any less, three of the most important problems facing man.

These are statistics from 1950. One would imagine that with the passage of ten years—and half a billion more mouths to feed and an environment more polluted than ever—the situation would improve. Table III shows the case.

A check of network television and radio newscasts during a six-week period from September 26 to November 7, 1960, reveals the same pattern of news priorities as newspapers.[8] [see TABLE IV]

When we advance another nine years, to 1969, we see that population and pollution still had very low news priorities although they are not so totally neglected as in the past. But it should be kept in mind that the slight improvement in pollution coverage in 1969 can be partially accounted for by the attention forced on the media by pollution spectaculars such as that caused by the Union Oil Company off the coast of California. [see TABLE V]

A more extensive study than the one we've just seen revealed that the *Honolulu Star-Bulletin* during a four and a half month period fared no better on its first three pages for both news articles and photographs than the two metropolitan newspapers did on their front pages alone. Fourteen of the 15 pollution items were about a pollution disaster off the California coast; this left 1 item for other pollution news. [see TABLE Va]

Population and pollution have also been neglected news items on *Huntley-Brinkley* and *Walter Cronkite,* each of which had more than 20 million listeners. On *Huntley-Brinkley* during two months in 1969, the items which had a higher priority than population and pollution were Senator Kennedy's tragic car accident, other accidents (not including the hurricane disaster), plane hijackings, stock market, personality trivia, and other trivia. The great problems fared just as badly on *Walter Cronkite* during the same period. Moreover, *Walter Cronkite* gave rock festivals and sports more time than population and pollution. Table VI gives the breakdown in detail.

Most Americans get their news from television but many Americans, especially teenagers, get their impression of what's happening in the world from the three-minute radio headlines that interrupt song and commercials on music stations. An analysis of two network on-the-hour newscasts show that two of man's greatest problems, overpopulation and pollution, were not newsworthy in the summer of 1969, the period of time selected at random for our sample. These two

TABLE III

THE FREQUENCY OF POPULATION AND POLLUTION NEWS: NEWSPAPERS, APRIL AND MAY 1960, FRONT PAGE

Newspaper	Population, Birth Control		World Hunger		Pollution	
	items p.1	photos pp.1,2,3	items p.1	photos pp.1,2,3	items p.1	photos pp.1,2,3
Los Angeles Times	0	0	0	0	3	0
New York Times	0	0	0	0	0	0

	Accidents*		The Entertainment World*		Other Trivia*	
	items p.1	photos pp.1,2,3	items p.1	photos pp.1,2,3	items p.1	photos pp.1,2,3
Los Angeles Times	120	80	17	61	40	73
New York Times	18	14	4	0	7	3

*Includes stories of both local and national distribution or interest

TABLE IV

THE FREQUENCY OF POPULATION AND POLLUTION NEWS: NETWORK TELEVISION AND RADIO NEWSCASTS, 1960
September 26 to November 7

	Population Birth Control Items	World Hunger Items	Pollution Items	Accidents Items	Sports Items	Humorous Trivia Items
TELEVISION						
NBC, *Huntley-Brinkley*	1	0	0	12	12	11
CBS, *Douglas Edwards*	0	0	0	9	8	2
ABC, *John Daly*	0	0	0	8	14	17
RADIO						
NBC, *Peter Hackes*	0	0	1	13	19	2
CBS, *Lowell Thomas*	0	0	0	9	14	40
ABC, *Edward P. Morgan*[9]	0	0	0	7	2	1

38

TABLE V

THE FREQUENCY OF POPULATION AND POLLUTION NEWS: NEWSPAPERS, JUNE AND JULY 1969, FRONT PAGE

Newspaper	Population Birth Control		World Hunger		Pollution	
	items	photos pp.1,2,3	items	photos pp.1,2,3	items	photos pp.1,2,3
Los Angeles Times	1	0	0	0	10	3
New York Times	1	0	0	0	2	1

	Accidents*		The Entertainment World*		Other Trivia*	
	items	photos pp.1,2,3	items	photos pp.1,2,3	items	photos pp.1,2,3
Los Angeles Times	17	19	3	11	2	45
New York Times	10	11	4	2	7	3

*Includes stories of both local and national distribution or interest

TABLE Va

HONOLULU STAR-BULLETIN, JANUARY 12 TO MAY 31, 1969

Population Birth Control		World Hunger		Pollution		Accidents		All Other Trivia	
items	photos	items	photos	items	photos	items	photos	items	photos
1	0	0	0	15	3	6	3	90	63

TABLE VI

THE FREQUENCY OF POPULATION AND POLLUTION NEWS:
NETWORK TELEVISION NEWSCASTS,[10] JULY 10 THROUGH SEPTEMBER 10, 1969

SELECTED SUBJECTS	NBC – HUNTLEY-BRINKLEY		CBS – WALTER CRONKITE AND CBS SATURDAY EVENING NEWS	
	Number of Items Out of a Total of 899 (52 days) Ave. 17.3 per day	Amount of Time Out of a Total of 1160 min. Av. 22:16 per day	Number of Items Out of a Total of 901 (53 days) Ave. 16.9 per day	Amount of Time Out of a Total of 1210 min. Ave. 22:44 per day
Population and Birth Control	3	:51	1	2:13
World Hunger[11]	0	0	0	0
Pollution	5	11:44	4	6:24
Conservation	3	7:21	3	6:29
Stock Market	40	8:48	42	10:09
Vietnam War[12]	135	148:08	150	149:55
Arab-Israeli Conflict	29	21:27	29	25:45
Hurricanes	19	27:20	21	29:54
Other Accidents	8	7:52	13	14:18
Kennedy Auto Accident	31	58:13	28	60:04
Plane Hijackings	10	3:54	7	3:44
Sports[13]	4	:44	18	54:10
Rock Festivals	3	8:57	6	13:08
Personalities (Trivia)	18	13:47	8	4:10
Other Trivia	23	32:00	13	39:07

newscasts can be considered among the best of the hourly newscasts. [see TABLE VII]

Some defenders of the media say that there are many good reasons for this neglect—mainly that such problems just don't qualify by news media standards. The reasoning has at least a surface validity: certainly chronic social ills like population increase and pollution are not easily covered by news technology nor do they lend themselves to the type of man-bites-dog stories the media has conditioned the public to accept as news. But stories about pollution and those guilty of causing pollution can be developed by an enterprising news staff. Monthly reports on efforts to curb population, world hunger and pollution could be featured as priority news. Photographs of overcrowded conditions and the signs of starvation and misery could be made into grim but significant news. Stories describing the efforts of church officials and politicans to promote causes that keep the birth rate high could certainly arouse much interest. Why don't news agencies do stories like this very often? Its simple. They lack the intent—the intent to responsibly inform the public in cases where to do so might conflict with the special interests of mass media owners or the large corporations who profit from increased population and an environment free for the polluting. We'll examine this phenomenon in detail in this book.

The important thing is this: through this news-neglect Americans are given a distorted view of what is important to them and to their country. We can see the result in polls: if we had had brought home to us the urgency of the population crisis, would 41 percent of us think four or more children an ideal number for a family? In a poll taken in 1968, 41 percent of Americans sampled did. In contrast, people in other countries appear much more aware of the danger of overpopulation. This Gallup poll revealed that in all other countries polled, the public was less than 24 percent in favor of such large families.[14]

TABLE VII

THE FREQUENCY OF POPULATION AND POLLUTION NEWS: FIVE-MINUTE ON-THE-HOUR NETWORK RADIO NEWSCASTS — WEEKDAYS, AUG. 22 TO OCT. 22, 1969

TOPIC	MUTUAL – KRKD Los Angeles 7:00 a.m. Announcer: Joe Campbell & others [15]		ABC – KABC Los Angeles 9:00 a.m. Announcer: E. P. Morgan & others	
	ITEMS 43 Day Total of 355, Average 8 Items Per Day	TIME Total Time 121 Minutes Average 2:49 Per Newscast	ITEMS 43 Day Total of 421, Average 10 Items Per Day	TIME Total Time 136 Minutes Average 3:09 Per Broadcast
Population and Birth Control	0	0	1	:17
World Hunger[16]	0	0	0	0
Pollution	2	:22	3	:35
Stock Market	2	:18	18	2:08
Vietnam War[17]	94	36:00	80	26:40
Arab-Israeli Conflict	42	13:12	22	8:32
Accidents	21	6:28	20	4:39
Kennedy Auto Accident	3	:28	15	6:31
Plane Hijackings	4	:52	6	1:44
Ireland Civil Strife	10	3:02	6	1:50
Trivia	3	:26	8	2:22

6 News Bias: Is the Vice President Off Target?

> The American people should be made aware of the trend toward monopolization of the great public information vehicles and the concentration of more and more power over public opinion in fewer and fewer hands.
>
> Spiro T. Agnew

> News reporting should be factual, fair and without bias.
>
> *Television Code*

> News reports should be free from opinion or bias of any kind.
>
> *The canons of Journalism*
> (the professional and ethical standard for American newspapers)

Considering media's neglect of the problems of hunger, smoking and auto safety, it is at first glance surprising that the performance of news media itself had never emerged as a major national issue. On November 13, 1969 in Des Moines, Iowa, with one speech, Vice President Spiro Agnew accused major news agencies of favoring liberals, and thus made bias in news media the number one national controversy. *Time* and *Newsweek* both promoted the issue to a front-page cover story. One network even pre-empted a regular program in prime time to debate Agnew's charges. Every news commentator in the country had something to say about Agnew and the issue he raised. His charge received banner headlines at the top of Page One in hundreds of dailies. For ten days every daily followed the issue, continuing to feature as priority news the debate between Agnew supporters and network defenders. Nearly every newspaper felt the matter important enough to take an editorial stand on the issue. For the first time in recent history, bias in news media became the number one controversy for an extended period. The journalists and scholars who for years have been criticizing the media for its bias must have been puzzled to note the auspices under which the issue finally emerged to claim public attention.

Why, after so many years, has a single speech so dramatically brought to the limelight an obscure issue? Some answers are not hard to find. Most criticism of the news media in the past has involved liberals attacking the conservative bias and domination of the press. As is human, those who were attacked did their best to hush the critics. They succeeded in this of course, since they control the media. A second probable reason Agnew's attack received such priority news treatment is that it expressed the ultraconservative viewpoint of the vast majority of media owners who, like Agnew, feel the networks to be too liberal. For the networks the attack was almost made to order. It was an attack unsupported by impressive evidence or long investigation, and its terminology was such that the networks found themselves to be liberal defenders of free speech against implied threats of government censorship. Network spokesman Frank Stanton and others who are ordinarily seen as pillars of the status quo such as Huntley, Brinkley, Cronkite, Sevareid, Smith and Reynolds found themselves under attack for being courageous and liberal journalists who opposed any restrictions on free speech. These men may have been bemused; for this was quite a switch for them. The past thirty years they were used to cries of "bias" from liberals, not conservatives, and they were used to answering charges accusing the entire communications industry, including the networks, of presenting news which was biased and censored to favor wealthy advertisers and media owners. Agnew's attack redefined the issue into one determining whether bias was being used to favor liberals—instead of conservatives.

By chance, a few days before Agnew's speech, a very significant survey of broadcast journalism had been made public. This report, titled: *Survey of Broadcast Journalism 1968-1969*, finds much wrong with the industry. It was based on inquiries sent to the networks and 500 different stations, reports of 40 correspondents across the nation, studies by 500 chapters of the League of Women Voters, and a canvas of 1,200 political candidates. It got little notice by the media. Neither *Huntley-Brinkley* or *Walter Cronkite* newscasts mentioned the survey.[1] The *Los Angeles Times* buried it on the last page of the entertainment section and the *New York Times* put it in the middle of Page 78.[2] The

Survey condemns the entire broadcasting industry to such an extent that we can imagine that broadcast officials were happy to kill the story. The *Survey* reports that the broadcasters' relentless search for profits pollutes the communication system just as a factory pollutes a stream:

> Of all those Americans who are trying to get more out of life than they have put into it and who are laying waste their country in the attempt, none in recent years has appeared more successful as a group than the broadcasters.[3]

Summarizing the performance of electronic journalism during the last year the *Survey* said: "Good intentions have been deplored and ridiculed where special interests were threatened, dedication has flagged in favor of profits, nerves have failed when stockholders have grown restive."[4] The 40 correspondents described coverage of local problems as "superficial," "event oriented," "dreary and unimaginative" and "marked by gross timidity." Reviewing these descriptions, the *Survey* stated:

> From the tenor of these comments, as well as from other data gathered by the survey, it seems clear that television, although increasing its probing, could often be accused of reluctance to undertake hard hitting exposes, particularly where these might be expected to arouse major controversy. Only rarely during the year studied by the Survey did a television station attempt to expose wrong-doing by a public official, or to challenge the actions of powerful forces in the community.[5]

This comprehensive survey sees the state of affairs in the broadcasting industry a bit differently than does Spiro Agnew. Where Agnew felt that the media was going out of its way to take editorial stands against the status quo, the *Survey* sees broadcasting timidly bending to the pressures of the conservative establishment. Where Agnew saw too much coverage of dissent and conflict, the *Survey* found that ". . . not nearly enough happened" last year on the television screens compared to the reality around us.[6] In fact, the *Survey* found the coverage of threatening conditions so inadequate that disaster could come unannounced: "Radio and television, which could be a periscope to alert us as to when and where we might safely rise, threaten to become the opencock that very well may sink us."[7] As if to anticipate Stanton's response to Agnew's intimidations, Sir William Haly, Editor of the *Times* of London and a Juror for the *Survey,* claimed that network presidents defend free speech eloquently in principle but not in deed.[8]

One of the communication industry's recent deeds was to try to suppress the most important study on communications policy ever undertaken by the United States government.[9] Apparently the attempt succeeded, but only for a while. *Final Report: President's Task Force on Communications Policy* was completed in December of 1968; President Johnson refused to make it public before he left office. President Nixon held up its release for another four months until May 1969. The *Report* was prompted by President Johnson's concern over the need for a long range communication policy for America. Expressing his belief that man's use of communication technology may mean the difference between man's survival or extinction, he appointed a task force in 1967 to take a "long hard look" at the nation's communication situation for the purpose of suggesting a foundation for a new national policy. The task force was made up of distinguished government officials who relied on expert counsel by government and non-government communication experts.

When the task force's *Report* was finally made public, the media resorted to their usual techniques of suppression. The *New York Times* gave the *Report* a very small headline in the middle of Page 95 and only touched on one aspect—the recommendation that all international communications carriers be merged into a single corporation—an aspect that the public could not be expected to easily understand.[10] The *Los Angeles Times* covered the task force's 475-page *Report* in a two-inch article on Page 2 under the daily news roundup.[11]

The communication task force described the greatest challenge to be the creation of a television communication system to insure a diversity in ideas and taste so that all minorities and majorities can be represented. The *Report* stated: "We must seek to make it available to as many people as possible, rural as well as urban, poor as well as affluent." The task force criticized the present system for not achieving this diversity and specifically for not meeting the communication needs of minority groups or reflecting their cultural values. Most important, the task force saw in the present system little potential for achieving diversity or realizing the potential benefit of communication technology. The *Report* recommended a vastly expanded government role on the executive, administrative and legislative levels. It suggested a great expansion of the role of the Corporation for Public Broadcasting and encouraged the promotion of pilot projects allowing minorities access to and control of television: "Additional television channels and facilities dedicated to their problems and to the expressions of their concerns are of critical importance." For the underdeveloped world, the task force suggested that our policy be aimed to encourage educational broadcasting—not commercial broadcasting.

In short, *Final Report: President's Task Force on Communications Policy* was a criticism of the nation's present commercial television system. It found present government policy totally inadequate and made urgent pleas for greatly expanded government and public participation and regulation so that telecommunications can "offer a maximum social and economic contribution to the national welfare and security."

Another plea for urgent change in the communication system was issued many years earlier in 1947 by a distinguished group of scholars and university deans who undertook an extensive study of the press in America at the request of Henry Luce, owner of *Time* and *Life*, and *Encyclopaedia Britannica*. They found free speech to be in grave danger, not so much from the government as from those who controlled access to the media. They noted:

> Protection against government is now not enough to guarantee that a man who has something to say shall have a chance to say it. The owners and managers of the press determine which person, which facts, which version of the facts, and which ideas shall reach the public.[12]

Unlike the redoubtable Spiro Agnew, they discovered that news bias came from the personal interests of the owners and the pressure applied by wealthy pressure groups—such forces that have consistently championed conservative, as opposed to liberal policies. As the Commission on Freedom of the Press stated it:

> Freedom of the press is in danger. Mainly in the hands of gigantic business units, the media of mass communication, vital to the life of our democracy, have failed to accept the full measure of their responsibility to the public. Newspapers, magazines, radio and motion pictures are not providing the current intelligence necessary for democratic government. They do not provide the free forum for discussion of diverse views which an informed public requires. They do

not represent accurately the constituent groups and major goals in our society.[13]

They made it quite clear who was preventing this "free forum for the discussion of diverse views":

> One of the most effective ways of improving the press is blocked by the press itself. By a kind of unwritten law the press ignores the errors and misrepresentations, the lies and scandals, of which its members are guilty.[14]

The press didn't exactly ignore this important 1947 report since they had sponsored the inquiry, but they didn't draw much attention to it either. The *New York Times* put it on Page 24 and the *Los Angeles Times* put it on Page 6.[15] What should have become, and what was meant to become, a national issue was treated with apathy. Dr. Robert M. Hutchins, director of the Commission's investigations, wasn't too happy with the way editorial writers covered the report, *A Free and Responsible Press:* "Some treated it unfairly, some used untruthful headlines and some just plain lied about it."[16] But Hutchins and other dissenters could not make their own headlines to compete with the "untruthful headlines;" they had to be content with having their views colored, masked and filtered by the conservative bias of the owners who controlled access to the media. While the *New York Times* gave Mr. Hutchins' complaints space on Page 10, the *Los Angeles Times* ignored them completely.

The 1947 Commission on Freedom of the Press wasn't the first group to attack the press for bowing to conservative financial pressure. In 1941, a two-year Senate investigation of the concentration of economic power in the United States also concluded that the (very conservative) National Association of Manufacturers, which was controlled by and representing many giant corporations, and the United States Chamber of Commerce were getting favored treatment from the press. The investigation found:

> Through the press, public opinion, and pressure groups it is possible to influence the political process. While all three of these factors have played a part in the process since our beginnings as a nation, the extent and consciousness of their use has grown inordinately. They are employed by all contestants in the struggle for control, but reflect the viewpoint of business more accurately than that of others. . . .
>
> In this connection the business orientation of the newspaper press

is a valuable asset. . . . Even where editors and publishers are men of the highest integrity, they are owners and managers of big business enterprises, and their papers inevitably reflect, at least to some extent, their economic interest.[17]

The Senate Committee explained why there is not much controversy when the big corporations are having their way:

> Because business controls the instruments of propaganda, the periods when the control struggle favors business seem relatively quiet. When business seems to be losing ground, the struggle becomes more vociferous.[18]

The Committee thought that the people should be made aware of the pressure applied on government by the National Association of Manufacturers and other industry organizations. To accomplish this the Committee proposed government-owned and operated radio stations to offset the powerful bias through which the commercial media were able to hide from the public the antisocial policies of the big corporations.[19] These revelations about the bias in the press were buried among the volumes of reports filed by the Committee. But if the press had had any desire to reform itself, now it had the evidence, and it could easily have focused the public's attention on the matter.

Some interesting examples of the clever ways in which conservative bias was channeled through the press had been revealed a few years earlier, in fact in 1939, by another Senate Committee, a group set up to investigate violations of free speech and rights of labor. At this time, even Uncle Abner, the cartoon character, served as a mouthpiece for NAM propaganda: "Seems t'me like business could stand on its own feet a lot better if the politicians would get off'n its back."[20] As the La Follette Committee on Education and Labor noted, every facet of media was exploited:

> The National Association of Manufacturers has blanketed the country with a propaganda which in technique has relied upon indirection of meaning, and in presentation upon secrecy and deception. Radio speeches, public meeting, news cartoons, editorials, advertising, motion pictures and many other artifices of propaganda have not in most instances disclosed to the public their origin with the association. The Mandville Press Service, the Six Star Service, Uncle Abner cartoons, George Sokolsky's services, the 'American Family Robinson' radio broadcasts, 'Harmony Ads' by MacDonald-Cook Co., 'civic progress meetings' and many other devices of molding

public opinion have been used without disclosure of origin and financial support by the National Association of Manufacturers.[21]

It is only natural that the big corporations would use propaganda to promote policies that would help them in their quest for profits. But the important point to be noted here is how the media cooperated and served willingly as a channel for this propaganda. This is clearly shown by their use of NAM written editorials and editorial cartoons as their own without mentioning the source. One-fourth of the newspapers in the country so used such editorials.[22] The media were more than a willing channel for corporation propaganda: they were an active contributor in a way that disclosed their shared values. A million dollars of free radio time a year was given to the NAM. Newspapers obliged in one three month period by giving the NAM one million dollars worth of free newspaper space.[23] (Not to labor our point, it should be pointed out that the media never bothered to give that type of "public service" on behalf of the poor, the minority groups or the critics of NAM's conservative policies.) The Committee explained

that the purpose of this prodigious effort is in part to forestall union organization, and in part to sway public opinion in favor of a legislative program approved by large corporations which control the association, and to influence the electorate in the choice of candidates for office.[24]

The NAM and the media owners were not satisfied with simply using their control of mass media to suppress labor's point of view. They often resorted to the use of spies and company police forces using guns and tear gas to keep workers from exercising free speech. The Committee noted that these (illegal) violent tactics were so successful that in some areas of the country the workers' "freedom of action, of speech, and assembly is completely destroyed."[25]

Was this propaganda and intimidation successful in shaping public opinion? It seems so. The Committee discovered that "officials of the association have boasted that its propaganda has influenced the political opinions of millions of citizens, and affected their choice of candidates for Federal offices."[26]

The media most blatantly reveals its bias when it dares to take the bold step of outright censorship. In a 1958 analysis of over 250 items censored by news media, Professor Warren Breed found that two-thirds of the items dealt with the behavior of a wealthy or powerful individual or group (usually from the business world) obtaining a privilege through a non-democratic means. Next to items exposing the wealthy and powerful, Breed found that items reflecting unfavorably on religion, foreign policy and doctors were frequently censored by the news media.[27] Such news protection indicates and establishes if anything a conservative not a liberal bias.

Spiro Agnew's claim of a liberal bias is contradicted by all the major studies of bias conducted during the last thirty years. That the people were not shocked by Agnew's accusations is itself testimony to the fact that for over thirty years the media have been using their power to spread corporation propaganda, protect the establishment from unfavorable news, and prevent a true competition among ideas. The subsequent popular support for Agnew's position is a function of media's intentional failure to communicate the most basic ideal of democracy—that all ideas, popular or unpopular, should be given a chance to compete fairly for public acceptance.

A single example may shed light on how the conservative bias of the news effects a story. In the late 1940's, A&P grocery company was found guilty, beyond reasonable doubt, of nationwide restraints of trade. On appeal the conviction was upheld by a United States Court of Appeals. These restraint practices had caused customers to pay millions more for food than they would have under real competitive selling. A&P was fined $175,000, a drop in the bucket to A&P. Aware of this, the government also filed a civil suit as a more effective means of preventing future restraints in trade. A&P then placed full-page ads in an estimated 2500 daily and weekly newspapers claiming that some of the accusations (already proven in court on two different occasions) were not true. The National Federation of Independent Businesses felt that the false statements in A&P ads should be answered with the facts as proven in court. They ran into a few stumbling blocks. Representatives Wright Patman who followed the whole episode revealed that three out of four newspapers in Washington D.C. refused to accept the Federation's paid advertisement even though they had carried and were still carrying A&P ads concerning the same issue. Only the *Washington News* accepted the ad. A member of the staff explained why in an interview:

> It's perfectly clear why we published the reply and three other papers refused to do so. The other three get grocery advertising from A&P every week. We don't get any. I have no doubt whatever that, if we carried A&P ads regularly, we also would have refused the ad.[28]

The story about the three newspapers refusing the Federation's advertisements was sent to newspapers by the wire services. Most papers killed this story. In addition, statements about the case made by the Attorney General and his assistant were either totally suppressed or buried in the back pages. A&P written editorials were printed in many papers without identifying A&P as the source. The result was that A&P ended up with a good public image despite the fact that they short-weighted the customers, made the customers pay the advertising expense by charging it against business, and corrupted the people's communication system.[29]

Huntley-Brinkley had the following item on their November 2, 1960 newscast:

> Financier Alexander Guterma was sentenced to 8 to 24 months in prison today for acting illegally as an agent for Dominican dictator Trujillo.[30]

What was omitted from this item were, very simply, all the important facts. Guterma wasn't just an ordinary Trujillo agent; he was a special kind of agent. While president of Mutual Broadcasting Corporation, he made an agreement with Trujillo whereby his 450 affiliated stations would carry 425 minutes of news favorable to Trujillo "in the guise of genuine news" for a period of eighteen months in return for $750,000.[31] The *Huntley-Brinkley* coverage was inadequate and misleading, but most news media suppressed the item completely. The other two network newscasts, along with the three network radio newscasts studied earlier, suppressed the item entirely. It didn't appear in either the *New York Times* or the *Los Angeles Times*.[32]

In early 1967 the American public responded with shock and disbelief to grisly details concerning American bombing of civilians in North Vietnam. These facts appeared in stories under the byline of *New York Times* correspondent Harrison Salisbury who had gone to North Vietnam to investigate for himself. The reason for the public's reaction wasn't that the bombings had just begun—or that the facts were not available before Salisbury's journey. As Salisbury explained it to the Overseas Press Club, Americans were surprised and shocked about his reports of civilian bombing casualties because the American press had been ignoring European press reports that had been detailing the casualties all along. The Overseas Press Club shouldn't be too hard for reporters to find, but apparently some got lost, for no hint of Salisbury's comments was reported in the *Los Angeles Times*. The *New*

York Times gave it six inches on Page 14, though Salisbury was their own correspondent.[33]

The *Los Angeles Times* also decided to completely censor a Federal Communication commissioner's charge that the networks were guilty of censorship. In a UPI dispatch Commissioner Nicholas Johnson was quoted as saying:

> There is censorship in this country, all right, make no mistake about that, but also make no mistake about its source. . . .
>
> While the government will not censor, apparently the networks will. The irreparable damage to the public is the same. The stifling weight of censorship is to be found, not in the hearing rooms of the Federal Communications Commission, but in the conference rooms of this nation's large television networks.

Johnson claimed the networks were resorting to this sort of censorship to support the establishment's war in Vietnam. The *New York Times* covered the story on Page 47 using a mild headline stating:

TV INDUSTRY VIEW ON SPEECH SCORED[34]

Mason Williams, sculptor, poet and at one time chief writer for the "Smothers Brothers," testified before the FCC hearings on the question of whether to restrict network domination of prime-time programs. Williams told the FCC that the "Smothers Brothers" were kicked off by CBS " . . . for not pacifying. It didn't divert your attention away from social problems."[35] Williams read aloud parts from his book:

> Network television is the art of electronic 'trash' mission. Getting an emmy for television is like getting a kiss from somebody with bad breath. You can't fight the system from within because the system is from within. The truly socially conscious television network is the network which warns you against watching it all the time. Network television wants to keep you stupid so you'll watch it.[36]

Testifying at the same hearing was Robert Montgomery, distinguished producer of many television dramas and former Special Consultant to President Eisenhower. He accused the networks of presenting a false picture of American life. He claimed: "You cannot get on the air today with a program unless the networks want that program on the air." These hearings were open to the press. What these two critics had to say was both important and entertaining. Montgomery, however, feared that the hearings would be censored by those he was attacking. He asked the Commission: "I want to know how well these hearings on network domination of programs are going to be reported."[37] He found out quickly—neither *Huntley-Brinkley* nor *Walter Cronkite* even mentioned the hearings; the *Los Angeles Times* suppressed the testimony of both even though there was an AP wire on the hearings; the *New York Times* carried two articles on Pages 75 and 95, giving fairly good coverage. One out of four was the overall record of these major news agencies. It seems Montgomery's fear of censorship was well justified.

A few months earlier Montgomery appeared on the Johnny Carson show and read parts of his book criticizing network domination of the air waves. But the public didn't get to hear all of what he had to say because NBC executives cut out four different statements he had made. One was a charge that CBS had faked a news story.[38] Another censored portion was his statement to Johnny Carson: "I want to compliment you for having the courage to be the first network to review this book."[39] It's obvious that the networks stick together in protecting themselves against any criticism from liberal sources.

In view of this evidence that the media uses bias to serve moderate and conservative powers of great wealth, Spiro Agnew was a godsend: it was indeed fortunate for the media that they were attacked by someone claiming the absurd. Agnew made the networks look like sponsors of hard-hitting journalism and thus diverted the public's attention from the monopoly of control over access that is enjoyed by conservatives and moderates.

7 The Bias in Technology and Finance

> We are all robots when uncritically involved with our technologies.
>
> Marshal McLuhan

Neglect of important news is not always the result of deliberately suppressing or playing down certain news events or conditions. Many of the significant trends or events in our history just don't cause any newsworthy events or for other reasons don't lend themselves to easy coverage. Events that happened an hour ago, events that have a beginning and an end, events that can be photographed or recorded—that is what makes news. The great threats to mankind are mostly unsensational trends and are ignored because they don't conveniently fit mass media's definition of news. In this chapter we examine how the technology and finance of news production and presentation can and does produce a decided bias.

The drain of scientific and medical experts from the poor to the rich countries produces no single noteworthy event that would attract cameramen, sound recorders, or reporters. Yet these poor countries cannot afford to lose such people if they are to make progress. Rich nations welcome the talent from the poor countries because they are also short of such people. In the United States alone, some 50,000 more physicians are needed. The shortage of physicians and scientists has produced few events in the last twenty-five years that would draw news media's attention to the problem. To give another example, a photographer would have a hard time getting a photograph of a balance of payments deficit. Also, a deficit produces no sounds that can be recorded.

Some important events would make sensational news if only they could be witnessed. In his book *The Half Shut Eye,* correspondent John Whale points out that the very essence of politics—political decision making—is neglected because cameramen or reporters are not allowed to be near when the real decisions are made. Whale notes that there were no reporters

> in the hotel sitting-room where Senator Strom Thurmond and the Reverend Billy Graham helped choose Governor Spiro Agnew as candidate for vice president; and if there had been, the discussion would have been moved somewhere else.[1]

Only the carnival atmosphere of nominating conventions and other superficial political shows are witnessed. Senate committees may allow the press to witness some hearings, but never the decision making that is supposed to result from them. The successful efforts of Cardinal Spellman and John Foster Dulles to convince President Eisenhower to back the Diem regime and oppose free elections in Vietnam were likewise never covered by the news media, because they happened "behind the scenes".

Illiteracy never produces a demonstration, riot, catastrophe or any other exciting event that can be directly attributed to it, yet it remains a serious problem in the United States. An estimated 24 million Americans over seventeen years of age are classified as functional illiterates by the United States Office of Education. Another 10 million school children have such serious reading problems that they too are likely to become functional illiterates.[2]

I can amplify this point through personal experience. In one high school history class I taught there was a shy black student who never handed in any assignments. Yet when I gave him an individual oral examination on topics discussed in class such as population explosion and agricultural problems in underdeveloped countries, he showed a better understanding than any of the other students in class. Here was a student with great potential who was severely handicapped because of illiteracy. His was not an isolated case; there are many like him. Illiteracy effectively denies an individual many rights and opportunities even though he has the legal right to them. Too, it is costly to society and a tragic waste of human potential. Yet little headway is being made in combating the problem either in the United States or in the world.

The United Nations published figures in 1969 from ninety-two countries showing that during the last decade the percentage of adult illiterates has decreased slightly, but the total number of illiterates has increased 60 million to reach a new high of 800 million.[3] This shows clearly that programs to wipe out illiteracy are not even keeping up with the population increase. Nevertheless, there is no sense of urgency or demands for an all-out crusade to wipe out illiteracy. This is largely because the public seldom hears about the problem, and so it assumes present programs are adequate.

Most everyone is aware that human societies could not cope with the results of nuclear, biological or chemical warfare. But there are other inventions of science and biology that can produce situations that could bring about political, social or economic disaster unless we prepare to cope with them. Gordon Taylor, in his book *The Biological Time Bomb*, shows that man's present and future biological knowledge and application will result in revolutionary changes that will create problems and crises for which governments and societies are at present not prepared to handle.

Taylor quotes a Nobel Prize-winner, Sir Macfarlane Burnet of Australia, who claims that "work in the field of molecular biology not only ignores possible medical aspects, but exposes the world to terrifying dangers."[4] Taylor goes on to state: "The practice of cultivating viruses and looking for new mutants creates a risk that a dangerous new mutant might escape and set off an epidemic against which the population of the world would be helpless. . . . "[5] Recent accidental laboratory deaths from deadly lassa fever and marburg virus give credence to his warnings.

Taylor also describes how techniques for dramatically raising intelligence could create great demands by parents that their child be so treated. Wide application would demand a revision of the whole educational system. New intelligent elites could quickly develop and the difference between the rich and poor nations would be accentuated. Regarding another problem—the possible effects of advances in transplant surgery—Taylor states:

> It is estimated that in the U.S.A. 1,500 transplant operations a day may eventually be called for. If society is slow to meet this demand the response could be violent. People are powerfully motivated where their health and survival and those of their children are concerned.[6]

The entire problem raises the question of whether certain types of research and biological abilities should be undertaken when the results could lead to situations or dangers that societies and the human species cannot cope with.

While news of organ transplants and other new biological break-throughs make the front pages, societies' capacity to deal with their revolutionary implications produces no events and is therefore largely neglected. Yet the social consequences of these biological break-throughs are obviously more significant in their implication than the iso lated events that symbolize the dramatic breakthroughs.

The above problems have not yet become newsworthy, but they may bring about crises that will make people inquire into causes. When this happens, politicians and editors must pay attention to situations that they've previously ignored. This actually happened with the issue of priorities (societies decisions as to where to allocate its money and talent). Ten years ago few people understood what the word meant. Today there is a lot of talk about the nations priorities, and recently the topic has been front-page news. Thus people are belatedly coming to realize that it is because of past priorities that medical care today is inadequate for many Americans, and education of their children to-day is often second-rate, and the air and water are polluted. The past priorities which neglected the quality of American life—in favor of moon landings, intervention in an Asian civil war and our stockpiling weapons to secure a supposed military "superiority" —were not estab-lished knowingly by the people. These priorities were established by establishment politicians with the encouragement of the military-in-dustrial-space complex and the help of the media. It is likely the com-mon people would not have made or approved of such priorities if they had been told the price they would have to pay. But they weren't told. The issue of priorities was never newsworthy. When President Kennedy decided to spend 30 billion of the taxpayer's dollars to land an American on the moon, he didn't tell the people that this would mean less money for cleaning up our filthy environment, curbing pop-ulation growth, fighting cancer and improving education. The press didn't bother to tell the people either. When President Nixon decided to go ahead with the supersonic transport (SST) and the manned space program, he didn't tell the people he was—in effect—taking the money away from education and cancer research.

If Americans had been given a clear choice among these alterna-tives, it seems likely they would have chosen clean water and clean air rather than a moon landing—cancer research instead of supersonic transports. It is these types of choices that are never given to the people through the mass media or political process. The announced decision to do something and the claimed benefits are newsworthy.

That funds have to be diverted from medical care and pollution control to pay the tab is scarcely newsworthy because there is no event or presidential announcement to draw attention to the fact. Too, the media have their own interests to consider. Very often they gain when they keep the public from knowing the true cost of programs because many media agencies profit from receiving defense or space contracts that devolve from such priorities. Other media agencies profit indirectly from supporting the same priorities.

It should be pointed out that a news story on government spending, budget proposals or congressional appropriations is not itself a news item about priorities unless the main point of the story focuses on the choice between two or more programs. In recent months, the tragedy of the Vietnam War has caused some politicians to take a fresh look at this matter of priorities. So the issue is receiving more attention through the media, but it is still a rare occasion when the subject makes the front page. Sample analysis of the *New York Times* and the *Los Angeles Times* during February and March 1950, April and May 1960, and June and July of 1969 (the periods I selected at random for examination) reveals that not one item whose main subject was priorities made the front page. The first three pages of the *Honolulu Star-Bulletin* from January 12 through May 1969 contained only 1 news item on priorities. Moreover, in these newspapers during these months there was not one news item on the front page about the brain drain, illiteracy, or on society's difficulty in coping with breakthroughs in biological science. In contrast, on one single day in 1960 the *Los Angeles Times* had 5 different stories about accidents on Page One.[7]

In trying to assess who is responsible for bias in news coverage it is important to take into account the role of the technology of news coverage as this influences any definition of what is news and creates as we have seen, a bias as significant as a politically motivated decision to play down or suppress a news item.

As we shall demonstrate in this section of the chapter, money, as well as technological and political bias, influences determinations of what shall be news. The agencies of communication are companies that are in business for the purpose of making a profit. They must make money to survive. Informing the public is secondary to this. Contrary to normal business where producing a good product often increases customers and profits, the best journalistic efforts often decrease audience and profit. Documentaries, news specials and live coverage of news events consistently lose great sums of money.[8] ABC spent 2 million dollars producing a four-hour color documentary on Africa in 1967, but they had to eventually sell it to an advertiser for $750,000.[9] Some documentaries have a hard time being sold for anything because so many sponsors don't want to associate their name with certain programs or get involved in a controversy.[10] If this type of news coverage loses money for the networks, why do they bother to broadcast even the few that they do? The answer is simple; they are forced to do it to maintain their "prestige" and convince the public and the Federal Communications Commission that they are operating in the public interest. Since the networks don't like to lose any more money on news than they have to in maintaining their image, news coverage will often be influenced or determined by profit and loss considerations.

Financial considerations determined that CBS viewers didn't need to see the Senate hearings on Vietnam—our nation's number one foreign and economic problem. One executive, Fred Friendly, quit his job as head of CBS News because he was not allowed to cover the hearings live. Instead, the listeners were offered "I Love Lucy." Newspapers and magazines make similar news decisions based on profit considerations. To attract readers in order to sell advertising, newspapers cover trivia magnificently. We have already seen how, in a two month period in 1960, the *Los Angeles Times* had 120 accident stories, 17 celebrity stories and 40 human interest stories on its front page—this compared to no stories on population, world hunger, illiteracy, or the brain drain.[11] Admittedly, accidents lend themselves to easy news coverage, but the placement of such items on the front page is testimony to the economic necessity of attracting readers who will respond to newspaper ads.

How many crusades or exposes a newspaper launches may also be affected by the profit motive. Oxie Reichler, newspaper editor, told a group of AP editors:

> Crusading is a rich man's game. . . . You lose advertising, you lose circulation, you even lose prestige. People begin thinking you have a personal ax to grind, and that the publisher himself is working for some ulterior motive.[12]

A crusade for legalized abortion may bring about an unofficial boycott by a church pressure group. The managing editor of a metropolitan daily said he figured that a well-organized pressure group, displeased by his newspapers' policy, brought about a drop in circulation of 50,000.[13] Small newspapers have been ruined financially after crusading in the public's interest. The *Morrelton Democrat* in Arkansas had to shut down its presses for lack of money after exposing voting frauds and corruption in the local area.[14] The *Rocky Mountain Journal* exposed the pricing practices of a supermarket chain and suffered financially as a result.[15] A woman photographer from Whitesberg Kentucky's *Mountain Eagle* had some of her film taken away and her life threatened by three men while she was taking pictures of the illegal strip mining being done by Bethlehem Steel Corporation. She nonetheless got some photographs. When they were published along with stories about the ravages of strip mining, editor Tom Gish lost substantial advertising money. When the same *Mountain Eagle* tried crusading for a TVA-type development program for Appalachia, the Kentucky Power Company stopped advertising in his paper. The result is that the once profitable paper is barely able to make ends meet.[16] J. R. Freeman who has crusaded to prevent the government from giving away shale-rich land to the oil corporations, usually publishes at a loss.[17] Hazel Smith's small newspaper in Lexington, Mississippi lost thousands of dollars fighting to end the violence and intimidation of blacks by the local sheriff.[18] Such newspapers seldom get financial assistance to help make up for the losses that result from exposing politicians or corporations. As journalism professor Bryce Rucker has noted, the large foundations don't hand out any money to crusading newspapers.[19] Whether it's a small weekly, a tabloid specializing in sensation, or the *New York Times,* profit considerations determine to some extent what type of news will be printed.

Most people get their news from television, and most people consider television the most reliable source of news.[20] It is in television where the great conflict between journalistic responsibility and profits becomes most dramatic. In his book, *Due to Circumstances Beyond our Control,* Fred Friendly documents some of these conflicts. Friendly notes that William Paley, chairman of the Board of CBS, was quite concerned that unscheduled news coverage of events like Winston Churchill's death and the civil rights issue had cost stockholders six cents a share.[21] Another time Paley explained why CBS had to keep making more money every year; his explanation reveals what counts most with a communication company, as well as with any other business operation:

We have many small shareholders across the country and within the company. Some of our employees have worked for us for a long time. Their entire security is tied up in their equity; many of them have stock options. Management's obligation is to protect the interests of those stockholders.[22]

It is not the networks or their executives who are at fault for allowing financial considerations to outweigh the importance of informing the public. The failure lies in a national policy that permits the communication system to be utilized for profits instead of for a lively journalistic competition between various viewpoints and perspectives. After quitting as head of CBS News, Friendly was aware that it was the system, not the men in it, that is responsible for sacrificing public interest programs for profit makers:

> Whatever bitterness I feel over my departure is toward the system that keeps such unremitting pressure on men like Paley and Stanton that they must react more to financial pressure than to their own taste and sense of responsibility. Possibly if I were in their jobs I would have behaved as they did. I would like to believe otherwise, but I must confess that in my almost two years as the head of CBS News I tempered my news judgment and tailored my conscience more than once. . . .
>   The fact that I am not sure what I would have done in these circumstances, had I been chairman or president of CBS, perhaps tells more clearly than anything else what is so disastrous about the mercantile advertising system that controls television, and why it must be changed.[23]

Even though the bias that results from profit pressures is not the result of an editorial decision based on one's political beliefs, it is nonetheless a bias which does favor certain policies and values. The timidity of some media owners to crusade for a cause which may harm their own financial interest, or to expose or embarrass powerful corporations or pressure groups is a timidity that favors the status quo. Likewise, the technological bias discussed earlier also happens to be—coincidentally—one which supports the status quo. It is a bias that unintentionally ignores the dangers to man and society, dangers which demand that man change in order to cope with the new realities he is creating for himself. Mass media owners rest on the status quo as their foundation, and so have not seen fit to correct imbalances that they can blame, with a superficial sense of justice, on financial pressure or the technology of news making.

8   For Sale--Free Speech

> The press of this country is now, and always has been,
> so thoroughly dominated by the wealthy few of the
> country that it cannot be depended upon to give the
> great mass of the people that correct information con-
> cerning political, economic and social subjects which it
> is necessary that they shall have in order that they shall
> vote and in all ways act in the best way to protect
> themselves from the brutal force and chicanery of the
> ruling and employing class.
>
> Edward W. Scripps
> founder, Scripps-Howard Newspapers

In early 1969 the people of Cheyenne, Wyoming were almost
entirely dependent upon one family for their ideas of what was happening in their community and the world. The Frontier Broadcasting
Company, controlled by Robert S. McCracken, with his wife and family, owns the city's only full-time AM radio station, the only television
station and the only daily newspapers. The family held a franchise to
operate the only community antenna television system and held a
construction permit for the city's second FM radio station.[1] This is
not a unique situation; there were seventy-three communities in the
United States in which one company or person owned or controlled
all newspapers and local broadcast outlets as of late 1967.[2]

Few communities have their mass media under the control of such
absolute monopolies like these, but such monopolies illustrate the
trend toward concentration of ownership in the communication industry as a whole—a concentration similar to that existing in other areas
of the economy. It takes millions of dollars to even think of buying a
daily newspaper or operating a television station, that is, assuming
one could get a license. As a result, newspapers, mass-circulation magazines and broadcasting ownership is concentrated into relatively few
hands. Professor Bryce Rucker, in his book First Freedom, accumulated

63

data showing national patterns of ownership. As of the middle of 1967, half of the nation's 1767 daily newspapers were owned by chains. These chain newspapers controlled 61.8 percent of total daily circulation compared to 46.1 percent in 1960. Eighty percent of the circulation of the largest twenty-five dailies was controlled by chains.[3] Scripps-League, Newhouse, Gannett, Donrey Media and Lord Thompson are some of the larger chains that own over twenty dailies each. Nine other chain owners own fifteen to twenty dailies.[4] If people don't like their daily newspaper, chances are there is little they can do about it; in 95.9 percent of American cities there is no competition between commercial dailies.[5] There is no competition among Sunday papers in thirty-four states.[6] Mass-circulation magazines are even more dominated by chains: eighteen of the nineteen magazines with circulation over one million are owned by chains.

Chains and newspapers have other economic interests which can easily create conflicts of interest which may influence news and editorial policies. Newspapers have economic interest in 9.5 percent of AM and 14.5 percent of FM radio stations.[7] Newspapers own 47 television stations affiliated with NBC or CBS.[8] The *New York Times* and the *Los Angeles Times* are two of the newspapers who have investments in newsprint mills.[9]

Many radio stations have difficulties making ends meet—but not the most powerful, widest-coverage stations. Rucker notes that 11 out of 12 of these stations

> . . . are in the hands of special-interest groups, chains and newspapers. Of the nations seventy-three 50,000-watt day and night stations, only five are licensed to independent broadcasting companies with no apparent special causes to plead. Fifty-three are owned by chain broadcasters.[10]

Commercial television is also dominated by chain broadcasters. They own 73.6 percent of all stations.[11] Rucker discovered:

> In the top ten television markets, which incidentally include almost 40 percent of all television households, 37 of the 40 VHF stations are owned by chain broadcasters. The remaining 3 are licensed to companies owning daily newspapers in the same cities
>
> Only 8.5 percent of the 156 VHF stations in the top fifty markets are owned singly by broadcasters who have no other obvious special interests.[12]

The networks have glaring conflicts of interest which may influence top level news and programing decisions. Harry J. Skornia, former president of the National Association of Educational Broadcasters, details their conflicts in his book *Television and Society*. Besides the profit motive itself, he sees natural conflicts of interest regarding labor and defense contracts:

> If the corporation were to give labor good program time and favorable news coverage, its position at the bargaining table would weaken. The corporation, as most managers see its role, cannot afford to do this. Therefore, it is inappropriate and naive to expect the business corporation to be able to synthesize and represent the public's interests when they conflict with its own profit interest.
>
> . . . Another question revolves around the stake which present broadcast owners have in continued armaments, cold-war tensions, and defense contracts. In view of the fact that RCA, CBS, Westinghouse, General Electric, and scores of other broadcast firms receive from 10 to 40 percent of their income from government contracts related to defense efforts, how whole-heartedly and sincerely can they be expected to press for genuine and lasting peace? How much recognition do United States broadcasters give to the fact, stated in the UNESCO preamble, that wars begin in the minds of men? How peace-oriented is United States broadcasting?[13]

Perhaps the most important conflict of interest is that of United States broadcasters and business firms owning or having interests in foreign broadcasting stations. Although the United States forbids foreigners from owning any stations in the United States, many countries have no laws to prevent U.S. firms from owning stations in their countries. Where such laws do exist, they do not deal with the other methods by which U.S. communication corporations are able to distribute their programs and services. The result is that while no Americans receive their news and entertainment from foreign communication sources, increasingly large numbers of people in foreign countries receive their news and entertainment from American sources. This expansion of the American communication system into foreign countries may be viewed as a potent force of imperialist influence supplanting and perhaps making unnecessary an invasion by the Marines.

In his book *Mass Communications and American Empire*, Professor Herbert Schiller lists some of the international holdings and activities of the American networks.[14] ABC is the most active. It has investments in telecasting in Latin America, Asia and the Middle East. Its international television network, Worldvision, operates in 26 countries and reaches an estimated 60 percent of television homes outside the United States. CBS owns television stations in Latin America and Canada. Its 72 overseas subsidiaries distribute CBS products and services in 100 countries. NBC has investments in stations in Australia, Latin America and Asia. It distributes film series and services for more than 300 television stations in 83 countries. Accompanying the electronic invasions of other countries are U.S. advertising agencies who have established 21 ad agencies in England, 20 in West Germany, 12 in France, 15 in Brazil and many in other countries. Schiller views the extension of the American communications system as a powerful tool of corporate forces in the United States:

> Mass communications are now a pillar of the emergent imperial society. Messages 'made in America' radiate across the globe and serve as the ganglia of national power and expansionism. The ideological images of 'have not' states are increasingly in the custody of American international media. National authority over attitude creation and opinion formation in the developing world has weakened and is being relinquished to powerful external forces. The facilities and hardware of international information control are being grasped by a highly centralized communications complex, resident in the United States and largely unaccountable to its own populations.[15]

Any trend on the part of foreign nations to prohibit or restrict this electronic invasion by the U.S. commercial communication system would certainly displease the networks. With such a vested interest in what foreigners think and the type of communication policy they develop, can the networks be depended upon to present an unbiased picture of international affairs to either their American or foreign audience? For example, how fairly will U.S. news agencies report on a foreign government that has nationalized its communication system or prohibited advertising or the showing of programs produced in America?

It's not easy to find out just how big the giants of the communication industry are and where their tentacles extend right here in the United States. The editors of *Atlantic* magazine had quite a bit of difficulty trying to discover what they termed "domains" of the big "media baronies," but they were finally able to get enough information to give some facts about their profits and holdings.[16] NBC, subsidiary of giant congolomerate RCA, had a profit of $71 million in

1967. CBS, the major part of a smaller conglomerate, netted $77 million in 1967. ABC made a $12 million profit in 1967. The Federal Communications Commission recently reported that the three networks combined had profits of $226 million in 1969, up 12 percent from the 1968 total of $179 million.

Besides owning *Time, Life, Fortune* and *Sports Illustrated,* Time-Life Inc. owns 5 television and 8 radio stations, 13 cable television systems, 600,000 acres of timberland and minority interest in foreign broadcast stations. In November 1970 it agreed to sell its 13 radio and television stations to McGraw-Hill Inc. for $80.1 million. The Gannet Company owns 30 newspapers, 2 radio and 2 television stations, and made a $8.6 million profit in 1968. Samuel I. Newhouse owns 20 newspapers, 6 television and 7 radio stations along with 9 cable television systems, and his estimated net worth is $200 to $250 million. An affiliate of the Mormon Church, Bonneville International, has 1 newspaper, 9 radio and 4 television stations, and is valued at $60 to $75 million. The Hearst corporation is worth about $250 million and owns 9 newspapers, 6 radio and 3 television stations. The *Chicago Tribune* owns 7 newspapers, 5 radio and 4 television stations whose total value is about $250 million. *Atlantic* magazine notes that the Los Angeles Times-Mirror company owns 8 book publishing concerns and 2 newspapers, and had a total profit in 1968 of $24.1 million. Some other giants in the industry are Westinghouse Broadcasting, RKO, Metromedia and the Mutual network.

It's obvious that it would take large sums to break into the communication industry. Those without a great deal of money are therefore excluded from making the very important ownership decisions which determine how and what information shall be communicated to the people. Needless to say, none of the millions of hungry Americans have ever owned any daily newspapers or stations. Out of the over 6,900 radio stations in 1971, blacks owned only 11. The other 169 "black" radio stations were owned by whites. Of the 848 television stations, blacks owned none.[17] Indians and Mexicans fare no better.

A communication policy that gives money the power to determine who will control access to mass media is *bound* to favor the political viewpoints and policies of conservative elements in society. The radical right has enough money to make itself heard throughout the nation. Neil Hickey writing in *TV Guide* reveals the slogans that were constantly heard over their broadcasts in 1967:

. . . abolish the United Nations, emasculate American labor unions, impeach Chief Justice Earl Warren, abrogate nuclear test-ban
treaties, abolish all foreign aid and domestic social-welfare programs, repeal the 16th Amendment (income tax), clamp down on
immigration, sell off the Tennessee Valley Authority to private interests, and invade Cuba.[18]

The radical right's latest obsession is in attacking any form of sex
education that is not based on the Bible. And they also stand behind
the military-industrial-space-media complex, and the priorities this
group has fashioned and sold to the American people. They are ener-
getic flag wavers, are often extremely religious and want the government to stay out of the way of the business community. These last
positions are identical to those of the giant corporations and their
foundations, thus explaining why the radical right elements in our
society get ready acceptance and financial support from many moderates and conservatives. Corporations and foundations might openly
denounce radical right extremists in public in order to create a good
public relations front, but many quietly support them in the way it
counts—with money. Arnold Forster and Benjamin R. Epstein, in their
book *Danger on The Right,* noted that in the early 1960's 70 tax
exempt foundations, 113 business firms and corporations and 25 public utilities contributed a substantial portion of the radical right's 14
million dollar yearly propaganda budget.[19] Such respected companies
as Abbott Laboratories, Armour and Company, Greyhound Corporation and Monsanto Chemical Corporation contributed to Edgar Bundy's Church League. And many firms aid the propaganda campaign
by placing advertising in radical right periodicals and by sponsoring
radio and television broadcasts. Forster and Epstein note that

. . . over and above the foundations and the corporate contributors, a group of approximately 250 men and women appear to constitute the major individual contributors. A fair proportion of these
individual contributors are themselves the owners of business firms,
corporation officials, or corporate directors. Some are prominent at-
torneys, retired men of wealth, or former political figures.[20]

There is also a direct tie-in between the corporate world and the
radical right. Senator Metcalf has documented one such case showing
that many officials of power companies also serve as officials in extremist groups.[21]

As a result of support and sympathetic treatment from media owners, the radical right is able to compete at about a hundred to one
advantage over the radical left. As *Newsweek* admitted, "large parts of
the U.S. are awash in a diet of far-right broadcasting."[22] Hickey
found that in 1967 they made over 10,000 television and radio broadcasts each week across the entire country. In comparison Hickey notes
that "the left have no voice on American TV and radio similar to that
of their rightist opponents."

Father Daniel Lyons, radical right priest and supporter of establishment priorities and wars, was able to announce in 1970 that "243
stations in over 40 states are carrying our programs free."[23] Father
Lyons is only one of many radical right spokesmen whose programs
were carried free evidently because many media owners like their message. No stations carry spokesmen for solid liberal views free, much
less spokesmen for the radical left.

In an August 1971 survey and comparison of the major radical groups
on both sides, the Institute for American Democracy found that the
top ten radical right groups had 1806 radio and 150 television
outlets compared to 44 radio and 1 television outlets for the ten
top radical left groups. On the right the Institute placed the John
Birch Society, the Liberty Lobby, Carl McIntire, H. L. Hunt, the
Christian Freedom Foundation, the Voice of Americanism and others.
On the far left it placed the Communist Party USA, WEB Du Bois
clubs, Progressive Labor Party, Socialist Labor Party, SNCC, SDS,
Black Panthers, Black Muslims and others.[24] There is no question that
as far as extremist ideas are concerned the public is exposed to very
little if any competition. The radical left may make the news often
because of their demonstrations—but this news is reported chiefly
through outlets owned by status-quo conservatives, who can slant coverage in order to descredit the demonstrators' cause.

A little closer to the center on the right of the political spectrum are
what I would describe as the respectable conservatives such as J. Edgar
Hoover, Spiro Agnew, Richard Nixon, most Southern politicians, The
Reverend Billy Graham, William Buckley and Paul Harvey. [In this
book they will be termed "solid conservative"]. They have almost as
great a media advantage over their equivalent opposition on the left
as does the radical right. A majority of television and radio stations
and daily and weekly newspapers are owned by and expound a solid

conservative viewpoint. On the opposite side are the respectable radicals such as Father Groppi, Dick Gregory, Dr. George Wald, Professor Paul Ehrlich, I. F. Stone, John Gerassi and William Winter [They will be termed "solid liberal"]. People with their viewpoints own no daily newspapers and their only broadcast outlets are those afforded occasionally by NET or the very few non-commercial radio stations. They too make the news often but this news is seen only after having been edited by those who disapprove of their viewpoints.

The only real competition among ideas allowed in the mass media is between elements usually described as moderate conservatives and moderate liberals. Self-styled or ostensible moderate liberals like Hubert Humphrey, Edward Kennedy, most Washington and foreign correspondents, newspapers such as the *Washington Post, St. Louis Dispatch* and the *New York Times* are still at a media disadvantage, but at least they have in their own hands some of the agencies of mass media. Moderate conservatives like Nelson Rockefeller, many Republican congressmen, the *Los Angeles Times, Time, Newsweek* and the networks have the biggest communication guns. It is not surprising that it is their priorities that have prevailed in policy decisions ranging from the Vietnam War and the ABM to the moon. And in advocating their priorities, they are helped by the solid conservative and the right extremist elements who push for basically the same priorities and for government non-interference with the giant corporations. In sharp contrast, because of the media owners and the commercial nature of the communication system, the solid liberal and the radical left are not allowed to compete fairly. The moderate liberals compete alone against the combined mass media power of all three segments of the conservative camp. This moves the middle ground on any issue considerably to the right of where it is in reality. The limits of controversy, then, include the radical right at one end and the moderate liberals at the other. This shuts out the solid liberal and the radical left and allows for example, Spiro Agnew to attack middle-of-the-roaders and moderate liberals as more liberal than they in fact are. In this way the conservative establishment can hardly lose since even moderate liberal policies—the most extreme policies on the left that are presented as respectable through the mass media—are policies that the conservatives can live with and profit from if they must. Elections like the Nixon-Humphrey contest are meaningless to many exactly because even the most liberal candidates still have to support establishment selection of priorities and establishment foreign policy in order to have a chance of being elected in the opinion environment nourished—or malnourished—by the media.

The fact that money buys and operates the media, as we have seen, works to the advantage of those with conservative viewpoints. This is a critically important fact—even more so than the concentration of media into the hands of large chains and corporations. Because even if the concentration were broken up and economic competition increased, real competition among all viewpoints still can never come about so long as access to the media is determined by ability to purchase rather than by the right to be heard. Chicago has four competing dailies, but they are all so conservatively oriented that a group of solid liberal Chicago journalists felt it necessary to establish the *Chicago Journalism Review* to point out myriad instances of suppression and bias in the Chicago press.

9   The Boss Is Sure to Have His Say

> And it is time, too, for recognition of the stark, naked
> but almost never spoken truth that hundreds—perhaps
> thousand—of reporters and even copy editors who
> draw their pay from the orthodox press are disgusted
> with the policies of their employers, but the economic
> necessities of their situation force them to vent their
> frustrations in the bars, in letters to friends, in their
> homes or wherever they gather with fellow profession-
> als. What finally, can they do? Where finally, can they
> go?
>
> Nathan Blumberg, Montana Journalism Review, 1969

If you ever doubt that owners of mass media are conservatively
oriented or that this fact influences what you hear and read, just take
a look at the editorial positions of the newspapers you read. The
Boston Globe analyzed the editorial positions of 39 of the nation's
major newspapers on the subject of Vietnam.[1] Four of them took a
position on the radical right and called for an all-out win policy.
Sixteen supported the Johnson Administration policy without reserva-
tion—holding what I term the solid conservative position. The remaining 19 took a moderately conservative or moderately liberal position
by supporting the United States commitment but favoring de-escalation and increased peace efforts. None favored an immediate and
orderly withdrawal of Allied troops. So the extreme limits of policy
alternatives as presented by the media in their editorial positions excluded completely both the solid liberal and radical left viewpoints.
The most liberal position presented was one of de-escalation with the
possibility of indefinite continuation of the war—a policy that even
President Nixon, no liberal certainly, found acceptable.

Those of the radical right prove very strong in Southern California
elections; they also control a significant portion of the mass media in
the area. In 1966 when an attempt was made through Proposition 14

to prevent the California legislature from enacting any fair housing measures, and in effect, legalize segregated housing, it found great editorial support. Fourteen of the 15 suburban dailies studies by Professor Jack Lyle favored the proposition—which was later declared unconstitutional after being approved by the voters.[2] Much earlier in California, Governor Earl Warren's proposed compulsory health insurance program was opposed editorially by 432 California papers and supported by only 20—more than a 20 to 1 competitive advantage for those opposed.[3]

A recent national survey of small dailies and weeklies revealed that 84 percent took a stand against any government-sponsored medical or hospital aid to the aged. The vast majority were also opposed to Federal aid to education.[4]

The private power companies in the northwest were able to obtain the support of almost every paper in their attack on the Columbia Valley Authority. Newspapers with 990,000 circulation backed the power companies while those favoring the CVA accounted for only 35,454 a 26 to 1 competitive advantage.[5]

Politicians who advocate policies approved by media owners are usually rewarded by endorsement at election time. The *Editor and Publisher* surveys of endorsements of presidential candidates gives us a clear picture of the enduringly conservative orientation of the press.[6] In both 1948 and 1952, newspapers accounting for nearly 80 percent of the daily circulation endorsed Dewey and Eisenhower as against 10 percent for Truman and Stevenson. In 1956, newspapers endorsing Eisenhower accounted for 60 percent of the circulation compared to 10 percent for Stevenson. Circulation endorsing Nixon in 1960 outnumbered that backing Kennedy 4½ to 1. Nixon again was favored heavily by the press in 1968, this time by a 3.7 to 1 margin over Humphrey. In all these elections it was a choice between a moderate or solid conservative Republican and a moderate liberal. The 1964 election offered a different choice, one between Goldwater, a solid conservative who is at times on the radical right, and Johnson, a moderate conservative in foreign affairs and a moderate liberal in domestic matters. Newspaper circulation endorsing Johnson outnumbered that backing Goldwater by 3 to 1.

These surveys of editorial endorsement show the same pattern that emerges on every issue. Radical left and solid liberal politicians are not even represented. In contrast, a politician like Goldwater, who

lines up with the solid conservative and radical right, can get endorsement from as many as 34 percent of daily newspapers, and those who
are solid and moderate conservative can get endorsements from 75
percent or more.

Many owners claim that this imbalance of editorial endorsement is
not important because they make no attempt to conceal the bias and
because it is restricted to the editorial column. But we can easily see
that only a few newspapers perform in a way that would support this
claim: most deliberately allow their bias to influence the regular news
coverage in the newspaper.

An editor's choice of which columnists to print also indicates the
conservative orientation of the press. In a study of newspapers representing 85 percent of the country's daily circulation, most were found
to clearly favor columnists and political cartoonists who supported the
stands taken in the newspaper editorials.[7] Of the papers that used
columnists in a biased manner, 7 out of 10 favored conservative columnists. A panel of newpaper editors divided columnists into three
categories on each side of the political spectrum. At the ends of the
spectrum they found that what they termed "very conservative" columnists (like Fulton Lewis, Jr.) made up 29 percent of the 1,861
columns classified, compared to 1 percent for what they termed "very
liberal" columnists (like Eleanor Roosevelt). Going up toward the
middle on each side, "conservative" columns accounted for 20 percent
compared to 8 percent for "liberal" columns. The columns taking a
position near the middle of the road, written by mildly liberal or
mildly conservative columnists—either of whom is acceptable to establishment leaders—made up 42 percent of the total. This study shows
the same pattern that emerges again and again on every issue: There
is plenty of competition of ideas between liberals and conservatives
near the middle ground, but solid conservative and radical right viewpoints have at least a 5 to 1 competitive advantage over the solid
liberal and radical left viewpoints.

Commentaries are to broadcasting what editorials are to newspapers. But where newspapers are not required by law to print opposing
editorials and viewpoints or to give equal space to someone attacked,
broadcasters are required by law to do so under the Federal Communications Commission's Fairness Doctrine. To sidestep these requirements, the owners pick newscasters with ideas similar to their own
who mask editorials by using phrases such as "many think" or "it is
thought," in place of "I think". In the early days of radio, CBS Vice

President Edward Klauber explained to newscaster H. V. Kaltenborn how to hide an editorial:

> Use such phrases as 'it is said,' 'there are those who believe,' 'the opinion is held in well-informed quarters,' 'some experts have come to the conclusion.' Why keep on saying 'I think,' and 'I believe,' when you can put over the same idea much more persuasively by quoting someone else?[8]

Instead of proposing a course of action or attacking another viewpoint, a reporter can merely imply the need for a certain policy and cleverly ridicule those opposing it. Howard K. Smith learned the art long ago and has used it in his editorial support of a very conservative policy in Vietnam. Instead of saying "I think we should escalate," Smith said: "There exists only one real alternative. That is to escalate, but this time on an overwhelming scale."[9] On another evening he ended the newscast by stating:

> From the first days of 1965 when President Johnson ordered massive intervention, he begged for a political solution. . . .
> Our political offering of a political settlement by internationally supervised free elections makes some sense. Their political solution that we surrender to them who cannot win an election, is not.[10]

Smith showed little mercy toward critics of the war in late 1969 as he came to the defense of Spiro Agnew. But instead of saying "I think," he stated:

> A portion of Americans . . . believe that Senator McGovern is impudent, and Senator Fulbright of *Arrogance of Power* fame, is effete. Many believe that those spokesmen have had more than their share of time to state their argument and should be answered back, and Agnew's answers are not more offensive than Dr. Spock's speeches.[11]

Two weeks later Smith felt that a Senator was over-reacting to the American atrocities in Vietnam. He first attacked a British journalist and then added:

> The other 'instant Solomon' is Senator Stephen Young of Ohio who said today that this is just like the Nazi atrocities. Well, it's not! Nazi atrocities, like the daily ones of the Viet Cong, were acts of national policy. This, if it happened, is a violation of national policy.[12]

As with the other Smith editorials disguised as commentaries, there were no competing commentaries stating the views of Senator Young, Senator McGovern or the many others who have argued that much of the combat in "free fire zones" (areas in which everyone in the vicinity including civilians is a target) and B-52 napalm bombings of villages are official policies which legitimize atrocities on civilians.

In another commentary Smith lectured Moratorium backers:

> Constructive criticism of a President with reasonable proposals and alternate policies is essential. Too much of the criticism today is harassment—senseless demolition of authority. With October the 15th at hand, critics should exercise care. Knock a hole in the Presidential end of the boat and we will all sink with him. [13]

The important thing isn't whether one agrees with Smith or not; it's that those who see the United States policy in Vietnam as a boat inevitably heading the nation for a crash over the waterfall were not given a chance to have their views heard in a competing commentary.

ABC claims that their commentaries are balanced, that there are just as many commentaries critical of the Vietnam policy as there are that favor it. Even if this were true—which it is not—it doesn't address itself to the crucial question of whether all viewpoints were given an equal chance to compete as far as commentaries are concerned. Whatever balance that exists over the networks is between moderate liberal and moderate conservative or solid conservative to the exclusion of a radical left, solid liberal and radical right viewpoints. But even from the network's own arbitrary and misleading idea of balance, ABC fails the test of fairness. An eleven-month survey of 1969 *ABC Evening News* conducted by a former journalist aided by seven of ABC's own newswriters and researchers, disclosed that there were 33 minutes of commentary favorable to the Administration's Vietnam policy compared to 14 minutes of commentary opposing that policy. In other international news, there were 14 minutes of commentary favorable to the Administration against only 1½ minutes of commentary opposing the Administration. [14] And even those comparisons are deceptive as it is very likely that "opposition" commentary was from a moderate point of view.

Eric Sevareid dominates commentary time on the *Walter Cronkite* evening newscast. He is generally a supporter of White House policy and establishment priorities and can be depended upon not to stray too far away from moderate conservative or moderate liberal policies.

This, by itself, is no shortcoming of any kind until it is realized that, like ABC, CBS excludes entirely commentaries from more extreme viewpoints. From July 10 to September 10, 1969, Sevareid was given 44 minutes of commentary time to expound the political views of the establishment. No commentary time whatsoever was given to those opposing Sevareid's viewpoints. On his 30th anniversary as a CBS newscaster, he spent 3 minutes congratulating himself and other newscasters for trying to achieve "objectivity." Like Smith, Sevareid is a master at covering up editorial viewpoint and personal attack. He therefore avoids the need to give opposing viewpoints an opportunity to reply. On the day of the October 15th Moratorium in 1969, Sevareid wrapped up coverage by commenting:

> Proponents for a quick and immediate withdrawal do not help; that is a practical impossibility. There is truth in the observations of the Spanish philosopher who said youth tends to be right in what it opposes and wrong in what is proposes.[15]

No spokesman for youth, or anybody else for that matter, was allowed to challenge this comment by arguing, for example, that the proposal for an immediate and orderly withdrawal is considerably better than the establishment's proposal to intervene in the first place, or that the present policy of Vietnamization would allow an indefinite extension of the war.

Coming to the support of President Nixon's first major policy speech on Vietnam, Sevareid again criticized the idea of immediate withdrawal:

> . . . That is a physical, practical impossibility as even the North Vietnamese enemy admits. . . . No doubt a precipitous withdrawal would for a time damage world confidence in American steadfastness and Americans' faith in themselves, but no sane person has suggested it.[16]

Men who have advocated immediate withdrawal, including former Congressman Allard Lowenstein, ADA spokesmen, General David Shoup, Dr. Benjamin Spock, Reverend Ralph Abernathy and many others may not be upset because CBS' pundit has implied they are insane because of their views. They may, however, object to the fact that CBS allowed no one representing their viewpoint to have his say—to comment that nothing is more damaging to world confidence in America, or to youth's confidence in America, than its steadfastness in pursuing a senseless and unjust war whose stated objectives have already been lost. And even though the radical right's proposals weren't attacked as insane, they too, might have liked equal time to propose their policy of an all-out military effort. But by excluding all but moderate viewpoints in their commentaries, CBS effectively decided for its audience which viewpoints it could or could not consider.

As we see, management bias can easily be determined by studying editorials and commentaries, but there is no way of discovering the cumulative bias that results from many other more significant ownership decisions. By hiring newsmen he knows will not go too far astray from his own views, an owner, without any special instructions, can determine the political orientation of the news department. The public is only made aware of this powerful tool of creating bias when the owner makes a mistake and hires a reporter who is more liberal than he had bargained for. When this happens, the owner may resort to ordering his newsmen how to report the news or what to suppress. Perhaps the most notorious edicts of this kind were given by radio tycoon George Richards, friend of Ty Cobb, Eddie Rickenbacker and J. Edgar Hoover and owner of 35 stations at one time during the 1940's. Richards, an extremist on the right, particularly disliked President Roosevelt who, according to Richards, was a "Jew-lover" whose objective was to bring about communism. Erik Barnouw, in his book *The Golden Web,* records some of the orders that Richards gave his news staff in order to "get rid of that bastard in the White House."

> Richards gave his news staffs orders to carry no items favorable to Roosevelt. Several newsmen testified to orders by Richards to 'tie in' items about Roosevelt with items about communists or criminals, so that they would seem related. After the death of Roosevelt the policies remained in effect for all members of his family. Concerning Mrs. Roosevelt he told staff members to 'give her hell' whenever possible—'the old bitch.' When she had an automobile accident in 1946 he called Robert Horn at KMPC to ask if he couldn't report the news in a way that would give the impression she was drunk. Horn felt this would be difficult.

Richards often ordered newsmen to add nicknames when referring to liberal politicians; "pig boy" or "tumbleweed" were to be used for Henry Wallace, and "pipsqueak" for Harry Truman. Richards stated his policy in a letter he wrote to newsman Clete Roberts at KMPC, Los Angeles:

> We should learn to beat the New Dealers with their attacks on
> business and other issues. . . . Beat them to the punch—accuse
> them of everything under the sun. Put them on the defensive instead
> of allowing them to be on the offensive. . . .

Richards reportedly had to fire seven news editors in three years.
Nevertheless, the FCC regularly renewed his licenses, and the Du Pont
Company gave Richards its 1945 public service award.[17]

Barnouw also tells of cases where owners ordered newsmen whenever possible to quote from and use *Counterattack,* an extremist peri-
odical which kept a ready list of liberals for use by communist hunters.[18] In 1935 one owner issued a memorandum to his newscaster:
"No reference to strikes is to be made on any news bulletin broadcast
over our stations." When the newsman complained that it would be
difficult to ignore a front-page strike story, he was fired.[19]

One modern-day media tycoon who apparently gave orders to his
newsmen in the George Richards manner is Walter Annenberg, head
of Triangle Publications Inc., which includes in its holdings many
newspapers, magazines (*TV Guide, Seventeen*), TV and radio stations,
cable television operations and horse racing dailies. Annenberg seemingly used his position as publisher and editor of the *Philadelphia
Inquirer,* one of the six largest morning dailies in the nation, to manu-
facture, slant and censor news in the attempt to produce public opinion that would serve his own personal, financial and political interests.
Writing in the May 1969 issue of *Philadelphia* magazine, Gaeton
Fonzi discloses some of the orders that Annenberg's employed newsmen received from the editor's office. One reporter was ordered to
change his story about *Holiday* magazine so that it appeared the magazine was in more difficulty than the reporter's investigations revealed.
This certainly didn't help out the owner, Curtis Publishing Company,
who at the time was looking for investors to help it out of a financial
crisis.

No one knows why, but Annenberg used his press powers to ignore
Philadelphia's professional basketball team, the 76ers. Both his Philadelphia newspapers "were ordered to extensively curtail their coverage
of the team, drop all features about its players and not print any pre-
game information." Two paragraphs were allowed to note a team
victory, one paragraph to record a loss. Telecast listings of games were
also dropped. During the month of newspaper neglect, the attendance
dropped from an average of 4,000 to 1,000 per game. A boxing promoter refused to increase the contribution that one of Annenberg's

charities was to get from a boxing match. Annenberg's two newspapers then blackballed his fights.

Inquirer reporters were ordered to write articles attacking businessmen who had financial interests which were in possible conflict with those of Annenberg. Annenberg's assistant editor told one reporter to write an article about a businessman that would "knock the hell out of him." It's obvious that financial interests were also what motivated Annenberg to launch his media attack against Democratic candidate Milton Shapp in the 1966 gubernatorial election. Shapp has financial interests in an electronics firm that is in competion with Triangle's cable television operations. He was successful in blocking Triangle's attempt to push through the legislature an amendment which would have given Triangle exclusive rights for cable television in Philadelphia. Annenberg himself traces back his all-out journalistic campaign against Shapp to the day Shapp claimed that the merger between the Pennsylvania and New York Central railroads "was a legalized multi-million-dollar swindle which put the robber barons of old to shame." At the time, Annenberg was the largest individual stockholder in Pennsylvania Railroad. There may be no evidence of the editor ordering newsmen to do a hatchet job on Shapp, but it's unlikely that no such concerted and consistent manipulation of news to descredit a candidate could have been accomplished without orders from above. Fonzi notes that the newspaper, in addition to carrying out "one of the most vicious editorial campaigns ever conducted against any political candidate by any newspaper, . . . consistently slanted news stories, distorted reports of the facts" and used "outright untruths" in its attempt to defeat Shapp.

The *Inquirer* ignored the presence of Ralph Nader when he came to town, but apparently one of the *Inquirer* reporters hadn't received an order; He wrote a story about Nader's speech. The story was killed. Annenberg ordered his television stations not to carry Howard K. Smith's program on Richard Nixon because it included, as part of a relatively balanced program, two minutes of Alger Hiss' critical comments about Richard Nixon. Annenberg's newspaper, radio and television stations were then told to censor wire service and network news reports about the furor over the program. One station blacked out a network commentator in mid-sentence.

Fonzi also discloses that Annenberg has ordered his staff not to use the names of certain people in the *Inquirer*. The blacklist was referred to by some *Inquirer* reporters as "Annenberg's shit list." Many famous people such as Imogene Coca, Zsa Zsa Gabor and Dinah Shore have made the list for varying periods. When Matt McClosky owned an opposition newspaper in town, he was on the list. He was also cropped or brushed out of group photographs published in the *Inquirer.* Harold Stassen made the list for attempting to take the vice presidential nomination away from Richard Nixon in 1956. Apparently Richard Nixon has been duly impressed with Walter Annenberg's management of news in service to conservative interests—he appointed him ambassador to England.

Another case of "orders from the boss" apparently took place in Wilmington, Delaware, where the Du Ponts own two daily newspapers. In 1964 news editor Creed Black claimed he received orders from H. B. Du Pont to censor certain items touching on some Du Pont special interests. Friction developed and Black was demoted. In Black's letter of resignation he stated: "I, for one, need no further evidence that the ownership wants the *Morning News* and *Evening Journal* operated as house organs instead of newspapers." H. B. Du Pont would not allow Black to publish his letter of resignation in the newspaper; announcement of the resignation was all that appeared. H. B. Du Pont denied the charges, but his denials included no journalistic evidence that could be used to refute Black's specific accusations of censorship.[20]

Steve Holbrook, a Mormon and former press secretary for the NAACP, was told by his friend, who was a newsman for the Mormon-owned KSL station, that he and other news personnel working for KSL were instructed not to put out any news about NAACP on KSL unless they had the express permission from the first presidency of the Mormon Church.[21]

KRON-TV in San Francisco would not allow coverage of the merger between the *San Francisco Chronicle* (which owns KRON-TV) and the *San Francisco Examiner* in 1968, according to former KRON cameraman Albert Kihn.[22] The *Chronicle,* who earlier criticized General Motors for using private detectives to snoop on Ralph Nader, then sent its own spies to snoop on Kihn. Apparently the news departments of the *Chronicle* and KRON-TV were ordered to ignore this story: they didn't mention it until after the snooping had been exposed in another newspaper and the *Chronicle* admitted to the FCC that it had occurred.[22]

Naturally, most owners hesitate to give orders to newsmen even if they would like to have the news slanted to support their political viewpoints or economic interests. Friction often develops in such cases. In a survey of ninety-nine television news directors, Per Holting found that 49 percent admitted that newscasts had caused friction with the station management.[23]

If other techniques fail, owners can and have resorted to firing reporters. Very few newsmen have ever been fired for being too conservative to suit their boss, but there are numerous cases of liberals being fired. As can be expected, owners seldom admit that the real reason they fire a reporter is because of his liberal ideas. CBS claimed that William L. Shirer's news program in the late 1940's was dropped because of programing considerations, but the famous author of *The Rise and Fall of the Third Reich* saw it definitely as an attempt to silence him for his liberal ideas.[24] He had an audience of over 6 million at the time.

Bryce Oliver, writing in the *New Republic* in 1947, noted that twenty-four liberals had been dropped or had their air time slashed. They included Orson Welles, Henry Morgenthau, Max Lerner and Fiorello La Guardia. Oliver felt the reasons were obvious: such broadcasters dealt with topics such as the political power of the Catholic Church, monopolies, dollar diplomacy and political power. Both the sponsors and the networks resorted to firing liberals. Robert St. John had a sponsor but was still unable to find a radio spot. Even before the firings of liberal radio commentators, conservatives outnumbered liberals. *Variety* made a comprehensive survey of radio commentators in 1945 and found there were 5 reactionaries, 5 conservatives, 10 middle-of-the roaders, and only 4 liberals.[25] After liberal commentators had been fired or had their time reduced in 1947, George Seldes made a survey of network radio newscasters at the extremes of the political spectrum as allowed on radio. He found there were only three newscasters who could be considered moderately or solid liberal—Cecil Brown, Raymond Swing and Leland Stowe. They had combined weekly time of only 105 minutes compared to 465 minutes for seven radical right newscasters.[26]

Sponsors of Drew Pearson's radio broadcasts fired him when Senator Joseph McCarthy threatened them with an anticommunist attack if they did not do so.[27] Another well-known journalist who got the axe was Howard K. Smith. Even though a moderate hawk on Vietnam, Smith has traditionally been a moderate liberal when it comes to domestic affairs. Smith was disturbed when he witnessed Sheriff "Bull"

Connors' police idly stand by while civil rights workers were brutally beaten. He concluded a special report on this Birmingham episode by quoting Edmund Burke: "The only thing necessary for the triumph of evil is for good men to do nothing." This, according to Fred Friendly, disturbed the top brass at CBS because of the possible effects it might have on affiliated stations in the Deep South. This caused disagreements about CBS news editorial policy to come to a head, and as a result Smith's resignation was requested by William Paley and Frank Stanton.[28]

A leading editorial writer for the *Providence Journal* had his weekly column dropped because of an article opposing the war in which he said that critics of Martin Luther King didn't understand civil rights or the war in Vietnam. Censored columnist James P. Brown said the episode:

> . . . is symptomatic of a larger problem that affects most if not all American newspapers today. This is a problem of preserving a vigorous provocative forum for discussion, and, if need be, dissent on the editorial pages of the newspapers which are increasingly dominated by business-oriented corporate boards enjoying monopoly status in their local communities.[29]

Life magazine reporter Chris Welles recently spent months digging into what is called the oil shale controversy. Potentially a front-page issue and scandal, it had never been brought into the open by a mass-circulation magazine. In his story, Welles related how the government seemed more intent on giving away billions of dollars worth of shale-rich land to the oil companies than on protecting the public's right to these lands. *Life* killed the story. Welles wasn't too happy over having his story censored: "I was outraged that the story had been killed. This is the biggest story I've ever worked on." When they found out that Welles had sold the story to *Harpers,* they fired him. Nobody knows the real reason for *Life's* timidity, but Chris Welles thinks it's because *Life* envisioned a $5 to $10 million loss in advertising from the oil companies if they printed the story.[30]

Newspapers and radio and television newsrooms throughout the country get much of their news about Chicago politics and crime from the cooperatively-owned City News Bureau in Chicago. Gene Corey, a newsman for the Bureau, cooperated with the *Chicago Journalism Review* in exposing how the City News Bureau censored reports of the disorders at the Democratic convention of 1968 before giving them to the National Commission on Violence. The Bureau management deleted a reporter's account of how he had been threatened by a police commander as well as parts of the story describing the treatment of a photographer: "The policemen halted, calmly kicked the photographer in the groin and walked on." The reason given by the executive for censoring was: "We have to work with the police." Three months later both Corey and reporter Terry Mullin, one of those whose reports were censored, were fired by the Bureau. Corey thinks the reasons for the firings were his cooperation in exposing the censorship, not the official reasons that were given by the management.[31]

The city editor of the *Waterbury Republican*, Floyd Knox, was fired for running, on Moratorium day, a front-page list of Vietnam casulaties from the Waterbury area. Ted Hall, managing editor of the Passaic-Clifton, *New Jersey Herald News*, was fired when he refused his publisher's orders to stop investigating a murder case involving charges against the son of a publisher of a nearby suburb newspaper.[32]

In Los Angeles, Mort Sahl, Les Crane, Bob Arbogast, Jack Margolis, Jill Schary and Stan Bohrman, although not reporters, were trying to deal with controversial issues from a liberal point of view. Their talk shows were all cancelled.[33] At the same time, Los Angeles radio and television are filled with numerous radical right talk shows and newscasters. Even moderate conservatives seem too liberal to get a fair break in Los Angeles media land.

The management of *Time* magazine, long-time supporters of the Vietnam intervention, were so upset by articles which they thought were damaging to establishment policy in Vietman that they publicly questioned the accuracy and loyalty of the reports filed by two of their own reporters, Charles Mohr and Mert Perry. This caused the two highly-respected reporters to quit.[34] This would seem an unusually clumsy technique for owners to take, usually bosses find a way to modify or bury the reports of correspondents that go against management policy. The clumsiness might have served as a clever way of forcing the resignations.

Many management decisions regarding programing are really acts that censor unpopular viewpoints for political or economic reasons. Naturally, this would be difficult for anyone to prove, and the public is usually not aware and has no way of knowing that such decisions have been made. Since the day Cuba's Fidel Castro expropriated U.S.

private business holdings in Cuba, the commercial press has not even attempted to be objective or to present liberal viewpoints regarding Cuba. In 1968, non-commercial KQED allowed the showing of a documentary favorable to Castro, but the response of educational stations indicates that they don't believe in allowing the public to see all sides much more than the commercial press. Out of 165 NET stations, 111 refused to carry the program. New York City's NET outlet carried it but only with the proviso that an hour-long panel discussion immediately follow in order to specifically counter the supposedly pro-Castro bias.[35] Such panels (filled with conservatives) do often follow the very few documentaries or interviews presenting a solid liberal viewpoint, but there are seldom if ever any follow-up panels specifically designed to counter the bias in the numerous documentaries presenting solid conservative viewpoints. This practice obviously tends to make the audience question the responsibility of solid liberal programs much more so than solid conservative programs.

The *Columbia Journalism Review* noted that another NET documentary, "Who Invited US?," a program which focused on a half century of United States military intervention abroad, was refused by NET stations in Washington D.C., Norfolk and Richmond, Virginia, Austin, Texas, Redding, California and other cities.

Network specials on Vietnam have had either a moderately liberal or a moderately conservative bias. Even so, 70 percent of NBC affiliates refused to carry a special on Vietnam scheduled for prime hours in 1966, and 58 percent of CBS affiliates refused to carry a special on the war the same month.[36] The audience had no way of knowing they were being kept from seeing the programs. Not all public affairs programs are turned down by such a high percentage of affiliates. About 25 percent of the affiliates consistently refused "CBS Reports," "Chet Huntley Reporting" and "David Brinkley's Journal" in the early 1960's. In a 1962 study of 2000 network public affairs programs, it was discovered that 25 percent were turned down by affiliates.[37] Even today, CBS' "Face the Nation" and other network interview programs are kept from the public by nearly a quarter of the affiliates.[38]

Edward P. Morgan noted that an October television interview of Premier Khrushchev by David Susskind was carried in New York City and about six other cities, but was not carried by the NBC-TV affiliate in the nation's capital.[39] This management decision deprived the nation's lawmakers of a chance to see and learn first hand something about the Premier's thinking and response to questions. Ironically, only five months earlier the White House had challenged Russian leaders to permit the Russian people to hear President Eisenhower's speech on the summit conference.[40]

The people of Boston, Providence, Buffalo, Rochester and New Orleans, because of CBS affiliate censorship, were not allowed to see a drama on "The Defenders" that included a trial in which a physician pleaded for legalized abortion.[41]

Instead of fighting the affiliate censorship, the top management at the networks actually abet it. Fred Friendly tells how Frank Stanton and Richard Salant instituted a system whereby affiliates could screen in advance each "CBS Reports" to see if it offended them in any way.[42] As Friendly noted, this can kill any enterprising producer's zeal to do a hard-hitting program. Since the more controversial and liberal programs are censored more often than others, producers and reporters are subtly encouraged to produce documentaries that will offend no one, documentaries that most or all affilliates will accept. This helps explain why the networks, each with ample talent and facilities for producing at least once a week a hard-hitting documentary like CBS' "Hunger in America" or NBC's "Report on CBW," instead end up featuring documentaries which, as critic Cecil Smith notes, have "been largely given over to studies of animal behavior and geography, valid and intelligent but scarcely subjects at grips with the issues of this society."[43]

TV Guide in a June 1969 editorial stated:

> Every so often the television networks dip their toes into the cold water of controversy that surrounds us in America today. But not very often.
> Once or twice during the past season, the networks have done shows on hunger, on the plight of the cities, the college revolution. But these few stand out in lists that are notable only for their studied avoidance of today's crucial problems.[44]

A "studied avoidance" of crucial problems in the planning stage is only one method of keeping controversial documentaries to a minimum; another is censorship of, or refusal to telecast, documentaries that are already made and available to the networks. Financed by ABC, Truman Capote produced "Death Row, U.S.A.," a documentary dealing with deplorable prison conditions and the individual plight of prisoners facing the death penalty. ABC has refused for three years to show the documentary even though a former ABC president, *Newsweek,* and the *New York Times* praised its quality. CBS and NBC showed no interest in buying the rights for $100,000. Thus for several years the American public has been kept from seeing this documentary, produced by one of America's great authors and producers.[45]

Despite its telecast in Japan and many other countries, all three networks have, since May 1968, refused to show a historical documentary film that Professor Sumner J. Glimcher of Columbia University characterized as "perhaps the best argument for people to live in peace." The film shows the destruction of Hiroshima and Nagasaki after U.S. atomic bombings. Also depicted are the bombs' horrifying effects on individual Japanese victims. The U.S. Army had censored the two-hour and forty-five minute film for twenty-three years. It was released by the United States in March 1968 at the insistence of the Japanese Government. As the networks told the Columbia University Center for Mass Communications (who had made a shortened version of the film)—they just weren't interested.[46] In August 1970, Public Broadcasting Service became the first network to show the film.

For a simple reason, the networks seldom find themselves in a position of having to censor or refuse to show a documentary. This is because decisions at top levels usually insure that network talent and resources will be spent producing documentaries that will offend no one. ABC's first three documentaries in 1970 were "Golden Age of the Automobile," "Last of the Westerners," and "Saga of the Iron Horse," fare that is not at all unusual for network documentary broadcasting in general.

In surveying the year ending in June 30, 1969, the *Survey of Broadcast Journalism* found network documentary efforts in 12 vital issues "comparatively infrequent, considering opportunities and proven capacities." The *Survey* noted that no network documentaries dealt exclusively with poverty and outside of the Czech crises, there was little on international affairs.[47]

In their monitoring of television in 40 different communities, the *Survey* found that locally-originated documentary programing had hit an all-time low:

> . . . correspondents reported no documentary coverage of international affairs in 12 communities, negligible coverage in 11 more. The subject of birth control and population was totally ignored in 13 communities, disarmament and the military-industrial complex in 19.

There was no or negligible coverage of the urban crises in 14 communities, of environmental problems in 16, of poverty in 15, of race and minorities in 14, of science and space in 23, of medicine in 20.[48]

Of the 173 stations responding to the *Survey's* queries, 68 reported that they had done no investigative reporting at all during the year.[49]

News reporters and producers can't help being influenced in their own work as they note the type of programing condoned by the brass. They usually learn either not to bother producing documentaries at all or to stay away from the hard-hitting investigative type.

Censorship by conditioning also occurs on a significant scale in the other news media. Unknown to the public, owners and their editors make decisions which prevent many situations from being exposed or investigated in the first place. An eleven-man Associated Press investigative task force interviewed 36 crew members who had first-hand knowledge of the alleged attack on U.S. destroyers by North Vietnamese torpedo ships in the Gulf of Tonkin. They filed a story which raised questions about the credibility of the official version. The story was refused by so many newspapers that it caused one AP executive to remark: "One of the problems is getting this new enterprise copy past crusty old telegraph editors and into the papers."[50] Both the *New York Times* and the *Los Angeles Times* chose not to publish the story on the day the wrap-up was released for publication.[51]

The AP will no doubt try other investigative efforts, but it is hardly reasonable to expect an individual reporter to keep digging into controversial situations if his stories are turned down. Urban affairs reporter Christopher Chandler quit the *Chicago Sun Times* because they refused to print his story detailing evidence on the bidding for a renewal project that pointed to graft on the part of top men in Mayor Daley's Administration. For months he had been encouraged by his editors to pursue this investigation, but the story never made it into print. Chandler thinks the story illustrates that: "Increasingly, important decisions are made above the level of editor."[52] Two other Chicago newspaper reporters also quit newspapers when their stories exposing political corruption were not printed.[53]

The marvels of communication technology enable all Americans to be involved directly in the most momentous cultural events of our times, whether it's the landing on the moon, funerals of great leaders or the Super Bowl. Certainly no one would criticize the use of our technology to enable people to witness these great events. However, this does raise questions as to why this same communication capacity isn't utilized to provide live coverage of events that are of vital significance to the welfare and future of the American people. Seldom are United Nations sessions or Senate investigations covered. The priorities of live coverage resemble very much the military-industrial's distorted priorities for the nation in general. Spectacular events like moon landings, the inauguration, presidential trips and political conventions are given maximal live coverage at whatever cost while many significant events are ignored.

This distortion in news priorities of live coverage is not entirely due to financial or technical considerations. A subjective decision is required when it comes to deciding what shall be covered live. Live coverage of events at the United Nations can provide one example. President Nixon has spoken of man's capacity for destroying the human species through chemical or biological warfare. On November 25, 1969, he made the issue the top story of the day as he renounced the use of germ warfare and asked the Senate to ratify the 1925 Geneva Protocol which bans the use of chemicals in warfare. This afforded news media a great chance to turn the people's attention to the investigations, hearings and resolutions on chemical and biological warfare that were taking place at the UN during the whole month of December. No greater threat confronts man than the possibility of chemical or biological warfare, yet the networks ignored the UN proceedings. Was it merely coincidental that during these proceedings UN scientific experts and voting members expressed their opposition to President Richard Nixon's CBW policy of using tear gas and defoliants in Vietnam by almost unanimously voting that the use of such chemicals was prohibited by the same Geneva Protocol that the President wanted the Senate to ratify?[54]

On November 15, 1969, the Vietnam Moratorium brought out the largest group ever to demonstrate in the nation's capital. The police estimated a minimum of 250,000 people, but others claimed the crowd to be close to a million.[55] No matter what the exact count, it was a notable event, yet not one television or radio network covered the demonstrations live.

Decisions about live coverage, like other news decisions, are being made by people who all have similar viewpoints. The political extremes are excluded from making these important news decisions. Liberals and radicals certainly would have decided to cover the Moratorium live if they had had their own network. The radical right would have covered live their Veterans' Day pro-administration demonstration if they had controlled a national network.

It seems incredible that a citizen can turn on his television or radio day after day and not be able to witness any of the vital government and non-governmental meetings where our country's politicians and experts are debating the issues that affect every American. In January of 1970, Senator Gaylord Nelson's Senate Small Business subcommittee was investigating the danger of using birth control pills. The hearings were lively and informative; they certainly would have held the interest of many millions of viewers if covered live. In the same month the Consumer Federation of America was holding an interesting conference that touched on matters affecting every American's pocketbook and health. Neither of these significant events was covered live. It seems incredible that the economics of television, or the decisions of only a few men, will determine the live coverage that Americans are offered. One might expect that in a democracy a citizen would have the opportunity, daily, of turning on his set and watching a few of the many important meetings, investigations and conferences that take place every day in our nation. That a relatively few people might watch such programing should never be a reason for eliminating the audience's right to witness and participate in democratic processes.

It would be difficult to prove that top level news decisions are made on the basis of the owner's political viewpoints instead of financial, technical or journalistic considerations, but occasionally the media brass are forced to make decisions which lay open to view their real biases. A nonpartisan group of scientists, politicians and celebrities called the "Citizens Against ABM" offered all television networks the $250,000 required to purchase a half hour of television time for presenting their case to the American people. All three networks refused to allow the group to buy access to the media.[56] None of the network television evening newscasts bothered to inform their listeners that they had refused the request. The Citizens group held a rally at the Palladium in Hollywood, but no local or national commercial stations felt it merited live coverage. Is it just coincidental that Southern California has more military-industrial defense contracts than any other area in the world?

All three networks again revealed their bias in May 1970 by refusing to allow the Democratic National Committee to buy time to reply to President Nixon's numerous televised statements on the Vietnam War.

10 Prostitution: A Problem in Definition

> The American press, with a very few exceptions is a
> kept press. Kept by the big corporations the way a
> whore is kept by a rich man.
>
> Theodore Dreiser

> While television is supposed to be 'free,' it has in fact
> become the creature, the servant and indeed the prosti-
> tute of merchandizing.

If a person or group has enough money they can buy favorable news coverage in the press. Some may accuse the press of "prostitut-ing" journalistic standards by selling this service, but as we shall see, when the nation's communication system itself legitimizes the buying of access to media—and thus favorable news treatment—it is some-times difficult to determine when such practices are flagrant enough to constitute unquestionable prostitution of journalistic standards. The sports pages of many newspapers are for sale. Irwin Ross mentions a few of the more flagrant examples in his book *The Image Merchants*. Twenty-six newspapermen representing two wire services and nine newspapers were paid $30,000 by New England racing tracks in 1953. Another sportswriter was being paid $150 a week by a boxing promoter.[1] This practice hasn't been dated; the *Chicago Journalism Review* revealed in November 1971 that sportswriters and broadcasters were accepting myriad forms of payment (including cash) for favorable coverage of horseracing.

In broadcasting, promoters avoid the necessity of having to pay off sportcasters because in most cases they—not the station—decide for themselves who the sportscaster will be. Writing in the January 1970 *TV Guide*, Stanley Frank outlined the TV sports scene by stating:

> Few fans are aware that sportscasters are hired directly by each
> local team and are answerable to it. Radio and TV stations that carry
> the games have no control over the play-by-play and 'color' men.

> Slanted accounts of games not only are allowed; they are demanded by promoters who sell the air rights to their events. An announcer who fails to shill for the home team and suggest that the local heroes can walk on water soon has ample leisure to reflect on the high price of integrity.

Frank notes that the networks select their own sportcasters, but only after approval by the league and teams they cover.

CBS, with its financial interest in professional athletics, can hardly be expected to cover sports in any other way than that of a public relations agent. WCBS radio in New York (owned by CBS) was upset because its own reporters weren't turning in Yankee baseball scores fast enough. To inspire faster coverage, it sent a memorandum to its new staff: "If I have to spell it out for you I will: CBS *owns* the New York Yankees."[2]

John Hohenberg provides many examples to show that what is printed in the sports section as well as the travel, real estate and women's sections of many newspapers is influenced more by money than by journalistic standards. In his book *The News Media,* he quotes Ferdinand Kuhn:

> In all but a few big city newspapers, one has only to look to know that the press adulterates its news with unlabeled advertising. The line between news and salesmanship is hard to find in the pages and sections that deal with food, fashion and travel.[3]

One editor admitted, "Product plugs don't sneak into our news columns any more; they march in with banners flying, trumpets blaring and drums beating."[4] Only the naive could imagine newspapers giving such service without some kind of remuneration.

Peter Bart notes that the Securities and Exchange Commission discovered some of the different forms of payments made to newspapers:

> Financial reporters and editors in many cases have held stock in companies about which they have written, or have accepted gifts, junkets and other favors from these companies.
> Financial sections often fail to distill truthful and important news from the dishonest and trivial; as a result, the financial press has been used over and over again by stock touts and manipulators to mislead the investing public.[5]

Professor William Hubbard, in a survey of business and financial editors from 162 dailies, found that 22.6 percent indicated that, as a matter of routine, they felt compelled to "puff up or alter or downgrade" business stories at the request of advertisers.[6]

The press has also sold its power to manage news to politicians. Fifty-one publishers, editors and other pressmen were paid $480,000 to print favorable articles about Illinois Governor Dwight H. Green's Administration from 1941 to 1949. It was later discovered that newsmen in Georgia, Alabama and New York were also being paid by politicians.[7]

Senate hearings in 1963 revealed that for a fee the United Press International provided a special news service to big corporations. The client could thus be assured that favorable news about corporation activity or comments by the company head would be included in UPI press releases.[8]

Not all of the press either demands or accepts fees for producing news favorable to the speical interests of the business community; many do it because they have the same political viewpoints and values as those in the business world. William Allen White, respected journalist and editor, explained the reasons for this similarity in viewpoints:

> The publisher associates on terms of equality with the bankers, the merchant princes, the manufacturers and the investment brokers. His friends unconsciously color his opinion. If he lives with them on any kind of social terms in the City Club or the Country Club or the Racquet Club, he must more or less merge his views into the common views of the other capitalists. The publisher is not bought like a chattel. Indeed, he is often able to buy those who are suspected of buying him. But he takes the color of his social environment.[9]

A survey of newspaper use of canned editorials (editorials written by advertising agents or company public relations departments and given to newspaper editors) also reveals shared values and, in addition, indicates the willingness of a large part of the press to let itself be used as a propaganda agent in return for legitimate advertisement money. For over fifty years the private power companies have been using part of the public's monthly utility bill to pay for its propaganda campaign against community owned power companies. Director of the Utility Information Committee in Missouri, J. B. Sheridan, noted the results of increasing the amount of advertising in 1924:

> This has a splendid effect upon editors. . . . The result is that we now stand very well with the editors, and the press of the State. I

may say that the newspapers are 99 percent with the privately-owned utilities.[10]

Actually Sheridan underestimated what his success would be. He claimed six years later that he was able to line up 599 out of 600 newspapers by the use of private utility blandishments of one type or another. Another public relations official, Lee Jones of the Kansas Public Service Association, claimed that even without ads he had equal success in getting the AP to send out utility propaganda: "Whenever we have had occasion to use the Associated Press, our material has gone over with a batting average of 1000."[11]

Forty years later the percentage of editorial support wasn't as high as earlier, but it was high enough to give the private utilities a considerable propaganda advantage over the community-owned utilities. During 1964 one million canned editorials were distributed by the Industrial News Review. Senator Metcalf notes, "A survey of use of these editorials in one state—Colorado—showed that about a third of the editors used the editorials, frequently as their own and without change."[12] A director of the Tennessee Valley Authority, Frank E. Smith, noted that in the first nine months of 1967, 75 of the 125 editorials unfavorable to the TVA were canned editorials distributed by the Industrial News Review. Only 1 editor bothered to inform his readers that the editorial was canned.[13]

As we have seen, automobile manufacturers through the years have consistently taken stands against legislation requiring auto makers to make safer cars. On such a controversial issue almost everyone has something of his own to say, but not some small California newspapers which ran canned editorials supporting the safety viewpoint of the auto manufacturers.[14]

For every four minutes of cigarette commercials broadcast in 1969 and 1970, stations were required to give one minute free time for anti-cigarette ads. Broadcasters tended to present these health ads at the least desirable hours such as early in the morning or in the afternoon when the audience is small. Few were shown during prime time. Still, media owners objected. Many newspapers took an editorial stand against giving anti-smoking groups, like the American Cancer Society, this free time. One in five papers ran canned editorials backing the station owners in opposing the free ads; many of these editorials were not labeled to indicate their source.[15]

Everyone knows that drug and food manufacturers are big advertisers. Are they able with their advertising money to buy special or protective news treatment in the coverage of stories concerning their products or the politicians that protect them from consumer reformers? It certainly seems so. On a KPFK radio newscast in August 1969, it was reported:

> A democratic study group released a report by its consumer task force under the Chairmanship of Congressman Ben Rosenthal, Democrat of New York, broadly criticizing the Administration's consumer policy and offering a counter-program of its own. The report notes cut-backs in the budget for consumer protection, failure to propose new consumer measures and general failure to fill several important Administration consumer posts. The report criticized President Nixon for appointing as Under-Secretary of Agriculture the man who led the National Association of State Departments of Agriculture against meat inspection legislation.[16]

The *New York Times* covered the study group's report on Page 19. The *Los Angeles Times* ignored the report completely, and there was no mention of it on either *Huntley-Brinkley* or *Walter Cronkite* newscasts.

As early as 1962 a joint committee of experts from the UN Food and Agriculture Organization and the UN World Health Organization issued a report strongly urging that baby foods be prepared without food additives.[17] This includes the most common additive—monosodium glutamate. This report was covered by the *New York Times* on Page 5 in a small article and caused little fuss. For the next seven years, little or nothing was heard about additives in baby foods. Probably 99 percent of American mothers were not aware of the warnings from these experts, and the baby food manufacturers kept using monosodium glutamate and other additives until the issue again raised its head in 1969. This time it was too big for the press to ignore, but some apparently kept on trying—a great pleasure, no doubt, to the baby food manufacturers. The *New York Times* reported on Page 33 that Dr. John Olney's research showed that monosodium glutamate had caused brain damage in mice. The Doctor warned pregnant women not to eat monosodium glutamate pending proof that it would not harm the foetus.[18] There was no report of this at all in the *Los Angeles Times*. Two months later at hearings concerning food additives and labeling, Ralph Nader was testifying before the Subcommittee on Hunger. He argued that the committee needed the power of subpoena to force food manufacturers to testify before the committee. He also accused the Department of Agriculture of employing secrecy to protect food processors. Nader added:

> Silent forms of violence . . . attacking cell or tissue doesn't attract attention like street crimes. . . . The more significant sources of violence, types of violence attached to corporate power or to profit interest, is not likely to be a concern.[19]

Huntley-Brinkley covered the hearings, focusing on Nader's sharp criticism of the hot dog, but failed to mention any of the above comments. Both *Walter Cronkite* and the *Los Angeles Times* ignored the hearings completely from July 15 through 17. On July 17, five medical scientists told the committee that monosodium glutamate was potentially harmful and served no nutritional purpose. One doctor testified that representatives of two baby food manufacturers told him their "hands were tied by their sales departments." They said that mothers would stop buying the products if the salt were taken out. Gerber's predictably denied this, claiming that "profits are secondary."[20] *Huntley-Brinkley* didn't mention the above testimony, but did have a forty-five second coverage of the hearings which focused on the hot dog issue again, and ending with a humorous comment cleverly implying that the hearings needn't be taken seriously. *Walter Cronkite* made no mention of the hearings. The *New York Times* reported what the five doctors had to say on Page 18, and the *Los Angeles Times* finally decided that at least this part of the hearings were important enough to make Page 13.[21] After July, television did a farily good job on the issue and brought out the fact that the FDA had been warned by doctors as early as January but had not acted. Dr. John Olney on a *Huntley-Brinkley* interview related how he had caused brain damage in mice with the same percentage dosage of monosodium glutamate, proportionate to body weight, that is put into baby foods. Many mothers and expectant mothers would certainly find all this news interesting, but they might also find it interesting to know that from 1962 to 1969 the issue was ignored by the press.

As early as 1951, Food and Drug Administration scientists reported investigations that revealed a high incidence of cancer among animals that were fed cyclamate, an artifical sweetener. Had these findings been published it is doubtful that the unrestricted use of cyclamates could ever have been permitted by the FDA or accepted by the public. However, they weren't published; FDA officials, presumably in order to protect FDA policy decisions and the food additive industry from embarrassment, censored this information discovered by their own scientists, along with many other findings on the safety of food additives.[22]

News media's record on cyclamate is no better than the FDA's. The National Academy of Sciences in November of 1955 said that there was no evidence that the use of cyclamates posed a hazard when used for special dietary purposes; however, they said that there was not enough information to deem it safe for unrestricted use. But it was used without restriction until 1969. As early as 1964 the number of cases of cyclamate-sweetened soft drinks sold in the United States reached 200 million.[23] This was the same year that some doctors became suspicious of the potential harmful effects of cyclamates. Martin Cohen, writing in *Fact* magazine in 1966, was able to cite considerable medical evidence indicating cyclamates should definitely not be used without restriction.[24] Americans were caught completely by surprise in late 1969 when cyclamates were taken off the market. Their surprise can be attributed to the fact that until 1969 no newspapers or broadcasters showed an interest in looking into the available material which showed the potential hazard in the unrestricted use of cyclamate.

Even when cyclamates became an issue, the newspapers did not go out of their way to call attention to it. In an AP release Senator Gaylord Nelson said there was scientific evidence that cyclamates can cause a variety of ailments, including liver disease, high blood pressure and skin irritation. The Senator added:

> Tens of millions of children and adults across the nation are unwittingly being exposed to potentially serious hazards by the unnecessary consumption of cyclamate-sweetened soft drinks, cereals, desserts and sugar-coated pills.

He said that some soft drinks contain so much cyclamate that one bottle exceeded the daily limit for children set by the FDA.[25] The *New York Times* cut this article down to two inches and placed it on Page 17. It competed in size with the most inconspicuous item in the paper. The *Los Angeles Times* also gave it only two inches, but placed it as one of the more important news items of the day on Page 2.[26]

Another AP release told of a FDA report detailing the animal evidence of a potential cancer hazard from the use of cylamates. The *Los Angeles Times* gave this story a good position on Page 4; The *New*

York Times suppressed the entire article.[27] This can't be considered merely an accidental oversight by the *New York Times*. When it comes to printing news unfavorable to the drug industry, the *New York Times* seems to have a blind spot. Morton Mintz of the *Washington Post* has a special file of articles on the drug industry that were either buried, inadequately interpreted or suppressed by the *New York Times*.[28]

In July 1969 there were three smoking stories that would have interested both smokers and taxpayers, but *New York Times* readers were only able to read one of the three. In the one the *Times* did cover, it omitted the part in the government report that called charcoal filters useless.[29] In the second, a UPI release, Senator Gaylord Nelson cited that studies done at North Carolina State University showed very high levels of pesticides in tobacco. Nelson said: "Now there is evidence that the smoker's health is also besieged by poisonous pesticide residues flowing into his throat and lungs with cigarette smoke." Nelson noted that tobacco is the only consumable crop that is not subject to a government-established limit on the level of pesticide deemed safe. The study showed DDT residues found in tobacco were up to seven times the tolerance level set for lettuce and spinach.[30]

The third story was also a UPI release telling of Senator Frank Moss's request that the Nixon Administration stop spending $50 million a year subsidizing overseas advertising of U.S. cigarettes, tobacco exports and tobacco farm prices. Nixon's Secretary of Agriculture, Clifford Harden, indicated he did not plan to change the program.[31] The *New York Times* was not alone in considering the above releases entirely un-newsworthy. *Huntley-Brinkley* and *Walter Cronkite* also ignored all the above smoking news even though they mentioned the government report.

Walter Cronkite told about scientific findings disclosing that many products are worthless in terms of the virtues claimed for them in advertisements. Omitted was that part of the news item which noted that most mouthwashes are useless. A few minutes before, an advertisement for Scope mouthwash had been presented.[32]

Many mothers won't allow children to drink coffee because it contains the stimulant caffeine. Coca Cola also contains caffeine but, like the dairy industry, the company has never been required to put on the label the ingredients of its product. A 1969 *Life* magazine article on Ralph Nader told of how two telephone calls received by the FDA— one from Senator Richard Russell and one from a White House staffer—were received just before the FDA ruled in 1966 that cola drinks did not have to list caffeine. The article mentioned that Senator Russell was from the home state of a large cola company. What *Life* omitted was the company's name and brand name—Coca Cola.[33]

An April 1969 UPI release reported that the public health service warned color television owners to sit at least six to ten feet away from their sets to minimize potential radiation hazards. The warning was based in part on a survey in Suffolk County, New York, which showed that 20 percent of nearly 5000 color sets emitted X-rays at a level above the maximum safe limit. Mothers of children who for hours on end sit a few feet away from color sets would certainly think this item newsworthy. However, even if the mothers had read every page of the *New York Times* or the *Los Angeles Times* they wouldn't have been able to find out about the warning; neither newspaper published it.[34]

In March 1963, two women died from botulism poisoning as a result of eating A&P brand tuna. The FDA found that there were additional tins of tuna canned by the same packing house on the shelves of California markets. These cans also contained the deadly poison. The FDA felt it their duty to warn housewives not to buy A&P and Taste Well brands with certain code numbers on the can.[35] Any housewife would be glad to know such information in order to safeguard her family. Housewives reading 15 out of 22 newspapers checked by Dr. Edward Glick and his study group were unable to read the FDA's warning because their papers had suppressed the news item.[36]

A significant wire service news dispatch in 1963 reported the testimony by a Food and Drug Administration physician charging his own agency with laxity in policing of certain drugs. Only 7 of 22 large newspapers placed the item on Page One; 6 suppressed it entirely.[37]

Protecting the consumer's pocketbook from the ravages of corporate greed is also a secondary consideration of the press whenever it conflicts with business profits of advertisers. Because local used car dealers complained, the *Houston Post* suddenly stopped printing a series of articles on what to look out for when buying a used car.[38]

Although the private power companies spend millions each year telling the public what a bargain electricity is, Senator Lee Metcalf has evidence to show that some families are overcharged as much as $5 a month by some private power companies.[39] It's understandable, then, that the companies like to avoid informing the public about their profits. Since the power companies enjoy a monopoly status, regulation of the industry is essential to hold profits to a reasonable level of around 6 percent. On March 30, 1965, the Federal Power Commission for the first time released a report detailing the uniform rate of return for major electric utilities. As Metcalf notes, the FPC study was proof that the regulation of the rates of the nation's largest industry had broken down. The press release was ignored by almost every newspaper, including the *New York Times* and the *Los Angeles Times*. Both, however, found room to print public relations material from the power companies on the following day. The FPC report showed that out of 188 private utility companies, three had profits over 10 percent, seventeen had profits between 9 and 10 percent, thirty-five between 8 and 9 percent and fifty-six between 7 and 8 percent—all excessive profits for a government-regulated monopoly.[40]

The food bill is a big part of everyone's weekly budget. The press doesn't help to make it any smaller. Behind a facade of "consumer affairs editors," the press does its best to keep the public ignorant of the sizable amount of cumulated loss that shoppers suffer because of deceptive packaging and measurements. A. Q. Mowbray, writing in the *Nation,* revealed how the press shaped up nicely when asked to cooperate in defeating the Hart Packaging Bill. Senator Hart's bill was designed to give the FDA and Federal Trade Commission the authority to standardize net contents in areas where packaging was so chaotic that it was impossible for shoppers to compare prices without a slide rule. The president of the Grocery Manufacturers of America had a little visit with the publishers of sixteen national magazines. The president related:

> We suggested to the publishers that the day was here when their editorial department and business department might better understand their interdependency relationships as they affect the operating results of their companies; and as their operations may affect the advertiser—their bread and butter.[41]

He was later able to point to press performances in eight magazines to show how well the publishers had paid attention to his message.

Both the *Saturday Evening Post* and the *Reader's Digest* commissioned articles about the bill but never published them.[42] Mowbray points out that during the five years in which Congress kicked the Hart bill around, none of the leading magazines had told their readers anything about this proposed legislation. Senator Hart sent background material to twenty-one magazines, but no articles resulted. *Look* found room, however, to print an article titled: "Let's Keep Politics Out of the Pantry," written by a food industry spokesman. President Johnson's special assistant for consumer affairs, Esther Peterson, and Senator Hart both felt this article so greatly misrepresented the bill that they asked *Look* for an opportunity to present their side. Publisher Gardner Cowles forbade this competition in ideas because, as he told Senator Hart, the public doesn't feel any need for labeling regulations. This may have been so, but the question was *why* the people felt no need. Considering *Look's* and other media coverage of Senator Hart's bill, that's not a very hard question to answer.

11   How to Become Newsworthy

> The eithics of salesmanship have infected every area
> of life. Politics has become a branch of public rela-
> tions. Persuasion has been substituted for debate and
> the search for the right image has replaced the search
> for the right policy.
>
> Stuart Hall and Paddy Whannel, *The Popular Arts*

Ford Motor Company's public relations agent estimated that if
Ford had had to pay regular advertising rates for the free news publicity they received from the press during one nine-month period in
1953, it would have cost them $2,200,000. Irwin Ross details some of
the public relations successes during Ford's fiftieth anniversary cele-
bration in 1953. During a six-month period, Ford was featured in
fourteen different articles in mass-ciruclation magazines; one article in
Life was fourteen pages long. In a three-month period, there were
enough news stories on Ford printed in newspapers to fill 332 pages
of the *New York Times*. The big accomplishment of the public relations campaign was having both CBS and NBC televise a two-hour
special on the Ford anniversary. It reached an estimated sixteen million homes.[1]

Public relations firms often do outstanding jobs; however, they begin with a big advantage. As businessmen, mass media owners naturally idolize those who have reached the heights of wealth, status and
power—heights symbolized by owners and managers of the giant corporations. Media owners want the public to respect the things they
themselves stand for. But instead of building themselves up, they find
it less embarrassing and more successful to give publicity to corporations and individuals that represent owner ideals. The makeup of
newspapers is designed to give business free access to the public under
the guise of news. In 1967, there were 434 business and financial
editors on daily newspaper staffs compared to 12 labor editors.[2] A
similar situation exists in broadcasting. This places the 80 million

working men and women at a distinct competitive disadvantage when it comes to getting free favorable publicity disguised as news. This pro-business bias is one reason the mass media offers youth few working men as idols for them to emulate, compared to the thousands of idols representing management or the military-industrial-space complex. The images that are selected to represent labor are almost always channeled through editors openly or secretly hostile to labor. Mass media presents those who favor very liberal causes in an even worse light than it does labor. While not completely ignored, solid liberals and radicals are often ridiculed. They are never set up as models for youth to emulate.

The conservative orientation of the press makes it hard to tell who or what is responsible for business publicity being classified as news. It could be the newsman's own choice or the clever efforts of a public relations agent. Chet Huntley reported on October 14, 1960:

> This year's automobile show—the American economy's most spectacular spectacular—opens tonight in Detroit. Here is a film preview from NBC news reporter Floyd Kalber.

Kalber took over with the film crew and continued in the tone set by Huntley's introduction. He noted:

> This year the compact car comes into its own and it's expected to deal the crushing blow to foreign imports. Ten different makes, about 35 different models of compacts are available featuring economy of cost and operation. This is also the year for the 'luxury' compact. . . . [3]

Kalber made no mention of safety features—and this at a time when cars had neither safety belts nor padded dash boards as standard equipment. To indicate what a subjective selection this news item was, the two other network evening television newscasts decided that the automobile show wasn't news for this day.

Despite Detroit's and Kalber's efforts "to deal the crushing blow" to foreign imports in 1960, the Japanese and German auto manufacturers were still doing a booming business in 1970. One of Ford's answers to stem the import car sales was introduced in April 1969 as the subcompact Maverick. An Associated Press release from Carefree, Arizona, was sent out over the wires. Having the AP do that was the initial success; next would be to get papers to print the item. The *Honolulu Star-Bulletin* not only printed it, they paraded it on Page 2 with a big headline at the top of the page.[4] Next to the story was a large photograph of Ford Motor Company's vice president standing alongside two new Mavericks. The photograph was not an AP photo. Having no listed source, it was undoubtedly a public relations release. The layout and placement on Page 2 may not have been great journalism, but it certainly was great publicity for Ford.

The automobile and oil industry are major polluters of the environment, and they have fought legislation and court action aimed at controlling their various polluting activities. But according to the mass media, these industries are the ones who are fighting pollution, not causing it. The *Los Angeles Times* featured its own story on February 15, 1968 with the headline:

AUTO, PETROLEUM FIRMS
JOIN IN U.S. SMOG FIGHT

The *New York Times* featured on Page One, December 11, 1969 its own story with the headline:

HENRY FORD VOWS INTENSIFIED
EFFORT TO CURB POLLUTION

Articles such as these can serve as models for public relations agents.

Defense and space contractors do as well or better than auto manufacturers when it comes to getting their public relations releases handled as news. NBC's 1968 documentary on the future uses of outer space, "Beyond the Sky," depended upon the opinions of commercial companies involved in space technology.[5] To depend on the opinions of companies who stand to lose or gain millions of dollars from national space policies is questionable journalism practice, but it's a big boost for the companies.

On September 26, 1969 the *Los Angeles Times* featured the following headline on Page One,

ADJUSTMENT TO SONIC BOOMS PREDICTED

Written by a *Times* staff writer, the tone of the article was set by the quote of a pilot: "People will get to the point where sonic booms are a way of life." That statement unfortunately is probably true. It is also true that similar news treatment of the pollution issue by the *Los*

Angeles Times has helped people living in Los Angeles to accept poison air and polluted beaches as a way of life. It would take a good conflict-of-interest detective to pinpoint whether this article was inspired by the *Times's* editorial stand backing the controversial supersonic transport or the prompting of Southern California's aircraft industry.

Many publicity agents are hired to make right-wing dictators look like enlightened benefactors. In this they have the willing cooperation of the media since the conservative owners are usually staunch supporters of any government—no matter how dictatorial or brutal it is—so long as it's anti-communist and it provides fertile ground for American corporate investment. One of the most disgraceful performances of the media, in my opinion, was its almost unanimous support for the Fascist government of Generalisimo Franco in his war against the Spanish people in the late 1930's. In this case the public relations agent was the Catholic hierarchy.[6]

The media hasn't changed character since then. Without U.S. military and economic assistance many dictatorial governments in Latin America would fall. Realizing the importance of United States public opinion in influencing foreign policy and U.S. overseas business investments, dictators know that every cent spent to buy favorable coverage in the U.S. press will pay for itself a hundred times over. If possible, dictators resort to outright bribery of American media owners. For years the Dominican Republic Information Center paid the International News Service (which later merged with United Press to form UPI) $6000 every three months to distribute stories favorable to the Trujillo regime under the guise of news. The INS received $2000 of this from Trujillo's publicity agent in the United States.[7] Sometimes an even more direct bribe is accepted by media owners. Alexander Guterma, while head of the Mutual Broadcasting Corporation, accepted $750,000 in exchange for broadcasting Trujillo's propaganda as legitimate news.[8] However, bribery is the exception. For legal or moral reasons American pressmen seldom will touch outright bribes. To get around this propaganda roadblock, dictators resort to various methods of legalized bribery such as providing all-expense-paid trips for journalists and their wives, and paying for the publicity services of America's top public relations firms. These firms make sure their client gets frequent favorable coverage in newspapers, radio, television, newsreels and travelogues. News distributing firms like the United States Press Association are also hired to send out canned editorials to thousands of dailies and weeklies. One such editorial presented in the *New Bedford Standard Times* serves as an example of the basic theme behind the news peddled by the right-wing dictators:

> Today the Dominican Republic . . . is a bulwark of strength against Communism and has been widely cited as one of the cleanest, healthiest, happiest countries on the globe. Guiding spirit of this fabulous transformation is Generalisimo Trujillo who worked tirelessly. . . . [9]

Because they owned no news agencies, the vast majority of Dominican people who hated Trujillo for his executions and torture chambers, plus the very liberal groups in the United States who opposed U.S. military and economic aid to Trujillo, were placed at a considerable disadvantage in trying to expose Trujillo and his butcheries.

Those who oppose the United States support of the Greek dictatorship also have to compete under a considerable media handicap. On May 13, 1967, the International Commission of Jurists in Geneva condemned the new Greek military dictatorship that had taken power after ousting a democratic government. The Commission asked the Council of Europe, made up of representatives from NATO and non-NATO countries, to investigate the Greek regime for violating the European Human Rights Convention. Every newspaper checked by publisher I. F. Stone apparently decided the public would be better off without knowing that the Greek military merited condemnation.[10] Not one word of this appeared in the *New York Times* or the *Los Angeles Times*. However, news about the Church of Greece getting a new Archbishop made Page One in the *New York Times*.

The media's kindness toward the Greek regime was surpassed only by the United States Government's quick restoration of full diplomatic relations and limited military aid, in February 1968, to the newest anti-communist dictator.

The task of investigating the Greek regime was taken up by Amnesty International, an organization with branches in twenty-five countries whose purpose is to aid political prisoners in all countries. Amnesty International has consultative status with the Council of Europe. In January of 1968 they sent an investigation team to Greece and made a report of its findings. On the basis of this report, the Council voted on January 31, 1968 (before the U.S. restored full military aid), to exclude Greece from the Council unless it restored parliamentary democracy.

The report gave the world a picture of the regime in action. It said that thousands of prisoners without being tried were being held in police stations and prisons throughout Greece, and that at the end of January 1968 the islands of Deros and Yaros alone were home for 2,777 such prisoners. Reporting about these prisoners, Amnesty International said, as quoted in I. F. Stone's weekly:

> It is believed that of these detained some 500 may have been active or potentially active Communists. The remainder cannot be described as 'Communist' in any accepted European sense of the word, and large numbers of them are old and infirm, having been arrested on security files prepared in many cases 20 years ago. . . . The prisoners come from all walks of life and include parliamentarians, professional people, intellectuals and artists.[11]

The investigating team took the testimony of sixteen persons who had been tortured by the regime and gathered evidence about other cases. One method of torture was described: "The prisoner is tied to a bench and the soles of his feet are beaten with a stick or pipe." This practice is called the "falanga." The report explains:

> . . . common methods accompanying 'falanga' are pouring water down the mouth and nose while the prisoner is screaming with pain; putting 'Tide' soap in the eyes, nose and mouth. . . .

Numerous incidents of sexually-oriented torture were also reported, and psychological methods of torture were described by former prisoners. Prisoners were forced to hear others being tortured. There were threats to kill, maim and rape prisoners. Others were pressured into signing a sheet of paper denouncing parents, wife or political beliefs.[12]

The press does its job well when it comes to exposing brutalities committed in some countries. When even a single case of torture by a communist country is discovered, it gets front page priority. But this systematic torture on a massive scale perpetrated by a right-wing military regime supported by the United States, was suppressed by most U.S. news agents. The *New York Times* and the *Los Angeles Times* ignored the report completely.

Symbolic approval, implied by official U.S. recognition of the military regime, coupled with the silence of U.S. news media, apparently convinced the Greek generals they were doing a fine job. In a London newspaper, The *Guardian Weekly,* Terence Prittie notes that ten months after the above report:

The military regime in Greece is evidently continuing to use torture of the most brutal kind as a means of intimidating its political opponents and critics. There have been fresh reports of cases of torture since two political prisoners appeared last week before the European Human Rights Commission in Strasbourg and gave evidence about the treatment meted out to them. . . .

It is now learned that the regime, which has repeatedly denied using torture in the past, is continuing to use it on political prisioners.[13]

This new evidence also failed to impress the *New York Times* to any significant degree. They gave it four inches on Page 3.[14] The *Los Angeles Times* passed up this Reuters story completely.

The same week former Premier Papandreou accused the United States of complicity in the Junta's destruction of democratic government in Greece. The Armed Forces network in Europe reported this news item, but it was suppressed by both the *New York Times* and the *Los Angeles Times*.[15]

The American press doesn't ignore Greece all the time; on the contrary, it often gives items on Greece front-page priority. But unlike the suppressed news, these items could have been written by the new dictatorial Greek government; such is their tone. On September 17, 1968, the *New York Times* featured this Page-One, two-column headline:

GREEK REGIME SAYS IT WILL FREE POLITICAL PRISONERS MONDAY

Another story in the *New York Times* proclaimed atop Page One:

GREECE RESTORES SOME CIVIL RIGHTS: PRESS CURB EASED

The story continued on Page 15 with a four-column headline adorned with a photograph of Colonel George Popadopoulos.

Eight months later when a Greek editor said this ease on press curbs had been a farce and that the previous style of censorship would be less restrictive, the *New York Times* placed the story on Page 55, and the *Los Angeles Times* ignored it.[16]

Some dispatches from Greece read as if they were written by a public relations agent for the Greek regime. In January of 1970, Copley News Service correspondent Victor Walker wrote from Athens that Greece's voluntary withdrawal from the Council of Europe, in order to avoid being officially expelled, was considered in Greece "as a victory for Hellenic national pride."[17] Terming Greece's removal an "empty gesture," he then claimed as credible the regime's charge that the whole campaign in the Council was the result of European socialist governments who were acting for domestic political reasons. Walker notes that the regime has seen no indications of popular opposition, but he doesn't even hint that this may be due to the widespread torture and imprisonment of those who dissent. The article had a five-column headline,

GREECE SEES PROGRESS WITH U.S. SUPPORT,

which set the tone for the report that noted, with obvious satisfaction, that it was United States support of Greece against the rest of Europe that turned the Council's debate into a "mishap." On-the-spot correspondent Walker ended his Athens report with a quote from a high Greek official who claimed the ideology and principles of the April 21 military takeover coincided "with those of the American nation"—not an outlandish statement if America's Greek policy is considered instead of American expressed high ideals.

Like Greece and the Dominican Republic, the governments of Portugal and South Africa provide for safe and profitable investment of American corporation money by firms like GM, Ford, Chrysler, Esso, Caltex, Chevron, General Tire and Rubber, and Coca Cola. These are among nearly 300 U.S. firms that have about one billion dollars invested in South Africa alone. The Chase Manhattan Bank and the First National City Bank of New York have made direct loans of up to $40 million to help the apartheid government get through times of financial difficulty. The Bank of America has made similar loans to help Portugal's government. United States firms cooperate with the South African government's policy of strict racial segregation when it comes to employment and wage policies. American investors make considerable profits under the present governments. For this reason, corporations find it easy to overlook the brutal exploitation and suppression of the vast majority of black Africans by the small minority of whites. However, the blacks in South Africa and others around the world who are concerned about justice, equal opportunity and self-determination find the situation deplorable and intolerable.

In the United States there is a battle going on in the mass media between those who are trying to persuade Americans that the South African and Portuguese African governments are stable, progressive and anti-communist, and those who are trying to convince the people that these governments have no intention of changing unless they are forced to do so either by strict economic sanctions or by revolution. The black Africans claim that the United States government policy supporting these governments amounts to an endorsement of the racial suppression and exploitation of the blacks. One such support is the sugar quota allowance given to the South African white farmers. It enables them to get two to three times the price they would on the world market. The farmers often buy sugar from poor black countries which have no quota and then sell it to the United States at the higher subsidized prices.[18] In contrast to the economic restrictions placed on dictatorships of the left like Cuba or China, there have been few restrictions on U.S. trade or investments in South Africa. In the United Nations, the United States has refused to back meaningful economic sanctions against Portuguese Africa or South Africa. Most disturbing of all to those hoping for eventual self-determination for blacks is the United States military aid given to Portugal through NATO. These weapons are used by the Portuguese to fight against the black guerilla liberation movements in Angola, Mozambique and Portuguese Guinea. And despite a 1963 U.S. arms embargo, the Pentagon still sells weapons to South Africa. Representative Lawrence Coughlin disclosed this on the same day that he complained about the increased arms aid given the Greek dictatorship in fiscal 1969.[19]

Former journalist and now professor Leslie Whitten, writing in the *Progressive,* explains why the South African government has such an advantage over the black Africans in telling their side of the story in the mass media.[20] Taking advantage of a communication system that is for sale, the South African government spent $1,750,000 in less than three years to present a favorable image to the American people. The black Africans during this same period spent less than $8000 to tell Americans their story. This 200,000 to 1 advantage translated into mass media meant that Americans were only hearing one side of the story. The apartheid government got some part of their message across in 969 telecasts reaching an audience of more than 30 million. Rarely getting any exposure in the mass media, the black Africans have had to depend on pamphlets and speeches.

This media advantage does wonders for the South African regime. They are able to camouflage or hide many of the daily atrocities inflicted on the blacks in South Africa. Professor Whitten asks:

Who knows, for example, that the International Commission of Jurists has urged a United Nations investigation of jail suicides in South Africa that smell of torture and police murder? Who knows of the 119 executions by hanging that took place in South Africa last year (forty-seven percent of all executions in the 'free world,' according to a University of South Africa study)?

Whitten notes that the few stories of gross denial of human and legal rights that are reported usually involved the sufferings of white men, but the deeds against the black men, in South Africa as in America, seldom emerge from the darkness in which they are committed.

A press so closely linked with corporate interests by both economics and political orientation can hardly be expected to go out of its way to reveal the brutal nature of the South African government. Instead of trying to compensate for the lopsided bias produced by South Africa's propaganda budget, the media maintain a superficial objectivity that cleverly hides a subtle bias against the black man's view of life in white-ruled Africa. Two exceptions were NBC's "Angola: Journey to a War", (1961) and CBS' "South Africa: A Black Man's View" (1970). Two programs surely don't make up for years of the past and future neglect of news that reveals the brutality of racism and colonialism in South Africa and the indirect American support of it.

From July 10 to August 12, 1969, there were at least five possible news items that would have given some glimpse of the real character of white rule in South Africa. Both *Huntley-Brinkley* and *Walter Cronkite* passed up all five stories. There were three stories originating from the United Nations. In the first, the UN Security Council condemned Portugal's aggression in Zambia. The vote was 11 to 0; the United States abstained.[21] In the second, the Security Council protested and condemned South Africa for its policy in South West Africa.[22] In the third, the Security Council gave South Africa until October 1969 to end its administration of South West Africa or face possible UN sanctions. The vote was 11 to 0; the United States abstained.[23]

One of the most significant items during this period told of twenty-five United States congressmen who made a protest against South Africa's refusal to grant visas to two black representatives of the House because they wouldn't promise not to speak to student groups opposing apartheid.[24] Both the *New York Times* and the *Los Angeles Times* completely ignored the group's protest. The biggest story about South Africa during this period was a sensational and significant news item about a trial. After an 88-day trial, an anti-apartheid newspaper editor and one of his reporters were found guilty of publishing "false" information about prison conditions in South Africa without taking reasonable steps to verify their stories.[25] It's not hard to imagine what would have happened to the reporter's stories if he had attempted to verify them with government officials. The reporter wrote about beatings by guards, forced sodomy and electric shock tortures in South African jails. The news item not only revealed what probably were the conditions in the jails, but also the lack of press freedom in South Africa. The *New York Times* placed it on Page One, But the *Los Angeles Times* suppppressed it completely.

Of the five stories that each news agency could have reported during this 32-day period, the *New York Times* published 3, the *Los Angeles Times* 1, and *Huntley-Brinkley* and *Walter Cronkite* none—a total of only 4 out of 20.

Despite the news items that were available, the media's neglect of them indicates that probably the majority of Americans did not hear or read anything negative about South Africa during this time. These Americans certainly would not have any reason to question the United States policy toward white-ruled South Africa. With this kind of media performance, the job of South Africa's public relations agent is made that much easier.

12   Stories That Really Count

> Our history will be what we make it. And if there are
> any historians about fifty or a hundred years from
> now, and there should be preserved the kinescopes for
> one week of all three networks, they will find there
> recorded in black and white, or color, evidence of dec-
> adence, escapism, and the insulation from the realities
> of the world in which we live.
>
> Edward R. Murrow

Men in the United States have a life expectancy lower than men in
eighteen other countries. In infant mortality, thirteen countries have a
better record than the United States. In eleven countries women have
a better chance of living through childbirth than in the United States.[1]
For the poor and underprivileged in America, the situation is even
worse. The maternal mortality rate for non-white mothers is four
times higher than for whites.[2] And thirty percent of the infants who
die in the first year of life die from environmental conditions created
by poverty.[3] It is estimated that the United States is short 50,000
physicians, 85,000 nurses, and 1,000,000 health services technicians.[4]

The question naturally arises as to why the United States has fallen
down in these vital health areas and why there is such a shortage of
physicians and nurses. The answer rests primarily with the American
Medical Association and the mass media. An analysis of AMA behavior regarding just one piece of legislation in 1950 is indicative of the
AMA's consistent long-term opposition to legislation designed to improve the public's health. It also explains why, twenty years later, the
nation is short of physicians. Third, and most important for our purposes, it illustrates the subtle complicity of the mass media in its effort
to protect the powerful AMA at the expense of the health of the
American people.

113

President Harry Truman requested a five-year, $250 million program of federal aid to help build medical, dental and nursing educational facilities, and to help pay the tuition of students. The AMA vigorously opposed the bill. Speaking in the House of Representatives, Andrew Biemiller, a Representative from Wisconsin, urged that the bill be passed:

> It should be passed now, and all the stalling, twisting, turning conniving tactics of the AMA cannot conceal the stark need of this legislation. . . .
>
> At this moment, as at every recent critical moment in our history, we do not have enough doctors or dentists or nurses or public health personnel to meet peacetime requirements, much less the demands of our mobilizing armed forces and civilian defense. . . .
>
> Some of our medical schools, and by no means the weakest in an academic sense, are near to closing because of their desperate financial state. . . .
>
> Who is responsible for this inexcusable delay in meeting a vital national need. . . . The answer is always the same—the American Medical Association.
>
> Until recently I thought I had grown calloused to the AMA's dog-in-the-manger selfishness in its efforts to defeat almost every progressive public health measure offered in this Congress. I thought I had grown used to the double-talking, double-dealing methods of the AMA and its huckster representatives in their defense of a status quo riddled with inadequacies. I thought I had learned to brace myself against the overwhelming weight of the AMA hierarchy's $3,000,000 advertising and political slush fund.[5]

Despite the many reporters covering Congress and the importance of the proposed legislation, not a word of Biemiller's speech was printed in the *New York Times* or the *Los Angeles Times*.

A month later when the bill was killed by the House Commerce Committee, the *New York Times* gave the story a small headline on Page 11. It mentioned near the end of the article that Representative Beimiller accused the AMA of blocking the legislation, but none of his sharp comments were printed.[6]

Brigadier General Dr. James Simmons commented a few days later:

> I am confident if the American people realized what a crippling blow this negative action has dealt the nation's military and civilian preparedness program they would demand the tragic mistake be rectified. Total output of specialists is now one-fifth of the number

needed to operate the nation's peacetime health program. Its cost compared to the enormous outlays necessary for armaments is relatively minor.[7]

But the public didn't realize what a "crippling blow" this action was because the press played it down as a minor story. This item appeared on Page 11 in the *New York Times*.

Ten days later the House Committee again rejected the bill. The *New York Times* gave the story a total of two inches on Page 20. The headline was no larger than ordinary size print. It mentioned again that Biemiller blamed the AMA for defeat of the bill, but didn't bother to print the names of those on the committee who voted against the bill. The newspapers could have printed what Biemiller had to say that day to the members of the House and the press corps, but they suppressed his entire speech in which he stated, "As far as I am concerned the deaf, dumb, and blind attitude of the AMA on this subject is its number one crime against the public interest in this session of Congress."[8] Biemiller reviewed the AMA record for the benefit of his colleagues in the House and for the press:

> It is a record untainted by a positive act or progressive idea, a 99 and 44/100 percent pure record of negation, of opposition and obstruction on every legislative measure proposed to advance the nation's health, safety and security. . . .
>
> When that record is added to the steadfastly reactionary attitudes and actions of the AMA over the last 25 years, it is ample evidence that the AMA now stands with the NAM [National Association of Manufacturers]as the most reactionary forces in American life—not on matters affecting medicine and health alone, but on the whole social-political front. . . . [9]
>
> The AMA's calm indifference to the needs of women and children is on record in permanent fashion.[10]

Biemiller spelled out and attacked the AMA's past opposition to inoculation for smallpox by public health departments, to workmen's compensation, to Federal aid to states to reduce infant and maternal mortality, Social Security, creation of venereal disease clinics and free diagnostic centers for tuberculosis and cancer. He saw the AMA's "selfish economic interest" as the motivating force behind their opposition to these proposals.[11] He revealed their propaganda strategy by pointing out that the AMA had spent 2 million dollars in 1949 alone to plant their message in mass media through political advertisements.

During the next twenty years a crusading media could have dramatized in photographs and stories many of the personal tragedies resulting from the inadequacies of the medical system. Infant deaths, maternal deaths and the languishing horrors experienced by those unable
to obtain medical care—these facts if publicized could have aroused
the people to pressure the establishment's politicians to act decisively
despite the AMA's opposition. But because the vast majority of the
media stood firm with the AMA, they didn't bother to draw attention
to such tragedies as these. They used their power instead to suppress
many stories critical of the AMA as well as those which revealed the
inadequate medical care available to the poor.

In 1969, the crisis created by past AMA policies had become so
critical as to become a major issue despite the media. Nevertheless, the media continued selectively suppressing and playing down
important news items. A UPI story reported that a doctor accused the
AMA and Upjohn Pharmaceutical Company of perpetuating a $12
million dollar theft against the public. The doctor noted that the AMA
refused to publish an article claiming that the drug Panalba was ineffective, but at the same time, the AMA did allow two full-page ads
promoting the use of Panalba to adorn the back cover of their official
journal.[12] The *New York Times* placed this on Page 94; the *Los Angeles Times* suppressed the article.

Two hundred physicians—black and white—met in New Hampshire
to discuss ghetto medicine. The AP reported that one prominent doctor criticized "high-volume, fast turnover service" in the ghetto,
claiming that some patients wound up in hospitals because of kidney
diseases and tuberculosis which were undiagnosed or improperly
treated. Mayor Richard Hatcher of Gary, Indiana, told the conference: "By and large, American medicine has provided one of the most
shocking examples of discrimination against minority groups our society has witnessed." The mayor said that the shortage of black physicians caused by racial admittance policies of white medical schools
was one of the causes of premature babies, infant diseases and ill
health in the black ghettos. Also addressing the conference, Senator
Edward Kennedy said:

> In the United States today—the wealthiest nation in the history of
> man—millions of our citizens are sick. And they are sick because they
> are poor.
>
> Their sickness is the shame of America. . . .

> Of all the effects of poverty, it is the sickness of the poor that we could attack most easily had we the will.

The doctors felt President Nixon lacked the will. They adopted a resolution which they sent to President Nixon: "The Conference on Medicine in the Ghettos is distressed by the failure of your administration to attack the health problems of the poor. . . . " The Conference concluded that all Americans be covered by a Federally operated national health insurance plan.

The *Los Angeles Times* covered the story of the conference on Page 8.[13] The *New York Times* failed to print the story.

An event took place the next week that one would think was too important and sensational to ignore. Both the *Los Angeles Times* and the *New York Times* placed the story on Page One. Warned ahead about the possibility of disturbances, the press was on hand to witness seventy-five doctor, nurse and medical student protesters storm the meeting of the AMA's House of Delegates and take over the podium. Dr Richard Kunnes then delivered a speech to present and past leaders of the organization, telling them:

> You're the criminals, who rather than developing a preventive health program have prevented health programs. You're the criminals, who through your monopolistic, exclusionary racist practices have created a vast shortage of health manpower resulting in the needless deaths of countless millions.[14]

Some of the physician delegates responded by throwing ashtrays at the podium.

Of the speeches given during the whole episode, the staff written *Los Angeles Times* article gave most emphasis and space to the speech of the AMA president, which predictably implied that the AMA was concerned about the nation's health needs. The speech of Dr. Kunnes was omitted. The AMA couldn't have asked for a more favorable article given the events which took place. Incredibly neither *Huntley-Brinkley* nor *Walter Cronkite* mentioned a thing about the meeting.

By featuring a dramatic and symbolic story of a tragic or momentous event in one person's life, the media can move its audience to empathy, indignation, tears, joy or action. We should thus pay attention to the type of dramatic stories the media feature as contrasted to those it neglects. We will find that individual tragedies symbolizing poor medical care and the AMA's selfish policies are not the only symbolic stories the media intentionally neglect.

The Czech merchant ship "Vitkovice" had to depart from Los Angeles Harbor one crew member short in October 1969, because a Czech seaman, Jiri Vokrouhlik, had escaped from the ship on a Sunday "and pleaded for political asylum from communism." A few hours later the *Los Angeles Times* sent out a photographer to take a picture of the seaman standing on the dock with the Czech ship in the background. The next morning the million *Times'* readers saw this photograph at the top of Page One above the caption:

ON FREE SOIL[15]

On October 11, 1960, Mutual Network newsman Bob Siegrist devoted more than half of his fifteen-minute radio newscast to the story of Russian seaman Victor Jaanimets who had also jumped ship and asked for political asylum.[16] The three network evening newscasts, along with the three 15-minute network radio newscasts, all carried the original story; NBC's Peter Hackes made it the feature item of the day. Dramatic stories like these serve as a powerful communication device for exposing the people's lack of freedom in Communist countries. When Americans are asked how they know there is little freedom in Communist countries they will almost invariably cite examples of ordinary citizens trying to escape from Communism in order to come to the free world. In contrast, Americans will have a hard time citing similar dramatic escapes to indicate the lack of freedom in countries like South Africa, Greece, Spain or Formosa. Although there are many instances of people escaping to avoid suppression and torture at the hands of these governments, the media choose to suppress or ignore such cases rather than dramatize them on the front page.

When professors and artists ask for political asylum, it is thought to be a specially significant indication that the country left behind is intolerable in some aspects. Novelist Anatoly Kuznetsov's escape from the Soviet Union made the front page of almost every newspaper. CBS had a special hour-long prime-time interview with him. Artists and professors in the United States have a great deal of freedom, but some have still chosen to leave the United States as a protest against the U.S. policy in Vietnam. Instead of placing such events on the front page, the media plays down or suppresses the news.

Thomas Boynton, a sociology professor, left the United States and requested political asylum in Cuba. The *Los Angeles Times* gave the story less than two inches on Page 2, and omitted the fact that Boynton was a sociology professor; they did, however, find room to mention his impending divorce from a go-go dancer.[17] The *New York Times* did not print the story.

Hans Enzensberger, a German poet who had a teaching fellowship at Wesleyan University, left the United States in 1968 to live in Cuba. He praised Cuba and denounced U.S. foreign policy as an attempt to impose the will of America on smaller countries throughout the world. The *New York Times* gave the story four inches on Page 35.[18] The *Los Angeles Times* didn't mention the story.

News of only one tragedy—a story which can reveal in itself elements of a larger problem—can move a town, a country or the entire world to take action.

A mother in Granada Hills, California, needed $45,000 to rent an artificial kidney machine to save the life of her daughter. She received the help of newspapers and television stations to bring to the public's attention the life-or-death situation. She found out that people throughout the country wanted to help. A benefit football game was arranged, together with a rally attended by many famous movie stars. The Mayor proclaimed a special day to focus attention on the pretty sixteen-year-old girl's plight. Within 90 days $45,000 was raised.[19]

Every day many young and old people in a similar predicament die because they cannot afford a kidney machine or because none is available. Dr. Belding Scribner in his presidential address to the American Society for Artificial Internal Organs, estimated that in a four-year period 10,000 Americans with Kidney disease—those who were ideal candidates—had died for lack of treatment.[20] These figures are rarely publicized by the media. When they are published they don't often cause people to jump into action to do something about it. Only the personal human interest story has this power.

In 1960 poverty in Appalachia became an important issue for the first time. To show concern for the people's votes in this region, both Senators John F. Kennedy and Hubert H. Humphrey campaigned in this area. Previous to this election, Appalachia had been ignored by both the press and presidential candidates. It took stories of the tragedies of individual miners to arouse politicians to take notice of what they had previously ignored. A Senate committee in 1959 heard an editor of a small newspaper tell about one fifty-seven-year-old miner who had been out of work for three years despite his many efforts in looking for a job.

> For some two years he was forced to sit in idleness at home, watching the health of his children deteriorate from lack of enough food—watching their clothes wear out—with no money to replace them.

The miner then figured out that his family would receive social security benefits if he died.

> And so as a Christmas present to his wife and his eight children, the man took out his shotgun and calmly killed himself. It was the best Christmas present he knew how to give. Living he was of no help to his family. By dying he could feed them.[21]

A few years later CBS produced a documentary on Christmas in Appalachia. The audience was so moved by the poverty they saw in individual homes that they sent thousands of Christmas presents to Appalachia. In comparison, repeated statements by government officials that approximately 30 million Americans are living in poverty caused little public response in the early 1960's.

The media, and therefore the people, generally ignore the brutality of our prisons—that is until a story like the following is featured as priority news. Two teenage boys were proven guilty of truancy, trespassing and chicken theft. They were sentenced to serve time in the same jail that housed hardened adult criminals. The *Los Angeles Times* presented this story with a photograph of one of the boys on Page One.[22] People in Los Angeles were justifiably outraged. A famous actor even offered to place them in the California reform school where he was once an inmate.[23] Fifteen years earlier, Sherman Norman, director of detention services of the National Probation and Parole Association, stated that 100,000 children from 7 to 17 years of age were being detained in county jails that were "a disgrace to the nation."[24] A New York State Prison official, Dr. John Rowan, seeing the situation as still a disgrace in 1969 said: "We are keeping delinquent children in jails—many of them cages—which house adult inmates mainly."[25] These news stories placed on the back pages didn't arouse as much public concern as the story of the one fourteen-year-old boy featured on the front page.

A few photographs of starving children in Biafra have touched humanitarian feelings of groups and governments all over the world. But the published statistic that 10,000 people die every day from starvation and malnutrition—in addition to those in Biafra—evokes little press coverage or public response. In fact, many groups which are active in aiding the hungry in Nigeria oppose some of the most effective ways of limiting population and starvation—legalized abortion, sex education and massive distribution of birth control devices.

The response of people to single cases of easily recognizable human suffering or injustic shows what we already know—that the people as a whole are strong advocates of justice, decency, humanitarian concern and human freedom. This being the case, the question arises as to why Americans haven't responded to long-term situations of unnecessary sufferings in our own country. The answer to this lies chiefly in the media's failure to publicize the individual human tragedies that might have the power to create an awareness of the underlying factors, people or groups responsible for causing the sufferings. The history of mass media's coverage of venereal disease provides a telling example.

Thousands of Americans die from syphilis. Others are blinded for life or become permanently insane. The cure for syphilis is sure and simple to effect, so these deaths and sufferings are unnecessary. The tragedy for each affected person could easily be used by the press as a tragic and symbolic story for educating the public and creating an awareness of the costly price people and society pay for needlessly allowing syphilis to go undetected. Prior to 1936, the mass media wouldn't touch the subject. In 1934 CBS radio network censored the following from New York Health Commissioner Dr. Thomas J. Parran's prepared speech for WABC's program "Public Health Needs:"

> We have made no progress against syphilis, though its end results crowd our jails, our poorhouses and our insane asylums. Yet there are specific methods of controlling it, better known to science than the methods of controlling tuberculosis. We need only to do what we know how to do in order to wipe out syphilis as a public health problem.
>
> In my philosophy, the greatest need for action is where the greatest saving of life can be made. I consider then, that our greatest needs in public health are first, the leveling up of present services so that every community may receive the benefits that have long accrued to the leaders; and second, a frontal attack by all communities against maternal mortality and deaths among new-born infants . . . against cancer and syphilis where we have done little or nothing.[26]

The Associated Press wouldn't even use the word "syphilis" in its news releases until forced to do so in 1938 by the same Dr. Parran when he became Surgeon General. But from 1939 to 1950 the press did cooperate, and as a result syphilis cases declined to an all-time low in the early 1950's. In one year in Tennessee, 18,000 sought treatment because of information heard on the radio.

Thinking the disease under control, the press dropped the subject and the government cut expenditures and drastically curtailed its public health control program. But soon the disease was on the increase and by 1954 danger signals led experts to appeal to the government, schools and media to act decisively to prevent another resurgence of the dreaded disease. No one acted and the disease increased rapidly until it reached a high leveling-off point in 1966. Since 1969 it has again been increasing rapidly. In fiscal 1971 syphilis increased by 16 percent and gonorrhea by 9 percent. Experts now describe the situation as pandemic.

Public apathy about venereal disease since 1954 can be traced to a great extent to the media. With few exceptions, its performance in alerting the public since this time has been poor. There are various possible reasons why media shy away from featuring news about venereal disease. Many Puritan media owners feel that the disease serves a good purpose in that it may help deter acts of sex in the first place and serves as a just punishment as an aftermath. Then there is simple prudishness. A few years ago in Houston a television official was asked to help in a crusade against venereal disease. He answered: "Certainly not, after all, ours is a family station." With similar objections, newspaper editors in the same city refused to print articles about venereal disease written by their own reporters.[27] Another element of media owners have no moral or political reason for ignoring venereal disease; they merely fear offending their audience or advertisers. This is probably the reason NBC refused to show Dr. Kildare and Mr. Novak dramas dealing with venereal disease. It's difficult to pinpoint the real reason. NBC said that discussion of "sexual intimacies" wasn't appropriate for their audience.[28] Other owners don't want to stir up the public because they oppose in principle the government getting involved in medicine. Like the AMA, they see government involvement as dangerous because they feel this may lead to socialized medicine.

Media's failure in this area is particularly crippling to society because most of the nation's education systems have avoided the subject even more than the media. Chief of venereal disease education for the Public Health Service, Dr. William F. Schwartz, pointed out in 1966 that only five percent of students who should be receiving venereal disease education in six large cities were receiving it.[29] A quiz given to teen-age venereal disease victims in New York City revealed that over 90 percent were ignorant of the facts about venereal disease. Yet despite this ignorance, the media did not fill the gap left by the timid schools and embark on an education campaign of their own, nor did they launch any crusade for mandatory education in the schools. In 1962 Dr. Leona Baumgartner, head of the Surgeon Generals task force, pleaded with the press to engage in a national education campaign to tell the American people the facts about vencreal disease.[30] The *New York Times* printed her request on Page 53. Along with the rest of the press, the *Times* refused to take on the job, even though New York City's school system wouldn't touch the subject.

A few years later, in 1965, the media heard another request that it use its unlimited technological potential to help stem the rising tide of venereal disease. Noting that teen-age syphilis had risen 230 percent in the previous nine years, the venereal disease branch of the Public Health Service urgently solicited the "active support of all news media."[31] Most owners of media still refused to support efforts of those few men dedicated to informing the public; they were satisfied to print on the inside pages the few news releases reporting the yearly rates of increase. One exception was Westinghouse Broadcasting Company's superb six-part, two and one half hour, 1966 radio documentary on venereal disease.

The media very seldom focused attention on two of the most important factors causing the increase in venereal disease—factors that could have been eliminated overnight if the public had been made aware of them. Teenagers naturally avoid going for treatment if their parents will be notified, probably because parents can be expected to react with anger, condemnation and morality lectures. As a result, the infected teen-ager prolongs his eventual treatment and infects others in the meantime. Nevertheless, over thirty states still have laws requiring that the parents be notified by public health clinics before treatment can be given.[32] Few if any news agencies have crusaded to have these laws removed.

The second factor was mentioned by Dr. William Brown, Chief of the Venereal Disease Branch of the National Communicable Disease Center, who said that the number one reason for the increase in venereal disease was the failure of private physicians to report cases of the disease to authorities.[33] This failure to report cases prevents public health investigators from finding persons who are unaware they have the disease. Some estimates claim 800,000 Americans who have the disease are unaware of it. These persons go untreated until it's too late to prevent sterility, blindness, death or insanity. To help prevent these kinds of tragedies, all fifty states have passed laws requiring physicians to report cases to health authorities. This has not proved effective because most private physicians violate these laws. Only about 12 to 25 percent of the cases treated by private physicians are reported as required by law.[34] The media owners, self proclaimed guardians of law and order, choose to keep the public ignorant of these crimes. In a rare Page-One story in the *New York Times* reporting on the AMA's drive against venereal disease, there was no mention at all of the physicians' failure to report cases as required by law. This omission no doubt made the AMA doctors look like better crusaders than they are in actual practice.

If there is an epidemic of any other kind of communicable disease, even the flu, it makes the front pages—but not venereal disease. When Dr. William Brown, the nation's foremost authority on venereal disease, stated that "syphilis epidemics are raging at this very moment in 25 or 30 of our largest metropolitan cities," it didn't cause much of a commotion. One reason is that America's most prestigious newspaper in the city with the worst venereal disease problem placed Dr. Brown's statement on Page 73.[35] The *Los Angeles Times* didn't print the AP story.

Two critical years for veneral disease control were 1957 and 1958. If at this time the government and media had acted responsibly the ensuing epidemics that are still raging in our cities could have been averted. To indicate why the public was too apathetic to pressure the timid politicians to act, it is only necessary to look at the *New York Times Indexes* for 1957 and 1958. It records only 3 items on venereal disease for the entire 730 days, and this at a time when venereal disease was on a critical upswing.

In 1960, possibly as many as 1,000 persons a month died from syphilis.[36] While total local, state and federal expenditures to control venereal disease reached only $19 million, the cost of taking care of the victims was nearly $100 million. It costs nearly $50 million a year just to maintain the syphilitic insane in public institutions.[37] Despite these alarming facts, venereal disease never made the front page of newspapers and was seldom if ever mentioned on radio or television newscasts. Table VIII gives some idea of this neglect.

As a point in comparison, during April and May of 1960, the *New*

TABLE VIII
NEWS ITEMS ON VENEREAL DISEASE, 1960

NEWSPAPER OR NEWSCAST	Time Period	Total News Items	Number on Venereal Disease
Los Angeles Times (Front Page)*	April & May	900+	0
New York Times (Front Page)*	April & May	700+	0
NBC-TV Huntley-Brinkley	Sept. 26 to Nov. 7	450+	0
CBS-TV Doug Edwards	Sept. 26 to Nov. 7	450+	0
ABC-TV John Daly	Sept. 26 to Nov. 7	450+	0
ABC Radio Edward P. Morgan	Sept. 26 to Nov. 7	450+	0
NBC Radio Peter Hackes	Sept. 26 to Nov. 7	450+	0
CBS Radio Lowell Thomas	Sept. 26 to Nov. 7	450+	0

*Includes stories of both local and national distribution or interest

York Times found room for 18 accident and 11 trivia items with 17 photographs, and the *Los Angeles Times* made front page space for 120 accidents and 57 trivia items accompanied by 214 photographs.

In 1969 venereal disease was epidemic, but as shown in Table IX, it didn't rate priority coverage in the news media.

In contrast to the blackout of venereal disease news, the *New York Times* found space on their front pages for 10 accident and 11 trivia items with 16 photographs, and the *Los Angeles Times* had 17 accident and 5 trivia items with 75 photographs. The *Honolulu Star-Bulletin* had 90 items on trivial matters during the time it ignored venereal disease. *Huntley-Brinkley* had 41 items taking 45 minutes for trivia and *Walter Cronkite* had 21 items taking 43 minutes for trivia. *Walter Cronkite* and CBS *Saturday Evening News* had 54 minutes on sports during the time it failed to mention venereal disease.

With such neglect of the venereal disease epidemic, the public will continue to tolerate the tragedies caused by ignorance and inaction along with the conditions which prevent syphilis from being eliminated and gonorrhea from being controlled.

Our penal system produces many tragedies—individual tragedies—that if widely and prominently publicized could make everyone aware of the larger issue of inadequate prisons and the archaic attitudes that allow prison brutalities to continue. An 18 year old boy, Ismael Nieves, was arrested in 1968 for being truant from school. According to an article in the *Saturday Evening Post,* he wrote to his mother that he couldn't stand the beatings he was taking from other inmates. That night someone set fire to Nieves' mattress and locked him in his cell. Nieves, who did not smoke and had no matches, was severely burned and died a week later. The coroners, after listening to testimony, were unable to determine if it was an accident or not.[38]

A 1967 study of Cook County Jail detailed other atrocities:

> One 14-year old boy was dry shaved, producing about 50 cuts, and later sexually attacked by four adult offenders.
>
> Another young boy was repeatedly attacked sexually by various inmates and went into a catatonic state. He ended up in a mental hospital.[39]

These are not exceptional incidents. An investigation of three Philadelphia prisons in 1968 disclosed that there were a minimum of 2,000 sexual assaults in the previous two years.[40]

TABLE IX
NEWS ITEMS ON VENEREAL DISEASE, 1969

NEWSPAPER OR NEWSCAST	Time Period	Total News Items	Number on Venereal Disease
Los Angeles Times (Front Page)*	June & July	450+	0
New York Times (Front Page)*	June & July	700+	0
Honolulu Star-Bulletin (First 3 Pages)*	Jan. 12 to May 31	1500+	0
NBC-TV Huntley-Brinkley	July 10 to Sept. 10	899	0
CBS-TV Walter Cronkite	July 10 to Sept. 10	901	0
Mutual Radio On-The-Hour (7:00 a.m. P.S.T.)	Aug. 22 to Oct. 22	355	0
ABC Radio On-The-Hour (9:00 a.m. P.S.T.)	Aug. 22 to Oct. 22	421	0

*Includes stories of both local and national distribution or interest

Not all prison brutality comes from other prisoners. It was discovered in 1966 by a former superintendent of an Arkansas prison farm that prisoners were murdered, beat with barbed wire whips, blackjacks, and brass knuckles. Others had to endure an electrical torture device that ran "electrical current through two wires attached to the genital parts of the body."[41] Former Superintendent Thomas Murton said that the Arkansas prisons were among the worst but that there were others like them across the entire nation.

Two young boys, one a 13-year old Indian who had been in solitary confinement for forty-one days, hung themselves in Minnesota jails.[42]

Such brutalities as these—and many more examples—were disclosed during the Senate Juvenile Delinquency Subcommittee investigations in March 1969. Here the media had an opportunity to use the hearings as an educational tool to make a maximum impact upon all Americans. Television and radio stations could have covered the hearings live. Advertisements announcing live coverage could have been placed in the newspapers and over the air. Incredibly, not one radio or television station covered the hearings live. So Americans didn't have a choice of whether to watch the hearings or not. There was no competition among news decision makers on this point. Newspapers could have kept the subject on the front page for days, but they were content to *objectively* report the hearings on the inside pages. It's safe to assume that prison conditions would be ignored altogether if left to the initiative of the press.

Those that deserve credit for first drawing attention to the inhumane treatment of prisoners were the prisoners themselves. Having no access to media, which would have enabled them to tell their story, they staged twenty major uprisings in 1952. Five percent of the inmates were actively involved. The Director of Federal Prisons warned that improvement would not occur unless the citizens were aroused to the urgent need for drastic reform.[43] The media failed to dramatize personal tragedies or feature the news on the front page, and as a result there was little public demand for prison reform.

NBC radio produced an hour-long documentary on prison conditions in 1953, but there were few other efforts. Although the report was a hard hitting exposure of conditions, it still tried to discredit claims by ex-inmates. The views of inmates were given but introduced with the comment that some were "lying in their teeth." Jack Gould, television critic, noted that it was never shown where they had lied.[44]

Prisoners again tried to communicate to the outside world in the only way available to them—through uprisings. There were eighteen uprisings in ten states in the first eight months of 1955. It was clear that there hadn't been much change in prison conditions since 1952.

The 1969 Senate Hearings indicated that the United States Prison system in 1969 was still so deplorable it turned out, according to one expert, "finely honed weapons against society." And Committee Chairman Senator Thomas Dodd said that the nation's prisons did little but "achieve the degradation and dehumanization of offenders."[45] In November 1969, a Congressional Commission, after a three year study, pinpointed public attitudes as the basic reason why the nation has tolerated this torture and dehumanization of inmates for so long. The Commission stated: "The American public has never quite made up its mind as to whether it is more important to punish offenders . . . or try to change them into useful citizens."[46] This is an attitude communicated to the people through the media's own laziness, neglect and suppression of news exposing prison conditons and policies. Many mass media owners, being very conservative, see prison brutalitics as justifiable punishment for those who break the law. Other owners oppose the needed appropriations because they are in principle against "big government" or increased federal expenditures. The Congressional Commission said that nothing could be done in the area of prison reform without more money. This is a political shortcoming. It is the political shortcomings that the press fails to bring to light even more than the conditions themselves. A few days after the Commission report was published, President Nixon asked for an immediate and dramatic reform of the nation's prison system, but he didn't bother to ask for the necessary money.[47] As usual, studies were proposed—as if there weren't already enough facts to justify immediate action. The press headlined the President's proposal for reform instead of exposing the fact that more money, not further studies and eloquent oratory, is what is needed.

When former prison superintendent Thomas Murton revealed that Governor Winthrop Rockefeller told him he "shouldn't talk so much" about prison conditions, it didn't even make a headline.[48] He later accused the governor of being an accessory "after the fact to the crime of murder," and pointed out that the state was suppressing "the truth about atrocities within the prison."[49]

In 1950 the prisons were quiet on the surface and the newspapers were making no great effort to dramatize or publicize the plight of the abused inmates. During February and March of 1950, there were no items on prison conditions on the front pages of either the *Los Angeles Times* or the *New York Times*.

In 1960, eight years after the prison uprisings brought conditions to the media's attention, prison conditions were still given little attention. The same newspapers and 6 network newscasts that completely ignored venereal disease during the period in 1960 as shown in Table VIII, had a total of 1 item on prison conditions.

After the sensational subcommittee investigations in March of 1969, it would be natural to expect a lot of follow-up publicity, but as Table X shows, the performance was lukewarm except for *Walter Cronkite's* six-minute coverage of prison conditions and racism at San Quentin.

Dramatic human interest stories are not always ignored by the media. Episodes which emphasize man's successes—the moon flights, heart transplants, solo sailings, mechanical inventions—get plenty of coverage. This might not be entirely unplanned. The dramatization of man's successes makes people satisfied with the status quo that the media owners find so profitable. Failures are just as important as man's successes because awareness of them allows man to adjust and reevaluate his priorities in order to prevent more serious consequences in the future. This basic reevaluation of priorities is exactly what the media owners are against. As a result, they seldom if ever dramatize human interest stories symbolizing man's great failures. There are few items symbolizing man's failure to curb the population explosion. There are none exposing politicians who do nothing to combat the problem. There are few dramatic examples that make clear the failure of communication systems to inform people of the dangers that lie ahead. There are few dramatizations that would make people aware of man's failure to deal with what U Thant calls the greatest problem facing man—the increasing gap between the rich and poor people of the world. The world provides no end of human interest stories that would serve as symbolic dramatization of man's failures, but the media intentionally passes them by.

On purely domestic problems the media's performance is the same. Walter Rugaber noted in a *New York Times* article that "1000's of American Industrial concerns violate the Federal government occupational safety and health requirements each year, but the available penalties are almost never invoked against corporate offenders." Rugaber notes that only about 1 out of 1000 offenders is ever punished. At least thirty-eight workers die each day from job-related injuries

TABLE X

NEWS ITEMS ON PRISON CONDITIONS, 1969

NEWSPAPER* OR NEWSCAST	Time Period	Total Items	Number of Items on Prison Conditions	Photos pp. 1, 2, 3, or Minutes
Los Angeles Times (Front Page)	June & July	450+	0	0
New York Times (Front Page)	June & July	700+	2	0
Honolulu Star-Bulletin (First 3 Pages)	Jan. 12-May 31	1500+	1	0
NBC-TV-Huntley-Brinkley	July 10-Sept. 10	899 +	3	1:25
CBS-TV-Walter Cronkite	July 10-Sept. 10	901 +	4	8:07
Mutual Radio On-The-Hour (7:00 a.m. P.S.T.)	Aug. 22-Oct. 22	555 +	0	0
ABC Radio On-The-Hour (9:00 a.m. P.S.T.)	Aug. 22-Oct. 22	421 +	0	0

*Stories of national distribution or interest only

and accidents, and 5500 per day suffer from disabling injuries. The rate of disabling injuries has increased markedly from 1958 to 1968. The resulting loss of man-days of work is ten times the amount lost due to strikes.[50] Many of these injuries could be avoided if there were safer equipment and working conditions as required by federal regulation. Dramatizing the individual deaths, disabling injuries, and corporate violations of safety and health standards could be a powerful media tool for forcing industry to act in a more responsible manner, but such stories are seldom featured by media owners. By not dramatizing these tragedies, the media shows itself to be on the side of the mine owners and other industrialists who place worker safety behind company profits.

As the National Commission on the Prevention of Violence reported, the courts favor the rich even in the few cases where the poor can scrape up enough money to go to court. The failure of American society to guarantee the poor equal justice is seldom dramatized by the press, yet there are thousands of personal injustices suffered by the poor every day that could be used to show the lack of equal justice afforded to the poor. The media owners show their determination to safequard the special legal privileges they have for themselves by not publicizing cases that would arouse the public.

America has failed to provide equal access to mass media, but the media would be the last to dramatize the way in which solid liberal and radical left viewpoints are denied equal access.

The failure of 80 percent of American industry to end policies of racial discrimination provides mass media with thousands of potential stories, but the media seldom choose to use their power to dramatize personal cases of discrimination. It can hardly be expected that they would do so since the media themselves are guilty of racial discrimination in the employment of technicians and other workers behind the screen. Chairman of the Equal Employment Opportunity Commission, William F. Brown, reported in 1969:

> Our hearings in California indicated to us very clearly that the television networks are very derelict in the duties they are performing as it relates to elimination of discrimination in their own industry.[51]

A week later the Federal Communications Commission felt it necessary to order all the nation's television and radio stations to eliminate racial discrimination.[52]

More than one half of the nation's auto deaths are caused by drunk drivers; that's two to three times the percentage caused by drunk drivers in Scandinavia where they have tougher standards and penalties.[53] Millions of Americans are tragically addicted to the expensive habit. Nevertheless, while the media dramatizes thousands of tragedies symbolizing the hazards of marijuana and LSD, they dramatize comparatively few tragic cases involving alcohol. While mass media donates free time for anti-drug advertisements which often feature personal tragedy, they give no time for anti-drinking advertisements.

We have seen how one of the most powerful techniques of persuasion—the use of dramatic or tragic human interest stories to symbolize a larger social or medical condition—has been used selectively by the media for the purpose of having us focus our attention on some conditions and factors while ignoring others which might embarrass the supporters of the status quo.

We shall next examine the numerous additional techniques used by those who control the media.

13   A Catalog of Hidden Bias

> Trying to determine what is going on in the world by
> reading the newspaper is like trying to tell the time by
> watching the second hand of a clock.
>
>   Ben Hecht

Man's mind is the daily target that receives the shotgun-like blasts
from the news barrels of mass media. On August 7, 1969, Chet Huntley fired off 7 different news stories at his audience in 58 seconds. On
October 16, 1969, Edward P. Morgan assailed his radio listeners with
9 news items in 63 seconds. A reader of the first two pages of the *Los
Angeles Times* has more than 50 news stories pass through his mind
each morning. A thorough reader of the *New York Times* has to make
room in his mind for over 300 stories daily.

Man is capable of absorbing all these news items—events disassoci-
ated in time, space, and subject matter—but it is impossible for him to
make any meaningful order out of the never-ending kaleidescope of
world events that make up the day's news. What philosopher Erwin
Edman says of newspapers applies even more to the total output of all
news media.

> . . . the worst possible way of getting a coherent picture of the life
> of our time. It is a crazy quilt, a jazz symphony, a madness shouting
> in large type. . . . The mind of the newspaper reader, if it could be
> photographed after ten minutes reading, would not be a map, but an
> explosion.[1]

This explosion is a threat to man's sanity. Merely to survive and function normally he must somehow grapple with the explosion in his
mind caused by the daily input of disordered news. He must put
things back into some type of coherent picture of the world in order
to have bases for his opinions and actions.

This situation enables the clever newsman to slip his bias into the
news, unnoticed by the news fan whose attention is focused on the

event itself. The reader or listener is lucky if he can understand the news item and fit it into some kind of pattern; he can hardly be expected to analyze carefully the elements of bias inserted by the communicator. Jacques Ellul, in his book *Propaganda,* sees a close connection between the technology of news and the propagandist:

> To the extent that propaganda is based on current news, it cannot permit time for thought or reflection. A man caught up in the news must remain on the surface of the event; he is carried along in the current, and can at no time take a respite to judge and appreciate; he can never stop to reflect. There is never any awareness—of himself, of his condition, of his society—for the man who lives by current events. . . . One thought drives away another; old facts are chased by new ones.[2]

Faced with the daily onslaught of news, man unconsciously latches on to any order that may be within the news itself. Bias is the order that is within the news. It is bias that saves man from chaos by giving him emotional themes and structured patterns within the news. Without bias in news, man would be like a child trying to cope with unpatterned stimuli without learning a language with which to give some order to new experiences. Each different language has within it a hidden bias which determines how the learner makes sense out of his experiences. When a child learns a language, he also unknowingly accepts the view of the world that is inherent in the particular structure of that language. As a child grasps for language to cope with the world, so man grasps for the bias—no matter how slight—to cope with the unstructured kaleidescope of news that daily assails his senses.

In *American Democracy,* Harold Lasky describes what a powerful tool hidden bias can be:

> The real power of the press comes from the effect of its continuous repitition of an attitude reflected in facts which its readers have no chance to check, or by its ability to surround those facts by an environment of suggestion which, often half-consciously, seeps its way into the mind of the reader and forms his premises for him without his even being aware that they are really prejudices to which he has scarcely given a moment of thought.[3]

The messages secretly implanted in the news are used to create and maintain views and attitudes favoring the establishment. Since those advocating solid liberal or radical left viewpoints own no mass media outlets, they are effectively denied the opportunity of deciding what story shall become news, who to interview or which photograph to select. They make no headlines or captions for news going out to the millions of average American citizens. They are restricted to using the techniques of implanting bias in their own small pamphlets and magazines which, by the way, reach fewer than one half of one percent of Americans.

Bias in the Source of News

The news that is available to the owners, editors and broadcasters may be biased even before they receive it in their news offices. In my opinion, the most objective news is sent to news agencies over the wire services of the Associated Press or the United Press International. But while this news is relatively objective much of the time, in many cases it is blatantly biased. John Gerassi, Latin American correspondent for *Time* magazine from 1957 to 1961 and later an editor of *Newsweek* magazine, sums up his experience with these wire services in Latin America:

> I have found Associated Press and United Press International completely unreliable in Latin America. To the people of Latin America AP and UPI are United States Government agencies. And it is not hard to see why: Their dispatches turn every politician that criticizes the United States into a 'Leftist,' most peasant leaders that demand a better living standard into 'demagogues,' and all Castro supporters into 'communists.'[4]

One example of wire service bias given by Gerassi is the failure of all U.S. wire services to report that the United States had intercepted and confiscated a Swiss arms shipment bound for Guatemala in the early 1950's. Reuters, the British wire service, reported the incident.[5]

Wire service reporting from Washington D. C. can be just as biased as that from Latin America. Robert H. Yoakum, frequent contributor to the *Columbia Journalism Review,* noted how the wire services chose to cover up for the wrongdoings of Senator Thomas Dodd: "A Senator was up to his clavicle in ill-gained dollars, but the wire services were unable to spring even one of their 141 Washington reporters to interview the ex-employees who had the story."[6] Yoakum points out the UPI dispatches

> often sounded as though they had been processed in Dodd's office. 'For eight years, he has been one of the most respected members of the Senate,' a UPI background story reported inaccurately in April

1966, compounding the error later in the piece by referring to Dodd as ' . . . a man respected for his views on foreign affairs.'[7]

A National Education Television analysis of news coverage of a demonstration in Washington D.C. by the Women's Strike for Peace found bias in UPI's selection of words to describe the women taking part in the demonstration. Jeannette Rankin was referred to as "dowager queen" and "peacock"; others were described as "hippy".[8]

As we've noted already, whatever bias there is in the wire service reports is especially significant because more than 5000 news agencies around the world use the services of the AP alone. The vast majority of daily newspapers and stations can't even choose between different wire service accounts of the same story because they subscribe to only one wire service.[9]

Handouts by government agencies and departments are another main source of basic news. No one except a few government officials will deny that such press handouts are biased. Often the people are not fooled by government news handouts and speeches. A Gallup poll taken in October 1967 showed that 70 precent thought the Johnson administration was "not telling the public all they should know about the Vietnam war."[10]

Another source of basic news is public relations information received from corporations and other organizations. These news handouts are decidedly biased in favor of the sponsoring organization.

The significance of all this is that news is often biased before it even gets to the news agency that will transmit it. The transmitters of news—those who control access to mass media—take this already biased news material and manipulate it further, using various consciously applied techniques of implanting bias in the attempt to make the American public think, feel and respond in certain ways. Each technique can be analyzed separately, though the techniques are used in various combinations simultaneously.

Bias Through Selection of News

One of the most effective and easy ways of implanting bias is one that the public could never be aware of. We have no way of knowing what news stories the editors decide not to print on any given day. We cannot see the film or the interview segments that were not selected for inclusion in the day's news. Newspapers handle more news than any other news medium, yet what finally ends up in the paper is only a small portion of the news that is available. A large newspaper will receive more than a hundred photographs a day from the wire services plus many more from local sources and its own staff photographers. Only a few will be chosen as newsworthy: the public has no way of knowing which photographs were excluded. Radio and television must be even more selective than newspapers: naturally they cannot be expected to cover as much as newspapers. A three-minute radio news summary includes a small fraction of the available news; the public will just have to trust that the rest of the news was not as important.

Nobody could expect (or want) newspapers to print, or newscasts to broadcast, every bit of news they receive; it would be lengthy, costly, boring and chaotic. But we-the-public should be aware that many decisions are made by editors who select news in a way designed to support certain viewpoints, to be entertaining at the expense of "hard" reality or not to antagonize the audience. Regardless which reason, the bias that results is one that favors conservative viewpoints and the status quo. Chet Huntley admits how subjective these decisions are:

> In our sometimes zeal for shooting film with interesting facades and lovely landscapes, and in our fear of dullness and the low rating, we arbitrarily rule out a long and imposing list of awesome subjects and conclude that they were just not meant for television and radio.[11]

A study of 1800 news items covered by *Huntley-Brinkley* and *Walter Cronkite* during two months in the summer of 1969 reveals a high percentage of entertaining but unimportant news items.[12] Robert MacNeil, former NBC correspondent studied in detail the three network television newscasts for a three day period in 1967 and concluded:

> They perform wonders of technical competence, but their journalistic achievement is still erratic. Their content demonstrates capricious selection due not only to news judgment, but to the unshakable belief that picture must come first.[13]

One July morning in 1968, famous Hawaii disc jockey Aku-Head Pupule reported "to the moment, the latest news of the world." He told his KGMB listerners: "Not much news. Ky and Johnson to meet—that's all."[14] On the local scene Aku mentioned that there had been seven traffic accidents. He wrapped it up quickly with a weather report and got back to the commercials and discs. Network news-on-the-hour is unquestionably more responsible than this, but a two-month study of 776 news items from Mutual and ABC shows that their selection of what is newsworthy is very capricious from a journalistic standpoint.[15]

Professor Jack Lyle checked the selection of news by seven different television stations in Los Angeles. He found that together they covered a total of 103 stories, but only 5 of these appeared on all seven stations. Of the 103 stories, 65 were presented on only one station.[16] These different selections by these stations demonstrates clearly the capriciousness of the selections which determine for the public their view of the world for one day.

Our previous examination of the front pages of newspapers for three two-month periods in different years showed that what newspaper editors decide to put on the front page is governed by the same subjective political and commercial considerations that predominate in news broadcasting.[17] The content of the rest of the newspaper is even more whimsically selected than the front page.

George Turnbull Jr.'s analysis of newspaper stories about the Vietnamese fight for independence from the French showed, without doubt, that there were not enough stories presented through our media to enable us Americans "to think adequately about it."[18] During the 208 weeks from 1946 through 1949, the *New York Times* presented 38 news stories about the war—mostly spot news. *Time* magazine had 4 during this period. Of the three newspapers and one newsweekly checked by Turnbull, only the *New York Times* covered the announcement in 1949 that the United States was increasing its support of France's colonial war by agreeing to pay one-third of the cost.

An analysis of three television network evening newscasts for a six-week period in 1960[19] shows a similar neglect of the (then potentially dangerous) situation in Vietnam, though by 1960 the United States had committed itself to the Diem Regime. *Huntley-Brinkley* had 1 item consisting of eleven words telling about a "Communist" attack on a road-construction project. CBS and ABC had no items at all on Vietnam. During this same six weeks, the *New York Times* had 14 items on Vietnam, mostly spot news slanted in favor of the Diem regime.

In another study, ten daily newspapers together covered 69 different stories of national significance. A majority of the ten papers ran stories on only 7 of the 69 items. Only 3 of the 69 items were covered by all ten newspapers. Three of the ten newspapers decided that news of the physicians draft was not important enough to mention.[20]

Dr. Edward Glick made a study of twenty-two newspapers to see how they covered health news.[21] He concluded that the majority of twenty-two newspapers—including all the dailies in seven major cities—did not publish many of the stories made available to them by the AP and UPI. Selection on the part of individual editors varied greatly. While the *Washington Post* and *Washington Star* both printed more than 30 stories each, the *Chicago Tribune* printed only 5. The newspapers studied covered seven cities. Only one newspaper outside of Washington, D.C. published the AP story reporting the Surgeon General's statement that more than one half of all American children of pre-school age were not adequately protected against polio. Nineteen of the twenty-two papers, including those in air-polluted Los Angeles, passed up the story of a government report which showed a link between the common cold and air pollution.

Despite complaints of too much coverage of radical dissent at the 1968 Democratic Convention in Chicago, the networks actually devoted very little time to showing the demonstrations. As noted in a staff report to the National Commission on the Causes and Prevention of Violence, CBS alloted 32 minutes to demonstrations out of a total of 38 hours and 3 minutes. Out of 19 hours and 37 minutes of convention coverage, NBC devoted only 14 minutes to film or tape coverage of disorders involving demonstrations and police.

Nevertheless, (perhaps due in part to the conservative complaints that too much attention was given to protests at that Convention) the networks used their power of arbitrary selection to ignore dissent that took place along the Presidential Inauguration route. NBC ignored the dissent almost completely; CBS reported some incidents, but repeatedly apologized to its audience for doing so.[22]

Sometimes in their desire to keep ideas they dislike off the air, media owners will conspire to ignore certain events which otherwise would be selected as news. Newspapers, radio and television outlets in Medford, Oregon, in agreement with the state police, suppressed coverage of an anti-Vietnam war vigil in 1967.[23]

Decisions to select items as newsworthy or un-newsworthy must make the total picture of the day's events very biased to begin with. As we try to absorb the numerous images and headlines that compete for our attention, there is no way for us to evaluate this hidden bias, for all we see is what the editors think we should see.

Bias Through Omission of News

After an editor decides a story shall become news he can give the story a considerable bias merely by omitting the part of the story he doesn't want the reader or listener to know about. The citizen can't possibly be aware of what was left out even if he stopped to analyze the shortened news article. The editors leave no blank spaces.

Dr. Jean Meyer, Director of the White House Conference on Food, Nutrition and Health, said on "Meet the Press" in 1969 that one of the biggest roadblocks to feeding the poor was to get Americans to be concerned about the issue. He noted that Congress received very few letters or telegrams urging Congressional action on the matter. And he noted another roadblock: many politicians were actually opposed to feeding the hungry. He cited as an example the case of New Hampshire's State OEO official losing his job because he showed that there was hunger and malnutrition in the state. In the AP release sent to newspapers the above points were omitted.[24]

Omission of important points like these and the playing down of certain news items about hunger keeps the public satisfied with the status quo, though today 15 million Americans don't have enough money to buy food for an adequate diet. News of vocal complaints about the President or local officials doing little or nothing to feed the hungry is either buried or omitted. On the other hand, to make the people think that establishment politicians are acting decisively to meet the emergency, the media gives priority attention and presents as decisive the stop-gap measures of the President that are seen as inadequate by critics.

The media gave a big headline on Page One to Nixon's proposal for an increase in the food stamp program.[25] But six months later in December 1969, Senator George McGovern in a "Face the Nation" interview accused the Nixon administration of actively lobbying against passage of a newly proposed food stamp bill. This was given only six inches and placed with a very small headline in the middle of Page 26 in the *New York Times*.[26] This is obvious playing down of the news item. Sunday interview shows usually are priority news items: "Face the Nation" received first or second-page coverage in the *New York Times* for all 52 of its interviews in the year ending June, 1969.[27] Besides burying the McGovern interview on Page 26, the *Times* omitted McGovern's statement which summed up what he thought to be the real reason why the poor were not being fed:

> We have had the kind of leadership both in the executive branch
> and in the Congress that has been too much concerned about special
> interest in this country and not enough concerned about the broad
> range of human need. That's really the problem.

However, the *Times* in this inconspicuous story did mention
McGovern's contention that the administration was guilty of "double
talk" in that it had actively opposed passage of a food stamp increase
and then applauded when the appropriation was passed.

The AP dispatch as printed on Page 17 of the *Los Angeles Times*
omitted completely any of McGovern's comments about hunger.[28] Instead it focused exclusively on the other topic covered by McGovern
during the interview—the massacre at Songmy. And its coverage of
this part of the interview omitted McGovern's strongest statement:

> Now really, what is the difference between a bombing plane or an
> artillery piece destroying a village and destroying its inhabitants,
> men, women and children, and what Lt. Calley did? The difference, I
> suppose, is that Lt. Calley and his people, if they are guilty as
> charged, were operating at closer range. But the moral issues, it
> seems to me, [are] the same.

The *New York Times* report of the interview omitted all of the
Senator's comments on the significance of the Songmy incident.

One of the reasons Dr. Jean Meyer could truthfully claim the American people are not concerned enough about hunger is because of
news coverage that protects from exposure to public view the mechi-
nations of politicians who resist measures designed to help feed the
hungry. A UPI release in July 1969 told of the Senate Agriculture
Committee's rejection of proposals to give free food stamps to families earning less than $40 dollars a month. It included the names of
the five committee members voting for the bill but omitted the names
of those seven who voted against the bill.[29] The *New York Times* coverage also mentioned the five who voted yes but omitted the names of
the other seven.[30] Politicians may now be doing more than ever in
combating hunger, but this does not exonerate the past inaction or
obstruction by politicians, or media's use of bias to protect those who
acted in no great haste as millions of Americans went hungry.

Senator William Knowland in a 1953 "Meet the Press" interview
stated that South Korea's Syngman Rhee "was not sufficiently consulted [on Asian policy matters] during the Truman Administration or
during the Eisenhower Administration." The AP dispatch, omitting

the reference to the Eisenhower Administration, reported that Knowland "said today that we might not be faced with the present 'unfortunate' situation in Korea if the Truman Administration had consulted with Syngman Rhee."[31]

The bias implanted by the wire services is minimal compared to the news agencies they serve. The *Pottstown Mercury* on September 5, 1968, omitted from its published news reports enough statements to make up almost an entire newspaper page. The parts omitted were those critical of the President, the United States Government, the local government and the U. S. policy in Vietnam.[32]

Most news agencies use this tool for creating bias less frequently than the above newspaper, but vital information is still omitted from important stories by even the more responsible agencies. In October 1960, Chet Huntley reported: "Premier Fidel Castro said counter-revolutionaries fighting his regime are stronger than were the Batista forces but he will win."[33] This report would perhaps lead television viewers to think that there was a substantial opposition to Castro by Cubans inside Cuba—a concept pleasing to the establishment at that time. What Chet Huntley left out was the key part of the news release as received from the wire services. Edward P. Morgan included it as he reported that same evening: "Fidel Castro *accused the United States of mobilizing* his political enemies into a force more powerful than the Batista dictatorship he overthrew."[34]

Huntley-Brinkley's 20 million viewers were shown films of President Nixon at his desk up to his knees in the thousands of telegrams that citizens had sent expressing their support for his Vietnam speech.[35] What the audience was not told is that these letters were actively solicited by the Republican National Committee through its newsletter. That same evening Walter Cronkite included this information.[36]

When Black Panther leader Bobby Seale was on trial for conspiring to cross state lines with the intent to incite riot, his hands were tied and mouth gagged at the order of Judge Julius J. Hoffman. The Judge had become annoyed by Seale's interruptions of the trial with outspoken demands that he be allowed to defend himself.

After a tireless effort he somehow managed to free a hand, yank off the gag, and shout at the Judge: "You fascist dog, you. You rotten low life son of a gun." *Walter Cronkite,* which spent more than two minutes on the episode, omitted these words and merely told its viewers that Seale had yelled "obscenities" at the judge. *Huntley-Brinkley* apparently didn't consider "fascist" as obscene; they used the word in describing what Seale had shouted to the judge.[37]

Actor Hal March had been a smoker until he quit only three years before he died from lung cancer at the age of forty-nine. *Walter Cronkite* in reporting March's death made no mention that March had been a smoker or that he had given up smoking before his death.[38] When *Walter Cronkite* and *Huntley-Brinkley* reported the death of Robert Taylor from lung cancer, they omitted the fact that since childhood he had smoked three packs of cigarettes a day—a fact included in the wire services' reports.[39] Is it only coincidental that tobacco companies at this time were paying as much as $25,000 a minute to advertise on network evening news programs?

Former Health, Education, and Welfare Secretary Robert Finch's first choice for Assistant Secretary for Health and Scientific Affairs, Dr. John Knowles, said in July 1969, that "the White House under President Nixon is in the grip of the arch-conservatives and progress is at a complete standstill." KPFK, listener-supported radio in Los Angeles, and the *Los Angeles Times* chose this as the main point of Knowles' statement, but the *New York Times,* which gave more than 40 inches of coverage to the story, omitted it.[40] *Huntley-Brinkley* and *Walter Cronkite* didn't cover the story at all.

In a speech to the National Press Club, Wright Patman, Chairman of the House Banking and Currency Committee said:

> It is an open secret on capital hill that many campaign chests are swelled by contributions from the banks. Members of the House Banking and Currency Committee have been offered huge blocks of bank stocks free of charge and directorships on bank boards. Freshmen members have been approached within hours of their arrival in Washington and offered quick and immediate loans. In one instance that was reported to me, the bank told the member, quote, 'just write a check, we will honor it'. . . .
>
> Today's economy which has the highest interest rates in the nation's history is largely the result of the banking and monitary policy written by the special interests for special interests.

Patman drew attention to the fact that banks were denying mortgages to middle income families at the same time they were

. . . issuing credit cards by the tens of millions, sending them to people who never asked for them or didn't want them, making credit easier while all the time claiming to fight inflation. . . .

Through their newly found toy, the bank holding company, they are moving into all lines of business using the special privileges of the bank to force their competitors to the wall. They are now into everything from pizza parlors to green stamps. This movement, left unchecked, will change the face of the entire American economy, sharply concentrating power in the hands of a few. . . . This new Nazi style economy, should it become a reality would destroy this nation.

Patman also claimed Federal Reserve Board Chairman William Martin had cost the American people $300 billion dollars through his tight money policy.[41]

Huntley-Brinkley failed to mention the Patman speech. *Walter Cronkite* took 25 seconds to report briefly Patman's charge that lobbyists were trying to influence Congress with campaign contributions, but Patman's statements about credit cards, pizza parlors, William Martin and the Nazi-style economy were omitted. The *New York Times* and the *Los Angeles Times* both omitted the same statements from their coverage.

President Nixon's trip to India in 1969 was given priority coverage by the media. Both the *New York Times* and the *Los Angeles Times* covered his trip on the front page. Television featured satellite-relay coverage. That same day Mrs. Indira Gandhi, Prime Minister of India, gave a press conference that was attended by members of the U.S. press. In her talk Mrs. Gandhi said she felt the United States was moving toward India's policy in Vietnam, but then she made some statements that showed that her thinking about the Vietnam war was fundamentally different than that of President Nixon. She commented that she had always felt the Vietnamese should be left to solve their own problems, that foreign troops should be withdrawn, and that all outside interference should end. She added: "Left to themselves, the Vietnamese would not want to be under the Chinese or anyone else." She emphasized that the strongest force in Asia was nationalism. Another important part of the Prime Minister's speech was covered in a Reuters dispatch as broadcast over KPFK radio:

She said if the whole of Vietnam went Communist, it would not effect India very much. She said it was up to the Vietnamese to decide on their own government and that there were different forms of communism, some of them even liberalizing.

The *New York Times* mentioned the Prime Minister's press conference but omitted the above statements except the one about the United States moving toward India's policy in Vietnam. The *Los Angeles Times* covered the above statements but burried the coverage at the end of the report on President Nixon's trip to India.[42] *Walter Cronkite* allotted 2:48 minutes on President Nixon in New Delhi but didn't mention a thing about Mrs. Gandhi's press conference. *Huntley-Brinkley* alloted 3:40 minutes but omitted all of Mrs. Gandhi's comments except the one about the United States moving toward India's policy. Lest you think the story was knocked off the news by other pressing stories, we note that *Huntley-Brinkley* did find time the same day to allot a minute to coverage of a humorous item about a stolen car.

On July 11 and 12, 1969, President Thieu made the front page of almost every newspaper with his proposal that the National Liberation Front join in free elections to decide South Vietnam's future. The proposal was thoroughly covered by the media. Also reported were favorable responses made by several U. S. politicians, but the *New York Times,* the *Los Angeles Times,* and *Huntley-Brinkley* all omitted the controversial response of Senator George McGovern. This should have been the response most significant and newsworthy since the Senator had just spent four hours talking with National Liberation Front delegates in Paris. Senator McGovern said the NLF would not participate in any election with the Thieu-Ky government administration "holding the ballot boxes."[43] *Walter Cronkite* newscast, also ignoring McGovern's comments, found time to slip in a hidden editorial by one of its own reporters, Robert Pierpoint, who tried to persuade his 20 million listeners that, "at least a basis for political negotiations have been put on the table and if Hanoi and the NLF refuse to negotiate, they are on the defensive, in Paris and around the world."

On December 9, 1969, President Thieu, the man Richard Nixon had called one of the four or five *great* statesmen of the world, attacked three members of the lower house of the South Vietnamese legislature who had advocated neutralism. He said he might "cut off their heads" if they continued their ways.[44] But neither the *Los Angeles Times* nor *New York Times* readers will ever know about this *great* statesman's threat to cut off the heads of his political opponents because both newspapers omitted that part of President Thieu's warning.[45] The statement was made available to both newspapers in a Reuters dispatch.

The Art of Interviewing

The treatment and use of interviews is another way in which an editor can slip his bias into the news. Ben Bagdikian made an analysis of the use of interviews by *U. S. News & World Report* and discovered:

> In the first six months of 1958 . . . there were verbatim interviews with 27 representatives of large corporations. There were almost none from labor or the opposite wing of domestic economics. On auto-workers' demands there were textual reprints from heads of the car manufacturing corporations, none from the union. On prices, wages and profits there were full texts from Harlow Curtice, head of General Motors; Roger M. Blough, chairman of US Steel; and Benjamin F. Fairless, president of the American Iron and Steel Institute; but none from the opposite side.[46]

During this six months the magazine printed 12 speech texts from politicians: 11 were from conservative or moderate conservative politicians. Hubert Humphrey was the one liberal. Bagdikian noted that in addition to being out-numbered, the liberals were out-spaced. In a debate-like coverage of views of some candidates in the '58 political campaign, Republicans were given 82 percent of the total space while Democrats were given 18 percent.

Bagdikian also found that the magazine selected or excluded interviews in a manner which clearly favored the deep South's position against integration. The use of such bias led Bagdikian to conclude:

> If one characterized the treatment by *U. S. News and World Report* of integration—and of other issues with which the editor strongly disagrees—one could say that it records dutifully the official news and some of the opposition. And it pursues with enthusiasm, imagination and overwhelming space the ideas dearest to his heart.[47]

When the white press decides to interview a black man they disapprove of, the end result often comes out to the black man's disadvantage. Malcolm X was aware of the difficulty of trying to communicate through the opposition's news media:

> I don't care what points I made in interviews, it practically never got printed the way I said it. I was learning under fire how the press, when it wants to, can twist and slant. If I had said 'Mary had a little lamb,' what probably would have appeared was, 'Malcolm X lampoons Mary.' I was trying to cope with the white newspaper, radio,

and television reporters who were determined to defeat Mr. Muha-
mad's teachings. I developed a mental image of reporters as human
ferrets—steadily sniffing, darting, probing for some way to trick me,
somehow to corner me in our interview exchanges.[48]

Blacks in Africa are similarly placed at a competative disadvantage
by the white media when it comes to interviewing. *Huntley-Brinkley*
had a 3:10 minute filmed report on Rhodesia near election time in
June 1969.[49] The report was a very favorable portrayal in film of a
wealthy white businessman, his home, wife and children, and business. NBC's dialogue was also favorable, characterizing the businessman as "hard working," "fast moving," "technical," and "Western."
The NBC reporter noted that the businessman had little in common
with the "underdeveloped," "primitive," black Rhodesian. Two thirds
of the report focused exclusively on the businessman and his family
and included a 45 second interview in which the businessman and his
wife expressed their political and segregationist viewpoints from the
patio of their luxurious home. A portion of the report was devoted to
describing the situations of the businessman's black employees, but
not one of them was interviewed as to his viewpoints on politics or
the racial situation. In all, the entire report and especially the unbal-
anced interviewing would have won a stamp of approval from the
whites in Rhodesia—but not from the blacks. During the next two and
one half months during which *Huntley-Brinkley* was monitored there
were no reports to counter this bias.

In June 1969, *Walter Cronkite* news had a 4:30 minute report from
Vietnam on the U. S. pacification effort.[50] The reporter began his
report by noting that it was a "hopeful development" and then he
interviewed three persons, all of whom spoke favorably about the
program. One was the U. S. Ambassador, and the other two were
pacification project advisors. No one who was critical of the pacification program—and there are many who claimed it a futile effort—was
interviewed. The report ended with a CBS correspondent giving his
subtly editorialized evaluation: "at least solid evidence of beginning
of a change." The report certainly would have won the applause of
the Pentagon. During the next two and one half months there were no
filmed reports on pacification from Vietnam that included any interview with those who were critical of the pacification effort. A few
seconds of isolated news items covering dissident protestors in the
United States does not begin to balance the persuasive power of a
4:30 minute public relations type report from Vietnam.

When it comes to covering dissent in the United States, *Huntley-Brinkley's* selection of those to interview parallels the network's biased selection among persons in Vietnam. It seems to me there is even less excuse for their sad performance on the home front. While it may be difficult for a correspondent to find a dissenter in Vietnam willing to speak out, no such handicap exists at home. October 15, 1969, was Moratorium day. *Huntley-Brinkley* gave over 12 minutes to coverage of Moratorium activities on that evening's newscast. Most of this time was alloted to film showing dissenters marching, handing out pamphlets or singing—the spectacle type aspect of the demonstration. Only 3:20 minutes was given over the actual speeches or interviews. Four dissenters got to have their say for short periods totaling 1:37 minutes. Of these four, only Senator McGovern's 20-second segment stated a clearly understood idea expressing opposition to the war. In contrast, even though it was Moratorium day, four anti-Moratorium interviews were included. They totaled 1:43 minutes, and all four segments selected expressed very clearly their oppositon to the Moratorium. This group included two GI's and President Thieu who himself was given more interview time than any of the dissenters. In addition to the four anti-Moratorium interviews, NBC alloted over 52 seconds to Governor Lester Maddox's solo performance singing God Bless America on the steps of the Georgia State Capital building. This was also more time than that alloted to any of the dissenters interviewed. NBC then switched to Vietnam to cover a Saigon-arranged mass funeral for civilians allcdgedly murdered by the Viet Cong. Coverage such as this may explain why those opposed to the Vietnam War find it necessary to demonstrate to be heard.

Three weeks later *Huntley-Brinkley* covered the Veterans' Day demonstration backing the administration's Vietnam policy. They interviewed three persons favoring the Vietnam policy and attacking the dissenters. In contrast to the coverage of the Moratorium, not one person was interviewed who spoke for the other side.[51]

November 15, 1969 witnessed probably the largest demonstration ever seen in the nation's capital. Protesters of the war arranged to have more than twenty prominent and respected speakers in Washington, and many others in the companion protest in San Francisco. *Huntley-Brinkley* alloted a total of 7:47 minutes for coverage on their evenings news. Of this time, only 22 seconds was allotted to statements of speakers explaining their opposition to the war. New York Senator Charles Goodell was given 12 seconds and Senator McGovern was given 10 seconds. The rest of the time covered the demonstration not as an expression of dissenting ideas on a basic issue, but as a spectacle-like event similar to an athletic contest or a carnival. If the news decision makers had favored the viewpoints of the demonstrators, it can safely be assumed that the 22 seconds out of 7:47 minutes allotted for speeches would have been changed to 3 or 4 minutes to cover the highlights of many speeches.

Even when the media does interview an even number on each side of a controversial issue, the result is often biased because of the way the media sets up the format. This is especially the case when special interests are attacked. The media often presents those who are in the pay of special interest groups as if their testimony were as valid as that of a disinterested scientist who gets no profit for his research or testimony. Howard K. Smith cites CBS' documentary on smoking as an example:

> On that program there were doctors, who had every reason to be objective, who maintained that cigarettes have a causal relation to cancer. On the other side there were representatives of the tobacco industry, who have no reason to be objective, who stated persuasively the opposite.[52]

Writing in the *Montana Journalism Review,* Professor Nathan Blumberg revealed the nearly unanimous wire service and newspaper suppression of the statements made by a returning GI whose story made the front page of many newspapers.[53] P. F. C. John W. Guinn was buried in funeral rites. It was then discovered that the Army had made a mistake—Guinn was alive! On returning to the United States, he said to Ed Rabel in a CBS interview: "I ain't going to re-enlist, and I hope they bring all of the United States boys out."

RABEL: Why do you feel that way, Sir?
GUINN: Cause it's not no war over there—its just a tragedy.
RABEL: You don't think we ought to be there?
GUINN: No, Sir.

Rabel concluded by saying: "Guinn, who must serve eighteen more months in the Army before his discharge, said his opposition to the war was shared by most of the men with whom he served."

When asked by an ABC reporter how many of his fellow soldiers felt the same way as he, Guinn replied: "I guess all of them does."

From all of Guinn's statements above, the AP reported only his

"No Sir" in response to whether he wanted to return to Vietnam. The UPI ignored all of Guinn's comments.

Out of 40 newspapers checked by reporters, only one reported what Guinn had said in his interviews. The *Louisville Courier Journal* carried a twenty-paragraph article on the story but omitted any reference to Guinn's anti-war attitude. On the same day they carried on Page 2 an AP story which was headlined:

GI MORALE, VIETNAM AID IMPRESSIVE, COWGER SAYS

In December 1967, fifty-two million television viewers witnessed what appeared to be President Johnson's spontaneous responses to the questions of three network reporters, one from each network. It is true the interview was not rehearsed and there was no attempt to restrict the inquiries of the reporters. But then before the interview was broadcast, 38 minutes of the 98 minute interview was cut, much of it at the request of President Johnson and the State Department. Neither NBC or ABC bothered to inform its audience that the interview had been edited under the Administration's supervision. The Administration naturally claimed that care had to be taken lest the President accidently divulge some secret information that may aid the enemy, but the real reason for editing was probably to make the President and his foreign policy look as good as possible.[54]

Ordinary citizens don't get such special treatment when it comes to having any say on how their statements will be edited, especially if they say something the moderator or program director may not like. A young woman, a college graduate who had had syphilis, wanted to do her part in attacking Puritan attitudes that prevent many people from discussing and treating the disease like any other disease. She consented to take part in a television program on venereal disease. As reported in a Westinghouse Broadcasting Company radio documentary "Conspiracy of Silence," she wasn't too pleased with how her statements had been handled:

> The whole point of this show was to take the moralism out of the discussion of syphilis. Well, I was asked a number of questions and justice was done to my replies except for the last one which, I must say, I considered the most important. The final question had to do with my opinion as to the validity of social ostracism for people who have become infected with venereal disease. My response to that question was that venereal disease was like any other disease and the

fact that it was now easily curable would make it all the more imperative that this disease should be talked about in unemotional and unmoralistic terms. I ended my response to this question by saying:
> 'All right, so I had syphilis and many other people have had syphilis. Why talk about it as if it is a matter of sin or morals or what have you—so what.'

And in the final version of the show, I was portrayed as saying:
> 'Well, so what, if you have syphilis, if you had syphilis, why bother with any kind of precautions, who cares,'

which is not only what I did not say, but what I would not say. My comment was taken as the springboard by the moderator to go into a long peroration which put this whole discussion right back into the moralistic terms they were trying to eliminate in doing the show in the first place.[55]

When a network suppresses an interview, it has the same importance as a wire service suppression: it affects hundreds of news agencies. Top management at CBS cut out Howard K. Smith's interview of Dr. Robert Oppenheimer, renowned physicist, from the "Where We Stand" program because of their fear of being branded too liberal.[56] Fred Friendly notes that it wasn't till four or five years later, in the early Sixties, that CBS tried broadcasting a Dr. Oppenheimer interview again and this only after the "climate had changed."[57]

According to *Variety* magazine, actor Robert Vaughn and Dr. Benjamin Spock were definitely scheduled to appear on "Meet the Press" in September of 1967, but the interview was squelched by NBC's top brass.[58]

Those who control access to mass media clearly and unmistakably select, exclude, edit and distort interviews in such a way that establishment viewpoints have a decided competitive advantage over those viewpoints critical of the establishment.

Bias Through Placement

Many major news breaks are too big for editors to ignore, even if the story might reveal something they would rather keep from the public. The suppression of a big story might be discovered or repercussions felt from persons involved in the incident. The suppressing news agency would then lose its credibility and prestige. However, news editors can minimize the attention such events receive by placing the article in the back pages of newspapers or allowing only five to ten seconds in a newscast. This is another technique of implanting bias that is hard for the public to detect. The mere appearance of the item on the back page, in itself, persuades the reader that it's insignificant. Conversely, if an item appears on the front page, for this reason alone, readers assume it has significance. The continual placement of hunger, car safety, smoking and venereal disease stories on the back pages is ample example that editors use this technique successfully without the public being aware of it.

Ted Poston, reporter for the *New York Post*, revealed that the

> . . . *Birmingham News* headlined the bloody riots in Cyprus while finding only brief space at the bottom of page 4 to make mention, without details of the local rioting then going on between Birmingham's Negroes and Bull Connor, with his police dogs and fire hoses.[59]

On December 11, 1967, in a Page-One article in the *New York Times* reporting on a battle in Vietnam, one officer was quoted as saying: "there was evidence that the attacking enemy soldiers had been using heroin before the battle." An investigation later proved that the enemy soldiers were not using heroin. The white powder found on dead enemy soldiers turned out to be disinfectant, fungicide, water purifier or ordinary soap. The AP report noted: "There have been numerous reports of enemy soldiers using drugs, but, so far as could be determined, none of these reports have ever been confirmed." The *New York Times* placed this article which corrected the previous front-page error in the bottom left corner of Page 11.[60] The *Los Angeles Times* reported the original account of the battle on Page 2:". . . field doctors said the enemy troops were under the influence of heroin." This statement left no doubt that enemy troops were drugged. When the AP sent the correction out five days later, the *Los Angeles Times* suppressed it completely, leaving its million readers with just one more media-created myth about the war in Vietnam. The same day the *Los Angeles Times* did find room for a Pentagon-type public relations article headlined:

AID ADVISER HELPS PACIFY VIET VILLAGERS

During the October 1967 anti-war march on the Pentagon, soldiers used tear gas against the protestors. The Pentagon claimed that they had at no time used tear gas but, that instead, the demonstrators had. The *New York Times* placed the Pentagon's denial and counter accusations on Page One. The next day when there was news proving that the Pentagon had lied, the *New York Times* put this on Page 32: "Some newsmen said today that they observed soldiers using tear gas against the demonstrators."[61]

Bias Through "Coincidental" Placement

Another technique of implanting a hidden bias is to be seen particularly around election time. An editor chooses a headline or photograph that is favorable to one candidate and right next to it on the same or next page he places a headline or photograph unflattering to the other candidate.

Since Richard Nixon had the support of 634 daily newspapers compared to 146 backing Hubert Humphrey,[62] we would surely be wise to expect that he was given the best of this kind of treatment from the editors who used the technique. The American-owned *International Herald Tribune* cleverly placed next to each other items that coincidentally made Richard Nixon look good compared to his opponent:[63]

HUMPHREY   Rejects 'Passive Presidency'
DRAWS BOOS   NIXON PROMISES TO BUILD
IN BOSTON   BIPARTISAN ADMINISTRATION

In comparison, the news treatment of the two events by the *New York Times* was favorable to Humphrey despite the boos. They placed on Page One a favorable photograph of Senator Edward Kennedy greeting candidate Humphrey. There was no photograph of candidate Nixon on Page One. Below the photograph, the headline emphasized Kennedy's endorsement as well as the boos:[64]

KENNEDY HAILS   NIXON PROMISES
HUMPHREY: JEERS   TO HEED DISSENT
MAR RALLY IN BOSTON   IN MAKING POLICY

On another day the *International Herald Tribune* placed a large photograph of Richard Nixon with hands outstretched in the victory signal. This very favorable photograph was placed above three smaller face shots of Hubert Humphrey. The *Tribune* caption for Nixon was

"GROOVY"

It told of Nixon's acknowledging "the cheers at a packed rally." Humphrey's face shots had a caption

"TRAILING"

It noted "his desperate effort" to bring all Democrats back into the fold.[65]

Newsweek magazine used the same technique to Nixon's advantage. A very flattering photograph of Richard Nixon in his famous outstretched "V" stance riding atop a car was placed on the same page with a considerably smaller unflattering photograph of Humphrey. The caption pointed out that "While Humphrey plotted strategy with O'Brien, Nixon took Chicago by confetti-storm."[66]

A week later *Newsweek* placed two unflattering photographs of Humphrey, one with him pulling his pants up, on Page 14. On Page 15 were two very favorable photographs—one of Richard Nixon and the other of Spiro Agnew.

Bias in the Headlines

A good headline is a short poetic image that gives the reader the gist of the story along with an attitude about the event. Many readers get whatever impression they will get of what occurred just from scanning the headlines. Even the most circumspect news readers seldom have time to read every story in a newspaper. Millions of people, especially younger people who receive their news from the radio, form their views and attitudes about national and world affairs from radio headlines alone. Every person must depend on the headlines for impressions about stories that he doesn't read. The headlines establish the mood and the value system of the paper. Tests have proven that even the most educated readers can be influenced one way or the other by headlines.[67]

The wire services send only the news story; news editors make up the headlines on their own. This provides an opportunity for an editor who desires to shape public opinion to sneak in an emotional or factual bias into the story. And even if the editor is attempting to be as fair as he can, some personal bias will be implanted whether intended or not. Many stories include information that demands a subjective choice on the part of a headline maker. In 1952, the United States agreed to pay one third of France's cost to maintain its hold over the people and natural resources of Indo-China. The *New York Times* didn't interpret this as aid to help France crush the Vietnamese in their drive for independence; they interpreted it as primarily a fight against world communism. Their headline reveals this biased interpretation:

U.S. AGREES TO STEP UP AID FOR INDO-CHINA WAR ON REDS[68]

This kind of headline helped politicians like John Foster Dulles and Richard Nixon convince the American people that it was in their interest to help France wage war against the Vietnamese independence movement. A copy editor who was critical of this policy could just as easily and justifiably have used a headline such as:

U. S. BECOMES FULL-FLEDGED PARTNER IN FRANCE'S IMPERIALIST WAR

The *Los Angeles Times* gave the following headline interpretation to a story about the elections in Saigon-controlled territory:

VIETNAMESE BRAVE RED TERROR TO VOTE

The same day the *Washington Post's* headline gave the event a different emphasis:

JUNTA CRACKS DOWN ON EVE OF VIET VOTE[69]

The *New York Times* interpreted a speech by Edward Reischauer with the headline,

REISCHAUER CRITICAL OF VIET POLICY

The *Washington Post's* headline interpreted the same speech quite a bit differently:[70]

REISCHAUER BACKS U. S. VIET POLICY

In 1968 the United States Department of Agriculture made an assessment of ecological consequences of the ongoing defoliation program in Vietnam. The assessment was vague enough to leave a lot of freedom for the copy editor as is evident from the different headline interpretations:[71]

Los Angeles Times	*New York Times*
STUDY FINDS NO LASTING HARM FROM DEFOLIATION	STUDY FINDS ECOLOGY HURT

The *Los Angeles Times'* headline probably pleased executives in the U.S. pesticide industry, which makes millions by providing materials for the defoliation policy. Such headlines also helped keep the American people apathetic so that the Pentagon was able to continue the unrestricted use of the defoliants. A year later the results of more extensive studies left no freedom for headline writers to please the Pentagon. After investigating in Vietnam, biology Professor E. W. Pfeiffer reported that "the number of abnormal births is increasing so dramatically that the Saigon Health Ministry has classified the files on malformed babies as secret." He also stated that the Pentagon lied when it claimed the use of such chemicals would be limited to uninhabited areas. He viewed with his own eyes their use in densely inhabited areas.[72]

Huntley-Brinkley introduced a report on President Nixon's budget proposals for fiscal 1971 by noting that it proposed no drastic change in priorities. Brinkley demonstrated this by showing a chart which dramatically illustrated that the $73 billion proposed for defense was twenty-nine times more than the $2.5 billion budgeted for natural resources and pollution control.[73] Despite these figures, the *Los Angeles Times* seems to have been taken in by—or wanted its readers to be taken in by—the Nixon rhetoric. They headlined on the top of Page One,

NEW BUDGET: MORE
FOR LIFE THAN WAR
NIXON BEGINS REORDERING OF U.S. PRIORITIES

Many experts on the environment, such as Professor of biology Paul Ehrlich or Senator Gaylord Nelson could certainly have chosen a more fitting headline for the budget story. Ehrlich has estimated that $50 billion, and Nelson $25 billion, a year is needed just to begin to win the fight against environmental destruction, not President Nixon's proposed $2.5 billion.[74]

When stories are such that they can be honestly interpreted either way, it is difficult to determine if the editor was purposely choosing a headline according to his own bias. But there are some examples which demonstrate beyond doubt that the editor is trying to influence public opinion by his selection of a headline. When the story itself contradicts or has the opposite meaning of the headline chosen by the editor, it is evidence of a deliberate attempt to manipulate the news.

Take this case: During George Romney's campaign for the Republican candidacy, he said that the war in Vietnam would be the number one issue in the election. The CBS radio affiliate in Honolulu gave the story this lead:

> Romney is the only candidate to put the
> Negro in second place

The news item which followed didn't mention Romney's stand on the racial issue or even the word "Negro."[75]

Senator Charles Percy said he thought the poor people's Resurrection City set up in 1968 had done some good because it dramatized the problem of hunger. He said: "Perhaps this is a good thing to demonstrate nation-building has to begin right here at home." When asked whether he would have the people stay on in Resurrection City or go back home, he replied:". . . when they have made their point, when they have made the dialogue," they should leave. The *Honolulu Star-Bulletin* emphasized the one aspect of the Senator's comment that made the poor look like they had been totally rebuffed. The headline read:[76]

> GO HOME, POOR PEOPLE ADVISED

The text of a *Los Angeles Times* story evaluated the results of Resurrection City in this manner: "The government made some meaningful concessions. Undoubtedly, because of Resurrection City poverty has been brought to the American consciousness as never before."

Considering the wealthy media owner's historic neglect of poverty and contempt for the poor, this is no small accomplishment. But the *Times* headline writer saw little of value achieved by Resurrection City; he gave this story the headline:

> Buried in Mud

> FOUNDED ON HOPE
> RESURRECTION CITY
> DIES IN IGNOMINY[77]

Senator James Pearson, concerned about the increasing militarization of U.S. society, made a few comments about the military. He said: "We must have it, but we must control it. . . . We must be vigorous in our efforts to see to it that it is a servant of peace and prosperity rather than the servant of war and destruction." The *Los*

Angeles Times seemed to miss the main point of Senator Pearson's comment. Their story was headlined:

SENATOR CALLS U.S. MILITARY FACT OF LIFE[78]

The Pentagon and the arms industry certainly wouldn't find anything wrong with that headline.

In 1969, Senator George McGovern repeatedly criticized President Nixon's response to the problem of America's hungry. In a March AP dispatch the first paragraph told of McGovern's complaint "that a food program reportedly being worked out by the Nixon Administration would amount to half hearted tinkering with the needs of the poor." The *Los Angeles Times* chose to save President Nixon from a critical headline by making the poor think that something was being done. They accentuated the positive by focusing on the part of the story which told what action McGovern was taking as a result of President Nixon's inaction:

McGOVERN TO PROPOSE FREE FOOD STAMPS[79]

The following headline appeared in the *Los Angeles Times:*

ABC NEWS CALLED 'FAIR, BALANCED'[80]

The story underneath reveals that it was none other than the President of ABC News, Elmer Lower, who called the presentation of his news department fair and balanced. He said that a year-long survey proved this. Included in the article were survey results that showed the opposite. In the use of commentaries—a very powerful tool of bias in broadcasting—ABC was decidedly not fair. It had 33 minutes of commentary favorable to the administration's policy in Vietnam compared to only 14 critical of the policy. On other international news, ABC commentaries favored the Nixon Administration by an 8 to 1 ratio. The story was actually a public relations release by ABC, but the *Los Angeles Times* didn't bother to tell its readers the source of the story; that would have made the misleading headline look too much like an advertisement for ABC news.

Bias in words

Through the use of a carefully chosen word a reporter, editor or broadcaster can discredit people and organizations he dislikes, or on the other hand exalt those he wants the public to respect. Robert O'Hara describes the strategy of this technique of implanting bias in the news:

> It is the choice of just the right objective or verb to sum up a situation that evokes from the receiver the response the mass communicator feels should be adopted toward a story. . . . The word and the situation it describes become almost inseparable, so that the use of the word triggers a standardized response in the receiver. . . .
>
> They use stock words and phrases to describe the same situations, which give the news an appearance of sameness. The event being described is news, but it is described in terms applied over the years to similar events. The impression of sameness obscures understanding and limits the range of possible responses for the receiver.[81]

Fulton Lewis Jr. minced no words in describing Fidel Castro, one of his villains in 1960:

> Just a big phony punk. . . . An opportunist, a mountebank, a charlatan, and more than that a physically repulsive guy. You don't have to be mangy in order to be a hero and soap is cheap, even in Cuba.[82]

Nikita Khrushchev fared no better with Lewis when he pounded his shoe on the desk at the United Nations:

> And that's what the whole performance reminded one of really: an act of an animal, a captive monkey putting on a display of fury because he has been denied a banana. How do you deal with these people? They have no sensibilities, no inhibitions, they are not restricted by any of the rules of society or manners that control other people. They are indeed, just animals and they act that way. And we try to reason with them.[83]

Mutual's Lewis had different words for Barry Goldwater whom he described as: "a very courageous, and hard fighting statesman of the highest quality."[84]

Joe Rose, reporting an item about four U. S. soldiers being allowed to stay in Sweden, began the item with the lead: "Rats—four of them."[85]

The use of biased words is usually much more subtle, but every writer or broadcaster uses such words. When Fidel Castro was attracting more than a million people to hear his speeches in Havana's main square, the UPI said the crowds were "mustered" by Castro. Castro was reported to have made "bellowing" demands. The crowds were called "mobs."[86]

On *Walter Cronkite,* Attorney General John Mitchell was described by a CBS correspondent as "cool and urbane."[87] If liberals were selecting words for the same news item, they certainly would have chosen two different words.

Network correspondents never describe Pentagon or administration statements or news releases as "propaganda," but the word is often used to describe statements originating from unfriendly countries. Bernard Kalb of CBS reported that China: "turned its big propaganda guns on President Nixon."[88] William Cole, CBS correspondent in Moscow, described the position-statements of the Communist summit meeting as: "tired cliches of anti-Americanism."[89] They may be tired cliches, but this phrase or similar ones are never used to describe what many feel are the very, very tired cliches of President Nixon, the Pentagon and the State Department.

The University of Syracuse School of Journalism undertook the task of searching for word bias in the news coverage of the 1956 political campaigns. The survey judged that *Time's* words were 75 percent biased to favor the Republicans, *Newsweek's* 28 percent to favor the Republicans, *U.S. News and World Report's* one percent to favor the Republicans.[90]

Finding other techniques of bias equally effective and easier to hide, *Time* no longer loads its news stories with so many biased words, but it used to be the acknowledged master at using words to further its owner's political viewpoints. Looking through ten issues of *Time,* John Merrell compared the words describing President Eisenhower with those describing President Truman—all in the context of reporting the news. He found 47 negatively biased words and no positively biased words referring to Truman. In contrast there were 40 positively biased words and no negatively biased words used in covering Eisenhower stories. *Time* used these words in describing President Truman:

> said curtly—said coldly—flushed with anger—the petulant, irrascible President—publicly put his foot in his mouth—with a blunt finger he probed

For Eisenhower they used:

said with a happy grin—cautiously pointed out—said warmly—devastatingly effective—serene state of mind—frankness was the rule—brisking aside misunderstanding[91]

David Brinkley, unlike most newscasters, writes his own reports. He referred to the "shouting speeches" and "bloody tactics" of the North Vietnamese.[92] Brinkley uses no such words to describe the speeches by American spokesmen or the tactics of U. S. forces even in "free-fire" zones—areas where bombs and artillery are used on anything and anybody in the area, regardless of age or sex.

Newsweek referred to "Hanoi's duplicity in skillfully launching another phony peace offensive."[93] None of the obviously superficial peace gestures by the Johnson or Nixon administration are ever described in *Newsweek* as "phony".

All news agencies frequently refer to Viet Cong activities as "terrorist". American military activity, even the slaughter at Songmy, is never termed "terrorist".

The Pentagon is well aware of the power of words to affect the public's response to news stories. Most of the Pentagon's terminology is accepted willingly by the news agents even though they cannot be forced by the Pentagon to avoid the use of words which really describe what's going on in Vietnam. The Pentagon can and does, however, force Army publications to avoid using certain words. Instead of "ambush," "engagement" is used. Vietnamese family "huts" are "V. C. structures," and "sampans" are "waterborne logistic craft."[94] The Army has sniper schools in Vietnam, but as one army journalist admitted:

> I'm not allowed to talk about snipers. The Army tells me we don't have any flame tracks, which is very interesting. I was out yesterday burning what used to be a rubber plantation with four flame tracks.[95]

According to Robert Lifton, Professor of Psychiatry at Yale, the use of these and similar words by mass media and the Pentagon to cover up the brutality of defoliation, napalm bombings and other tactics "helps psychically numb people to what's happening on the other side of the weapon."[96]

Subjected to thousands of words of news each day, the American citizen can hardly be expected to stop and analyze the hundreds of subtly chosen words that are designed to persuade him to think and feel the way media owners and the military-industrial complex want him to.

Bias in News Images

Images created through the use of words can be used to persuade readers or listeners to hate, condemn, disapprove or laugh at persons representing a position contrary to the favored policies and special interests of the communicator. Conversely, word images can evoke in the reader an attitude of respect and approval toward those who represent a position favored by the establishment. Chet Huntley *objectively* reported an airport departure of a head of state in 1960: "Fidel Castro boarded his Soviet hand-me-down airliner followed by his bearded entourage—his admirers, their cardboard boxes, and their teddy bears."[97]

David Brinkley *objectively* reported the Russian leaders response to President Nixon's big reception in Romania: "The Russian leaders don't like this much, but they keep their mouths shut."[98] Governor Rockefeller's hostile receptions in Latin America and the massive Okinawan demonstrations against the presence of B52 bombers in Okinawa caused very little comment by President Nixon, but Brinkley didn't bother to observe that the President had kept his "mouth shut."

Two black athletes, Tommie Smith and John Carlos, bowed their heads and raised their clinched fist in gestures of black power defiance of the establishment during the 1968 Olympics. *Time* magazine showed its disapproval through biased images. In reporting news of the event, *Time* described the scene as "angrier, nastier, uglier." and noted:

> Two dissaffected black athletes . . . put on a public display of petulance that . . . turned the high drama of the games into theater of the absurd. . . .
> A wave of boos rippled through the spectators as the pair left the field. Smith and Carlos responded by making interesting gestures at the stands.

Time obviously approved the behavior of another black athlete, one who didn't embarrass the establishment. As *Time* saw it, he "stood straight and tall and proud on the Olympic pedestal."[99] In contrast, the *London Observer* applauded the black athletes for their dignity, and *Ramparts* noted that many of the Third World athletes applauded the two black athletes. But since *Time* reporters were probably in the middle of the mostly white audience from the United States who had the money to go to the Olympics, they may not have heard how the rest of the world responded.

Time could win any propaganda contest for the favorable images it has created for politicians that serve its special interest. Despite Richard Nixon's claims of bad treatment by the press, the media have always given especially fine treatment to the hometown boy from Whittier. Ben Bagdikian, surveying the biased images in *Times* "news" reports, discovered this poetic profile of Richard Milhous Nixon in 1952:

> . . . the most up-to-date attraction at the Illinois State Fair last week was a goodlooking, dark-haired young man with a manner both aggressive and modest, and a personality to delight any political barker. He seemed to have everything—a fine TV manner, an attractive family, a good war record, deep sincerity and religious faith. . . . He was Richard Milhous (pronounced mill house) Nixon, Republican nominee for Vice President. . . .

The Democratic nominee for Vice President the same year didn't fare so well in *Time:*

> John Jackson Sparkman . . . stopped grinning, fished a cough drop out of his mouth and slipped it through a crack in the platform floor. . . . Sparkman in fact, is so resolute a compromiser that it takes a political micrometer to tell just where he stands. . . .

During the 1956 campaign, Democratic Vice Presidential candidate Kefauver was featured in a cover story that "started with a reference to Kefauver pitching manure and thereafter put the words 'shovel' and 'pitch' in the text of his speeches." In contrast, Bagdikian notes a 1956 news report of the Republican Vice Presidential candidate:

> . . . while he is a politician to his fingertips, Nixon is a man of consistent principle, whose values are as sound and fundamental as any in U. S. politics today. . . . Had Nixon been the weak, unprincipled character that his more choleric enemies make him out to be, he might well have given up. . . . [100]

With this type of media treatment no one need ever give up.

The March on the Pentagon, like every other demonstration by anti-establishment groups, inspired the mass media to tap its best artistic talent to produce news images to discredit the demonstrators and their cause. Nathan Blumberg in his article "A Study of the 'Orthodox' Press: the Reporting of Dissent," revealed many examples from coverage of the March. The *Los Angeles Times,* setting up its society page standards on the news page, reported that only one-third of the crowd had a respectable appearance:

> The balance of the crowd was composed of the wildest mixed bag imaginable; communists, hippies and flower-power advocates, unkempt, scraggly youths and girls. . . . Some seemed to view the demonstration as anything from a lark to an opportunity for romance or an occasion for flaunting an obscene poster.

The *Washington Post* referred to the "shaggy doves and the sweet smell of pot."

Newsweek, the magazine that claims to separate fact from opinion, referred to the "artists freak out" and a "gaggle of hippies."

Time found a newsworthy gardener to quote in their report: " 'You should see what we found out there' said one worker. 'Nothing but bras and panties. You never saw so many." "[101] *Time* didn't bother to comment that the bras must have come from CIA infiltrators who became quick converts to the anti-war, pro-life cause, because women in the radical movements seldom bother with such bourgeois apparel.

The 1969 Veterans Day demonstration supporting President Nixon's Vietnam policy inspired the establishment to produce different news images. Typical was correspondent Keith Brinkley's description of the crowd at the Washington Monument rally, as heard one evening by ABC *Evening News'* audience:

> Effete—it certainly was not. The crowd was orderly, well scrubbed, liked the sometimes funny speeches, and very sincere.[102]

The activities of dissenting generals such as Lt. General James Gavin, Brigadier General Hugh Hester, General David Shoup, Rear Admiral Arnold True and others who oppose using the Armed Forces for what they view as unjust and senseless wars don't evoke mass media's finest efforts at favorable image making. In sharp contrast, generals who support the establishments foreign policy and conservative viewpoints inspire the media to produce its most inspired poetry. In their book *Television and Politics,* Kurt and Gladys Lang made a survey of the television coverage of General MacArthur's return to the United States after President Truman had found it necessary to relieve him of his command in Korea. With the use of thirty-one on-the-spot observers, the authors established as best they could the different reasons why people came to MacArthur's welcoming-home parade in Chicago. They found that 48 percent came primarily to get a look at the general, 42 percent had only passive interest in the spectacle, and only 9 percent came to express hero worship of the general. However, in the television view of the crowd as portrayed in its photographic and verbal images, hero worship and tension were the dominant moods of the crowd. One announcer reported:

> You can feel the tenseness in the air . . . you can hear that crowd roar. . . .
> The whole city appears to be marching down State Street behind General MacArthur.

Another broadcaster reported:

> The air is electric . . .
> There is the feeling you just can't wait.
> Never such a thrill . . .
> Look at that chin! Look at those eyes!

After their thorough study of parade coverage, the two authors concluded that television

> interpreted the crowd's motivations in accordance with their own preconceptions. Later they seized on anything that could be interpreted as enthusiasm. . . .
> Television disseminated an image of public sentiment that was overwhelmingly in favor of the general and, by implication his politics.[103]

Bias in Photograph Selection

Mark Davidson, producer of television documentaries and news programs for twelve years, in an article titled "One Picture is Worth a Thousand biases" states: "Pictures always have exercised power that is unique:power to influence illiterates, seduce sophisticates, and manipulate the minds of everyone in between."[104] More people look at photographs than at anything else in newspapers and magazines.[105] The editors of all news agencies are well aware of the powerful bias that can secretly be implanted by careful selection of television footage or photographs.

Time magazine selected 21 photographs of Dwight D. Eisenhower during 13 weeks of the 1952 campaign: all showed the candidate in a favorable light. During the same period 13 photographs of Adlai Stevenson were selected for publication: about half of these showed him in an unfavorable manner—eating, drinking or grimacing.[106]

Arthur Rowse compared the front-page photographic treatment that 36 newspapers gave candidates in the 1952 election. He found that

> nearly every paper studied gave more space to candidates it supported on the editorial page. Some froze out the opposition completely from page 1. Photograph partisanship was most evident in selection and display of candidate pictures.[107]

While newspapers often feature photographs of civilians killed or injured by Viet Cong artillery or terrorist activity, photographs of civilian casualties resulting from U.S. bombings, artillery or terrorist activity seldom made their way into print until news of the Songmy massacre was published. From the numbers of civilian casualties depicted in newspapers' photographs, a citizen would assume that at least 90 percent of such casualties resulted from activity of the North Vietnamese and Viet Cong. This is a gross misrepresentation of the facts as disclosed by even the most avid supporter of the U.S. policy in Vietnam.

Time magazine had a five-page story on the South Vietnamese election of 1967. It selected 3 very favorable family photographs of President Thieu and Vice President Ky plus 2 more favorable photographs depicting the election process. There were 2 neutral photographs. *Time* selected none that might displease President Thieu or the Pentagon.[108]

The *New York Times* suppressed the first photograph of a Buddhist Monk immolating himself as a protest against the Saigon regime. Later, when the *Times* was not such an avid supporter of the war, they printed another photograph of a similar suicide protest.[109]

Robert MacNeil revealed that the network television newscasts have refused to show the vast majority of real brutalities of the Vietnam war even though the news decision makers do see such footage: "The grisly truth has been shown in the screening rooms of the network news departments." [110]

The photographs in *Life* magazine's May 27, 1966 article on white-ruled Rhodesia add up to a colorful ten-page photographic advertisement for Prime Minister Ian Smith and his policies based on white racism. Out of a total of 18 photographs, 7 depicted the Prime Minister in a very favorable light—at social functions, walking his pet dogs, having coffee with his wife, talking with blacks. There were no unfavorable photographs of Smith. There were 7 additional photographs depicting Rhodesia in a way that would please the Smith regime. The remaining 4 photographs depicted blacks—having a white nurse give them a hygiene lesson, working, relaxing at a concert in the public park, strolling beneath modern government-built housing for blacks. Out of the entire 18 photographs, there wasn't one which was unfavorable to the Smith regime and what it represents in Africa.

The most important, noteworthy and widely seen news photographs published each week in America are those appearing on the front cover of *Time, Newsweek* and *Life* magazines. There are few Americans who are not exposed to these photographs. A study of the photographs and paintings selected by these magazines shows that a very distorted selection process determines what issues deserve a front cover photograph. Table XI shows the number of times that certain topics were featured with a photograph or painting on the cover of the respective magazines during a seven and one half year period.

The selection of cover subjects shows that news decision makers seldom if ever bothered to use cover photographs to focus the public's attention on vital issues which Americans should have been dealing with.

On controversial subjects such as Vietnam the selection was very biased. *Newsweek, Time* and *Life* all selected many more pictures that were favorable to the U.S. Vietnam policy than those that depicted the policy in an unfavorable manner.

The selection also indicates, beyond any question, that those in position to select cover topics have similar viewpoints regarding which issues to ignore. Whether their motivations are economic or political makes little difference: Americans still receive a distorted picture of what is important. There clearly is no competition in ideas in deciding what topic will deserve front-cover photographic attention.

Bias in Captions

Every news photograph has a caption; every segment of T.V. news film has an accompanying dialogue. People want to know who is in the picture, what they represent, what they are doing, and when and where the event took place. Also, everyone needs some assistance in

TABLE XI
COVER PHOTOGRAPHS, 1962 THROUGH JULY 1969

SELECTED TOPICS	*Time* Total Covers 390	*Newsweek* Total Covers 390	*Life* Total Covers 390	*Look* Total Covers 198	TOTAL
POLLUTION	2	1	0	0	3
POPULATION & BIRTH CONTROL	1	2	0	0	3
WORLD HUNGER (excluding Biafra)	0	1	0	0	1
HUNGER IN UNITED STATES	0	0	0	0	0
ILLITERACY	0	0	0	0	0
BRAIN DRAIN	0	0	0	0	0
PRISON BRUTALITY	0	0	0	0	0
VENEREAL DISEASE	0	0	0	0	0
CHEMICAL-BIOLOGICAL WARFARE	0	0	0	0	0
MILITARY-INDUSTRIAL COMPLEX	1	1	0	0	2
ABORTION	0	0	0	0	0
ATHLETICS	13	9	13	0	35
ENTERTAINERS	20	20	73	69	182
SPACE	15	20	28	1	64
RELIGION	15	9	10	6	40
VIETNAM	30	27	31	3	91
BUSINESS CORPORATIONS	30	25	1	0	56

placing what they are seeing in a larger context. But, along with getting the necessary explanations, the public unknowingly absorbs hidden bias contained in captions or dialogues. Different researches done among groups of college students prove that different captions under the same photograph can significantly affect a person's attitude toward the subject of the photograph.[111] William L. Lederer, in his book *A Nation of Sheep*, points to a misleading caption sent out by the UPI in March 1960:

> TAIPEI-PRESIDENT CHIANG KAI-CHEK WON AN
> EXPECTED LANDSLIDE VICTORY FOR
> RE-ELECTION IN THE NATIONAL
> ASSEMBLY LAST WEEK. . . .

As Lederer notes:

> . . . the average reader inferred that Chiang had been brought back to office by a popular clamour. In the first place, the reader was not told that it was contrary to the Nationalist constitution for the Generalisimo to serve as Chief of State again. Nor did the reader realize that members of the National Assembly who elected Chiang were his own appointees.[112]

Newsweek magazine had two photographs of Harold Stassen—one of him bald and one with a wig. The caption wasn't one that imparted any dignity to Stassen:

> NOW AND THEN; CAN A FORMER BOY WONDER
> FIND
> POLITICAL HAPPINESS IN A TOUPEE?[113]

Time magazine dislikes black militants even more than the black athletes who made black power gestures at the Olympics. The caption under a picture of best-selling author Eldridge Cleaver read:

> AS QUALIFIED AS ATTILA

Time, in this case, derived the caption from a statement made by Max Rafferty who commented: "Cleaver is certainly as well qualified to lecture on urban unrest as Attila the Hun would be qualified to lecture on international mass murder."[114] It is certain that if any black person was selecting the caption he wouldn't look to someone like Max Rafferty. But blacks have little or no power to choose headlines for any photographs in the mass media.

A *Newsweek* cover had the caption headline:

"IS DR. SPOCK TO BLAME?"[115]

The photograph cleverly associated Dr. Benjamin Spock with the buttons that were pinned on the baby featured on the cover. The buttons read:

"DON'T TRUST ANYONE OVER 7"
"ANYTHING GOES"
"KINDERGARTEN POWER"
"DOWN WITH MOM"
"THE PERMISSIVE SOCIETY"

These are not quite the principles Dr. Spock has dedicated his life to, but *Newsweek* seldom depicts in a favorable way those who fight the establishment.

In early 1970, CBS morning and evening newscasts showed a film portrait of North Korea taken by Wilfred Burchett, communist journalist from Australia.[116] Instead of having Burchett—who was on the scene in North Vietnam describe his own film, CBS had one of its own reporters, who had not been there, supply the dialogue. He did an acceptable CBS job by emphasizing in almost every sentence how the North Koreans used propaganda. The film depicted many other interesting facets of life in North Korea, but the dialogue was so concerned with pointing out communist propaganda that other aspects were ignored. And of course no one except CBS could know how much of Burchett's film was shown and how much was not shown.

Time magazine never has liked unions or the idea of union teachers going on strike. They expressed their feelings with a caption under a photograph of teachers voting to strike:[117]

THREE STRIKES AND THE CHILDREN ARE OUT

Under a photograph of Diamond Head monument in Hawaii a *Time* caption read:[118]

EVERYBODY'S CRAZY ABOUT SAVING SOMETHING

This was obviously an attempt to cast doubt on the seriousness of those trying to save Diamond Head from real estate interests who wanted to put high rise buildings on the slopes of the majestic landmark.

Time interpreted a photograph of President Johnson sending off airborne troops to Vietnam as:[119]

DIFFICULT PREMIUMS FOR THE NECESSARY INSURANCE

An editor against the U.S. policy in Vietnam would probably have chosen a caption such as:

INVESTING AMERICAN LIVES IN AN UNJUST WAR

The Use of Editorials to Distort Facts

Editorials by radio and television broadcasters are a world apart from the seldom read editorials in magazines and newspapers. Broadcast editorials reach 100 percent of the radio or T.V. audience who are tuned in. And when editorials are delivered by highly respected authorative newscasters like Chet Huntley, David Brinkley, Walter Cronkite or Eric Sevareid, they become powerful tools of persuasion. Such editorials often include references to actual factual situations. These broadcasters are respected for their alleged objectivity in presenting the news; they are seldom suspected of misrepresenting facts in an editorial. Editorials can thus serve as an ideal cover for distorting facts in order to persuade the listeners to think and feel as the broadcaster wants them to.

Chet Huntley used this technique of bias in trying to convince his listeners that the Wholesome Meat Act inspection program "is a farce." Irwin Knoll points out in the *Progressive* magazine that on May 27, 1968, in his radio editorial Huntley claimed: "The public has been sold the false notion that 'U.S. Inspected' is a guarantee of cleanliness."[120] In other allusions to factual situations he announced:

> In New York, this reporter knows, truck drivers and other employees of the wholesale district are now quitting their jobs to become Federal Inspectors, and they talk openly of the 'fringe benefits.' The fringe benefits are monies under the table in return for that misleading inspection stamp.

On June 10, 1968, in another radio editorial, Huntley told his listeners:

> Sure, let's face it, there is such a thing as dirty meat, but any city

or any community, or any state with any kind of sanitation, could have eliminated the real culprit in the dirty meat business and without putting another cost factor on the product

The fact is that 99.9 percent of all meat has always been clean, . . .

Huntley then must have felt it was his duty to warn the nations' housewives: "Mrs. Consumer, your meat is now so clean you may choke on it." The housewives probably will not choke on Federally inspected meat, but they may gag a bit when they chew uninspected— and inspected— luncheon meats, hot dogs and sausage from the meat of dead, dying, disabled or diseased animals. After spending fourteen months investigating packing houses, Neil Peck, Assistant U.S. Attorney, revealed the wretched state of some meat:

> On *many* occasions the 50-pound blocks of meat contained hide, teeth, pieces of hooves, whiskers, and other indigestible parts of the animal. A number of times there was excrement in the package. In one instance we found that *every single block of meat in an entire truckload* was contaminated with one or more of these filthy or inedible materials.[121]

Neil Peck was not arguing for passage of the new meat inspection bill; he was arguing that the new bill still doesn't protect the public.

How do the other factual statements made by Huntley in these editorials hold up? Knoll points out that Huntley has so far not documented even one case of New York meat inspectors taking bribes—as he claimed— and his statement that truck drivers were being hired as meat inspectors is false. Of the twenty-one meat inspectors hired in the New York area, none of them were truck drivers.

Can the states clean up their own packing houses as Huntley claims? In January 1970, almost two years after Huntley's claim, the Federal government revealed that only three states had so far met "clean meat" standards.[122] It could just be possible that Chet Huntley's editorial performance was influenced by his own $35,000 financial interest in the livestock industry. This is only two percent of Huntley's claimed net worth. If only a two percent interest could produce this sort of self-blinding bias, one can only guess at how other facts may have been bent to accommodate the remaining ninety-eight percent of Chester Robert Huntley's special financial interests.

Chet Huntley was one of the more responsible newscaster editorialists. Most handle the facts much worse. The *New York Times* also slips in false facts through the cover of an editorial. In supporting the establishment's policy south of the border, one of their editorials concluded:

> What is wrong with the Alliance for Progress is not the concept, and certainly not the goals. On the contrary, the best minds and most experienced statesmen and economists in the hemisphere cannot come up with anything better or anything very different.

John Gerassi, Latin American expert, explains why the *Times* is factually wrong:

> There are literally hundreds of other suggestions available expounded by literally thousands of 'minds' both here and in Latin America. Indeed, no respected Latin American academician considers the Alliance anything else but a fancy, propaganda-packed plan for keeping the old structure intact in Latin America.[123]

The Hidden Editorial

Advertisements more and more are coming to look just like news items. Madison Avenue has realized that an advertisement accepted by the public as news has more power to persuade than an easily recognized advertisement. People are suspicious of ads but not of the news. Owners and editors are advertisers too—advertisers for establishment policies and wars. They are aware that an editorial disguised as news is much more effective in maintaining or changing attitudes than a genuine editorial. In addition there are other advantages. Disguised as news, the editorial doesn't have to be restricted to the seldom read and suspect editorial page, and broadcasters can avoid the necessity of giving equal time to opposing viewpoints.

Newsmen vary in their technique of hiding their editorial opinions. Joe Rose, newscaster at NBC's affiliate station in Honolulu, KGU, doesn't feel the necessity of hiding his opinions. It is impossible to separate them from the news he reports. The following are comments that were interjected by Rose during his 6:00 p.m. news report.

Reporting on the poor peoples' Resurrection City in Washington D.C., he interjected, "The temporary forces of chaos wallow in the mud . . . thiefs . . . that miserable enclave. . . . "[124]

Reporting on Attorney General Ramsey Clark's use of computers in analyzing civil unrest, Rose added, "You know what they call this guy in Washington?—the cream puff."[125]

After he announced that four Russian writers had been convicted by a Russian court he said, "In Russia they put 'em in jail; we send them to Sweden."[126]

Reporting an Air Force officer's court-martial for refusing an order to go to Vietnam, he interjected, "You know what's wrong with this cat? He's afraid to get shot."[127]

Announcing that three U.S. Army soldiers had asked for political asylum in Sweden, Rose interjected, "Red rats. . . . Russia sends deserters to jail; we send them to Sweden.[128]

After reporting that five retired generals had urged a bombing halt, Rose asked his listeners: "Isn't this surrender? What else would you call it?[129]

Most broadcasters in larger metropolitan centers couldn't dream of getting away with such blatant editorializing while reporting the news; they would receive challenges from various groups demanding equal time. They would also lose their prestige and reputation—precious assets which rest on at least a façade of objectivity and fairness. To maintain this façade, and sidestep requirements of the FCC's Fairness Doctrine, many of the highest paid newscasters have resorted to the use of innuendo and nuance, such as a sarcastic tone of voice, a derisive smile or a smirk, at points where these may convey respect or condemnation of some person or viewpoint. Professor Robert O'Hara takes note of some newscasters' techniques in an epitome:

> His reporting may be 'straight' in that it contains no overt expressions of approval or disapproval, but his vocal inflections, intonation, and significant pauses, as well as his facial expressions, can frequently have the same effect as an editorial comment.[130]

Such expressions are not verbal, so they cannot be analyzed or recorded in a book, but other subtle techniques of giving concealed editorial opinion can be detected.

In trying to discredit Fidel Castro's claims that the United States was planning an invasion of Cuba—claims that were subsequently confirmed as valid a few months later by the invasion itself—Peter Hackes on NBC radio news subtly cast doubt on the claims: "With Castro's invasion propaganda continuing to pour forth from Havana, invasion rumors—quite naturally— are on the increase."[131]

John Daly on ABC television news used the same technique to discredit the claims: "Some observers believe the phony invasion reports were started by the Cuban Government. . . . "[132] It was this type of biased news which helped the establishment, through the CIA, plan and launch, in secret, the disastrous invasion of Cuba.

In October 1960, an official United States Information Agency report detailed a decline of United States prestige abroad. The report showed that 51 percent of the British and 39 percent of the French had "not very much or very little confidence in American capacity for leadership in dealing with present world problems." The Eisenhower Administration classified the report as secret. Others were clamoring for release of the report, claiming that there was no justifiable reason for classifying it as secret. At this point David Brinkley cleverly expressed his opinion supporting the right of the government to arbitrarily classify documents as secret:

> Several members and committees in Congress have for some time been trying to get the paper out. But under the Constitution, the President and the entire executive branch have the absolute privilege of keeping from Congress, the public, or anyone anything they feel should not, in the national interest, be made public.
>
> That privilege is being exercised in this case and there is absolutely nothing Kennedy, Fulbright, or anyone else can do about it.[133]

They did do something about it. Public pressure caused administration officials to make it public.

NBC correspondent Ron Nessen wrapped up a report detailing how bad medicine for minority groups was by saying: "The problem of bad and expensive medical care cannot be cured quickly by some big new government program."[134] Many white and black doctors and poor people think that a big government medical program is exactly what is needed to improve medical care for the poor; they would certainly consider Nessen's comment an editorial.

Dr. John Knowles was too liberal for the medical establishment. After President Nixon advised him he would be appointed to a high post in the Department of Health, Education, and Welfare, the AMA and corporate interests put the pressure on. Subsequently President Richard Nixon decided not to appoint Knowles. A correspondent on *Huntley-Brinkley* concluded his report of the affair by saying: "Everyone is anxious that it should be forgotten."[135] That is obviously the reporter's opinion or desire; there are many others who think the public should keep the affair in their mind constantly to remind them of where political power really rests.

CBS correspondent Richard Threlkeld interjected this phrase in his report from Vietnam: "even though Ho is the man responsible for fifteen years of war here."[136] To claim that Ho Chi Minh is the person responsible for the war is opinion, not fact: there are many responsible politicians and historians who lay the blame for this war on the foreign policy of the American military-industrial-media complex.

A "Group W" correspondent reported that the North Vietnamese exploded a bomb in a South Vietnamese post office "like only they can."[137] Far from factual reporting, this is the reporter's opinion. B52 bombings, defoliation, the Songmy massacre, and South Korean atrocities in Vietnam demonstrate that it is not "only" the other side that can do such things.

Many critics of the Vietnam war, including senators and congressmen, claim the United States through its unwillingness to consider a coalition government in place of the dictatorial Thieu-Key regime has adopted a negotiating position that precludes any real progress at the Paris Peace Talks. This is an opinion—but it is never cleverly inserted in news reports as are the opinions of mass media owners, who by and large support the basic United States policy. NBC's Paris correspondent Garrick Utley, in presenting news of the Paris Peace Talks, inserted his opinions backing the administration's viewpoint that it's the other side that refuses to make meaningful concessions:

> For a year and a half they have refused to compromise on anything, and its worked. . . . For the Communist, there has been a great deal of progress here at the peace talks, not by bargaining or by making concessions, but by being intransigent. . . . [138]

Even more than newscasts, newspapers daily print as news the opinions of those whose viewpoints they agree with, while restricting opposing viewpoints to the editorial page. On April 7, 1969, Page One of the *Los Angeles Times* looked like the editorial page of an Army newspaper. At the top of the page was the headline:

WAR CURBS CITED BY WESTMORELAND: SAYS WHITE HOUSE LIMITATION BLAMED FOR LACK OF CLASSIC VIET VICTORY

In the middle of the page in large letters was the headline:

THIEU OFFERS 6-POINT PEACE PLAN, HINTS AT UNDER COVER TALKS

At the bottom right of the page was the headline:

U.S. BOMBING OF NORTH VIETNAM SUCCESSFUL, ADMIRAL SHARP SAYS

Often when a distinguished scientist writes an article in a respected journal on a topic relating to a controversial issue, it is considered newsworthy; a summary of the article appears as a news item. This is accepted journalistic practice even though the article may include the scientist's opinion. But when the wife of an administration official writes an article on a complex topic it belongs on the editorial page or in the letter to the editor column. However, the *Honolulu Star-Bulletin*, in its enthusiasm to sell the United States Vietnam policy, put this headline across the entire top of a news page:

VIET CROPS SAVED IN DEFOLIATION PROGRAM[139]

Underneath, taking up a third of the entire page, was an article written by the wife of an agricultural specialist working for the United States Agency for International Development in Vietnam. To help disguise it as genuine news, a photograph of planes spreading defoliants was included near the top of the page. No source for the photograph is listed (indicating it is probably a Pentagon handout). The main point of the defoliation article was expressed in a quote of her husband stating that the defoliants used were harmless to animals, humans and crops. That this was mere unscientific opinion has been proven by the scientific reports in 1969 tracing numerous deformed Vietnamese babies to the use of these pesticides—some so seriously deformed that many Vietnamese have termed them "monsters."[140]

Conclusion

The great volume of news, the way it must be processed and the public's need to make some kind of order out of the chaos of news events, make bias inevitable. Objectivity and fairness are impossible. Declarations of objectivity and fairness serve only as public relations devices intended to hide from Americans the great advantage of controlling the decisions and tools which create bias. To expose the techniques by which editors and broadcasters intentionally implant their bias in the news is not to condemn either the techniques or the persons or agencies using them. No human being would refrain from using the communication resources available to them to persuade others to their points of view.

Those who use the techniques of implanting bias in the news cannot be condemned. Rather, it is the communication system that is at fault, allowing the power to create biased news to be monopolized by those who advocate similar viewpoints and priorities. This places the overall bias decidedly to the right on the political spectrum. So those excluded—individuals of solid liberal and radical left viewpoints—are prevented from participating on an equal basis in a competition among ideas.

14　The Importance of Propaganda

American society is perhaps the best example of a social order in which direct coercion is at a minimum. Here those who wish to control opinions and beliefs turn less to physical force than to mass persuasion in the form of news and views and entertainment. They use the advertising campaign and the public-relations program instead of the threat of firing squad or concentration camp.

But even if modern democracies use psychological manipulation instead of totalitarianism's direct and violent forms of social control, the results are not necessarily less effective. Never before have such pervasive and ubiquitous means of communication existed; never before has public opinion been so completely at the mercy of whoever may control the instrument.

Theodore B. Peterson
The Mass Media and Modern Society

We might be the first people to go fascist by the democratic vote, and that would be something not even the Germans or Italians did.

William L. Shirer

Any attempt to influence public opinion can be considered propaganda of one sort or another. Some propagandists employ facts and history responsibly; others falsify or ignore facts and distort history. Some propagandists allow for at least the possibility of real choice and participation in opinion-making on the part of their audience; others try their best to keep people from thinking on their own. Propaganda is used to further good causes as well as bad causes, peace as well as war, brotherhood as well as hate. The use of hidden techniques of implanting bias by those who control mass media in the United

States is a form of propaganda. That it is used to further establishment policies and priorities can be seen readily. The question we take up here is this: How important is propaganda in shaping American politics and society?

First, let us examine the matter of editorial support of presidential candidates. In twenty out of forty-two presidential elections the candidate supported by the press has lost the election.[1] Those who control access to media often claim that this is proof that there is little advantage in controlling the means of producing bias. If this control was a significant advantage, claim the owners, candidates supported by the owners would always win elections. This shaky reasoning ignores three very important factors that must be considered when trying to determine the effects of attempts to influence public opinion. First, it fails to take into consideration how an election would have turned out had press support been the opposite of what it was. President Harry Truman had the support of only 10 percent of newspaper circulation compared to Thomas E. Dewey's 78 percent. Truman won by a relatively small margin. Would he still have won by only a small margin if he had had 78 percent support and Dewey 10 percent? What is remarkable in this election is not that Truman won without press support, but that a candidate such as Dewey was able to get close to forty percent of the vote. Through its use of propaganda, the press was able to convince millions of poor and middle-class people that their interests were the same as the very wealthy whom Dewey represented. One factor that helped Truman win despite news media's massive editorial opposition and pro-Dewey bias was the Democratic advantage over the radio; confident of victory, the Republicans allowed the Democrats to outspend them in purchasing radio time.

John Kennedy won in 1960 by a very small margin and he also had little press support—only 16 percent of newspaper circulation compared to 71 percent for Richard Nixon. The question is by how much more might John Kennedy have won had he been backed by 71 percent of the press instead of 16 percent? The 1964 election may suggest some answers. In this unusual election the more conservative candidate, Barry Goldwater, was deserted by the traditionally Republican press. For the first time the more liberal candidate was favored by the press. The election resulted in the most lopsided victory ever recorded in a presidential election in modern times. The next largest margins of victory ever achieved at the polls occurred during the depression years of 1932 and 1936 when enough of the conservative press supported the more liberal Franklin D. Roosevelt to give him 40 and 36 percent press support instead of the usual 10 to 15 percent received by the Democrats.[2]

Second, in addition to having newspaper support, the more conservative candidate has usually had considerably more money to spend for political advertisements in newspapers and over radio and television. If this propaganda advantage had been reversed, giving the more liberal candidate like Hubert Humphrey more money for propaganda, it too, may have significantly affected the margin of victory or defeat. Candidate Humphrey was sure that his financial handicap influenced the outcome of the 1968 election:

> Equal time access to television is an empty concept if the time must be bought. And without question there must be a better way, a better system, to guarantee equal access of candidates and parties to the television viewers of America.
>
> . . . Elections ought not to be decided on the basis of who has the most money.
>
> There is no surer way to corrupt American life and American politics than to have the great decision of this nation as to who will be its leader and its sense of direction determined by the size of a checkbook or a bank account.
>
> It's wrong; it is wrong, wrong, wrong to have to go around seeking large contributions from the few rich in order to conduct a campaign which you say is for the many. Can't do it. It's wrong.[3]

Humphrey did all this complaining because Richard Nixon received three times as much money as he did and outspent him $12.6 million to $7.1 million on broadcasting alone. For the 1970 elections Democratic candidates were even at more of a financial disadvantage: figures released in October 1970 showed that the Republicans received $18.3 million in contributions compared to the Democrats $3.5 million.[4]

The third factor ignored by owner interpretation of election results is much more significant than the first two. This is the effect of consistent and long term use of propaganda to create views of the world and attitudes which favor conservative priorities and politicians. Constant and subtle use of bias over hundreds of years has created racism, chauvinism, respect for the rich, contempt for the common laborer and the poor, and respect for religious leaders no matter how shortsighted or inhumane their use of political power is. At election time these basic attitudes are more important than political advertisements or the momentary endorsement of the press. If overnight all the mass media agents in the South supported politicians running on platforms of complete racial equality, they could still not prevent segregationists from winning the elections.

This long term bias on the part of news agencies might in some cases explain seemingly paradoxical political events. For example, until very recently the *Los Angeles Times,* through the use of blatant bias, had helped create racist and reactionary attitudes toward labor and the black man. When in 1968 the *Times* took the bold step of endorsing for mayor a black man, Tom Bradley, against Sam Yorty, a man who seemed to appeal to white racists, its position was rejected by the majority of voters. The *Times* long-term ultra-conservative propaganda had been too successful even for a *Los Angeles Times* that had become less conservative.

In recent times the *New York Times* has been a strong advocate of abortion reform for the state of New York, but the voters continued to elect politicians who defeated abortion reform year after year until 1970. The *New York Times* can take most of the blame for the previous defeats of abortion reform legislation. Their long term propaganda glorifying church leaders and doctrines has helped create in the public mind a respect for dogmatic church leaders and politicians—the very ones who have turned archaic and inhumane church dogma into laws which demand obedience from all citizens no matter what their religious beliefs. A newspaper can reverse political direction in midstream, but a human being doesn't so easily change his basic attitudes.

If, as some owners claim, control of the means of creating propaganda is no great advantage, why are dictators, politicians and advertisers so concerned with who gets access to mass media? Would advertisers spend up to $70,000 for one minute of access to television if it had only little power to affect attitudes and behavior? Would Spiro Agnew make such a fuss just because of a few mildly critical comments about President Nixon's half hour political speech? Would President Nixon's media advisors have gone to all the fuss that Joe McGinnis details in his book *The Selling of the President* if the use of hidden bias was not important? Of course not; none of these people would have put the money and effort they did into creating a favorable bias if it didn't pay off. In fact the reason that dictatorships in communist countries, as well as in South Vietnam, Spain, Greece and Brazil, are able to continue in power is that they control completely the means of creating propaganda through the mass media.

Governor Nelson Rockefeller's successful 1966 campaign for re-election demonstrates the powerful effect that a propaganda advantage can have. In early 1966, only 25 percent of the potential voters gave the Governor a favorable rating. The situation seemed hopeless. But instead of dropping out of the picture as friends advised, he hired a famous advertising agency to launch a campaign through the mass media. They made 35 different commercials—many of them indistinguishable from items on news programs—and had them shown more than 700 times. Nelson Rockefeller out-spent his opponent, Frank O'Connor, $4.3 million to $278,000—a 15 to 1 advantage. It worked: by September his favorable rating had gone up to 36 percent and in November he was re-elected.[5] In his 1970 election victory four years later, Rockefeller outspent his opponent Arthur Goldberg by a 5 to 1 margin.

"Buying" elections by outspending opponents by huge margins is not an isolated phenomenon. In the 1970 primaries, Senatorial candidates Howard Metzenbaum in Ohio, Richard Ottinger in New York and Lloyd Bentsen in Texas won elections in which they outspent opponents by as much as ten to one. In the 1970 Senate election, eleven of the fifteen major candidates were millionaires. The four non-millionaires all lost. In an attempt to salvage what integrity there is left in the electoral system, a law limiting election spending was signed in early 1972. While placing a limit on advertising, it places no limit on a candidate's total campaign spending. It is certain the new law will do little to change an electoral system designed to give a tremendous propaganda advantage to those with money.

Even though it appears obvious that the use of propaganda has considerable effect on public attitudes and behavior, the owners of media are still able to minimize its importance because it is extremely difficult to prove scientifically the exact effect of attempts to influence public opinion. No election could be held over again, reversing the newspaper endorsements, advertising money or long term use of bias. The results of such a hypothetical election can only be guessed at. Furthermore, there are other uncontrollable and unmeasurable factors which may influence people's attitudes very significantly. The unemployment and poverty of millions of Americans during the depression was a factor that helped Franklin D. Roosevelt get elected. The poor knew things were bad and had come to suspect the intentions of big business despite a more optimistic view presented by the Republican press. In Cincinnati, after a six-month propaganda campaign designed to increase support for the United Nations, the percentage of people supporting the United Nations was found to have decreased. It was reasoned that one of the causes for this decrease was that decisions and actions by the United Nations during this period were unpopular and thus offset the pro-UN propaganda.[6] The use of propaganda in mass media has its limitations: it would be impossible to convince a starving person he has plenty to eat. The propagandist won't even try to do this; instead, he will try to tell him who and what is to blame for his hunger or find spurious comparisons for him to rest in, such as "you're less hungry than you were ten years ago," or "the people overseas are worse off." But whoever actual conditions and events may tend to favor, it is still a great and unfair advantage for one politician to have more press support, money and access to media than his opponent. It is a situation that can't possibly be made consistent with the American idea of a fair election in a democratic society. That the people accept the situation seems to me an example of the success and power of mass media propaganda.

While communication experts may disagree on whether or not public opinion can be significantly changed by a particular public relations or election campaign, they have all agreed that a few underlying principles hold true in all situations involving persuasion and public opinion. There are two types of propaganda campaigns aimed at influencing people's opinions and behavior. One is a short term campaign, such as a project aimed at getting people now or in the near future to buy a product, to vote for a certain candidate or to demonstrate in the streets. The other type of campaign is a long term project designed not to affect any immediate action but to form or modify, over a period of many years, the basic values and self concepts of individuals and society. Professor Michael Choukas, in his book *Propaganda Comes of Age,* considers the short term effort as tactical propaganda and the long term effort as strategic propaganda.[7]

Tactical propaganda is sometimes successful at changing ideas that are not too important to a person, but it will in very few if any cases change ideas that are an integral part of an individual's self concept—his nuclear self. Propaganda attempting to change overnight a person's belief in God or white supremacy will fail, but that aimed at changing a person's belief in birth control or the Ku Klux Klan has a chance of succeeding because the person can change his ideas on these topics and still continue to believe in God or white racism.

It is much easier to persuade people to hang on to their present ideas and attitudes than to change them. In other words, those advocating the status quo have an easier job than those advocating change of any kind. In addition, attitudes which are reinforced by social groups like family, church, club, military organization, school, or society at large are much more resistant to change than attitudes that play no part in a person's social interactions.

While tactical propaganda will fail to change a person's basic attitudes, strategic propaganda carried on for years can be successful in developing, modifying or changing an individual's fundamental beliefs and self concept. Media owners' capacity to produce this kind of propaganda gives them their real power—much more potent a force than the power to endorse a particular candidate or help him with biased presentation of photographs at election time. Through their strategic or long term use of bias they can create basic public attitudes that will insure that both candidates—whoever they may be— will be acceptable to them. Candidates who advocate policies fundamentally at variance with the attitudes created over a long period of time by media owners will be lucky to poll 5 percent of the vote. Gilbert Seldes, media critic, describes the process of influencing basic ideas through the media as

> the slow daily and weekly creation of a climate favorable to certain ideas, the unnoticed gentle nudges and pressures that turn people in one direction rather than another, the constant supply of images to populate our subconscious minds.[8]

In the process of shaping attitudes that serve their own special interests, the media owners have created, sustained and confirmed racism, an unthinking patriotism, self blinding anti-communism and an acceptance of a communication system that prevents real competition between conflicting viewpoints. These undemocratic ideas have been implanted so deeply in Americans' concept of themselves that the ideas are highly resistant to propaganda aimed at changing them. J.H.C. Brown, in his book *Techniques of Persuasion,* states: "The most difficult thing in the world is to change minds in directions which conflict with the attitudes deeply embedded in the nuclear self."[9] The resistance is natural; it is based on man's instinct for survival. If man accepts ideas which destroy his value system—no matter how distorted his values may be—he has nothing left to live for. To destroy a person's self concept without replacing it with another, reinforced by the approval of social groups, is to risk destroying the person himself. In his book Brown includes many fascinating examples of how individuals made dramatic changes in their opinions regarding religion or social philosophies, but in each case there was a substitute system of belief that the individual could adopt in place of the old one.

Over a long period of time basic attitudes may be modified by strategic propaganda, but since all the means of creating strategic as well as tactical propaganda are in the hands of those who don't want basic changes, there is little hope for the creation of attitudes that will demand a basic realignment of priorities in America. Establishment ideas have been made even more resistant to change as the result of the media owners success in convincing the family, school, military, and church to reinforce these ideas in group situations. Nothing else can explain or exonerate the American peoples' acceptance of the racism, self-blinding anti-communism, censorship by mass media and the distorted priorities that the establishment has found so profitable. Nothing else can explain why the American people often choose very conservative individuals such as George Wallace, Spiro Agnew, Ronald Reagan, Everett Dirkson, Pope Paul and the Reverend Billy Graham to be on the list of the ten most admired men in the world while solid liberal or moderate liberal individuals such as Ernest Gruening, George McGovern, Eugene McCarthy, Paul Douglas, Father Groppi and Malcolm Boyd seldom make the top ten.

Research has indicated that intelligence is not an important factor in whether a person can be easily persuaded or not. What appears to be important is how inadequate a person feels.[10] Perhaps it is not entirely an accident that the poor, the laborer and the ordinary middle class workers are pictured in the media in such a way as to make them feel inadequate. The rich, the corporate owners and managers, the military and the establishment politicians, by comparison, are idolized even if they are unethical. The feeling of inadequacy that the ordinary man unconsciously picks up from images produced by the media make him easy prey for both tactical and strategic propaganda efforts. This partly explains the biggest miracle accomplished by media owners— the turning of the laborer and middle class against the hungry, poor, black and brown. It is the laborer and the man of the middle class who violently opposes welfare to the poor while supporting the giving of billions of dollars of "welfare" to the very rich in the form of subsidies, tax privileges and wasteful or unnecessary defense contracts. As Jacques Ellul points out, while the middle class is highly resistant to tactical propaganda urging agitation for some new cause, they are "ideal prey" of *integration* propaganda, the term Ellul uses to describe strategic propaganda.[11]

The voting behavior of the common American and the ease with which he is persuaded to vote for establishment priorities that are detrimental to his and his country's well being leads many liberals and scholars to doubt the reasoning ability and good sense of the common man. They claim that even if there was equal competition among varying viewpoints, the people would vote for establishment priorities and politicians. This may be true from a limited viewpoint, but no real test of the common man's capabilities can be conducted until all viewpoints have an equal chance to employ techniques of implanting bias on a long term or strategic basis. Competition among viewpoints is only fair when each position on the political spectrum has had a chance to affect the individual's basic nuclear attitudes from the first time he is exposed to the media. To grab a person at twenty, thirty or fifty-years-old, after he has been exposed to only establishment viewpoints, and expect him to choose intelligently among all viewpoints—when he has just then and for the first time seen them presented on an equal basis—is to ignore the basics of persuasion.

These are fundamentals that the conservatives understand much better than the liberals because of their experience in using and monopolizing the tools of propaganda that come with ownership of mass media.

15   Those Who Call the Tune

> The minority, the ruling class at present, has the
> schools and press, usually the church as well, under its
> thumb. This enables it to organize and sway the emo-
> tions of the masses, and make its tool of them.
>
> Albert Einstein

The establishment reaps huge profits from the arms-space race, special tax favors, congressional corruption and the present priorities as
expressed in the national budget. Some elements of the establishment
reap considerable profit from the low wages that accompany poverty
and racism. Others take advantage of weak government regulations in
order to increase their take. It is understandable that they use their
communication power to keep the public from demanding changes in
a status quo they find so rewarding. Naturally, they do not see themselves as the causes or even contributing to America's and the world's
problems. They have listened to their propaganda long enough to be
convinced that they are mankind's benefactors. The establishment's
greatest power rests in their being able to use their money and power
to insure that the means of producing propaganda will stay in the
hands of those persons whose interests coincide with those of the
establishment. Combining this power with the power they have
through controlling the giant corporations, banks and foundations,
they are able to govern — or have the United States governed — pretty
much the way they desire, whether or not this is in the interests of the
public, the country or mankind at large.

Who makes up the establishment? According to Ferdinand Lundberg who has spent years studying the subject, they are the ultra-
wealthy families who have billions of dollars and all the power that
goes along with it. In his book, *The Rich and the Super Rich,* he lists
the four top families and the value of their assets. First come the
DuPonts, who are worth an estimated $7.5 billion dollars. The Rocke-
fellers and the Mellons are close behind, having about $5 billion each.

Fourth place goes to the Fords who are worth about $2.4 billion. [1]
This is the top floor; there are thousands of other rich people who are
near the top. They are the one-half of 1 percent who own about 32
percent of all assets.[2] They are the 1.6 percent of the population that
own "80 percent of all stock, 100 percent of state and local government bonds and 88.5 percent of corporate bonds."[3]

These are the people who can, by their concentrated investments,
gain much more power than their money indicates. Lundberg explains
how:

> A man whose worth lies in 5 percent of the capital stock of a
> corporation capitalized at $2 billion is worth only 100 million. But as
> this 5 percent . . . usually gives him control of the corporation, his
> actual operative power is of the order of $2 billion.[4]

Lundberg makes clear that even the money of the small stock holders, who own about 20 percent of all stock, adds to the power of the
wealthy:

> The actual power of such concentrated ownership, therefore, is
> much greater than its proportion in the total of investment assets.
> The corporate power of the top 200,000 and certainly of the top
> 700,000 is actually 100 percent. The power of this top layer corpora-
> tively would be no greater if it owned 100 percent of investment
> assets.[5]

Establishment leaders are the active members of the very rich who
belong to the elite clubs such as the Links or Knickerbocker in New
York City. Lundberg discloses it is at these clubs that the wealthy
corporation, bank and foundation owners and managers discuss and
decide how, when and where to use the power they have at their
disposal in order to protect what they consider to be their vital interests.[6] Lundberg notes that not all the wealthy belong to the clubs or
participate in establishment policy. Many of the wealthy are women
and there are many wealthy infants who have inherited great sums
that are put in trust. Their money is still part of the concentrated and
combined assets which give control to the elite who see to it that only
certain policies safe for their interests are carried out. They delegate
power by determining the memberships of the bodies which manage
the large corporations, banks and foundations.

By analyzing the power and influence of the very wealthy, Lundberg demonstrates that they run the country the way they want to —
for their own interests. William Domhoff, in his book *Who Rules*

America?, uses a different approach to determine who governs America, but he comes to the same conclusion as Lundberg. By showing that rich businessmen and their descendents occupy positions of authority, Domhoff proves that the power elite (the very rich upper class and their high-level employed talent) control the executive branch of government, the federal judiciary, the military, the CIA and the FBI. In addition they directly influence Congress and most state and city governments.

Domhoff claims that the establishment controls the presidency by its campaign contributions to both parties. Neither party can even begin to think of nominating a candidate who is not acceptable to either the liberal or conservative elements of the very wealthy. If they do, there will be so little money coming in that defeat is guaranteed. In the 1968 presidential campaign, the Republicans spent $30 million and the Democrats spent $20 million.[7] The Democratic Party found itself $8 million in debt as a result of their expenditures. This kind of money can come only from the wealthy upper class and the people and institutions under their control. While the giant corporations give mainly to the Republicans, other big businessmen, some oilmen and the "ethnic rich" give to the Democrats. Domhoff found that 66 percent of the 105 largest contributors to the Democratic Party in 1952 and 1956 were members of the upper class.[8] The two parties are not backed by different groups, but rather by different elements within the establishment: "The Democratic Party is controlled by different members of the same elite group. We cannot overemphasize the falsity of the stereotype of the Democratic Party as the Party of the 'common man,'. . ."[9]

Even the most liberal President in recent times, John F. Kennedy, was acceptable to the establishment even though most establishment people may have wanted the more conservative Richard Nixon. Washington reporter Bernard Nossiter clearly documents this in his book *The Mythmakers*. He states:

> Of all the myths in current political and economic literature, one of the most imaginative and furthest removed from reality portrayed President Kennedy as anti-business. In fact, in every significant area — wage policy, tax policy, international trade and finance, federal spending — the President showed a keen understanding and ready response to the essential corporate program. It is doubtful that a Republican president, historically vulnerable to the charge of 'business tool,' could have done so much. Indeed, Eisenhower didn't.[10]

Besides campaign contributions, Domhoff's analysis of presidential cabinets reveals the establishment's control of the executive branch: "A study of the Cabinets for the years 1932-1964 suggests that the power elite dominates the departments that matter most to them — State, Treasury and Defense."[11] There is no doubt that the military is controlled by the wealthy establishment. This is indicated by the type of men who have headed the military. Domhoff found that "of the 13 men who have been Secretary of Defense or Secretary of War since 1932, eight have been listed in the Social Register. The others are bankers and corporation executives, and clearly members of the power elite."[12]

In addition, all of those who have political power over the military — the President, his closest advisors, the Security Council, the Secretary of Defense — are clearly members of the power elite. It often appears as if the military is making the decisions, but these decisions are made by the establishment. If the establishment had decided not to intervene in Vietnam, the military would not be there. The military does not run America — it merely carries out the high level policy decisions of the establishment. In wanting more (unnecessary) arms and foreign adventures than the administration thinks is reasonable, the military is merely siding with one part of the establishment against the other. Its political influence depends on its being backed by the giant corporations as well as the more conservative establishment politicians.

Domhoff also finds that through presidential appointments and the cooperation of the American Bar Association, the power elite has been able to control the Federal Judiciary. It is very unlikely that a Judge will be appointed who does not share the economic and social values of the establishment. The actual decisions in each case before the court cannot be dictated by the establishment leaders, but having judges with acceptable outlooks on life guarantees that the judicial decisions will not stray too far from the desired path. Warren Burger, Harry Blackmun, Louis Powell and William Rehnquist, Richard Nixon's appointees to the Supreme Court, serve as examples of judges who can be depended upon to protect the special interests and values championed by President Nixon and the establishment.

The CIA is also seen by Domhoff as an extension of the establishment:

From its inception the CIA has been headed by members of the power elite. . . .

We believe that the social backgrounds and previous institutional affiliations of these five directors, in conjunction with the sociological composition of the Special Group, is enough to establish the fact that members of the upper class control the CIA.[13]

Besides its authorized task of collecting intelligence, the CIA is used by the establishment to keep much of its dirty work hidden and to avoid the check of democratic processes in decision making. There are certain activities and policies of the establishment which are so greedy and self-serving that even the mass media cannot be expected to make them respectable. That these activities are authorized and are not the result of the CIA acting on its own was testified to by Allen Dulles, former head of the CIA:

The facts are that the CIA has never carried out any action of a political nature, given any support of any nature to any persons, potentates or movements, political or otherwise, without appropriate approval at a high political level in our government outside the CIA.[14]

When the CIA does operate, make decisions and attempts to influence public policy on its own it usually lines up with the more conservative element of the wealthy establishment.

J. Edgar Hoover, besides being FBI Chief, is on the board of directors of Acacia Mutual Assurance Company of Washington, D. C., the country's thirty-seventh largest insurance company. It is natural for Hoover to be sympathetic to the business aristocracy. Fred J. Cook, in *The FBI Nobody Knows,* reveals that Hoover early in his career was probably instrumental in calling off an investigation of cheating on war contracts that allegedly involved millions of dollars.[15] But what most clearly links Hoover and his FBI to the very conservative wing of the establishment is the Bureau's lack of enthusiasm for fighting certain types of crimes. Violations of civil rights have never inspired the FBI to utilize its full expertise. A similar lack of enthusiasm helps allow organized crime to flourish. The FBI has opposed attempts to set up any kind of Federal program to combat organized crime, claiming that it is a State and local law enforcement problem.[16] It is obvious to anyone acquainted with syndicate crime that murders, intimidations, payoffs and rackets are perpetrated by groups that extend across state lines, and cannot be tackled until seen as a national problem — therefore an FBI responsbility. Even under the Nixon Administration, the FBI showed its reluctance to tackle organized crime by refusing to help the Law Enforcement Assistance Administration conduct its training conference for State and local police prosecutors who are attempting to combat organized crime.[17]

What the FBI lacks in enthusiasm for tackling big crime it makes up by its vigorous harassment of those who criticize the establishment, even though the criticism may be based on solid information. Nobody represents the widespread legalized bribery and betrayal of the public that flourishes in Congress better than Connecticut's Senator Thomas Dodd. He seems to have sold his votes and considerable political power to any special interest willing to pay for it in the form of gifts, campaign contributions or other forms of bribery commonly accepted by congressmen. Nevertheless, the FBI was more interested in Dodd's staff (those who had had the courage to risk their own jobs and future by revealing Dodd's public betrayal) than it was in Dodd's own wrong doing. The FBI investigated the lives of the staffers and authors who revealed how America's welfare was being sacrificed for the interests of the wealthy who were willing to pay Dodd's price.[18]

The FBI also harassed people contributing information to investigations and broadcasts in 1968 that proved beyond doubt that millions of Americans were hungry and malnourished. According to the *Progressive* magazine, the purpose of the investigations was "to intimidate these people into saying something that can be used to create suspicion about the reports and the groups who sponsored them." Father Ruiz provided the CBS documentary, "Hunger in America" with some instances of near starvation; he also told of FBI agents questioning the poor. Before a U.S. Civil Rights Commission he asked, "What do FBI agents know about hunger? What purpose can they have except to frighten . . . the poor and hungry who thought the government in Washington was their friend?"[19] The purpose is obvious to anyone acquainted with the history of the FBI's frequent use of investigations to harass those who attempt to criticize the FBI or expose establishment politicians and policies.

President Nixon's appointments seem to confirm the Lundberg and Domhoff claims that the establishment rules America. On every issue before Congress, Melvin Laird, the President's choice as Secretary of Defense, voted correctly according to the establishment-oriented U.S. Chamber of Commerce. The very conservative group, Americans for

Constitutional Action, approved of 85 percent of his votes. In contrast, the moderately liberal Americans for Democratic Action, founded by Hubert Humphrey, approved of only 7 percent of his voting record.[20] Laird's appointment was welcomed by defense contractors since he is a vigorous exponent of costly weapons systems and the obsolete concept of military superiority. The man Nixon chose for the number two spot in the Defense Department was multi-millionaire David Packard, head of Hewlett-Packard Company — maker of electronic equipment for the military. His company was found by a Federal court to have illegally refused to disclose cost data to the General Accounting Office.[21] Mr. Gilbert Fitzhugh was chosen by President Nixon to head a blue ribbon panel with the job of making an "objective and uninvolved" analysis of defense spending. As Senator William Proxmire pointed out, Fitzhugh's only experience with defense was in being chairman of the board of the Metropolitan Life Insurance Company which holds $1.4 billion of loans in the twenty-four largest defense contractors. The company also has over $34 million in stocks invested with defense contractors.[22] It's not surprising that Senator Proxmire questioned the wisdom of such a selection.

President Nixon also looked to the corporate world for his selections of those who would protect the national environment from the ravages of corporate greed. Harry L. Moffett was chosen to head the Office of Minerals and Solid Fuels in the Department of Interior. He was a former registered lobbyist for the mining industry. Loren Forman and Charles F. Luce were chosen to be on a commission drawing up priorities for environmental planning; they work for Scott Paper and Consolidated Edison—both pollutant-producing companies. Earl Butz, the new Secretary of Agriculture, has long been a booster for the giant farm corporations.

Senator Joseph Tydings noted that Peter M. Flanigan, a top Presidential Assistant and at the time a stockholder in Barracuda Tanker Corporation, a company directly affected by the oil import quota system, was selected by the President to supervise the preparation of a White House statement on the quota system.

Dr. Franklin Lang, Dr. John Knowles, and Dr. John Adriani were all advised by President Nixon that they would be appointed to high posts in the administration. When the medical establishment let it be known that they were not pleased with these choices, the President changed his mind and appointed others.

Appointed as Secretary of Labor was George Shultz, a man who in

1969 thought $1.60 an hour was high enough for a minimum wage. He is also appalled by strikes of public employees. One of the first things he did was suspend for ninety days new safety standards, some of which were meant to protect miners.[23] One of the first things Attorney General John Mitchell did after being appointed by his former law partner was to drop the anti-trust case against El Paso Natural Gas Company. Both Mitchell and the President had been lawyers for the gas company.[24]

The President appointed Charles Meyer of Sears and Roebuck to the chief foreign policy position dealing with Latin America. Meyer had spent years expanding American corporate interest in Cuba and in other parts of Latin America. Henry Kissinger, closely associated with the Rockefellers, is the President's chief foreign policy advisor.

In short, the men who have been chosen by the President to fill the most important posts have been and are still dedicated to preserving and furthering the interests, priorities and foreign policy of the corporate world — a world controlled by the very rich families, its hired lawyers and managers.

President Nixon's major decisions reveal, even more than his appointments, his dedication to serving the interests of the establishment-controlled military-industrial complex rather than the public. At the same time that he has approved additional billions for ABM, manned space program, super sonic aircraft, Navy shipbuilding and the Vietnam war, he has taken money away from the children and the sick by vetoing congressionally passed appropriations for education, health improvements and medical research. He has sided with the oil companies of the very rich by favoring an oil depletion allowance and oil import quota which amounts to the nation's largest single output of welfare for the rich.

The establishment does not have as direct a control over Congress as it does over the presidency, the military, the CIA or the FBI, where members of the power elite are in positions of authority. Only a small percentage of the 535 Congressmen are members of the upper class. But the establishment is not particularly restricted by this lack of direct representation. By various lobbying techniques it recruits the most powerful members to support its special interests and keeps those who oppose it from gaining power. As a result there is a recognizable "congressional" power elite which serves the establishment.

Though these officials might not make up a numerical majority, they effectively control and determine public policy as expressed in laws, appropriations and investigations. They run Congress by their dominance on important committees, their use of the filibuster and other procedural manuevers. The establishment politicians use this power to further the special interests of the establishment at the expense of the public when there is a conflict between the two. The establishment rewards their politicians well; there are many like Lyndon Johnson, Richard Nixon and Everett Dirkson who have entered politics poor and are now worth quite a bit — Johnson some $16 million and Nixon is approaching his first million. The rewards from the establishment are in the form of legalized bribes and payoffs, added power in Congress, help at getting re-elected, help in business and investment ventures, and favorable coverage in the mass media. The establishment obtains more than enough for its investments: dividends are paid in the form of favorable legislation and policies regarding taxation, regulation, foreign affairs and appropriations.

Mass media's role in serving the establishment is vital. It serves to convince the people that the very rich and their hired servants are very respectable and well meaning people. It keeps the public from being aware that the establishment runs the government. To hide their role of serving the establishment, the agencies of mass media have used their propaganda tools to create in the public's mind myths about the news media. It is these myths which persuade the people to accept a communication system prostituted to the special interests of a few. These myths allow the establishment to continue to shape public opinion in such a way that democracy has merely become a window-dressing of legitimacy for the corporate control of government.

16   The Mythology of News Media

> Every reporter knows that when you write the first word, you make an editorial judgment.
>
> Robert E. Kitner, President, NBC

The Myth of Propaganda

The agencies of news media unanimously cooperate to put over the idea that the term "propaganda" correctly applies only to Communist produced news. Whenever the claims of the North Vietnamese, the Viet Cong, the Russians or the Chinese are announced, correspondents characterize the message as propaganda. Hardly an hour passes without the term being used to describe "enemy" claims. In 1969 NBC showed a film of the Russian-Chinese border dispute produced by Communist China.[1] Instead of finding a Chinese translator to interpret the audio portion, NBC had one of its own correspondents narrate the film. He repeatedly used the word propaganda to describe the film and explained in detail, while the film was being shown, the actual photographic techniques of implanting a bias favorable to the Chinese:

> The shots are angled to make it look as though. . . .
> That scene was repeated to make everyone see how. . . .
> An old fashion 'freeze frame' makes them look. . . .

To make sure the audience didn't forget for one moment that it was watching Communist propaganda, the statement:

FILM FROM COMMUNIST SOURCES

was repeatedly shown at the bottom of the screen.

News media are doing their job when they correctly reveal the sources of their information. And the term propaganda certainly does correctly describe the information output of Communist news agencies. The only criticism that can be made of U.S. news media's handling of Communist information sources is that U.S. correspondents substitute their dialogue for the original. This is a hidden technique of implanting bias in itself. It is also an insult to the American people to treat them as if they must be protected from the original words of Communists even after the source is made clear.

The media are not always so conscientious about identifying the source of their information—especially when this information emanates from the propaganda arm of the Pentagon. Many television stations show Pentagon produced film of action in Vietnam without identifying the source. When U.S. Army officers in Vietnam are interviewed to supply much of the dialogue for network film coverage of Vietnam, the audience isn't warned that they are getting a one-sided view, nor are Pentagon news releases ever termed "propaganda" by U.S. correspondents. Most U.S. correspondents writing about Vietnam support the presence of the United States in Vietnam and oppose an immediate and orderly withdrawal of all U.S. troops. When their interpretive reports on Vietnam are shown or published there is no warning to audience or readers that the news item represents a point of view favorable to the Pentagon. In contrast, articles written by Australian journalist Wilfred Burchett, a Communist, are introduced by conspicuous notices identifying his point of view. As the *Los Angeles Times* warned its readers, this article "presents a Communist viewpoint and should be read in that light."[2]

This double standard of news treatment, identifying and classifying only the other side's news releases as propaganda, has been successful in making propaganda a bad word—and a word never to be applied to the news output of U.S. commercial news agencies.

This myth conveniently prevents the American public from focusing attention on the situation that makes propaganda important to begin with. The real question is whether the public is receiving one-sided propaganda or propaganda from all viewpoints—a situation where one news agent of propaganda can balance off and expose propaganda techniques used by news agencies advocating opposing viewpoints. In the Communist world the public is unquestionably propagandized because there is no counter propaganda. But Americans are also being propagandized because there are no news agencies in the mass media who use the tools of propaganda to advance viewpoints which are fundamentally at odds with those of the establishment oriented media owners. How often does one network expose the propaganda techniques of its competitor or advocate, with its use of hidden bias, opposite priorities and policies?

The myth that only the other side uses propaganda is limiting in another aspect that is relevant to the one-sided presentation of news. It doesn't deal with the decided bias that is introduced into the media by technical or financial requirements of the communication system, a bias we've explored earlier. There is little competing bias to counter such bias either in Communist countries or in the United States. As a result, all the people of the world are in a state of being propagandized by the very technical and financial nature of modern communications. This explains in part why newspapers and news programs around the world feature moon shots, transplant operations and accidents while ignoring the less dramatic and palpable problems of illiteracy, the brain drain, pollution, population increase, disparity between the rich and the poor, and arms proliferation.

The Myth of Objectivity

Another news media propagated myth put forth and used for many years is the idea that news can be presented objectively, free from opinion or bias of any kind. As long as the media owners were able to make the question of objectivity respectable enough for argument, they were able to keep the public from asking the right question. The right question is whether all viewpoints have an equal opportunity to use bias, not the already answered question of whether or not bias is being used by this or that news media.

Those researchers who have taken the time to investigate media's claim of objectivity in presenting news found extreme bias favoring the media owners' viewpoints. The newspaper judged the fairest and most reliable by members of the press failed the test of objectivity along with all the rest. Walter Lippman and Charles Merz examined over 3,000 news items from the *New York Times* reporting on the Russian Revolution from 1917 to 1920.[3] They found that the *New York Times* used hidden bias to advocate American intervention in the Russian Revolution. When the President of the United States suddenly decided against intervention, the *Times* then changed course and used its "organized propaganda" against intervention. Later when intervention occured, the *Times* again switched back and used its propaganda in approving the intervention. Lippman and Merz found so much bias in the *Times* news that the net effect was "almost always misleading," so misleading that "a great people in a supreme crisis could not secure the minimum of necessary information on a supremely important event." The two journalists concluded: "So blatant is the intrusion of an editorial bias, that it will require serious reform before the code [of objectivity] which has been violated can be restored."

A later 1947 study of the *New York Times* objectivity, or lack of it, in reporting on news about the Soviet Union from 1917 to 1947 revealed that the *Times* continued to use every technique available of implanting hidden bias to propagandize the nation.[4] Martin Kriesberg found that the amount of attention and the manner of reporting news were not determined by journalistic standards of objectivity, but "by the relationship between American and Soviet interest." During weeks when the Soviet Union was acting in a way contrary to the *Times'* conception of America's national interest, items about the Soviet Union were as much as 84 percent unfavorable. When the Soviet Union was fighting on our side, as during the battle at Stalingrad, hidden bias was used less often so that the unfavorable bias was considerably decreased. Kriesberg noted some of the themes that appeared in the *Times'* propaganda. Soviet leaders were portrayed as unjust, unreasonable and arbitrary. The Government was made to look as if it wouldn't succeed. Kriesberg felt that readers exposed to *Times* bias would tend to acquire or have reinforced the feeling that conflict with the Soviet Union was a likelihood and that it would be a just conflict.

Professor George Lichtheim made a study in 1965 and found that the *Times* was still committed to using hidden bias to further government policies—this time in Vietnam. He showed, among other things, how two of the most important expositions of French policy regarding Southeast Asia were buried in the *Times*. The reason is not hard to guess. One was a statement by President Charles DeGaulle which termed both Russian and American foreign policies as imperialistic. The other was a statement by Couve de Murville calling for independence from United States influence both in Asia and in Europe.[5]

A media analyst for the Commission on the Freedom of the Press, Leila Sussmann, published the results of a survey showing how the thirty-three top network radio news programs handled labor news in

665 newscasts during a seven-week period in 1944. Monitors discovered a total of 212 news items on labor. Of these, 22 percent were straight factual reports and the remaining 78 percent were opinion voiced either by the newscaster or someone he quoted. The analysis found that for every 1 item favorable to labor, there were 5 items unfavorable. There was clearly no competition among networks when it came to who they were cheering for with their hidden bias. [see TABLE XII]

These figures led Sussman to conclude: "They seem to prove beyond doubt that labor news was treated unfavorably on the top news programs of the four major networks during the period studied."

The *Los Angeles Times'* earlier hatred of labor as expressed through its biased news reporting made it notorious for being one of the worst newspapers in the country. Its dramatic improvement in recent years still hasn't changed its basic policy of news manipulation. The owners of the *Times* are some of the largest landholders in California and New Mexico. They profited financially from a farm labor policy that allowed the importation of cheap Mexican labor. Michael Pan, graduate student in journalism, analyzed the *Times'* news reports and editorials for the year preceding and the year following the expiration of the bracero importation program in December, 1964. He found that the *Times* was still far from being objective. However, its techniques of implanting a bias to favor the economic interests of its owners was more hidden and more clever than in the past. As Pan stated:

> The *Times* handled the event in a skillful way. . . .
> In the editorial pages, the *Times* consistently defended the owner's non-media interests. . . .
> In news columns, the *Times* had different attitudes. Opposition was spelled out only when there was a chance of success. When it became obvious that the cause was lost, they shifted their attitude to a position more in keeping with social rather than selfish interest.[6]

A study of the *Los Angeles Times'* news treatment of Richard Nixon in comparison with Harold Stassen during the time when Nixon was campaigning for the vice presidential spot shows that the *Times* used headlines, cartoons and other tools of propaganda to favor Nixon and ridicule Stassen.[7]

Lewis Donohew studied the news treatment that 17 newspapers accorded President Kennedy's Medicare proposal. He found that newspapers who opposed or supported medicare in their editorial

TABLE XII

BIAS IN NETWORK RADIO NEWSCASTS COVERAGE OF LABOR, 1944*

	CBS		NBC		BLUE		MUTUAL		TOTAL	
	Number of Items	Per-cent	Number of Items	Per-cent	Number of Items	Per-cent	Number of Items	Per-cent	Number of Items	Per-cent
Favorable	2	14	3	8	9	17	8	13	22	13.2
Unfavorable	7	50	26	70	3	61	41	64	105	63.2
Neutral	0	0	4	11	6	12	4	6	14	8.4
Balanced	5	36	4	11	5	10	11	17	25	15.0

*Source: "Labor in the Radio News: An Analyses of Content," *Journalism Quarterly*, September, 1945, p. 212.

comments also opposed or supported medicare with the use of biased news reporting.[8]

Newspapers are apt to be less biased in covering election campaigns than other events because they know their news treatment of candidates might be investigated or will antagonize readers of the opposing party. Nevertheless, they still fail miserably any test of objectivity or fairness. An analysis of the objectivity of 8 newspapers, 4 Republican and 4 Democrat, during the 1952 campaign showed that all 8 used hidden bias to favor the candidate endorsed on the editorial page.[9] A study by Nathan Blumberg of 35 newspapers during the same campaign found that 17 percent of them, including the *Los Angeles Times,* clearly showed partiality and another 34 percent showed slight partiality.[10] Blumberg termed the slight partiality insignificant, but this may overlook the fact that a slight bias is often more effective than the more blatant bias which might give itself away.

A more revealing examination of coverage of sensational news breaks about politicians found newspapers to be decidedly biased. Arthur Rowse studied the way 36 major newspapers handled particular news stories about Richard Nixon and Adlai Stevenson. He found that 35 out of 36 gave more favorable news coverage to the candidate they endorsed on their editorial page.[11]

UCLA Professor Jack Lyle analyzed 20 Southern California daily newspapers during the 1964 presidential election. He reported in his book *News in Megalopolis* that 12 of the 20 dailies used bias to support the candidate they endorsed on their editorial pages. Of these, 9 used hidden bias to support Barry Goldwater and 3 to support Lyndon Johnson.

Even the very foundations of news were found to harbor bias during the 1956 presidential campaign. An analysis of the wire service reports showed that AP, UP and INS all favored Eisenhower over Stevenson.[12] This bias was picked up and transmitted through every news agency in the country.

As might be expected the media has failed miserably in its attempt to report the Vietnam war objectively. In my study of photographs of Vietnam and of Vietnamese leaders, I found many more photographs that would please either the Saigon government or the Pentagon than ones that would displease them. The *Los Angeles Times* in March and April 1969, featured on its first three pages 6 photographs favorable to Saigon or the Pentagon compared to none favorable to the North Vietnamese or the National Liberation Front; 2 were neutral. During these two months, the *New York Times* featured on its first three pages 25 photographs favorable to Saigon or the Pentagon compared to 7 favorable to North Vietnam or the NLF; 2 were neutral.

My analysis of words, headlines and photographs used in news coverage of the war in Vietnam revealed a hidden bias favoring U.S. policy and depicting the United States as winning the war. [see TABLE XIII]

The study shows a considerable difference among the three newspapers. The *New York Times* bias ratio favoring the Pentagon was about 2 to 1, the *Los Angeles Times,* 3 to 1, and the *Honolulu Star-Bulletin,* 4 to 1. Stories originating from the *Star-Bulletin* itself were even more biased—10 favorable, 6 neutral and none that would have displeased the Pentagon. It can be assumed that every other newspaper and broadcasting station had at least a 2 to 1 hidden bias favoring U.S. policy and depicting the United States as winning the war. This was a great advantage to those wanting to continue the war, but the congressmen, professors, generals and others who opposed the war were in no position to create an opposing bias and were thus placed at a considerable competitive disadvantage in trying to rally the public to oppose U.S. policy. This also prevented the public making a decision based upon competing views of the situation in Vietnam.

The biased selection of photographs was also used to depict a slow-down in the war greater than the slowdown that actually took place after President Nixon's election. In September and October 1968, the *Los Angeles Times* featured 7 photographs of combat situations on its first two pages in contrast to 3 for March and April of 1969. Soon after President Nixon presented to 88 million television viewers his Vietnam policy, the *Los Angeles Times* had succeeded in bringing the war in Vietnam to an end—photographically. On its first three pages during December 1969, it featured only 1 photograph of combat situations in Vietnam—a photograph of a GI blowing out the candles on a birthday cake. Despite the "end of the war" as implied photographically by the *Los Angeles Times* during December, more than 260 GIs were killed during the month. During the same month, the *New York Times* did depict, photographically, that Americans were still engaged in combat; it featured 9 photographs of combat situations on the first three pages.

Despite the convincing evidence as far back as fifty years ago that achieving objectivity was impossible, the news agencies continued to convince most of the public that objectivity was possible. This served

TABLE XIII

PHOTOGRAPH, HEADLINE AND WORD SELECTION IN NEWS COVERAGE OF THE VIETNAM WAR. JUNE 18 TO JULY 31, 1968

	Los Angeles Times, First Two Pages*	New York Times, First Four Pages	Honolulu Star-Bulletin, Entire Paper
Headlines favorable to Saigon or the Pentagon, or unfavorable to North Vietnam or the NLF.	40	32	72
Headlines unfavorable to Saigon or the Pentagon, or favorable to North Vietnam or the NLF.	17	20	23
Photographs favorable to Saigon or the Pentagon, or unfavorable to North Vietnam or the NLF.	13	19	20
Photographs favorable to North Vietnam or the NLF, or unfavorable to Saigon or the Pentagon.	3	9	2
Words used to depict Saigon or the Pentagon favorably, or North Vietnam or the NLF unfavorably. (in headlines)	22	no significant bias	40
Words used to depict North Vietnam or the NLF favorably, or Saigon or the Pentagon unfavorably. (in headlines)	8	no significant bias	7
Number of times the word "Red" was used to describe North Vietnamese or the NLF. (in headlines) (in addition to the words used above)	22	0	8

*The vast majority of news about Vietnam occurs in the *Los Angeles Times* on pages 1 and 2, and in the *New York Times* to keep the public questioning whether or not news was being presented in an objective or biased manner. As a result, they were diverted from asking the most relevant and important question, that is, since bias cannot be eliminated, did all viewpoints have an equal opportunity to present news in a biased manner? By the time the public finally began to realize that the concept of objectivity was a farce, even the news agencies—the perpetuators of the concept—rejected it as impossible. In 1968, publisher of *Newsday* and former Press Secretary for President Johnson, Bill Moyers, stated: "Of all the myths of journalism, objectivity is the greatest."[13] Frank Reynolds, ABC-TV, admitted: "I think your program has to reflect what your basic feelings are. I'll plead guilty to that."[14]

The destruction of the myth of objectivity places the media owners in a precarious position because if objectivity is impossible, than it must follow that the only way to give people advocating different viewpoints a fair chance to compete for public acceptance is to endeavor to allow each an equal degree of control over access to the media. Media owners are naturally scared to death of this; it would deprive them of establishment-based profits and nullify their political power. Media owners and the establishment, would, I believe, fight the idea to the last man.

The Myth of Fairness

To keep the public from realizing the need for equal access the media owners have created another myth to function in the place of the myth of objectivity; it is the myth of fairness. The substitution of the one myth for the other is revealed in a statement made by David Brinkley: "Objectivity is impossible to a normal human being. Fairness, however is attainable, and that is what we are striving for—not objectivity, [but] fairness."[15] So far this strategy has worked; the public as well as the Federal Communication Commission are busy concerning themselves with whether or not the news is fair or balanced, when to present news fairly would seem as difficult as presenting it objectively. To achieve fairness, you'd have to eliminate personal bias in the decisions that determine whether all sides of public issues will be adequately and fairly covered. Since such subjective decisions can't be eliminated, the news presentations that result are going to be biased in any case. And biased news can never be fair if only those with establishment values are in positions to control the media, and so produce the bias.

It is the media owners or their handpicked reporters and correspondents who decide which issue to cover in the first place. They then decide how many sides there are to an issue. Further, they decide what type of coverage is balanced and then the who and where and what of the interview or photograph.

Newspapers and magazines cannot be required by the government to try to be objective or fair; they are a law unto themselves. But broadcasters, since they use the public airways, can be required by Congress or the FCC to perform in a manner ostensibly consistent with the public interest. Unfortunately, like every other governmental regulatory agency, the FCC represents the industry it is supposed to regulate, and not the public. It is pressured into doing this by the establishment politicians who have power over the agencies. Drew Pearson and Jack Anderson describe the FCC's dependency on Congress in their book *The Case Against Congress:*

> Of all the watchdogs, the Federal Communications Commission seems the most eager to sit up and beg or roll over and play dead at the command of Congress. The politicians on Capitol Hill have tamed the FCC until it has become little more than a retriever for the networks.[16]

President Nixon, a firm supporter of the present commercial communications system, has guaranteed FCC subservience to the communications industry by appointing Dean Burch as its chairman. Burch, Barry Goldwater's former campaign manager, is a solid supporter of the status quo in broadcasting.

The Equal Time Provision, passed in 1934, and the FCC's 1949 Fairness Doctrine are the government's tools and bases for forcing stations to be fair to political parties and to opposing viewpoints. The FCC has found it impossible to enforce these laws. The few FCC efforts in this area have been totally inadequate, ineffective and inconsistent. Moreover, the rulings it has made tend to reinforce the media owners and the status quo rather than the concept of fairness.

If any politician is given free time or allowed to purchase time by a station, that station must extend to his political opponent the same free time or opportunity to purchase time. There are few complaints based on this Equal Time requirement because broadcasters are very careful to abide by it. The requirement is stated so clearly that no broadcaster could hope to violate the provision without being called on it. But when the President of the United States is given free time (in effect whenever he wants it) to make proclamations or policy statements, there are usually numerous complaints based upon either the Equal Time Provision or the Fairness Doctrine. The Fairness Doctrine requires that, when an issue is a matter of public controversy, all sides must be presented "fairly". If the President uses the air waves to make a non-partisan declaration as head of state, then the Equal Time Provision does not apply. A declaration of war or national emergency, of course, are not considered partisan. If, however, he includes partisan attacks on his opponents or partisan defenses of his policies, the speech should not be exempt from either the Equal Time Provision or the Fairness Doctrine, as the President is usually a candidate in the next election, and will directly or indirectly be supporting one side in a controversial issue.

The important point, and the point we should note is that the media owners are the ones who have the power to determine whether a president's speech was partisan enough to require free broadcast time for opposing viewpoints or candidates. These decisions can result in a very powerful bias. For if the President gets to present his viewpoints to 88 million Americans for a half hour or 15 minutes and his opponents are shut out by media owner decisions, the people are merely being propagandized and an opportunity for real public dialogue is lost. Only the most obvious presidential announcement—about which there can be no debate as to whether or not it is partisan in nature— should be exempt from either the Equal Time or Fairness Doctrine requirements.

The willingness and the unanimity of the entire broadcasting industry in refusing to grant free time for opponents to reply to President Nixon's first five speeches on the Vietnam issue, as well as his television veto of the education bill, reveal the dedication of the broadcasting industry to establishment priorities and policies. These speeches were primarily defenses of administration policies and attacks on critics—thereby clearly demanding free time for opponents to reply. The network decisions to refuse, and their failure to offer, free time to opponents during prime time, make a mockery of any concept of fair play. The networks tried to put on the facade of fairness by having a few correspondents comment afterward, or by inviting the opposition to appear for a few minutes of comment and debate. But such window dressings did not constitute a balance: nothing short of free and adequate time for the opposition, not network correspondents, is even an attempt to achieve fairness. The advantage to the President was becoming so embarrassingly obvious that by the summer of 1970 (after the president had been on nationwide television more than 8 hours), the networks were making token gestures of fairness by offering some free time to "the loyal opposition" (the Democratic Party), and the FCC finally awakened to require under the Fairness Doctrine a fraction of free time for the opposition. But the long overdue and inadequate gestures of the networks and the FCC did not begin to achieve fairness to the opposition party, and even less so to the solid liberal and radical spokesmen—the ones the President attacked the most. They were given no time whatsoever.

In order to answer President Nixon's claim that dissenters were holding back peace (along with his other distortions of history such as his ridiculous claim that "the Marines alone this year have built over 250,000 churches, pagodas and temples for the people of Vietnam"), the opposition such as Senator Goodell and journalist Erwin Knoll had to write articles in small-circulation magazines such as the *New Republic* and the *Progressive*. Their dissent reached an audience of 200,000 instead of 80 million.[17]

House Democratic Leader, Carl Albert, responded to President Nixon's television veto of the health and education bill by stating on January 27, 1970:

> I call upon the President to use the awesome power of his office, not against the children, the sick, the aged, and the poor of this nation, but rather against the great monopolies which are the true culprits in causing inflation.

Albert requested free time from the networks in order to communicate his reply to the American people. His request for equal time was refused by all three networks. As a result Albert had to settle for yelling on the street corner, writing an article in a magazine that has possibly 200,000 circulation, getting fifteen seconds on a newscast or having his reply buried in ten lines on Page 14 of the *New York Times*. It exemplified the establishment's idea of fairness—a 400 to 1 advantage. It is small wonder that the media is able to produce majority support for establishment priorities and wars.

In 1954, President Eisenhower presented a partisan defense of the Republican's tax program over all three networks. The President's talk was carried during prime time on over 100 television stations. The next evening the three television networks refused to show the Democrats' reply. Of the only ten television stations that showed the Democrats' reply, two carried the program at 11:20 p.m. instead of during prime time. People in Boston, Chicago, Denver and Los Angeles were denied by media owners a chance to see on television the Democrats' reply. It was carried on radio by ABC, Mutual and NBC, but CBS even refused to provide radio time. The networks claimed that in their opinion the President was speaking as a head of state and therefore the Fairness Doctrine didn't apply.[18]

Barry Goldwater was too conservative for the top leaders of the establishment. This was reflected by the media's use of hidden bias to favor the more liberal presidential candidate for the first time in modern history. One example of this was the network's refusal to grant Goldwater equal time to respond to President Johnson's report to the nation about the Chinese nuclear bomb test and the fall from power of Nikita Khrushchev. Since Goldwater's views on foreign policy and his supposed willingness to drop the bomb were the main issues in the campaign, the speech took on a definite partisan character.

Mayor Richard Daley was given one hour of free time by 157 television stations to present a defense of Chicago City and police department actions at the Democratic National Convention.[19] The American Civil Liberties Union and two other organizations put together a rebuttal in order to balance the presentation; 145 of the 157 stations who broadcast Daley's defense refused to present the ACLU rebuttal.[20] From their subjective viewpoint, that was fair enough since the dissidents supposedly had received adequate coverage during regular newscasts.

Often the networks grant a propaganda advantage to establishment spokesmen in such a clever way that no one, not even solid liberals or radicals complains. On February 6, 1970, in an interview by Walter Cronkite, Lyndon Johnson was given an entire hour to promote an establishment version of the war and to criticize the war critics. Apparently CBS felt that having dutifully and objectively relayed for many years the former presidents' viewpoints on the war did not afford establishment viewpoints enough of an advantage. To make sure a maximum audience would hear the establishment viewpoints as channeled through this ex-president, CBS paid for full-page newspaper ads and made spot announcements over television and radio. CBS made a typical token gesture of fairness by allowing Senator Fulbright five minutes to reply to Johnson's attack on him. Would a solid liberal or radical network have considered it fair to give an entire hour in prime time to allow a former President to expound the establishment's view of the war and other issues without giving anti-war spokesmen equal time to reply?

A handful of individuals sitting in network offices by reason of business ambition, wealth or establishment endorsement are able to arbitrarily decide whether the world's largest and most important democratic nation will or will not have a public debate on vital issues. No President ever dreamed of such power. Only in the Soviet Union or Communist China is such power placed in the hands of so few.

If a station itself takes an editorial stand backing or attacking a certain candidate or policy, they are required by the Fairness Doctrine to provide for opposing viewpoints. This provides for a debate in which at least two sides of an issue may be heard. However, the Doctrine fails to deal with the decisions that bring about the greatest bias and unfairness. To remain silent on a vital issue is to endorse the status quo. This is exactly how most stations endorse the establishment; they fail to take an official position on many vital issues, and most stations take no editorial positions at all. The three networks never officially editorialize. There is thus no way for those opposing present policies on such issues as Vietnam, abortion, ABM or the SST to compel stations to grant any time at all unless there is first an official editorial.

Second, with more than 10,000 radical right broadcasts each week it is impossible for the liberals who are attacked to find out about it and respond. Stations often don't inform those attacked and refuse equal time when requested to do so. The task of enforcing the Doctrine is so great that the FCC doesn't even try.[21] Third, and equally important, most personal attacks are camouflaged in commentaries or interpretive reports, both of which are exempt from the personal attack provisions of the Fairness Doctrine. Howard K. Smith, Frank Reynolds, Eric Sevareid and the network correspondents can cleverly belittle ideas and politicians without ever having to grant equal time to opposing viewpoints. The 40 to 50 million combined network evening news audience hear only commentaries by network personnel.

When the media owners do make decisions about fairness in regular news programs they often appear to be protecting special interests from the truth rather than trying to achieve fairness. Howard K. Smith admits the attempt to achieve balance often hides the truth:

> If one man argues one way, we seem duty bound to get somebody, whether he's right or wrong, who will argue the opposite. They balance each other off, and leave the impression that the truth lies somewhere half way in between. The method is misleading in most cases, because truth is where it is and not between anything.[22]

Robert MacNeil of NBC had a major part in making a documentary which exposed the special interests of groups which were opposing new gun control laws. The documentary showed the "hypocrisy" of the position taken by the National Rifle Association and "the weakness of Congress in allowing itself to be pressured by an interested minority." Top NBC network and news department executives screened it and decided to reedit the film, cutting out an interview which tended to embarrass an NRA spokesman and toning down other parts including MacNeil's ending. The result was a program that would lead people to think the problem was not one of capitulation to special interest, but of finding a reasonable compromise. When presented, NBC of course didn't bother to inform its audience that the documentary had been censored by top brass at NBC. MacNeil believes the Fairness Doctrine was only used as an excuse to tone it down. As he put it: "One was left with the conviction that NBC had other reasons for wishing to avoid too forceful a presentation of this issue."[23]

Using the concept of fairness as a substitute for the discarded idea of objectivity has worked. Americans are still led to think that fairness in presenting news can be achieved through arbitrary and subjective decisions made by media owners and their handpicked employees. Until the public realizes that actual and true fairness is impossible, the most important decisions in society—ones which determine what people will talk, think and debate about—will stay in the hands of a few wealthy media owners who consciously or unconsciously serve the policies and priorities of the establishment's military-industrial-media complex.

The Myth That all Sides are Presented

As we have seen, news agents often claim they present all sides of controversial issues. So on news programs covering controversial issues, there are usually two sides with contrasting viewpoints presented.

But sometimes this seemingly fair technique is a front, behind which the agents can completely shut out sides of the controversy that they don't approve of. They present only those sides that they find acceptable or responsible—or those so bizarre as to be ridiculous. The public is thus deprived of any opportunity to consider all sides. Let's examine how the news media handled the controversy involving abortion and abortion laws to test news media's competence in presenting a controversial topic.

Each week in the United States many thousands of women choose to have an illegal abortion rather than give birth to and raise an unwanted child. It is estimated that 80 to 90 percent of these women are married with two or more children.[24] Many of the abortions are performed by unskilled amateur abortionists or even by the pregnant woman herself. The tools are often primitive, and many of the methods of inducing abortion are based on tragically wrong old wives' tales. Thousands of women die a painful and tragic death as a result. Prior to legalization in a few states, an estimated 100 women died each week from such abortions.[25] Almost 80 percent of these abortion deaths occurred among non-white women who couldn't pay the $500 to $1000 necessary to obtain an illegal but safe abortion from a physican.[26] Performed by a qualified physician, abortion is much safer than giving birth to a child. In Czechoslovakia, 140,000 legal abortions were performed in 1964 without a single death.[27] Modern vacuum techniques of abortion now being used in England take only three to six minutes and require no surgery.

Laws prohibiting abortion deter many women from seeking an abortion, and as a result millions of women, approximately 1 million a year, unwillingly give birth to unwanted children. Princeton Sociologist Charles F. Westoff in his study of 5,600 married women found 42 percent of the poor and 17 percent of non-poor births were of unwanted children.[28] Many young girls thirteen-years-old, as well as women forty-five and older, are forced against their will to give birth to unwanted children.

These facts—and the religious and "moral" arguments used to justify present day abortion laws—are what make the present abortion laws a subject of heated controversy. On one side of the controversy are those who advocate abolishing all abortions laws, leaving it a matter to be decided by the individual woman and her doctor. On the other side are those who want to retain the abortion laws which for so long have prevented any woman from having a legal abortion unless it was necessary to save her life. Also against the repeal of abortion laws are the reformers who advocate laws be reformed to allow abortion only in specific cases such as danger to the mental or physical health of the mother, incest, rape, or the probability of a deformed fetus.

Throughout the past and into the present there is little question which side in the controversy has had its argument accepted as the basis for public policy. Even though it seems merely a matter of time before legalized abortion wins out in both the courts and in some state legislatures, thirty-four states still prohibit abortion unless the mother's life is in danger, or even prohibit it altogether, and thirteen states have liberalized laws permitting abortion under conditions acceptable to those advocating reform. As of 1970, only women in New York, Alaska and Hawaii could obtain an abortion on the legal grounds that it is their individual right to decide whether or not to bear and raise a child.

The politicians in supporting the position of the Catholic Church have had the support of the majority of the public despite the great numbers of physicians, scientists and church leaders who oppose the laws. The major reason the Church and the politicians have for so long been able to maintain public support for restrictive abortion laws is that the news media until very recently have only presented one side of the controversy. An analysis of America's most responsible and thorough news agency—the *New York Times*—proves this. It can safely be assumed that 99 percent of the other news agencies gave the controversy even less fair coverage than the *Times*.

During the twenty-nine years from 1936 through 1964, the *New York Times Index* listed a total of 21 abortion items that included the arguments taken by one side or the other in the controversy. Of the 21 items, 12 included arguments advocating the position of the Catholic Church, 8 the reform position, and 1 for legalized abortion.[29] This 20 to 1 competitive advantage can hardly be termed fair. The one argument for legalization appeared in 1964 on page 36 as one paragraph buried in a ten-inch article on penal law.[30]

During these twenty-nine years there were 5 letters to the editor taking a side in the controversy. Of these, 2 sided with the Church, 3 sided with the reformist and none advocated legalized abortion.

A big uproar was heard in 1951 when Pope Pius XII announced to physicians and midwives: "To save the life of a mother is a noble aim, but direct killing of a child as a mean to that end is illicit even if sanctioned by public authorities.''[31] In the next ten days there followed 6 more articles dealing with the Pope's statement. While one criticized the Pope, it didn't advocate legalized abortion. The other five were all statements by the Pope or the Vatican expounding their position.

During the entire twenty-nine years there were 10 articles expounding the Roman Catholic position and only 1 attacking it.

More glaring than the shutting out of one side in the controversy was the almost complete neglect of the issue itself. During this twenty-nine year period (when, according to responsible estimates, at least 150,000 women—mostly non-white and poor—died as unwilling martyrs of a religious belief made into law), the *Times* featured only 21 news items and 5 letters stating a position in the controversy. More than 90 percent of the indexed news items on abortion dealt with the subject in its criminal aspects such as arrests, convictions and sentencing of those involved in abortion. Such articles tend to cast the blame for the ills of abortion onto those being arrested instead of those who make the laws and impose them on others. This sort of article diverts the people's attention from the real issue and for some readers at least, serves to reinforce support for the religious abortion laws.

The *Times* didn't bother to feature personal tragedies of women being forced to bear children against their will, or risk death. Such stories might have caused people to begin to clamor for change of abortion laws. Lawrence Lader describes one typical case—the type ignored by news media:

> A mother with three children was admitted to Boston's Massachusetts General Hospital with severe abdominal pain, vaginal bleeding, and a temperature of 105 after douching herself with a soap and bleach solution by syringe. 'She was alert and asking to go home and care for her children although she was gray and appeared about to die at any minute,' the attending physician reported. Despite blood transfusion and every emergency measure, she died twenty-six hours later.[32]

Those responsible for the laws which cause this kind of avoidable tragedy are not so much the Church hierarchy, but the mass media which has by its news coverage propagandized the public into accepting Church belief as society's law. This is borne out by the dramatic change in opinion since 1965 when those advocating legalized abortion began to receive at least a minimal coverage in the mass media.

The more they have been allowed by media owners to have their say the more the public has sided with them. In December 1965, only 15 to 21 percent favored legalized abortion.[33] By the start of 1972, percentage had risen to 60 percent.[34] When and if the day ever comes when those advocating legalized abortion have equal access to mass media, the public will realize the injustice and brutality of all present abortion laws which fail to leave the decision of abortion up to the woman and her doctor.

The Myth That all Controversies are Presented

Confronted with the facts of past bias, many media owners will admit that they have avoided controversies like car safety, hunger, tobacco and cancer, and abortion. Some may even admit that when they did cover a controversy they didn't present all sides. But most will assuredly claim that today in the 1970's all controversies are being covered in the mass media. They will point out with pride their coverage of racism, birth control, pollution, priorities, the Kennedy Assassination, the Songmy massacre and others. But what they won't point out is that they tried their best to cover up these controversies for as long as they could. They only covered these topics when it became impossible for them to ignore them without losing prestige and public confidence. Furthermore, these issues were finally forced on the news media, not by crusading media owners, but by dedicated individuals and scientists who were able, despite the owners' conspiracies of silence, to circumvent the mass media and alert the public.

Racism in the North is 300 years old; but as news it wasn't given much play in the media until the blacks burnt down Watts. President Eisenhower's and President Kennedy's policy of doing nothing about the population explosion wasn't considered controversial despite many grave warnings of future catastrophe made as early as the late 1940's. What was probably a conspiracy of auto manufacturers to ignore the problem of auto-caused air pollution wasn't covered until 1969. Despite the vocal criticism of many as early as 1960, it wasn't until 1969 that the media treated as controversial the spending of billions to go to the moon. The official theory of the Kennedy assassination was left largely unquestioned by the news media until Mark Lane and others, on their own, made the topic the number one controversy of the day. The lack of gun control legislation and the high rate of murders in the United States, compared with other countries, was not treated as a newsworthy subject until after the assassination of President Kennedy, and not as a full fledged controversy until after Martin Luther King and Robert Kennedy had been assassinated much later.

The CIA had for years been acting politically in an unauthorized fashion by secretly subsidizing organizations and engaging in extensive propaganda activities in the United States. Yet it was *Ramparts* magazine in 1967, not a mass news agency, that first exposed the fact that the CIA, aside from doing its authorized task of gathering information, was secretly engaged in many far flung and sometimes unsavory political activities.

Many activities of the FBI and its agents are clearly illegal. Its director, J. Edgar Hoover, has used his power in a despotic manner to attack, damage and intimidate those who don't agree with his very conservative political viewpoints. This was revealed not by agents of mass media, whose drama and news glorifies the Bureau and its Chief, but by Jack Levine, former FBI agent, who gave the facts in a two-hour interview over listener-sponsored non-commercial WBAI. Levine's very serious and sensational charges have been verified by authors Fred J. Cook and William W. Turner. Levine took his story to WBAI only because the *New York Times*, other newspapers, the wire services, and radio and television outlets refused to touch the story.[35]

Unknown to Congress and the American people, the U.S. Embassy secretly directed widespread military operations in Laos ("Project 404") for four years without the "watchdog" U.S. Press discovering or publicizing the fact. It was a Senate subcommittee which finally revealed this unauthorized U.S. military involvement in a second Asian war.

The oil industry for years has been given billions of dollars in subsidies through the oil import quota and tax privileges, yet scant attention was paid to this scandalous situation until the late 1960's. For years churches have been able to avoid paying billions of dollars in taxes as the result of unjustifiable tax privileges, yet there was little or no coverage of the topic until the late 1960's.

Former President Hoover, in 1949, claimed that 10 percent of the then 15 billion a year defense spending was wasteful and could be saved without sacrificing military strength.[36] H. S. Nieburg, in his 1966 book *In the Name of Science,* documents case after case of wasteful defense spending. But it wasn't until the late 1960's, when an estimated 20 billion per year was being wasted, that the media began to allow it to make the big time news.[37] After reaping the harvest of the hundreds of billions wasted, in silence, during the previous twenty years, the giant corporations and their cooperating news media could no longer cover up the increasingly critical comments.

Researches revealed as early as 1965 that color television sets emitted dangerous radiation, but the media kept the controversy buried until 1968. The examples of once ignored but now inadequately and unfairly presented controversies could go on almost indefinitely.

Today in 1972, there are still many controversial topics which the media won't present one way or the other; the topics are still taboo. One such topic concerns us directly. Wealth determines who shall control access to mass media. This allows the very wealthy, through direct ownership, indirect influence or coercion to use the country's communication system for their own selfish purposes. Their power is completely independent of any democratic checks or balances. Nevertheless, the question of who and what should determine access to mass media is never examined. Instead, the phony issue of whether there is bias or not is given big play, for which the media can thank Spiro T. Agnew. President Johnson, himself a multimillionaire media owner, felt the future communication policy of the country was of vital importance to the country's survival. His task force submitted their very controversial recommendations calling for a change in the nation's domestic and international communication policy. Presidents Johnson and Nixon both suppressed this report. When it was finally published, the topic was ignored by the media.[38]

Each year magazine and newspaper owners receive millions of dollars worth of welfare money from the government through mail subsidies which help them distribute cheaply their establishment propaganda through the U.S. mail system. Big advertisers are also given millions of dollars of welfare to send out their "junk mail" advertisements through the postal service. The poor, however, pay the full 8 cents per 1 ounce rate to send their personal letters through the same mail system. The tobacco industry is given $150 million dollars a year of taxpayers' money to help them produce tobacco and advertise cigarettes.[39] Defense contractors are given millions of dollars in subsidies to help them manufacture supersonic fighter planes for foreign countries.[40] The United States Government gives eight times as much money to wealthy farmers and corporations not to grow crops as it gives to the millions of hungry Americans.[41] These welfare payments to the wealthy can justly be termed scandalous, but they have not been made into a real issue by the news media. Public utilities have often been caught overcharging their customers, but the public utilities issue is never presented in the news. The three networks have never done a documentary on this potentially explosive issue. Other big issues such as the high percentage of non-competitive bids for defense contracts and the attempt by oil companies to get the government to give away land rich in oil shales should be given a public hearing, but the media have only touched the subjects.

Many smaller issues also deserve to be controversial, but news media has ignored them completely. News commentators and reporters often have financial investments affected by news items which they are reporting, yet they don't have to inform their audience of the fact. Chet Huntley's interests in the cattle and broadcasting industries is only one example of how the news can be affected by such interests. CBS has millions of dollars invested in professional althletics. It is to their financial interest to encourage enthusiasm in professional athletics. But when CBS News has a five-minute sports item as a regular part of its *Saturday Evening News,* no mention is made of their financial interests in keeping its audience interested in professional sports. When the *Los Angeles Times* reports on the grape strike they don't have to inform their readers that the *Los Angeles Times'* owners stand to make larger profits if the movement to unionize farm labor fails. This blatant conflict of interest problem is never presented as a controversial issue.

Cigarette advertisements have been banned from the air waves. But it would have been more effective and consistent with ideals of free speech to merely require equal-time or space for anti-cigarette ads. Today, both cigarette and alcohol ads are permitted in magazines and newspapers without the requirement of equal-space for opposing health advertisements, yet this isn't treated as a controversial topic. Instead, the mass media act as if banning cigarette ads from the air waves solved the problem in a self-sacrificing manner.

Ralph Nader pointed out that approximately 10,000 people a year are accidently electrocuted in hospitals, but to avoid malpractice suits physicians cover up the deaths by attributing them to "cardiac arrests."[42] This deplorable situation is never touched as a controversial topic by the news media.

The Myth of a Free and Competitive Media

A major propaganda success of the communications industry is convincing the American people that there is a fierce competition among news agencies. There is a fierce competition all right, but it is to make a larger profit or audience, not to compete in the realm of ideas or concepts in news coverage and presentation. The American people have been convinced that they are getting their news and entertainment free of charge. This is also untrue. Henry Skornia reveals that in 1961 the FCC estimated that the average family was paying $45 a year more for products because of commercial sponsorship of radio and television. This mass media tax is a form of taxation without representation. Whether a family watches television or not, they have to pay an advertising tax of $12 for their yearly supply of cosmetics and toiletries.[43] If the cost of the television, repairs and electricity is added to the advertising tax, the total cost for *free* television comes to $183 per year.[44]

Conclusion

These myths about controversy, competition and free television, like those concerning objectivity and fairness, are myths used to persuade the public that what they are hearing or reading via the media is really news of the world instead of a very subjective, distorted, one-sided fabrication of reality designed to shape public attitudes into programmed channels that can be exploited for profit and power. The media owners will do anything to maintain these myths. They will spend millions to cover live a presidential trip or a moon shot or a sporting event. They may even search out a new controversial topic if it will help them maintain their myths and earn prestige. They will do anything to keep the public from realizing that the establishment dominates society through its direct and indirect control of the nation's communication system.

The Reader's Digest: The Biggest Myth of All

> There is one copy of the Digest which not only will never be thrown away but is actually framed. It belongs to an oil geologist, working in a part of the Venezuelan jungle inhabited by Motilone Indians. As he and his party were returning to camp, they were attacked, and an arrow struck him from behind. Since the Motilones used poison arrows, he was sure he was going to die. In camp he found that he was unscratched. The arrow had been embedded in a copy of The Reader's Digest which he had put in his hip pocket.
>
> *Reader's Digest,* February 1969

The *Reader's Digest* was the first mass-circulation magazine to use the word "syphilis." This was a courageous act for a mass-circulation magazine because up to 1936 the word had been taboo. The *Reader's Digest* was one of the few out of thousands of mass media agents to crusade from the very beginning against the hazards of smoking. The *Digest* was alone in the middle 1960's in crusading against the vast sums of money being spent to send a man to the moon. And what the *Reader's Digest* does is important as probably no other single publication so effectively shapes the attitudes of its readers—who number an estimated 80 million world wide. For millions who pay little attention to regular news media, the *Digest* serves as a capsule guide to what's going on in the world. Every doctor's office, supermarket check stand and drug store prominently features the *Digest* with its quickly and easily read articles. The *Digest* is important for another reason—it stands alone without competition; no other magazine of this type has even one percent of its 28 million paid monthly circulation. If the *Digest* has a one-sided bias in its selection of articles from 500 different magazines, then its 80 million readers in effect are being propagandized. On the other hand, if the *Digest* is earnestly trying its best to, select and present a cross section of viewpoints as expressed in the nation's magazines, it is indeed offering its readers a valuable service.

The *Digest* claims that this is what it is doing—acting as a representative digest of the tens of thousands of articles published monthly in the nation's many magazines. On close examination this claim turns out to be grossly misleading. George Bennett, a statistician, classified all *Digest* articles and found there are three kinds. One is a genuine reprint of an article first appearing in some other magazine. Another type used is the plant—an article written by or for the *Digest,* but planted in another magazine first so that when it later appears in the *Digest,* it looks like a genuine reprint. These articles are often given free to smaller magazines such as the *American Legion Magazine,* the *Kiwanis* or others like them. This is a method of extending *Digest* influence even beyond its own readers to include the readership of about sixty other magazines which accept plants. The third type of article is a *Reader's Digest* original—one that is written solely for or by the *Digest* and printed nowhere else. Bennett found that from 1939 to 1945 genuine reprints accounted for only 42 percent of *Digest* articles while *Digest* originals or plants accounted for 58 percent.[1] Since 1945 the *Digest* has become more and more fond of its own articles, and as a result about 70 percent of the articles in the 1960's were *Digest* originals or plants, and only 30 percent were genuine reprints.[2]

Another *Digest* claim is that through its selection of articles it presents both sides on controversial issues. This claim turns out to be even more false than the claim of being primarily a digest. From 1950 through 1969, the *Digest* presented 84 articles dealing with Vietnam. Of these, 81 supported the U.S. policy in Vietnam while three were neutral. During this time there was not one single article criticizing the U.S. Policy, although many congressmen, senators and retired generals had written many dissenting articles which appeared in various magazines. Typical of the tone of most *Digest* articles was one in February 1956 on:

THE BIGGEST LITTLE MAN IN ASIA

who, according to O. K. Armstrong, a favorite *Digest* writer, was President Diem, South Vietnam's notorious dictator who was eventually overthrown by his own people. The subtitle for the article said:

HE SHOWS THE WAY TO PEOPLE WHO

ARE DETERMINED TO BE FREE

The article, which had Diem fighting colonial exploitation and "Red" agression, ended by stating: "In the midst of the dark storms that threaten Asia, President Diem stands like a beacon of light, showing the way to a free people."[3] The *Digest* ended its 81 article crusade for the war in December 1969 by featuring its own editorial backing the establishment's policy plus an article by the press corps' most enthusiastic supporter of the Pentagon, Joseph Alsop. In his article titled

THE VIETCONG IS LOSING ITS GRIP,

Alsop asked the American people for more patience. *Reader's Digest's* own editors wrote 18 of the 84 articles on Vietnam. Of the *Digest's* stable of favorite writers on the topic, Alsop was featured three times, Hanson Baldwin six times and Richard Nixon three times, beginning with his 1964 article:

NEEDED IN VIETNAM: THE WILL TO WIN

Another characteristic of the *Digest*—important in our understanding of its effect on its worldwide readership—requires the following background information, upon which I base my opinion concerning the role of private U.S. corporations in the Latin American economy. Each year U.S. corporations take out from Latin America much more in profits than they invest. In 1968 more than a billion dollars, five times the amount invested, was repatriated to the United States. In addition, the rich raw materials of the region are exploited to give Americans, not Latins, a higher standard of living. Furthermore, large U.S. corporations through their political power have been the authors of a U.S. foreign policy that sanctions using foreign aid money (and the Marines, if necessary) to guarantee the survival of dictatorial governments who are sympathetic to U.S. corporate interests. Critics of U.S. corporate activity and foreign policy use these facts to argue that the people of Latin America suffer from being exploited by U.S. corporate investments and corporate influenced political power. Even the very conservative leaders of the Latin nations are now complaining that Latin America gives to the United States more than it receives.[4]

In 1969, President Nixon, a long time supporter of corporate economic and political policies in Latin America, admitted to Chile's Foreign Minister, Gabriel Valdes, that U.S. private investment in Latin America was a matter of business, not aid.[5] The exploitative character of U.S. corporate activities in Latin America is the reason that even loyal supporters in Peru, Chile and Bolivia, as well as the establishment's enemy in Cuba, have nationalized large oil and mineral holdings of U.S. corporations.

As we shall see, the *Reader's Digest* apparently wants to keep its readers from being exposed to critical viewpoints based on these facts. From 1950 through July 1969, the *Digest* selected 99 articles favorable to U.S. foreign policy and corporate activity in Latin America compared to only 2 unfavorable and 10 neutral articles.[6] One of the more memorable ones, in a historic sense, was the December 1950 article titled:

DO YOU KNOW WHAT'S HAPPENING
SOUTH OF THE BORDER?

The subtitle carried the answer:

A DECADE OF PHENOMENAL PROGRESS . . .
PROMISES BETTER DAYS AHEAD

The author was Michael Scully, a *Digest* favorite, whose 14 articles constituted almost a third of the 43 articles on Latin America selected by the *Digest* in the Fifties. Most of the articles favorable to the U.S. presence in Latin America dwelt on the great benefits that Latin Americans received as a result of U.S. corporate investments, missionary activity or foreign policy. The two articles unfavorable to U.S. activity were both critical of U.S. foreign policy, not U.S. corporations. This left U.S. corporations with an unblemished twenty-year record of humanitarian portrayal by the *Digest* during a time when many journals and small magazines had numerous articles criticizing U.S. corporate activities in Latin America.

From 1950 through 1959 the *Digest* sided with investor-owned electric power companies against the customer-owned power companies. It published 9 articles dealing with the issue; all 9 either praised the private power companies or attacked the customer-owned companies and government policies which made them possible. William Hard, one of the *Digest's* own editors, wrote 6 of the 9 articles on the subject. In the very same issues there were full page advertisements from the investor-owned companies (which cost $55,000 per page).All tolled, the *Digest* receives about a quarter of a million advertising dollars annually from the private power companies.[7] It's not necessary to subject *Digest* articles to any rigorous analysis to decide where their bias is on this issue. Albert L. Cole, while General Manager of the *Reader's Digest*, told the Edison Electric Institute in 1961: "We are on your side. We have shown this repeatedly by articles published in *Reader's Digest* over a period of many years."[8]

From 1945 through 1959 the *Digest* presented 9 articles criticizing the concept of socialized medicine while shutting out completely the other side of the debate. Reo Christenson, writing in the *Colombia Journalism Review*, noted that the *Digest* attacked Medicare three times, at the same time shutting out those supporting Medicare.[9] The *Digest* presents so one-sided a view of government activity in helping the unfortunate that Christenson was able to state in 1965:"In none of these categories was I able to find a single article since 1945 presenting welfare state activities or concepts in a generally favorable light."

The *Digest* has always looked favorably toward "hard working men"—that is, as long as they don't join a union. Christenson found that from 1952 to 1965 the *Digest* had 49 articles critical of the labor movement, 5 neutral and 8 favorable. An earlier study by John Bainbridge found 13 articles unfavorable to organized labor, many written by *Digest* editor Willim Hard, compared to only 3 favorable.[10]

Christenson also found 5 articles favorable to the House Un-American Activities Committee and other Congressional committees investigating radical organizations, but none pointing out the abuses and violations of rights by these committees. Not all Congressional investigations were supported by the *Digest*. They printed a March 1963 article saying there were too many government investigations, claiming they "harassed industry" and were costly to the public.

The *Digest's* attitude as revealed by its treatment of controversial issues also expresses itself as conservative and ultra-conservative in the political arena, even though the *Digest* claims to be non-partisan. Christenson found that during President Truman's last four years there were 14 articles favorable to his administration compared to 44 which were critical. Bainbridge found earlier that articles critical of Franklin D. Roosevelt and his administration outnumbered those favorable by a 3 to 1 ratio.

While the *Digest* kept its readers aware of the hazards of smoking and had the courage to deal with syphilis before anyone else, it published only one article on hunger in America from 1945 through 1969, and this was not until November 1968.

The *Digest* has consistently through the years warned of the threat that labor unions pose to democratic processes. However, from 1960 through 1969 not one article appeared pointing out the danger posed to democratic processes by the military-industrial complex even though President Eisenhower had made it the subject of his farewell address to the nation in 1960. During this ten years there was not one single article drawing attention to military waste or the excessive stockpiling of nuclear arms.

From 1940 through 1959, there were many articles about automobile accidents and safety, but not one of them mentioned car design as a factor in causing accidents or making accidents less serious for the victims. In the 1960's there was mention of the need for seat belts, but no mention was made of auto manufacturers' lack of enthusiasm in designing safe cars. Typical of the *Digest* attitude toward the controversy was a September 1965 article titled:

HOW GOOD ARE AMERICAN CARS?

The subtitle read
THEY'RE AMONG THE BEST BUYS

IN THE WORLD TODAY

An April 1964 article asked
: WHAT ARE THE REAL CAUSES

OF AUTO CRASHES?

The answers were mechanical failure due to lack of maintenance, inadequate driving skills and poor highway environment. Mechanical failure due to poor automotive engineering or construction was not mentioned. The article did mention that at least half of those killed could have been saved if they had used seat belts, but there was no mention or complaint about the fact that the automobile manufacturers were not including seat belts as mandatory equipment in all new cars and had opposed legislation that would require them to do so. It wasn't until August 1966, more than two years after the *Digest* reprint, that Congress finally passed a law requiring seat belts as mandatory equipment in all automobiles.

A February 1964 article ended with the conclusion: "Today's cars are the safest we have ever had." That may have been true, but it wasn't saying much because the 1964 cars were still without the many life-saving safety features that critics had been suggesting for more than 25 years. As one engineer prominent in automobile crash research said in early 1965, "One has only to examine the current model automobiles to find many flagrant examples of complete disregard for the most rudimentary principles of safety design."[11]

The *Digest* didn't flinch when it came to exposing prison conditions from 1945 to 1959. However, the way in which the articles were written would tend to convince the reader that though the situation was deplorable, good men were in charge and something significant was being done to improve the prison system and its approach to rehabilitation—a very misleading idea since treatment of prisoners in United States prisons was and still is deplorable. There were 9 articles focusing on courageous prison reformers who had worked miracles. There were only two articles which exposed conditions and at the same time revealed that nothing much was being done. In my view, based on my research for this book, this is a standard technique used by the mass media when handling a controversial topic. The situation is painted in the blackest of terms with no holds barred, and then the article concludes by giving the impression that good intentioned men are in charge and progress is being made—so there's no sense in getting aroused or pushing for radical change.

The *Digest's* dedication to the establishment is also revealed in the way they treat establishment leaders and their corporations. Warren Boroson found that the March 1965 reprint of an *Esquire* magazine article on American gasolines omitted the sections exposing deceptive advertising gimmicks.[12] *Digest* protection of big business was also shown in its coverage of the issue of pollution. Back in 1962 the mass media were still able to keep pollution from being a big issue. It was even fashionable to question whether people like Rachel Carson, author of *Silent Spring*, were loyal Americans or were doing the country any good by exposing major polluters and embarrassing the pesticide industry. Boroson notes that the *Digest* selected an article from *Time* dealing with the charges in Carson's book. The reprint was featured in December 1963 with the title:

ARE WE POISONING OURSELVES WITH PESTICIDES?

The subtitle established the tone of the article by stating:

HERE ARE THE REASONS WHY MANY
SCIENTISTS DISAGREE WITH THE AUTHOR

The article concluded by claiming that, "many scientists . . . fear that her emotional outburst in *Silent Spring* may do more harm than good."

Advertisers spend $60 million each year to advertise in the *Digest*. This must affect the *Digest's* selection and editing of articles. The titles of many *Digest* articles appear to read like advertisements for establishment concerns. A few of these are: FROM HENRY TO EDSEL TO HENRY, HOWARD JOHNSON—HOST OF THE HIGHWAYS, UNITED FRUIT'S INTERNATIONAL PARTNERS, BANKS THAT BUILD NEW BUSINESSES, STEEL—OLD GIANT WITH NEW TRICKS, HEAVENLY WAY TO RUN A RAILROAD, and HOME SWEET ELECTRIC HOME.

The *Digest* permits advertisers to use the exact same layout, print, and style as regular *Digest* articles. This makes it hard to tell the difference between an advertisement and a real article (and reading the ads often won't help because the message of ads and articles is often the same). To discourage deceptive advertising, the Federal Trade Commission requires magazines to place the word "advertisement" on ad copy that could be confused with editorial matter so that the reader may have a way of telling the difference between the two. In November 1967, the *Digest* published a $240,000 advertisement from the Pharmaceutical Manufacturers Association. It was an eight-page section composed of four different article-like editorials glorifying the drug firms and attacking the practice of buying drugs—at a considerable savings—under their generic names. The first page had in small type the words "special advertising section." There were then seven pages and three more advertisement articles with no identification as advertisements. On the last page was the notice: "First in a series published as a public service by the Pharmaceutical Manufacturers Association." Wisconsin's Senator Gaylord Nelson, a critic of practices that sustain the high cost of drugs, described this and other advertising practices of the *Digest* as "calculated deception."[13]

One of the *Digest's* most arrogant acts in defense of its advertisers and the advertising ethic was its censorship, through its own publishing company, Funk and Wagnalls, of Samm Baker's book, *The Permissible Lie: The Inside Truth About Advertising*. Robert Shayon notes that after this setback, Baker bought the rights from the *Digest*-owned Funk and Wagnalls Publishers and sold them to World Publishing Company, a Times-Mirror subsidiary who promised full-page ads

which were to state: THE BOOK THAT *READER'S DIGEST* SUP-
PRESSED. World later decided this would be in "bad taste" and left
it out of their ads. Baker also claims that World failed to spend the
full agreed-upon advertising budget to promote his book. The *Digest*
found other companions in its effort to shackle the book. While Baker
received many TV and radio interviews in Europe, "Today," "To-
night" and the "Merv Griffin" show turned down repeated requests
for the author to discuss his book on their shows. Baker, a retired
advertising man with thirty years experience on Madison Avenue and
eighteen books to his credit, commented that he ". . . hadn't realized
the prevalence and overriding power of censorship by conglomerate
communications interests"

The *Digest*, in an obvious effort to avoid the need to censor any
future books, promised to exercise control over all future Funk and
Wagnalls manuscripts.[14]

An extra bonus for the establishment leaders occurs when the *Digest*
decides to honor them as highly respectable individuals. Bainbridge
found an average of 2 articles a year on Henry Ford. One pictured the
industrialist in most saintly terms by asking in a title: "ARE GAN-
DHI AND FORD ON THE SAME ROAD?" In the 1960's the *Digest*
still sees the leaders as great benefactors: "JOHN D. ROCKEFELLER
JR.'S GREATEST GIFT" was featured in September 1960. To round
out the decade ten years later in December 1969 was an article titled:
"WHY I BELIEVE IN PHILANTHROPY," written by John D. Rockefeller III. (Those reading the *Digest* might find it rather difficult to
reconcile these portraits with the hatred that millions of Latin Americans feel toward Nelson Rockefeller and what he represents.)

Since 1961, the *Digest* has had a "Press-Section." It's the first feature readers come across as they turn the pages. This section includes
various editorials from newspapers representing the entire spectrum
of the mass media press. The balanced selection of newspapers serves
as a cover for the selection of editorials with a bias favoring *Digest*
interests and values. It is an easy task to find among any newspaper's
editorials one or two that express the viewpoint of the *Digest*.

The *Digest* has condensed many great books over the years, but it is
careful not to reprint any books that attack its own special interests or
ultraconservative values. Some of the books the *Digest* runs have been
denounced by responsible reviews. The *Nation* magazine pointed out
that the *New York Times* denounced the right-wing book, *The Road
Ahead*. The *Times* saw the book as significant because it was one of:

". . . the latest and most extreme manifestations of endemic hysteria presently affecting a considerable segment of our society."[15] Apparently the *Digest* editors did not mind the possibility that this right wing hysteria might spread; when they introduced the book they printed only that part of the *Times* review that said it was one of the two "most important books about the contemporary American scene that we will have this year." The readers were left unaware that the *Times* thought it important only because they considered it a noteworthy example of hysteria.

The *Digest* apparently isn't satisfied with propagandizing its readers by selecting articles to favor its own views by 80 to 1, 20 to 1, 5 to 1, or 3 to 1 margins. Many of the articles it writes or selects contain flagrant errors. The Area Development Administration found twenty different instances where "IS THIS THE WAY TO FIGHT THE WAR AGAINST POVERTY?" was misleading or factually inaccurate. The article was written by a member of the *Digest* staff. Boroson also notes that another staff writer, James Daniel, wrote an article about unemployment that caused the director of the Bureau of Labor Statistics to reply: "I cannot recall having read a short article in which so many inaccurate statements were presented in support of such unwarranted conclusion."[16]

The *Digest* does not have to write all their misleading or factually inaccurate articles, for there are plenty to choose from—some of them by Congressmen. Representative Frank T. Bow's "THE GREAT MANPOWER GRAB" claimed that the U.S. Employment Service was undermining the people's right to choose the kind of work they want. After analyzing this article Reo Christenson stated:

> The author is able to provide no evidence whatever that the U.S.E.S. or anyone else had such a goal in mind, except that the service is helping many high school students about careers. . . . The *Digest* did not inform its readers that Representative Bow has close relations with private employment agencies, which have a special interest in restricting the U.S.E.S.[17]

Inaccurate articles plus the *Digest's* ultraconservative bias and Republican partisanship have not passed unnoticed by politicians:

> The *Digest* has been lambasted by President Truman for printing 'a pack of lies,' by Sen. Mike Mansfield for being 'irresponsible,' by Sen. Joseph Guffey for being 'a tool and toy of a power-crazed publisher,' by Rep. Elmer J. Holland for its 'hit-and-run-journalism,'

and by Rep. Emanuel Celler for refusing to print 'the views of the underdog, or that of minority groups.'[18]

Digest readers are unaware of widespread criticism of the *Digest* because its editors use one of the oldest propaganda techniques in the trade to convince its readers it is responsible, fair and infallible. The *Digest* steadfastly refuses to print any rebuttals or make retractions or corrections no matter how biased the article or glaring the inaccuracies. This technique has been so successful that even the *Digest's* most learned readers have been fooled. Teachers order 500,000 copies a month for use in American classrooms. If teachers used the magazine to help students learn techniques of implanting hidden bias the practice could be justified. But the *Digest* is seldom used for that purpose. It is used by teachers who don't warn students that the *Digest* is a masterpiece of deceit.

The American Education Fellowship Conference for Parents and Teachers made an attempt in 1947 to alert teachers about *Digest* deceit. They adopted a resolution calling the attention of teachers to the fact that ". . . the *Reader's Digest* carries the implication that it is unbiased and comprehensive in its selection when it is in fact otherwise." Teachers would have been lucky indeed if they found out about this warning. The *New York Times* placed this announcement in one small paragraph near the bottom of an article on Page 64 whose headline,

WIDER RECOGNITION OF SCHOOLS URGED,

carried no hint of the *Digest* condemnation buried below.[19]

Despite false *Digest* claims, the critics must admit the *Digest* is a vital magazine. Each issue contains fascinating tidbits, interesting episodes, informative articles and beautiful advertisements. It is a pleasant experience for the reader; nothing difficult is required of him. He does not have to edit, arrange, select, balance or deliberate on what is happening in the United States and the world—it is all done for him through the painless vehicle of entertaining selections. But the reader and society pay a price for being entertained and informed by the *Digest*. They receive and assimilate, unaware, a bias which gives them a view of the world that is so distorted it limits the alternatives they must consider in meeting their challenges. There is no opposite bias in mass media to compete, expose or balance *Digest* bias. No regulations exist requiring the *Digest* to give equal treatment to competing ideas, perspectives and selections. The result is that over fifteen million *Di-*

gest buyers in the United States are excluded—to the extent they depend on or believe the *Digest*—from taking part in deciding what is true from among competing interpretations and information. The *Digest* bias has decided what is true for them.

18 According to the Mass Media It's Not Crime

> A disturbing number of newspapers today see nothing wrong in publicly stating that they conceive their highest duty to be that of fitting themselves into the life of the community. This means, of course, that if a community is governed by a corrupt and corrupting group, the paper will fit in with it.
>
> Ralph McGill, 1965
> Publisher, Atlanta Constitution

Through the mass media the establishment has convinced itself and the majority of Americans that the large corporations act in a responsible and patriotic manner. But the facts indicate that they act first and foremost to increase profits no matter what the consequences are to individuals or to the nation. In response to a questionnaire, half of 1,300 men in top and middle management positions agreed that American businessmen are concerned chiefly with gain and tend to ignore ethical considerations. Four out of five agreed that their own industry accepted such practices as "lavish entertainment to seek favors; kickbacks to customer's purchasing agents; price fixing and misleading advertising."[1]

It is impossible to guess at the total amount of money that corporations steal from Americans and their government, but the amount is without doubt many times the property loss caused by individual and organized crime combined. Some ideas of the great sums involved can be imagined by considering the cases in which some corporations were convicted. Twenty-nine top electrical corporations and thirty-one of their officers were convicted in 1961 of illegally rigging bids, fixing prices and dividing markets for electrical equipment valued at $1.75 billion annually. In another case a Federal court convicted eight of the largest steel companies for fixing the price of carbon sheet steel which alone accounted for annual sales of $3.6 billion. Bell Telephone Company was forced to pay back to California phone users $80 million in overcharges collected between 1962 and 1965. Ten U.S. firms doing business with the U.S. Government in Vietnam doubled their money by illegal operations in Vietnam's black market. Three major drug manufacturers were convicted of price fixing which resulted in customers paying as much as 51 cents apiece for capsules that cost less than two cents to produce. These firms were among the five drug companies that, in order to avoid a trial, agreed to pay back $120 million compensation to groups and individuals who had payed the exorbitant rigged prices for antibiotics.

H. L. Nieburg notes that Boeing overcharged $23 million for its work in the Bomarc missile program. Bethlehem Steel overcharged $5 million for construction of a nuclear frigate. Westinghouse added $1.5 million of "unwarranted" cost for a job on the USS Enterprise.[2] Nieburg notes that it wasn't until after the companies had been caught that they tried to square accounts with the government. But since the government checks only about five percent of such contracts, the overcharge on the other 95 percent of the contracts is kept in company tills. From a Government Accounting Office investigation in 1965 of just 5 percent of contracts, $60 million in overcharges were discovered.[3] Representative Henry B. Gonzales disclosed that investigation of war profiteering from the Vietnam war found that fourteen defense contractors were responsible for 35 of the 88 overcharge cases during the last three years. The discovery by the GAO resulted in the companies being ordered to turn back $29 million to the government.

Corporations are required to share the benefits of inventions made under publicly financed research projects so that the government gets its money's worth and other companies are not put at a disadvantage in competing for contracts. Many corporations illegally avoid this obligation. The GAO reported that "Lockheed failed to disclose fifty-eight inventions that had been made under defense contracts during a two-year period; Thompson-Ramo-Wooldridge subsidiaries failed to disclose some eighteen inventions over a three and a half year period."[4] In another case Westinghouse charged the American public one million dollars for a technical data package, the rights to which had previously been acquired by the government under a defense contract.[5] Withholding such information is not only illegal, it hampers the nation's efforts to produce the best possible weapons at the cheapest possible prices.

There are more than 30,000 tax-free foundations in the United States worth an estimated total of $25 billion or more. Supposedly organized to promote educational, scientific, religious and charitable causes, they are primarily used by the rich to avoid paying income and inheritance taxes they might otherwise have to pay. Many think the nation would be better off if these foundations, even the best of them, were phased out of existence. The profits of the very rich could then be taxed and spent to finance non-profit publicly supported groups not under the absolute control of the very wealthy. It would place important priority decisions under democratic control and result in an overall total savings to the government. These establishment-controlled foundations make billions of dollars of profit by investing in stocks. Since the profit is tax-free they can easily afford to give some of it away for charitable causes and still come out better than they would have had they been required to pay taxes. Even though foundations are forbidden by law from retaining an enormous percentage of their profits, about half of the profits they do garner are retained and reinvested in order to gain more income, power and political influence for the controlling family. The Ford Foundation itself had retained $432,916,492 through 1960.[6] The Houston Endowment Charitable Fund, owner of the very conservative *Houston Chronicle,* had an income of $97 million from 1951 to 1964, but gave only $19 million to charities.[7] Other foundations don't even try to cover up their main purpose. An Associated Press survey in November 1969, showed that oil companies avoid $100 million in taxes each year by contributing to foundations which give little or nothing to charity.

It is a crime against the environment and the American people for corporations to pollute the waters and air of America. It is also a violation of the Federal standards established by the air quality act and the seventy-one year old Federal anti-water pollution law. Yet neither the mass media or the government decided to expose polluters and their criminal acts until they were forced to do so when ecology became a big issue in 1970.

The mass media seldom if ever touches on another aspect of establishment crime becasue it links legitimate business with organized crime.

Many industrialists and businessmen promote organized crime by seeking cheap blackmarket foreign laborers from the Cosa Nostra instead of from unions. One business paid the Cosa Nostra $5,000 to guarantee a non-union shop.[8] To avoid strikes or pickets, businesses will pay Cosa Nostra-controlled unions to sell out the workers by sacrificing wage and safety demands. The vice president of Spartan

Industries, operator of a chain of discount stores, sought out the aid of Cosa Nostra leaders to help him solve his labor problems.[9] Newspaper owners, not wanting to expose some of their social and country club companions, have purposely used their media power to keep the public unaware of business's participation in organized crime.

Donald Cressey, in his book *Theft of the Nation,* is very critical of mass media's coverage of organized crime. He claims that it focuses on gangland killings and famous big-name "underground" crime tzars while ignoring the close link between organized crime and legitimate business.[10] He suggests that the operation of organized crime should never be referred to as the operations of the "underworld" because,

> . . . the activities of Cosa Nostra members are so interwoven with the activities of respectable businessmen and government officials that doing so directs our attention to the wrong places.[11]

Very important in concealing the price that citizens, government and society pay for the various forms of establishment crime is the quantitative bias in mass media's coverage of crime. Although organized crime itself is covered less than adequately, still it gets more attention than establishment crime even though trifling amounts are involved compared to the enormous amounts involved in crime by corporations and charities with their price fixing, overcharging and illegally retaining foundation profits. Even though individual and mob crimes rob people of money and destroy property, the amounts involved are small compared to the billions stolen through established crime. And even though the violence and death caused by individual crime affects thousands, it is on a smaller scale than the silent and unseen violence inflicted on Americans by the illegal disposal of poisonous pollutants, poor auto safety design, uninspected meat, contaminated food, overuse of pesticides, misleading advertisements and violations of work-safety standards. Perhaps most important of all is the role played by establishment crime in undermining youth's belief in America. How can youth be convinced to act honestly and legally if many of those held up by media as society's idols are society's biggest thieves?

An analysis of which types of crimes and criminals are featured—and therefore brought to the public's attention—reveals distorted news priorities which must greatly please the establishment criminals. It also explains why the people don't clamor for something to be done to

put a stop to certain types of crimes and criminals, while on the other
hand they are willing to take urgent and drastic action to combat
individual crime. [See Tables XIV and XV]

The three newspapers studied featured individual crimes three
times as often as establishment crimes, and two times as often as
organized crime. If local crimes were included, the proportion would
be many times greater. The most distorted picture of crime was presented by *Huntley-Brinkley* and *Walter Cronkite* newscasts which alloted a total of 42:42 minutes for coverage of individual crime as
compared to only 2:45 for coverage of establishment crime. The two
network on-the-hour radio newscasts alloted no time at all for coverage of establishment crime.

The reason for this neglect isn't because there are few establish-
ment-type crimes being committed. Each day there are hundreds of
cases involving price-fixing, restraint of trade, mislabeling, false advertisements, removal of law-required markings, false weighing and
measurement, and various other violations both sensational and common place, violent and harmless. They are documented and frequently
made available to the news media by the Federal Trade Commission,
the Food and Drug Administration, The U.S. Securities and Exchange
Commission, the National Labor Relations Board, the Federal Communications Commission, the Federal Power Commission, the Interstate Commerce Commission and other federal agencies. The main
reason for news media's neglect of establishment crime is obvious; it
tends to make the public think establishment crime is insignificant.
The public is forced to focus its attention on individual crime, and
sometimes the Cosa Nostra while the criminal corporations rob individual Americans and the public treasury of billions of dollars each
year.

When the news media and the President talk about combating
crime, they don't mention establishment crime and the public doesn't
notice the omission. But if there were competing media owners who
crusaded against establishment crime by continually featuring the
criminal acts and the cost to the public pocketbook and health, politicians would address their attention to the problem and make the topic
a campaign issue. Instead of treating those who are responsible for
establishment crime as criminals, news media treats them as venerable
pillars of society and the free enterprise system. There is no demand
here that all establishment criminals be caught and duly punished

TABLE XIV

FRONT PAGE NEWS COVERAGE CF DIFFERENT TYPE OF CRIME

(items of national significance)

NEWSPAPER AND MONTHS	Individual Crime		Organized Crime		Establishment Crime	
	Items p.1	Photos pp.1,2,3	Items p.1	Photos pp.1,2,3	Items p.1	Photos pp.1,2,3
February and March 1950						
Los Angeles Times	10	17	2	0	4	0
New York Times	5	0	1	0	2	0
April and May 1960						
Los Angeles Times	8	8	0	0	0	0
New York Times	7	1	0	0	4	0
June and July 1969						
Los Angeles Times	10	6	1	2	2	0
New York Times	6	0	15	3	1	0
January 12 – May 31 1969						
Honolulu Star-Bulletin (first three pages)	21	4	6	0	2	0
TOTAL	67	39	25	5	15	0

TABLE XV
TELEVISION AND RADIO NETWORK NEWSCAST COVERAGE OF DIFFERENT TYPES OF CRIME

NEWSCAST	Individual Crime		Organized Crime		Establishment Crime	
	Items	Time	Items	Time	Items	Time
September 26 – November 7, 1960						
ABC-TV, *John Daly*	4		0		4	
NBC-TV, *Huntley-Brinkley*	8		0		6	
CBS-TV, *Douglas Edwards*	2		0		1	
ABC-Radio, *Edward P. Morgan*	2		1		1	
NBC-Radio, *Peter Hackes*	10		4		1	
CBS-Radio, *Lowell Thomas*	7		0		1	
TOTALS	33		5		14	
July 10 – September 10, 1969						
NBC-TV, *Huntley-Brinkley*	21	19:16	6	2:13	3	:56
CBS-TV, *Walter Cronkite*	27	23:26	6	5:49	4	1:49
TOTALS	48	42:42	12	8:02	7	2:45
August 22 – October 22, 1969						
Mutual-Radio, *On-The-Hour*						
7:00 AM, PST	2	:22	3	:55	0	0
ABC-Radio, *On-The-Hour*						
9:00 AM, PST	3	:51	6	3:18	0	0
TOTALS	5	1:13	9	4:13	0	0

even though some corporations have been convicted of criminal violations repeatedly, and still continue to operate with relative impunity. General Electric and Westinghouse have more than once been convicted of various antitrust violations and yet little or nothing is done about it. The problem here is compounded by the fact that the companies are permitted to own broadcasting stations. Back to our main point, there were no demands by the mass media to put in jail the network executives and program producers responsible for rigging quiz shows. There were no demands to put in jail the 297 disc jockeys who illegally took payoffs to play records.[12]

This power to focus the public's attention on individual crime and away from serious and widespread establishment crime is almost as flagrantly used as the power to hide from the public the means by which the establishment controls the government. It is illegal bribery to give a congressman money to vote one way or the other. To get around this roadblock, the establishment bestows on congressmen many different types of legalized bribery in return for their influence and support: loans can be arranged, campaign contributions are given, vacations are paid for, expensive gifts are given. Corporations pay high legal fees to a congressman's law firm whether or not the firm does much legal work for them. Bankers give stock tips. Plane trips across the nation are arranged in private corporation planes. High lecture fees are given whether the congressman is much of a speaker or not. Credit cards are given to congressmen, but the monthly bill is paid for by a wealthly special interest group. If a congressman throws a big gala birthday party, a corporation often picks up the tab.

One of the most powerful forms of bribery is preferential treatment by the home town radio and television station. Interviews or a "report from Congress" can be arranged, and neither will require equal time by an opposing candidate or those advocating opposing viewpoints. At least 60 percent of all congressmen make such television reports that are shown "as a public service." This is only one of the many forms of legalized bribery used by station owners in their efforts to maintain the present commercial communication system as it is. The job isn't too difficult. To begin with, many in Congress are willing supporters of the present communication system because of their own financial interests in broadcasting. At least twenty-four congressmen have significant holdings in radio or television stations.[13] No forms of legalized bribery are needed to persuade them how to vote on matters affecting the communication industry. Others, because of their vast wealth, tend to support a communication system that sells access and control because they can afford to buy it. An Associated Press survey revealed at least 20 millionaires among the 100 Senators.[14] Other congressmen respond to various forms of legalized bribery handed out by the National Association of Broadcasters which represents over 3600 station owners. To insure the present communication system against any reforms that would take away their power to make news decisions and profits, the Association has set up a $2.6 million office building in Washington D. C. They employ a staff of eighty to make sure the right congressmen get the proper treatment. In addition, broadcasters have retained the law firms of about half of all congressmen to represent them.[15] It's very unlikely such congressmen are going to act contrary to their client's will.

Legalized bribery from the NAB has paid great dividends, so great it's almost embarrassing. Senator John Pastore introduced a bill enthusiastically supported by the NAB. It was designed to give station owners their franchise to use the public airwaves in perpetuity no matter how badly they abuse the public interest. Twenty Senators signed as co-sponsors of the bill. The House rushed in to show the NAB its support by introducing eighty different bills to serve the same purpose. Another piece of legislation greatly troubled the NAB—it dealt with commercials. Between 1964 and 1968 the number of commercials in network prime time had increased 50 percent from an average of 1990 to 3022 per month.[16] In addition, many smaller stations openly allow more time for commercials than NAB's own code allows. Concerned about this trend, the FCC tried to limit the number of commercials. The House responded by voting 317 to 43 to take this power to limit commercials away from the FCC. The willingness of those congressmen who are not station owners to go along with the NAB prompted one Washington communications expert to comment: "Owners or not, it doesn't make a bit of differnce, they're all in the broadcaster's pockets anyway."[17]

Organized crime has learned from the establishment how to influence congressmen in a legal way. Besides outright bribery given to judges and public officials, it has adopted all the legal forms of bribery for the purpose of "influencing legislation on matters ranging from food services, garbage collection to invasions of privacy. . . ."[18] This influence can't be purchased cheaply. One analyst estimates that organized crime contributes 15 percent of the costs of local and state political campaigns.[19] The combination of illegal plus legal bribery has been such an effective combination that, according to Cressey, "They own several state legislators and federal congressmen and other officials in the legislative, executive and judicial branches of government at the local, state, and federal levels."[20] The results injure democracy. Cressey states: "The residents of some political wards no longer have an effective vote—their government officials represent criminals rather than law abiding voters."[21]

Organized crime is not alone in combining legal and illegal bribery. Many establishment bribes are on the borderline of legality, and some are clearly illegal. It is a violation of the law for a person to give, or for a congressman or official to receive, any money for favors done for any constituents or interested parties. Drew Pearson revealed a borderline case in which Richard Nixon wrote the American Ambassador in Cuba asking that he intervene on behalf of his friend Dana Smith to save him from a law suit. Smith had lost $4,000 on a gambling spree in Havana. He wrote a check for the amount and then stopped payment on the check. At another time Richard Nixon tried to use his influence with the Justice Department to help Smith in a tax case. Dana Smith, incidentally, had collected the $18,000 Nixon fund, the revelation of which imperiled Nixon's career in 1952.[22]

Many of the gifts given to Senator Thomas Dodd were obviously gifts that were in payment for services rendered. WALB in Georgia gave Representative Eugene Cox $2,500 to help it get a broadcasting license.[23] Despite these and many more obvious cases of illegal bribes and the thousands of borderline cases, no congressmen or their bribers are ever arrested or put in jail. If that happened there wouldn't be enough congressmen left to continue to operate the political system that forces politicians, many of them dedicated and honest men, to sometimes accept bribes of one sort or another in order to be nominated and elected. Senator Russell Long explained the effect of this system on even the best of men:

> I have seen men start out running for governor with the firm intention of promising nothing. Coming down the stretch, I have seen them making commitments that it made me sick to see. They did it because they could not pay for radio and television. Their sign boards were taken down, and the only way they could cross that finish line and make a respectable showing was to make promises

that they did not want to make, such as promising the highway contractors who the contract would be given to; promising the insurance companies as to who the insurance commissioner would be[24]

Of course politicians will never admit they are voting or acting in a certain way because of legalized bribes they accepted, but it would be obvious to even the most naive that these payments have considerable influence on what happens in Congress. It is therefore necessary to conceal or camouflage legalized bribery to save the system.

This is where the mass media play their biggest part. They have more than just one reason for covering up legalized bribery. Besides getting their politicians elected, they end up receiving the lion's share of the money given to candidates by contributors. Some $59 million was spent for political advertising in broadcasting alone in 1968, and the amount increases sharply every year.[25]

The news media will usually bury news items revealing the more blatant cases of legalized bribery. But many resort to outright censorship. In 1952, a group of very wealthy millionaire oilmen, defense contractors and real estate executives gave Richard Nixon $18,000 to help him pay his expenses as a congressman. This story was one of the ten top news stories of the year as selected by newspaper editors—certainly a front page news item. However, a check by Jean Begeman revealed that only 7 out of 70 newspapers in forty-eight different states chose to print the story on the front page the first chance they had. Out of the 7, two printed the vindication story without reference to the original story. All 5 of the Los Angeles dailies kept the story on the inside pages during the first two days. The *Los Angeles Times* named John J. Garland as one of the contributors but didn't bother to inform its readers that he was the brother-in-law of Norman Chandler, publisher of the *Times*.[26]

As previously noted, 35 out of the 36 newspapers studied by Edward Rowse used hidden bias to conceal two different cases of legalized bribery, one concerning the Nixon fund story and the other concerning a smaller fund for Adlai Stevenson.[27] An example of how the news owners defended their favorite politicians becomes clear when we compare the creation of headlines by two different papers, one favoring Richard Nixon and the other Adlai Stevenson. During the story and its followup, the *Los Angeles Times* featured these headlines:

EXPENSE FUND FOR NIXON
EXPLAINED BY FRIENDS

ATTACKS LEVELED AT NIXON DENOUNCED

NIXON'S DEFIANCE OF SMEAR HAILED (with the subhead:)
Crowd Roars Approval As He Warns Fight
To Rout Reds Will Go On

NIXON BLASTS 'BIG LIE' ON EXPENSE FUND

NIXON HERE TO TELL U.S. OF FINANCES

WE STAND BY NIXON

IKE PRAISES NIXON'S COURAGEOUS SPEECH

DOCUMENTS SHOW NIXON BLAMELESS

HOW TO DIRECT MESSAGES TO GOP CHIEFS

GREAT RECEPTION GIVEN NIXON

The headline creators at the *New York Post* (supporter of Stevenson)
saw the affair in a different light:

SECRET NIXON FUND

SECRET RICH MEN'S TRUST FUND KEEPS
NIXON IN STYLE FAR BEYOND HIS SALARY

DICK'S OWN WELFARE STATE

IKE ASKS NIXON BUT — I'M TRYING TO PHONE HIM

GOP BACKS NIXON

TAX MEN PROBING NIXON

IKE TAKES DICK NIXON UNTO HIMSELF,
AND A NEW GOP STAR IS BORN

THE NIXON FAMILY BUDGET:
A CASE OF GOP 'ECONOMY'

NIXON SINNED, DIDN'T REPORT, KERR CHARGES

POOR RICHAD'S ALMANAC

THE STORY OF 'POOR RICHARD' NIXON

Richard Nixon appeared to be in some trouble again—this time
concerning a $205,000 loan given to Nixon's brother Donald by How-
ard Hughes. The loan was secured by a mortgage on a small lot in
Whittier. The property was worth $4000 in 1923 and probably much
less than $60,000 at the time of the loan. Since the loan was never
repaid, the lot became the property of the Hughes Tool Company. At

the time of the loan the Hughes Tool Company was faced with an antitrust suit. The antitrust suit was later dropped. Soon after, Hughes' TWA airline was granted a new air route. The Justice Department denied that the loan to Donald Nixon was linked with the dropping of the antitrust suit. Drew Pearson in his disclosure of the facts didn't claim a direct link between the loan and the favorable treatment of Hughes; he merely raised the question of a possible conflict of interest. Donald Nixon denied his brother had anything to do with it, but one of his accountants said that Richard Nixon was secretly kept aware of the entire transaction. The loan story first appeared in "Washington Merry-Go-Round" on October 25, 1960. It was certainly an important news item whether or not the facts as disclosed by Pearson were true. If true, they indicated at least the possibility of conflict of interest worth further investigation. If false, the story should still have been featured and then rebutted to clear the air and expose the falsehoods.

Media owners came to Nixon's defense immediately. A group of editors found that 40 out of 43 New England daily newspapers that normally ran Pearson's syndicated column chose to censor it that day. They of course left no blank space in its place so that the readers would know about the deletion. The next day the AP and UP sent out a news release on the story which included Robert Finch's denial that the loan came from Hughes. He called the claim "absolute nonsense, another smear." The editors found that 19 of the 43 newspapers also censored these wire service reports. The next day Pearson had a follow-up story in his syndicated column charging that the Nixons had tried to keep the loan a secret and to avoid paying taxes on the profit from the sale of the property at $205,000—a capital gains tax of $50,250 adjusted in connection with the $4,000 originally paid for the property. This time 42 out of 43 newpapers that normally carried his column suppressed it. On the 30th, Donald Nixon admitted the loan was from the Hughes Tool Company, and Robert Finch admitted he had been "misinformed" when he had made his previous denial. Most revealing of all was that 21 newspapers who carried Finch's first denial refused to carry the AP story in which Finch admitted the loan was from Hughes.[28]

The 15 minute network television and radio newscasts also aided Nixon by suppressing the item. CBS's Douglas Edwards mentioned Pearson's charges and Finch's denial, but failed to mention Finch's later admission. *Huntley-Brinkley* passed up the story for five days before covering it on November 1st. ABC-TV's evening newscast made no mention whatsoever of the whole affair. Out of the eight 15-minute network radio newscasts checked, seven made no mention of the affair.[29] The *Los Angeles Times'* traditional public relations-type coverage of Richard Nixon was revealed in the creation of headlines:

CHARGE ON DON NIXON LOAN BRANDED SMEAR

PEARSON CHARGE DENIED
BY JUSTICE DEPARTMENT

DONALD NIXON TELLS OF
LOAN TO SAVE BUSINESS

DON NIXON LOAN CHARGE HELD ABSURD

In view of the fact that Pearson's account of the loan was proven correct, the *Times* headline writer could have qualified as campaign manager for Richard Nixon.

Senator Thomas Dodd accepted legalized bribes from almost every conservative special interest group in Washington. His activities on behalf of his benefactors were so flagrant that his own office aides felt these dealings should be exposed. Mike O'Hare was the chief witness in revealing Dodd's wrong-doings, and yet after the case broke, Robert Yoakum found that not one single wire service reporter bothered to interview O'Hare. The other ex-employees were interviewed only once by AP and the results never appeared in print. The *New York Times* headlined a UPI story,

PROBE CLEARED DODD ON TRIPS TO EUROPE

when, as Yoakum points out, it didn't clear him at all.[30] Yoakum notes that one of the reasons Dodd got such good press coverage was because he had previously sabotaged his own committee's investigation of NBC's and Metromedias' programming of violence on television.[31] The UPI felt it necessary to censor from its news report the words "arrogant," "insolent" and "brutal," words used by Robert R. Siegrist, Dodd's former press officer, to describe the Senator.[31]

Judge Abe Fortas was forced to step down from the Supreme Court, and Judge Clement Haynesworth Jr.'s nomination to the Supreme Court was rejected by the Senate because it was revealed they had accepted leagalized bribes which created conflicts of interest. They weren't the only judges to have accepted legalized bribes. Illinois Supreme Court Justice Ray Klingbiel ruled on a case involving Theodore

Isaacs shortly after being given $2,000 worth of stock in the Chicago
bank Isaacs helped to organize. He decided in Isaacs' favor. The daily
newspaper *Calumet* had the story first but censored it. Eventually, like
the Dodd case, it was widely publicized because it was too big to
sweep under the rug.[32]

Reporter Sidney E. Zion discovered that Federal judge Henry J.
Friendly sat in judgement on and made decisions favoring the interests of clients that had formerly hired him as a lawyer. The *New York
Times*, who had asked Zion to look for just this type of conflict of
interest in the federal judiciary, refused to print Zion's story. The
Wall Street Journal also refused to print the story. And *Time* suppressed the news story about the story of how Scotty Reston of the
New York Times had refused to print the story. An earlier column in
1966 by Drew Pearson, pointing out Judge Friendly's conflict of interest, was suppressed by the *Washington Post,* The *New York Post* and
many other east coast newspapers.[33]

Ralph Nader accused Senator Jennings Randolph of West Virginia
of betraying the mine workers in his state by not backing miner's
demands for better safety standards. Nader said Randolph was responding to the pressure of the coal owners' National Coal Association.[34] The *Los Angeles Times* didn't bother to print this story.

There are numerous cases of news agents censoring, playing down
or using hidden bias in order to protect their favorite politicians. But
even more significant than the outright manipulation of news on a
particular story is the lack of enthusiasm on the part of news agencies
for digging into the thousands of cases of flagrant conflict of interest
situations that occur every day. Pearson noted that the *St. Louis Post
Dispatch* was the only newspaper to dig into the Nixon fund story and
demonstrate the benefits that had been received by fund contributors.
Many owners may sponsor an investigation of a politician who is
voting against their interest or who is not in a position to help or hurt
media interests, but even these cases are usually token gestures to gain
some journalistic prestige and convince the public that media owners
are crusaders for honest government. Too many exposés might make
people aware that politicians are influenced more by legalized bribes
than by public opinion.

Most important of all in fooling the public is media's intentional
failure to identify a congressman's financial backers (or "legalized
bribers" as we've been calling them) when covering his voting record
or statements. This gives the appearance that congressmen are always

voting according to a sense of conviction or reason instead of according to special interests they represent. The late Senator Dirksen's position was always made clear by the press, but the press never let the public in on the fact that Dirksen almost always voted in a way that would please the large banking, insurance, oil, gas, mining and utility companies that paid his Peoria, Illinois law firm large sums of money to retain his legal services. When Representative William Harsha Jr. led the fight against the Mass Transportation Act in 1964, the news media didn't point out that Greyhound Bus Lines retained the law firm in which he was a partner.[35] When Senator Gordon Allott was favoring the 27.5 percent depletion allowance for certain types of mining, the news media didn't point out that the Plateau Natural Gas Company, who retained his law firm, did just this type of mining.[36] In a UPI dispatch passed up by both the *Los Angeles Times* and the *New York Times*, Representative James Burke revealed that some public officials had been paid $500 to $1,000 by state medical associations to make speeches against medicare legislation. Some made twenty-five to thirty such appearances.[37] When reporting the positions of politicians regarding medical legislation, does the press point out the source of any of their legalized bribes?

Exposed to news media, the public is left to assume that legalized bribery does not influence politicians or if it does, this happens rarely. Both the *New York Times* and the *Los Angeles Times* front pages during February and March 1950 had no items at all on legalized bribery. During April and May 1960, the *New York Times* had 2 stories while the *Los Angeles Times* had none. During June and July 1969, the *New York Times* had 1 story while the *Los Angeles Times* again had none. In comparison, during the same two months in 1969, the *New York Times* had 11 items on trivia, 10 on accidents, 50 on space and 14 on religion. A check of the first three pages of the *Honolulu Star-Bulletin* for a four and a half month period in 1969 turned up only 2 articles on legalized bribery, 1 on Abe Fortas and 1 on Justice William O. Douglas.

Focusing on scapegoats like Abe Fortas, Adam Clayton Powell and Thomas Dodd is a camouflage technique used by the media owners. They devote all their attention to a few individuals while ignoring all the other hundreds of judges and congressmen who also accept legalized bribes. This helps convince the people that such situations are not typical, and further, that something is being done about shaping things up and preventing recurrences. The media then pictures itself as a crusading force diligently keeping a watch on congressional ethics. The scapegoats are merely martyrs to the media-created myth that the government responds to the people rather than special interests.

The scapegoat-camouflage technique is illustrated in two on-the-hour newscasts monitored for eight weeks in 1969.[38] Mutual had 6 items and ABC had 14 on legalized bribery—not a bad showing. But all 20 items were on the Haynsworth case to the total exclusion of any items about the normal run of legal bribes offered and taken.

Walter Cronkite and *Huntley-Brinkley* newscasts had an excellent opportunity to delve into the possible influence of legalized bribery in influencing votes on the crucial ABM decision. More than almost any other vote, this issue lined up firm supporters of the military-industrial complex on one side. Both newscasts ran accounts of how senators were voting. Many were interviewed. CBS had 18 items taking 27:28 minutes and NBC had 16 items taking 25:20 minutes on the issue. But not once in the total of 33 items and 52:48 minutes was the subject of legalized bribery mentioned in connection with the positions taken by different senators. The public was left to think that the campaign contributions, loans, gifts, retainers and other legalized bribes handed out by the giant defense contractors had no influence whatever on how senators voted. Of the 873 other items on *Walter Cronkite* during this period, there were a total of 6 items taking 3:52 minutes on legalized bribery. Out of 873 items, *Huntley-Brinkley* had 2 items taking 1:45 minutes.

During a six-week period in 1960, ABC-TV and CBS-TV evening newscasts had only 1 item each on legalized bribery. *Huntley-Brinkley* had 4 items. E. P. Morgan, Peter Hackes and Lowell Thomas had a total of 2 items on their fifteen-minute network radio newcasts. Overall, for thirty days of news and more than 450 items for each of six reporters, the average of less than 2 items for each reporter amounts to a shut out of the subject. Legalized bribery, like establishment crime, is a way of life for the establishment; any day the news media want to they could find sufficient information for news stories on either topic.

If solid liberal journalists had equal access to the media it is certain that no mention of a congressman's voting behavior or a judge's decision would be reported without including information as to how much his voting or decision would help those who gave him legalized bribes. Such reporting would undermine people's confidence in the present congressional system by exposing the motivating factors behind many of the decisions of judges, government officials and congressmen. This is the value of a truly competitive media; it undermines those things which cannot take the exposure offered by newsmen who find the system intolerable. The whole system of legalized bribery needs to be undermined along with mass media's complicity in concealing it, so that Congress will respond to intelligent arguments rather than special interest pressure and rewards. Neither reason, practicality or response to the public, can possibly explain the behavior of Congress in ignoring pollution, hunger, auto safety, military waste, risks to worker safety, unjustified foreign interventions and the prostitution of the nation's communication system. This purposeful neglect can best be explained as a response to special interests. It can be concealed only by media owners who are willing to use their one-sided propaganda to keep the American public ignorant about the political and criminal situations that make the nation pay such a terrible price in men, money and quality of life.

19 To the Moon:
"There Really Isn't Any Argument"

> The next week may well be the most astonishing the world has ever known. Journey with us. And live it all.
>
> CBS Advertisement

President Eisenhower planned to scrap manned space flights after the Mercury project was completed.[1] Shortly after leaving office he warned the nation not to accept as a national goal spectacular space exploits such as putting a man on the moon:

> The United States should be highly selective in our space objectives and unexcelled in their pursuit. Prestige arises from sound accomplishment not from the purely spectacular and we must not be driven by nationalistic competition into programs so extravagant as to divert funds and talents from programs of equal or greater importance.[2]

Two years later, in 1962, the former President stated:

> What we need in this country is to set up some sensible priorities on spending projects — to put first things first. . . . Why the great hurry to get to the moon and the planets? . . . From here on, I think we should proceed in an orderly scientific way, building one accomplishment on another, rather than engaging in a mad effort to win a stunt race.[3]

President Eisenhower was not alone in his opposition to a hurry-to-the moon program. His advice was echoed by hundreds of the most noted scientific men in the country. The National Academy of Science's Space Science Board, established in 1958, advised that a manned lunar landing should have a low priority.[4] Director of Carnegie Institute's Geophysical Laboratory and editor of *Science* magazine, Dr. Philip Abelson, conducted a poll among members of the National Academy of Science and found that the overwhelming majority were opposed to the lunar program.[5]

Despite this advice, President Kennedy chose to commit the nation and 30 billion dollars to land a man on the moon by 1970. Many think his reasons were based purely on political rather than scientific grounds. After the failure of the Bay of Pigs invasion of Cuba and Russia's successful orbiting of astronauts, the President was looking for some spectacular accomplishments that would increase America's prestige.[6] Seymour Melman states in his book, *The Depleted Society,* that "the record discloses that the decision by President Kennedy to race for a lunar landing was a political decision for a political purpose, and had little relation to purely scientific considerations."[7]

President Eisenhower, most scientists, and others concerned with the nation's priorities and goals were not pleased by President Kennedy's decision, but the establishment's military-industrial-space-media complex was overjoyed. And as we shall see, to sell the moon landing to the American people they used all their propaganda tools to invent myths that would hide the enormous cost the nation would have to pay for the moon spectacular. Many Americans were led to believe the whole program was really free—that the so-called spin-off benefits would more than pay for the program. The then Vice President, Lyndon Baines Johnson, did his part in creating this myth: "it is estimated conservatively," he said in 1962, "that our space outlays will yield two dollars return for every dollar invested; for every nickel we put into it, we get a dime back."[8] Spiro T. Agnew, President Nixon's chief space advisor as well as Vice President—and advocate of putting a man on Mars by 1986 at the cost of $24 Billion—has claimed that "fall-out" from the space program may do more to solve ghetto problems than community action programs.[9] When asked to list some of what are termed spin-off benefits, Dr. Thomas Paine, head of the manned space program, pointed out that space spin-off helped produce a communication technology that "brought the voice of Frank Borman into the living rooms in Moscow at Christmas time when he read the opening words of Genesis."[10] This may have satisfied such influential Americans as the Reverend Billy Graham, but others of influence didn't think that this feat alone was worth $30 billion. Asked by a reporter to be more specific about how the alleged spin-off benefits would help man solve his problems on earth, Dr. Paine listed some of the tangible spin-offs benefiting man in the fields of weather forecasting, satellite observation of earth and ocean resources, and navigation. Space corporations public relations departments, such as the one at North American Rockwell, go much farther and list spin-off benefits to education, health, medicine, welfare, industry and public utilities.

Very few knowledgeable people or scientists have accepted these exaggerated claims of spin-off without voicing dissent. They point out that the vast majority of benefits listed by Paine and others are benefits deriving from the unmanned aspects of the space program—the part of our total space program that has the support of almost everybody. Benefits deriving solely from the manned aspects of the program, such as those in the field of medical knowledge and technology, are far fewer in number. Furthermore, such medical advances could have been achieved for much less money if that money had been spent directly for the purpose of advancing medical technology and knowledge. This was admitted by NASA's Director of Lunar and Planetary Programs, Donald Hearth, in 1969 when he stated: "There is no question a lot of spin-off. On the other hand, if we applied these monies to trying to get the spin-off in the first place, obviously we would get more."[11] A NASA-sponsored study concluded: "Relatively little importance can be attached to direct transfer of product from missile/space programs to the civilian sector of the economy. . . . "[12] Dr. Eugene Shoemaker, a principal investigator for Apollo and chairman of Caltech's division of geological sciences, upon quitting the space program in 1969, said that the scientific achievements of the Apollo program could have been gained with unmanned systems at "one-fifth the cost three or four years ago."[13]

Besides not having all the positive spin-off benefits that are claimed, the lunar program has many negative consequences. It is these negative aspects that concern most of the critics of the program. Physicians, scientists, technicians, natural resources and money being used to send a man to the moon and beyond cannot at the same time be used to help develop the knowledge, skill and technology needed to control population increase or pollution, reduce illiteracy, study the oceans, house and feed the world's poor, and provide more and better medical care for all people. Even President Kennedy, the man who made the decision to send a man to the moon, admitted the role of the space program in depriving society of its most valuable resources: "In the course of meeting specific challenges so brilliantly we have paid a price by sharply limiting the scarce scientific and engineering resources available to the civilian sectors of the economy."[14] Robert Finch, former Secretary of Health, Education, and Welfare, was in a position to know how badly human resources are needed to improve the quality of life. He commented that in sending man to the moon, "we used a great deal of expert talent that could have been used in other kinds of programs."[15]

The mass media have had a difficult job to do during the last ten years. They have had to generate and maintain the support of the people for the manned space program in the face of this widespread and substantial opposition by many of society's scholars and statesmen. The media's success in this endeavor of creating and maintaining the necessary public support is as spectacular as the moon landing itself. Scarcely a murmur of dissent was heard through the mass media until three astronauts were burned to death in 1967. And it wasn't until after the moon landing in 1969 that the media allowed more than just a murmur of dissent. Now that the space corporations and the mass media have reaped the full harvest of the 30 billion dollar lunar program, they are acting as if they are dedicated to questioning space priorities. For those who have studied mass media's coverage during the last decade this is a strange turnabout. Mass media's real performance has been a combined ten-year electronic spectacle and advertising campaign calculated to sell the moon landing to the American people.

The mass media have served as the willing partner of the NASA propaganda machine that spends some $20 million a year and hires some 400 publicity employees to produce television programs, motion pictures and other news services.[16] NASA news releases are shown with little or no critical comment and often without proper identification of source. With this kind of cooperation NASA has succeeded in convincing the American people that the nation's space program and moon extravaganza should be treated as one entity, indivisible. That is to say, the NASA-mass media combination have given the public the impression that to favor a space program is to favor the moon spectacular, and that to oppose the moon landing is to oppose the entire space program. They have intentionally failed to show the public that most of those who oppose the manned aspect of the space program do support the sound un-manned aspects of space exploration.

To conceal the great body of scientific and scholarly opposition to the lunar program the news media have used a simple technique—they ignore it. It is evident from a study of newspaper and broadcasting coverage that this technique was being used up to and through the first moon landing in 1969. [See TABLES XVI and XVII]

TABLE XVI
NEWSPAPER COVERAGE OF SPACE DISSENT

New York Times and *Los Angeles Times*, June and July 1969, Front Page

	Number of Items	Column Inches	Number of Photographs
Positive or neutral space coverage			
Los Angeles Times	55	466	19
New York Times	51	407*	32
Criticism of the basic reasons used to justify the lunar program			
Los Angeles Times	0	0	0
New York Times	0	0	0
Criticism of the priority given the lunar program, or elaboration of negative consequences			
Los Angeles Times	0	0	0
New York Times	1	16	0

Honolulu Star-Bulletin, Jan. 12, through May 31, 1969, first 3 pages

	Number of Items	Column Inches	Number of Photographs
Positive or neutral space coverage	49	615	57
Criticism of the basic reasons used to justify the lunar program	0	0	0
Criticism of the priority given the lunar program, or elaboration of negative consequences	0	0	0

*An estimate based on micro film projection

TABLE XVII   257

NBC AND CBS NETWORK NEWSCAST COVERAGE OF SPACE DISSENT

Huntley-Brinkley and *Walter Cronkite*
July 10 through September 10, 1969

	Number of Items	Time Allotted (in minutes)
Positive or neutral space coverage		
Huntley-Brinkley	48	95:00
Walter Cronkite	79	167:22
Criticism of the basic reasons used to justify the lunar program		
Huntley-Brinkley	0	0
Walter Cronkite	2	:51
Criticism of the priority given the lunar program, or elaboration of negative consequences		
Huntley-Brinkley	0	0
Walter Cronkite	5	6:21

NETWORK RADIO NEWS

ON-THE-HOUR COVERAGE OF SPACE DISSENT

ABC — 9:00 A.M. P.S.T., KABC, weekdays
MUTUAL — 7:00 A.M. P.S.T., KRKD, weekdays

August 22 through October 22, 1969

	Number of Items	Time Allotted (in minutes)
Positive or neutral space coverage		
ABC	9	1:36
Mutual	15	2:58
Criticism of the basic reasons used to justify the lunar program		
ABC	0	0
Mutual	0	0
Criticism of the priority given the lunar program or elaboration of negative consequences		
ABC	0	0
Mutual	0	0

The neglect of space dissent by *Huntley-Brinkley* (48 to 0) and *Walter Cronkite* (79 to 7) constitutes only a small part of the cumulative network bias that favored the lunar program and perpetuated the myth of near unanimous support. Added to the comparative figures of newscast coverage should be the endless hours of live space flight coverage in which space dissent is covered even less than in the newscasts. Since there has been so much live coverage, it seems a reasonable expectation that the newscasts' coverage of space could profitably focus on other facets than the flight itself—such as the issues and debates concerning the nation's space program. Instead we are treated to a rehash and summary of the live space coverage. From this point of view the two newscasts' 262 minutes of positive or neutral coverage compared to 7 minutes allotted to dissent is hard to countenance.

Front-cover space coverage by the mass-circulation magazines is similarly lopsided. *Time, Newsweek* and *Life* magazines together had 63 front-cover color photographs from 1962 through July 1969. All but 4 of these were photographs favorable to the space program. The 4 that cast an unfavorable light on the program all concerned the tragic death of the three astronauts—a topic that could hardly have been ignored. There was not one cover used to focus the public's attention on space dissent. It would have been very easy to occasionally feature renowned scientists like Ralph Lapp or Philip Abelson who constantly spoke out against the manned program, but no such efforts were made. It is obvious that the only efforts made were to ignore space dissent. Had there been a mass-circulation magazine which opposed the lunar program there certainly would have been some different cover stories regarding space.

Mass media's effort to sell the manned program is also demonstrated by the type of news stories it chooses to suppress. "Meet the Press" interviews are always covered by the wire services. Newspapers almost always print the story of the interview on the next Monday—often on page one or two. However, the news item covering Senator George McGovern's interview on December 29, 1968, was suppressed by both the *New York Times* and the *Los Angeles Times*. His statements about space may have been the ones that upset the establishment most. Complaining about the high priority that the moon landing enjoyed, he added,

> The money that we have spent on this program, while it has produced some very inspirational and wonderful results . . . has also

meant money that we have had to divert from the hungry, from the sick, from the uneducated here on earth.[17]

Shortly after assuming his post, George Romney, Secretary of Housing and Urban Development, said that to provide adequate housing for all Americans was more difficult than going to the moon.[18] Not a word of this appeared in either the *New York Times* or the *Los Angeles Times*.

Senator William Proxmire said that landing on the moon should be an occasion for putting limits on the space program and putting new priorities on national problems at home. He stated:

> The message of the moon mission is that the United States can achieve more hope if it sets goals and works diligently and energetically to achieve them, and it is more hope that we need now to rescue our cities from blight and from fear and to purify our air and cleanse our lakes and streams, to organize our care of the sick, the aged and the poor and most important, to free ourselves from the burden of ever increasing expenditures for the weapons of war.[19]

Walter Cronkite, Huntley-Brinkley and the *New York Times* ignored Proxmire's statement. The *Los Angeles Times* printed a UPI story covering congressional response to the successful moon landing which included the comments of eight congressmen, but Proxmire's response was not one of them. Representative Mendel Rivers of South Carolina, however, had his dissent registered. His complaint was that insufficient attention had been paid "to the fact that without the help of the almighty God our men wouldn't be there."[20]

Walter Cronkite and *Huntley-Brinkley* newscasts may be able to claim they just didn't have time to cover the above stories. But no such excuse can be given for their suppression of the following unquestionably important space story. Both the *New York Times* and the *Los Angeles Times* placed it on their front pages. It was the proposal by the Space Science Board of the National Academy of Sciences that future probes of outer planets should be accomplished with unmanned spacecraft. They said that the national space program could be carried out with unmanned spacecraft for "a fraction of the total cost" of a manned program. What made the scientist's request significant is that it is at odds with the NASA, Spiro Agnew and Richard Nixon approaches which favor the more spectacular manned space shots as well as space stations. Apparently the *Los Angeles Times* copy editor either didn't understand the main point or he wanted to hide it because his headline didn't even include the word "unmanned." Instead, it read as if the scientists wanted a further expansion of the present program:

PANEL OF SCIENTISTS CALLS FOR 'GRAND TOUR' OF OUTER PLANETS

The *New York Times* headline, noting the main point, read:[21]

23 SCIENTISTS ASK UNMANNED PROBE OF OUTER PLANETS

Representative George Brown, chairman of the House Science and Astronautics Committee, said in a house speech that the United States should delay five to ten years before determining to attempt a manned mission to Mars.[22] This was a significant statement because of Brown's position as chairman and his opposition to the administration's acceptance of a manned space program for probes beyond the moon. Both the *New York Times* and the *Los Angeles Times* ignored Brown's statement as did *Walter Cronkite* and *Huntley-Brinkley,* even though together they found time for 262 minutes of space coverage on their newscasts during the two months studied.

The mass media may neglect news of those who challenge the establishment's space priorities, but they go out of their way to publish stories which help promote the myth that fallout from the manned space effort pays off big back on earth. The *Los Angeles Times'* own financial editor wrote a long article which was featured at the top of a news page with the headline:

APOLLO FALLOUT PROVING USEFUL IN OTHER FIELDS

It had the subhead:

$24 Billion Program Produces Inventions, Applications, Ideas to Benefit Industry[23]

The *New York Times* had this headline atop Page One in August 1969:

MOON CREW SAYS MISSION CAN LEAD TO GOOD ON EARTH

The article continued on Page 29 under an eight-column headline atop the page reading:[24]

MOON CREW SUGGEST THAT LANDING
CAN LEAD TO SOLUTION OF
PROBLEMS ON EARTH

The *Honolulu Star-Bulletin* featured a series of five articles by the Gannett News Service detailing the fallout benefits of the space program. The first headline set the tone:

SPACE PROGRAM PAYING OFF ON EARTH

The article ended with a statement claiming that fallout-created production techniques "mean more efficient and cheaper items in the stores and will touch every person."[25]

Overwhelming bias in news coverage, news suppression and public relations type news articles are only part of the propaganda arsenal drawn upon by the mass media to convince the public it's to their advantage to spend great sums and utilize valuable resources to land man in outer space. One-sided editorials are also frequently aimed at the audience. Of course they are called "commentaries" so that the opposing viewpoints will not have to be given equal time. During the two months that CBS was checked, Eric Scvareid took a total of 10 minutes on *Walter Cronkite* to give four different commentaries favorable to the manned space program. He gave none against the program, nor did any other CBS commentator. The space commentary of the decade was a team effort by Walter Cronkite and Eric Sevareid who discussed the more philosophical and political aspects of the space program. Sevareid, describing the experience of seeing the lift off as "really a religious experience," went on to tell his 20 million viewers:

> All arguments, sociological arguments, philosophical arguments we've heard and talked about for weeks and months and years—should we do this instead of something else—somehow they all vanish in a cloud of smoke. This can be done and therefore it's done. There really isn't any argument.[26]

Sevareid is right—there really hasn't been any argument for ten years, that is, in the mass media.

Summing up the decade in NBC's two and one half hour "From Here To The Seventies," Chet Huntley commented on the meaning of the space effort:

> The national success in space was exceptional, and in it or out of it

we may find the way to achievements that now appear farther away than the moon itself. . . . Historians looking back over the past decade or century will find it hard to choose a more meaningful period than the last two weeks of July 1969.[27]

At times it's hard to tell the difference between our country's most famous professional journalists and Abigail Van Buren (Dear Abby). Abby was asked by a young mother:

> Since they haven't found a cure for cancer yet could you tell me why they spend so much money to get to the moon? I think the money they spent for this space foolishness could be put to better use for medical research for curing cancer and other fatal diseases.

Abby told the young mother, among other things: "Progress in science must go on, and putting a man on the moon may lead us to discovering as yet undreamed of benefits."[28]

The reason mass media feel it necessary to use overwhelming bias in smothering space dissent is apparent. The underlying reasons for sending manned spacecraft to the moon and beyond are as shaky today as they were when President Kennedy, against the advice of most scientists, committed the nation to land a man on the moon. It wouldn't take much dissent at all to topple the media-created myths. Just the murmur of dissent that began to get exposure in 1967 has been enough to alert most of the people to the colossal waste of resources and talent involved in manned exploration. An early 1969 Harris poll showed that 59 percent of the American people were opposed to the manned moon flight. Had there been media owners with the courage to use bias to oppose the lunar program and inform the people of the great body of dissent, the vast majority of Americans might have risen up to stop the establishment before the nation's wealth was lavished on going to the moon in the first place.

Ironically, what may stop NASA, President Nixon and Spiro Agnew from continuing the manned program is the very success the mass media has had in bringing, live, the moon spectaculars to 500 million people around the world. The stark photographs of the moon must make illiterate and starving peasants the world over, as well as young people, wonder why the United States has spent so much money to get to such a desolate place when this money could do so much here on earth. For most Americans, live color coverage of successful space exploits have taken away the fascination. As with any spectacular stunt, a space flight becomes a little boring to watch after awhile. The question naturally arises—well, what next? An answer suggesting more manned spectaculars will not sell so easily this time.

20   If God Only Knew

Attacks on religion and religious faith are not allowed.

Television Code

In this section we shall examine how the Pope, absolute head and ruler of the largest organization in the world outside of a few governments, is protected from criticism by the mass media. Further, we will see that as a result of this the Pope enjoys considerable respect despite his policies on abortion and contraception — policies which in the opinion of many cause misery, starvation and abortion deaths. If any other organization or ruler were responsible for such widespread violence and misery neither could hope for good press coverage. Some governments, like Greece, South Africa, Portugal or Spain, will receive at least minimal unfavorable exposure in U. S. mass media, but they couldn't begin to imagine getting the type of favorable coverage that is bestowed upon the Pope. The mass media act as synchronized cheerleaders supporting religion in general and the Pope in particular, and thus indirectly they abet the Pope's policies.

An analysis of front-page newspaper coverage of religion reveals very little news critical of religion or few exposes of unfair church privileges such as tax laws that benefit only religions. There is almost a total black out of news critical of the Vatican's ruler and policy maker. [See TABLE XVIII]

No publicity is more valuable to an organization or its cause than favorable photographs in the first few pages of a newspaper. As no other section or written item, they attract nearly 100 percent of the readers. Propagandists are well aware that one favorable news photograph and caption in a newspaper may be more effective in building up public support for an organization or cause than a $4,000 to $5,-000 full-page advertisement in the same paper. The willingness of the mass media to act as enthusiastic envoys for Catholic Church news (and propaganda disguised as news) is illustrated by special photographic treatment given the Church. From January through June of

TABLE XVIII

NEWSPAPER COVERAGE OF NEWS UNFAVORABLE TO RELIGION IN GENERAL OR THE POPE IN PARTICULAR*

NEWSPAPER	Positive or Neutral Coverage of Religion	Photographs pp.1,2,3	Items Critical of Religious Policies or Exposing Privileges	Photographs pp.1,2,3	Items Critical of Vatican Policies or the Pope	Photographs pp.1,2,3
	Items, p.1		Items, p.1		Items, p.1	
New York Times (Front Page)						
February and March, 1950	6	6	2	0	0	0
April and May, 1960	12	1	1	0	0	0
June and July, 1969	15	11	1	0	0	0
Los Angeles Times (Front Page)						
February and March, 1950	14	3	0	0	0	0
April and May, 1960	9	11	0	0	0	0
June and July, 1969	4	2	0	0	0	0
Honolulu Star-Bulletin (First three pages)						
January 12 to May 31, 1969	42	10	1	0	0	0

*Includes stories of both local and national distribution or interest

1967, the *New York Times* featured on its first three pages 12 photographs favorable to religion and 1 on dissent within the Church. Of these 13 photographs, 11 were favorable to the Vatican and 10 of these featured the Pope.

During March and April 1969, the *New York Times* featured 7 photographs on religion: all were favorable to the Catholic Church and 4 featured the Pope. During the same two months, the *Los Angeles Times* featured 6 photographs on religion on its first three pages. All were favorable to the Catholic Church and 5 featured the Pope.

Not to be outdone, mass-circulation magazines (with the exception of *Look*) seemed to compete to see who could give the Church the most favorable treatment. From 1962 through July 1969, *Time* magazine had 15 cover photographs on religion. Only 2 of these were not manifestly favorable, one with a caption "Is God Dead?" and the other drawing attention to rebellion within the Catholic Church. Of the 13 photographs that were favorable, 8 were about the Catholic Church and 5 were of the Pope.

Newsweek during the same seven and a half years had 9 cover photographs on religion. Of these, 7 were favorable to the Catholic Church and only 1 could be considered unfavorable; in this one, a caption brought up the topic of the Church and the pill.

Life magazine in these same ninety-one months had 10 cover photographs on religion. All 10 were favorable, and 8 of these featured the Catholic Church in public relations-type photographs.

The only magazine to treat the topic of religion with even a facade of balance was *Look*, which had 6 cover photographs on religion, 4 of which drew attention to political, economic or social policies of religions. Of the 3 covers featuring the Pope, 1 had an unfavorable caption asking: "Should the Pope Retire?"

The image communicated by mass-circulation magazine cover photographs during the seven and a half years was very favorable to religion in general and especially to the Catholic Church. The financial and propaganda value of cover photographs is so great that no price tag can be placed on it. Such treatment can only be purchased through good deeds in service to the establishment.

That's newspapers and magazines. But what about broadcasting? In examining this, we find that the broadcasting industry is second to none when it comes to protecting religions, and especially the Catholic Church, from criticism. This is evident from a study of network newscasts over a two-month period. [See TABLE XIX]

TABLE XIX

NETWORK TELEVISION AND RADIO NEWSCAST COVERAGE OF NEWS
UNFAVORABLE TO RELIGION IN GENERAL AND THE POPE IN PARTICULAR

TYPE OF COVERAGE	Huntley-Brinkley		Walter Cronkite		ABC Radio News-On-The-Hour		Mutual Radio News-On-The-Hour	
	July 10 to Sept. 10, 1969				Aug. 22 to Oct. 22, 1969			
	Items	Time	Items	Time	Items	Time	Items	Time
Positive or neutral coverage of religion	7	11:02	12	8:28	7	1:03	5	1:12
Items critical of religious policies or exposing special privileges	1	:11	1	:20	0	--	0	--
Favorable coverage of the Pope	3	4:19	7	6:44	4	:39	5	1:12
Stories Critical of the Pope	0	--	0	--	0	--	0	--

More important than the media's public relations campaign for the Catholic Church is its suppression of issues that expose the death and misery that are often thought to result from Church policies. During the seven and one-half years when the three mass-circulation magazines were repeatedly using their front covers to depict the Church in a favorable light, they used their front covers only one time to focus on the population explosion and one time on world hunger as related to population increase. Not once did the topic of abortion rate a cover photograph.

Magazines weren't alone in using hidden bias to keep these topics from becoming the issues they might profitably have been. The failure of the United States to deal in any way with the population explosion until the mid 1960's, and the continued tolerance of what I see as unjust abortion laws can be traced directly to the unanimity with which the mass media have used its propaganda services to suppress the issues, especially when the consequences of Church policies are up for airing.

The most significant protest ever made against the Vatican's birth control policy was placed on Page 20 of the *New York Times*.[1] It was a news item covering a statement of protest signed by 2,600 American scientists:

> We pledge that we will no longer be impressed by pleas for world peace or compassion for the poor from a man whose deeds help promote war and make poverty inevitable. . . .
>
> The world must quickly come to realize that Pope Paul VI has sanctioned the deaths of countless numbers of human beings with his misguided and immoral encyclical.

Not all articles about the Pope are relegated to page 20. On April 11, 1960, the *Times* placed this headline on Page One:

POPE MAKES PLEA FOR MORE
CHILDREN; REASSURES PARENTS

The article reported that the Pope in exhorting parents to have more children told them: "Don't be afraid of the number of your sons and daughters."

The 2,600 American scientists may "no longer be impressed" by the Pope's "pleas for world peace or compassion for the poor," but the *Times* is obviously duly impressed and wants its readers to be likewise impressed. In 1967, the newspaper featured on Page One a large photograph of a sister kissing the Pope's hand. The four-column headline read:

MILLIONS AT FATIMA HEAR
POPE PLEAD FOR PEACE.

All of Pages 46 and 47 were devoted to either photographs or articles on the Pope's visit.[2] The networks were so impressed that they carried the ceremony, live, to the United States. Just ten days earlier the *Times* had announced in a Page One headline:

POPE TO URGE PEACE AT SHRINE OF FATIMA

A UPI release in 1969 carried parts of a speech made by Baptist theologian Professor Wayne E. Ward. He accused the Pope of blasphemy for refusing to allow Catholics to practice birth control. He said such a prohibition reduced to mere procreative function the relationship between men and women. He added:

> Unless one is willing to say "let nature take its course and let infants die as they will without medical attention,' he certainly cannot deny the right and responsibility of medical science to use all its power to control the birth rate when it has been so effective in controlling the death rate."[3]

The *New York Times* suppressed this news release. Other stories did qualify as news. On the same day they had a six-column headline on Page 5 telling of the Pope's visit to Geneva, and another article without any identification as to source, announcing that the Reverend Billy Graham had arrived for a ten day crusade.

CBS employs a subtle form of censorship and bias to please religious leaders. The news department uses the leaders of the three major faiths in New York as editorial advisors. Programs about religion are often shown to the three leaders prior to broadcast.[4] With such an arrangement it's hard to imagine CBS producing or presenting anything that might displease the religious establishment. CBS along with NBC also provides the priceless publicity of presenting special programs on religious ceremonies such as the installation of Terence Cooke as the Archbishop of the Archdiocese of New York.

In NBC's two and one half hour "From Here to the Seventies," correspondent Aline Saarinen summed up the last decade on the topic of hunger and overpopulation and sketched the prospects for the future. Her performance was a masterpiece of subtle journalistic propaganda that could have emanated from the Vatican itself. After painting a realistic picture of the ravages of starvation, malnutrition and mental retardation resulting from overpopulation, she turned on what I'd call the usual network optimism, and gave the audience the impression that recent harvests in certain countries such as India and Mexico indicate that things are getting better. She stated that this so called "green revolution" has "silenced the cries of those predicting famine in the Seventies." She summarized the population-hunger situation by stating: "The green revolution has given the world a breathing spell of two, maybe three decades." Such statements, if believed, would allow Americans to avoid the necessity of demanding the drastic steps needed to even begin coping with the problem. Most experts in the field deplore attitudes fostered in such pie-in-the-sky journalistic coverage. Biologist Phillip Ashmole stated: "I join many biologists (and others) in the conviction that to lull the public into a false sense of security is the surest way to betray future generations by depriving them of a world to live in."[5] Professor George Borgstrom considers this type of optimism a "participation in a grand scale evasion of reality which bears all the signs of insanity."[6] Population expert Professor Paul Ehrlich had this advice for those like Saarinen who share and exude mass media's optimism on the topic:

> These clowns who are talking of feeding a big population in the year 2000 from make-believe green revolutions and the unlimited riches of the sea should learn some elementary biology, meteorology, agricultural economics and anthropology.[7]

Even the *New York Times* called the prediction of *Two Decades of Respite From famine* "too optimistic."[8] And one of the most optimistic experts and proponents of the "green revolution," Lester Brown, admits that in order to produce all the food needed, man may in the process have to destroy his environment with agricultural pollutants and ocean and land exploitation.[9]

Correspondent Saarinen's optimism can be excused, I think, but her failure to point out that, on the whole, progress is not being made is inexcusable. As the World Population Reference Bureau noted in January 1970, the euphoria over "green revolution" has blinded many to the fact that "more, not fewer, people suffer from malnutrition each year" and that this "circumstance prevails at a time when agricultural technology has already been making impressive strides." [10] The "green revolution" at best can only decrease somewhat the increasing rate of starvation; it doesn't begin to decrease the total scale of famine that takes place unnoticed every day. During the two and one half hour special program in which Aline Saarinen talked of the success of the "green revolution" in buying twenty to thirty years of time, 1100 human beings in the world, mostly children, died as the result of starvation or malnutrition.

Correspondent Saarinen also had something to say about a second issue where Catholic Church policy is a vital factor—abortion. She said:

> The vast majority of the world's women want to limit the size of their families, but they don't know how. So millions of them everywhere every day practice the crudest birth control method in the world—abortion. In this single hospital 2000 women who have been mutilated by abortions are admitted every year, one for every three deliveries. [11]

Woman reporter Saarinen failed to inform her large television audience that abortion instead of being "the crudest birth control method in the world" is actually very safe and simple when performed by qualified persons in countries where the Church has not prevented legalized abortion by use of its political power. It is not only safe, it is one of the most effective ways for a country and the world to quickly reduce its birth rate—a dire necessity for all but a few countries, rich or poor.

More glaring than her failure to point out that most mutilating abortions can be traced to the effects of Catholic Church policy, was her failure to mention the Catholic Church's opposition to birth control and abortion as one of the seven obstacles which stand in the way of reducing the population. She mentioned religious taboos as one factor, but this is a quite different factor from political pressure which quashes birth control efforts and prevents—by fiat—legalized abortion throughout the world. This has been shown by the readiness of millions of Catholic women all over the world to take pills and have abortions when the opportunity is available. The lack of laws, money and medical personnel that keep every woman in the world from having the chance to limit her child-rearing by contraception or abortion is the single most important obstacle to reducing man's suicidal birth rate. NBC's audience was given the impression that the Church's political policies were not even significant enough to mention. Taken by itself such journalism might seem harmless, but when we realize that no competing news agencies attack Church policies, such journalistic techniques are an important propagandizing instrument for the Catholic Church.

The mass media have also performed for the Catholic Church by either playing down or censoring important news items that reveal the overwhelming support of physicians, church leaders and others for repeal of all abortion laws. The American College of Surgeons came out strongly for repeal of all abortion laws.[12] This was covered by the wire services. However, both the *New York Times* and the *Los Angeles Times* failed to print the item. The *Los Angeles Times* can't even plead they weren't aware of the Surgeon's Conference because one of their own reporters attended it. He covered the surgeons' opposition to inadequately supervised Little League sports activities but made no mention of the position taken on abortion. This is consistent with the favored news treatment the *Times* has afforded the Catholic Church, and especially Los Angeles' radical right Cardinal McIntyre who was finally forced to retire. In late 1969, the *Los Angeles Times* in effect came to the defense of the Vatican by printing, on four successive Sundays, lengthy expositions and defenses of church policies.

The *New York Times* also failed to print a very significant news item sent out by the wire services noting that the 20,000 member American Women's Medical Association by an overwhelming voice vote took a stand advocating the repeal of all abortion laws. *Huntley-Brinkley* and *Walter Cronkite* also suppressed the item.[13] The *Los Angeles Times* gave the item two inches without a headline in the Page 2 news roundup.[14]

More important than the suppression or playing down of the few individual news releases of attacks on abortion laws is something we've hardly touched on—namely, the lack of initiative shown by mass media in making the topic a front-page issue demanding the public's attention. A study of both newspapers and newscast coverage of the topic shows how the media keep the topic from being a compelling issue—and incredibly, this neglect has taken place for years while 5,000 to 10,000 women unnecessarily died each year as martyrs to Church abortion laws.[15] [See TABLE XX]

The media owners always have some excuse when they are accused of handling news in a biased way. In the case of religion, which we have just discussed, they claim that it is unethical to attack religion.

TABLE XX

273

THE FREQUENCY OF NEWSPAPER AND NEWSCAST COVERAGE OF ABORTION NEWS*

NEWS AGENCY	Number of Items on Abortion
New York Times, Feb. and March 1950, front page	0
New York Times, April and May, 1960, front page	0
New York Times, June and July, 1969, front page	0
Los Angeles Times, Feb. and March 1950, front page	0
Los Angeles Times, April and May 1960, front page	0
Los Angeles Times, June and July 1969, front page	0
Honolulu Star-Bulletin, Jan. 12 to May 31, 1969, first 3 pages	3
ABC-TV *Evening News*, John Daly September 26 to November 7, 1960	0
NBC-TV, *Huntley-Brinkley* September 26 to November 7, 1960	0
CBS-TV *Evening News*, Douglas Edwards September 26 to November 7, 1960	0
ABC-Radio, 15 min. *Evening News*, E.P. Morgan September 26 to November 7, 1960	0
NBC-Radio, 15 min. *World News Roundup*, Peter Hackes September 26 to November 7, 1960	0
CBS-Radio, 15 min. *Evening News*, Lowell Thomas September 26 to November 7, 1960	0
ABC-Radio News *On-The-Hour*, 9:00 a.m. P.S.T., August 22 to October 22, 1969	0
Mutual-Radio News *On-The-Hour*, 7:00 a.m. P.S.T., August 22 to October 22, 1969	0
NBC-TV, *Huntley-Brinkley* July 10 to September 10, 1969	0
CBS-TV, *Walter Cronkite* July 10 to September 10, 1969	0

*Includes stories of both local and national distribution or interest

They have even included in their journalistic code of ethics a provision prohibiting attacks on religion. Few people would object to this code if it protected only those religious ideas and activities which don't affect politics or people outside the churches, but the code has been used by the media owners to justify their suppression and playing down of attacks on religious ideas and activities which can affect the life and death of every American, church member or not. Like the journalistic ethic excluding opinions or bias of any kind from news reporting, the part of the code that prevents attacks on religion merely serves as a public relations facade enabling media owners to conceal the widespread misery and death caused by Catholic Church policies, and the Church's interconnection with and loyalty to the corporate establishment.

The Church policies on abortion and population control are not the only political policies which need to be protected from criticism. The Vatican sided with Mussolini and Hitler in supporting Generalisimo Franco's Fascist war against the Spanish people. Pope Pius XII even went so far as to bless Italian aviators and soldiers who committed atrocities against the Spanish populace.[16] In the United States, Church political and social pressure was successful in convincing President Roosevelt's administration not to render aid to the Spanish people in their fight against Franco (with his allies Hitler and Mussolini). Through boycotts, letter writing campaigns, sermons from the pulpit and other tactics, the Church was able to marshal the force of the majority of American newspapers to use hidden bias to favor the Fascists in the Spanish Civil War. During World War II the Vatican supported Hitler and Mussolini rather than the Allied powers. After the war, the Church helped Franco win back his prestige and recognition from both the United States and the United Nations. The Catholic hierarchy in the United States, (Cardinal Spellman in particular) was secretly instrumental in convincing John Foster Dulles and Dwight Eisenhower to have the United States prevent free elections and back the dictatorial Diem regime in Vietnam.

There are other characteristics of the Catholic Church that the hierarchy would rather keep secret. Their enormous wealth is one such characteristic. The Church which symbolically represents a Jesus Christ who served the poor and downtrodden rather than the establishment, has assets and real estate holdings which exceed those of Standard Oil, AT&T and U.S. Steel combined.[17] This economic power is all subject to the control of the Pope through his appointments of the Church hierarchy around the world. Nino Lo Bello, in his book *The Vatican Empire,* estimates the Vatican's investments in stocks alone to be a minimum of $5.6 billion. [18] Others claim these holdings may amount to as much as $10 billion.[19] The Vatican itself claims it has a total of only $128 million in bank deposits and stocks.[20]

Total Vatican wealth is a closely guarded secret, but Martin Larson and Stanley Lowell, in their book *Praise the Lord For Tax Exemption,* show that the Catholic Church has property in the United States assessed at $54 billion and enjoys a yearly income of about $13 billion, including $5 billion coming from donations of the faithful.[21] The Church also likes to keep secret where they have invested their money. However, the German magazine *Der Spiegel* was able to discover that Roman Catholic orders and societies have billions of dollars invested in chemicals and armaments securities. Some of the companies favored by this Church money are Boeing, Douglas, Lockheed and Curtis Wright. The Society of Jesus was found to own the controlling stock in the Bank of America, Di Giorgio Farms Conglomerate with its steamships and banana plantations, Phillips Petroleum and Creole Petroleum. *Der Spiegel* estimated the Jesuits' annual stock income on investments to be about $250 million.[22]

What the Catholic Church wants to conceal more than anything else—in implication at least—is this: The income they as well as other churches receive from investments and profits from church-owned businesses such as radio stations, magazines, newspapers, hotels, farms, mines and myriad others is free from all taxation. No other organizations, not even educational or scientific foundations, have this special tax exemption. And church property is exempt from property taxes besides. This gives church hierarchies such an advantage over regular tax-paying business concerns that many businesses have sold to the churches for high prices and then stayed on as managers. Both the church and the businessman end up making greater profits this way, but these profits accrue at the expense of taxpayers who have to make up the difference by having to pay higher property and income taxes. Although there are now efforts in some state legislatures and in Congress to tax church profits from such businesses, there is no way retroactively to redistribute the billions of dollars of profits already gathered in.

Another unfair tax privilege that churches have involves their religious orders and societies. These groups are not compelled to furnish financial statements for audit. Therefore, the government has no way of moving against religious organizations that may abuse tax laws prohibiting foundations from spending excessive sums for administrative or other expenses. Treatment of churches and secular organizations is widely divergent. A tax exempt foundation like the Sierra Club has had its tax-free status taken away because it spent too much money on lobbying for conservation and pollution control. Yet religious organizations lobby extensively against legalized abortion and dissemination of birth control information without having their exemption taken away.

There are many nuns who are employed in public schools as teachers or in post offices as postal clerks. They are paid from the public treasury, yet they pay no income taxes. Priests serving as chaplains in the armed services or as administrators in anti-poverty programs are on the government payroll, yet they too, pay no income taxes. Protestant and Jewish chaplains in the Armed Forces are required to pay income taxes.

These facts involving preferential treatment make the constitutional separation of church and state in America merely a myth. In addition to tax laws favoring religion, education and welfare legislation has been passed which allows religious schools, hospitals, missionaries, nursing homes and welfare agencies to receive billions of dollars in direct grants from the government each year. The lion's share of this goes to the Catholic Church.

The mass media have been so successful in concealing the special privileges that are granted to churches that the public has not been aware of how much it is having to pay for these billion dollar tax subsidies. The media have failed to make clear to the public that such laws are clear violations of the constitutional principle of separation of church and state as well as the fundamental concepts of fairness.

The media have also failed to clarify or cover any criticism of church education itself. The spectre of having millions of children indoctrinated to oppose separation of church and state, tax reform, legalized abortion and population control certainly is no bargain for American society, even if Catholic schools allegedly take a burden off the taxpayer. In the first place, tax exemptions end up paying for these schools. In the second place, the burden of having a substantial part of a generation indoctrinated with attitudes which prevent a realistic approach to man's greatest problems is a price that no society can afford to pay if it is to meet its challenges.

There have been no media owners crusading against church privileges or policies. There is no competition between viewpoints regarding the good or bad that result from church policies. Acting as a choir, mass media have used all available propaganda power to glorify religious hierarchies at the same time they drown out criticism of church economic, political and social policies. They have been so successful that the public has accepted church policies which result in starvation, abortion deaths, long delays of federal aid to education, unfair taxation and violation of the constitutional principle of separation of church and state. Equally important, the mass media by its overwhelming bias have prevented that public scrutiny of church policy and wealth that could force churches to serve the same causes for which Jesus Christ suffered—justice, peace, and concern for the poor and downtrodden.

21 The Importance of Censorship

> In order to function effectively as citizens the people
> must have access to the unfettered truth. Without this
> access, our whole foundation of government will
> crumble.
>
> Mark Hatfield

The majority of American people very likely would not support the United States' presence in Vietnam if they were aware that the United States, in order to prevent the collapse of the Saigon regime and an American defeat, has had to resort to acts of terrorism against civilians as a matter of policy. Aware of this, the mass media, as a choir of support for the United States' presence in Vietnam have done their best to convince Americans that American atrocities such as those revealed in the Songmy incident are isolated acts and do not represent part of American strategic policy originating from higher up. The mass media has succeeded beyond any liberal's worst expectations; the majority of American people were still supporters of the establishment's Vietnam policy even after the Songmy atrocities received maximum publicity.

Although the media has censored many items revealing that atrocities are committed as a matter of policy, censorship has not been the main technique used in concealing the policy. News items which have included proof of a policy of terrorism have been repeatedly published and broadcast. As early as February of 1966, *Liberation* magazine compiled and footnoted numerous items of this sort taken from the pages of the establishment's news agencies. When the villages of Ben Suc and Ben Tre, along with their inhabitants, were bombed, burned and finally annihilated, news releases were published.[1] When Jonathan Schell's two books giving detailed accounts of such operations were published, they were reviewed in the news media.[2] Some news media coverage was given the nation's leading expert on nutrition, Dr. Jean Mayer, when he claimed that chemical destruction of crops in Vietnam took its toll of death mainly among the children, the aged, and pregnant and lactating women.[3] Although the *New York Times* and the *Los Angeles Times* suppressed it, some papers carried Peter Arnett's March 1969 AP review of the state of the war in which he explained how in the "Phoenix Program" U.S. officers directed the assassination of thousands of Vietnamese civilians sympathetic to the National Liberation Front.[4] The Bertrand Russell War Crimes Tribunal, after hearing testimony of numerous witnesses that indicated a general policy of terrorism, found the United States guilty of war crimes. This was duly reported in the press.[5]

It is the unanimous use of an overwhelming hidden bias, rather than censorship, that has succeeded in maintaining public support for the war and the indefinite extension of the United States presence in Vietnam. Nevertheless the censorship that has been used is of importance for other reasons: It indicates whether media owners are dedicated to high journalistic standards and freedom of the press as they claim, or whether they will sacrifice these principles and the public's right to know in order to serve the establishment. One proven case of intentional editorial censorship is often all that is needed to prove the real motivation of a news agency. For a media owner to claim that he or his hand-picked employees use censorship only one day out of the year is not much better than a convicted killer saying he murdered on only one day out of the year. The existence of a real public dialogue, the life and death of people, nations and the human species could conceivably be affected or determined by whether or not people are aware of a single important event or situation. When it comes to some of the most important stories in the last ten years, the mass media have unquestionably been guilty of censorship.

BIG LEAGUE CENSORSHIP

1. The Songmy Incident

Up until November 1969 the silent majority of Americans could rest assured that Americans did not commit the kind of atrocities that they had heard were being committed by the Vietcong. The story of the American massacre at Songmy changed all this—they were no longer so sure. Let us investigate the performance of the news media in bringing this important story to the attention of the public.

After interviewing surviving relatives and neighbors, a Quang Buddhist Church investigation unit revealed that 570 South Vietnamese had been the victims of U.S. Military actions and executions in Songmy on March 16, 1968. *Newsweek* magazine put the total of slain civilians at 567.[6] The massacre was censored by the mass media for months until it was no longer possible to cover up the story. No reporters were at Songmy on that day, and the news media reported the Pentagon's version of the day's combat by noting that 128 "Reds" had been killed. No mention was made of civilians. Nearly six months passed without the press or anyone else investigating the official Pentagon version of what really happened on that day even though NLF radio broadcasts heard in South Vietnam and NLF publications in Paris were describing the massacre soon after it took place.[7] Furthermore, long before the press was forced to show an interest in the incident, Ron Haberle showed photographs he had taken of the massacre to a Rotary Club in Ohio. Haberle's story aroused little interest and the public remained in the dark about it.

After investigating on his own for six months and finding witnesses glad to talk about the incident, a former GI, Ronald Ridenhour, put together a 2000 word letter detailing what he had found out and sent it to the President, Secretary of State, Secretary of Defense and numerous congressmen. Two months later, after response from the politicians was so disappointing that Ridenhour feared nothing would be done, he contacted literary agent Michael Cunningham. Cunningham sent telegrams to *Life, Look, Newsweek, Harpers* and *Ramparts* outlining the alleged atrocities. None were interested except *Ramparts*. Cunningham refused *Ramparts* bid because Ridenhour didn't want the story associated with a radical magazine. He then offered the story to major newspapers in Boston and New York, the two wire services and at least one of the networks. They weren't interested either. As Cunningham said: "No one wanted to go into it," though, as he noted: "We were trying to give the story away."[8]

By September 1969, David Leonard, a reporter for the *Columbus Enquirer*, had finally stumbled on to a lead. He asked the Pentagon about the case of a Lt. William Calley Jr. and dug up enough information to publish a front-page story in the *Enquirer*. This should have been enough to alert the supposedly "watchdog" press about the incident, but nothing happened. The pentagon expected the story would cause a big splash and was quite surprised when other news agencies passed it up. As a Pentagon lawyer commented: "We were amazed that story never went any place—absolutely amazed."[9]

In October, Seymour Hersh, a free-lance writer in Washington D. C., began investigating the incident and was able to put together a story. He tried to sell his story to several publications including *Life* and *Look*, but none were interested. He finally sold it to the Dispatch News Service who released the story about the atrocities on November 13, 1969. Even after newspapers were aware—since it was now being distributed by a news service—that the story would not be suppressed any longer, 13 out of 45 who had the chance refused to buy the story.

After the story broke in November, the wire services, newspapers and broadcasting stations all got in each other's way trying to cover the story. This delayed performance does not cover up or ameliorate the deliberate censorship of the story for many months. Rather, it indicates the lack of real competition that exists in a commercial communication system in which people advocating solid liberal or radical left viewpoints own no outlets. Would the story have been passed up by a network, magazine, daily newspaper or wire service owned by someone like I. F. Stone, John Gerassi, Dr. Benjamin Spock, Professor Paul Ehrlich or Ralph Abernathy?

2. The Bay of Pigs Invasion

The government and newspapers "should be natural enemies" according to Mark Ethridge, retired publisher of the *Louisville Courier-Journal and Times*. In contrast, James Reston of the *New York Times* doesn't see the government and the press at odds: "From both sides they have more to gain by cooperating with one another," Reston says, "than by regarding one another as the enemy."[10] During the 1960 Presidential campaign, six months before the Cuban invasion was to be launched, Reston said:

> Senator Kennedy would have done better to keep quiet . . . for we are now probably in for another big splashing debate involving not only Cuba, but Guatemala and the activity of the CIA, and a lot of other things that could well be left unsaid.[11]

It appears that Reston sees the press as an instrument to serve establishment policies rather than as a channel of "splashing debate" about vital policies. It was Reston who, when asked, advised the publisher of the *New York Times* to play down and censor parts of a Tad Szulc article which revealed that the United States was definitely about to launch an invasion of Cuba using CIA-trained Cuban exiles.[12] The story was originally earmarked as the number one story to be placed under a four-column headline at the top of Page One. Orders from top management played down the article by giving it a one-column headline instead, and important parts were cut. The CIA'S participation in the invasion preparation, the date of the invasion and the planned air strike from Guatemala were deleted. Most important, the part indicating that the invasion was imminent was eliminated. Instead, the *Times* deliberately misled its readers by using a subhead emphasizing that the invasion was not imminent:

QUICK ACTION OPPOSED[13]

Attached to the end of this article was another very small news item noting that CBS on its radio news had reported that there were "unmistakable signs" that an invasion would soon take place. But the over-all tone of the larger article would not give any reader the impression that the invasion was either imminent, a sure thing or planned and directed by the United States Government.

The *New York Times* censorship and playing down of this article was the last in a long series of efforts by mass media to conceal the United States plans to wage an aggressive war against Cuba. As early as October 1960, there were reports of a planned invasion.[14] These reports didn't inspire the mass media to play it up or crusade against such an aggressive act of war. The editors of *Nation* magazine tried in November 1960 to get all major news media interested in an article revealing that the United States was well along its way in preparing the invasion, but none of them took the story.[15]

The *New York Times* justified its censorship and toning-down by claiming that it was in the national interest to do so. They claimed that publicizing such information may have alerted the enemy and thereby endangered the lives of the men involved.

Many feel, and I agree—this type of reasoning makes a mockery of democratic processes. In reality it is often a rationalization for using censorship to allow the government to carry out in secret the establishment's foreign policy. In the first place, nobody has granted news editors the authority to decide what is in the national interest. They have arrogantly assumed for themselves this semi-official role as censor. In the second place, exposure of an invasion or Vietnam-type intervention ahead of time may actually prevent establishment plans from being carried out and thus result in saving thousands of Asian, Latin American or American lives. The media owners censor such items because they support establishment policy, not because of either security reasons or concern for American lives. If the *New York Times* or any other news agency discovered a secret United States plot to invade, let us say, Canada, Spain or Israel, would they have censored the news? Or would they have published everything in order to expose the plan?

It is never in the national interest to prevent the public or Congress from debating on whether this country should wage an aggressive war or not. In fact it was in order to protect the nation against leaders who would wage unjustified and unwise wars that the founding fathers included in the Constitution the provision that requires Congress to openly debate the matter before declaring war. President Kennedy, after the disastrous Bay of Pigs invasion, expressed his confidence that had the press done its duty it would have saved the nation from such

a disastrous decision. He told *New York Times* Managing Editor Turner Catledge: "If you had printed more about the operation, you
could have saved us from a colossal mistake." He later added: "I wish
you had run everything on Cuba. . . . I'm just sorry you didn't tell it
at the time."[16]

3. The Assassination of President John F. Kennedy

Whatever the truth may be about the assassination of President
Kennedy, the news media cannot justify the use of censorship in their
initial attempts to silence the critics of the official version. For two
years after the assassination the news media allowed very little questioning of the official version. Mark Lane, in his book *A Citizen's
Dissent*, records how his pleas for a national examination of the evidence was refused by, among others, *Look, Life* and the *Saturday
Evening Post*.[17] When the *National Guardian* published it and sent
advance proof sheets to the UPI, they replied that they "would not
touch it."[18] The later controversy over the Warren Report version of
the assassination was also ignored at first by the news media. When
Professor Andrew Hacker offered to write an objective study criticizing the workings of the Commission, the *New York Times* rejected the
offer, stating that "the case is closed."[19] When it became fashionable
to question the report, the news agencies joined in criticizing the report, but this was later.

The initial controversy over the Warren Report took place not in
the news media but in old fashioned debates. Though well attended,
these debates were systematically ignored by the press. The New York
debate between Melvin Belli and Mark Lane had a turn-away crowd;
one hundred and seven members of the press were on hand. A committee that was monitoring television coverage of the event found
only very superficial coverage. Lane was interviewed both before and
after the debate by two reporters from the *New York Times*. He
checked the six important daily newspapers in New York City the
next day and discovered that not one of them even mentioned the
debate had taken place.[20]

Mark Lane's first book, *Rush to Judgement*, almost never made it
into print. For fifteen months Lane could not find a publisher to print
his book. By the time the book was published the media had finally
decided to accept the issue as suitable for coverage as a controversy
and as a result the book received 450 reviews and Lane was invited on

numerous occasions to appear on local and national television. His book became the number one best seller. Normally a second book by a best-selling author gets very good coverage by the press, but Lane's second book, *Citizen's Dissent*, published in early 1968 got a very cold mass media reception. The book is the most exhaustive and documented study of mass media's use of hidden bias on one issue that has ever been undertaken. In contrast to the 450 reviews received by his first book, Lane could only discover 4 reviews for *Citizen's Dissent* after the same amount of post-publication time had elapsed. None of the networks had asked him to appear, and only one syndicated program, Les Crane's, extended an invitation. Up to this time Lane hadn't been able to discover one newspaper story in the mass media noting that the book had been published.[21] Lane recalled: "One television producer invited a number of media representatives to debate with me regarding the serious charges in my book. All declined and several of them explained why.'We will bury that book with silence.'"[22]

BUSH LEAGUE CENSORSHIP

Newspapers, and radio and television newscasts have so much information to choose from that it is hard to determine whether they have deliberately suppressed a news item or whether they have honestly considered the news item to be unimportant by journalistic standards. When an item is unquestionably front-page news and still doesn't appear, then it is obvious that an act of deliberate suppression was involved, but most items are not important enough to be classified as definitely newsworthy. Nevertheless, a study of a news agency's handling of news on a certain issue can often reveal a pattern indicating definite editorial decisions to censor information unfavorable to the owner's position on the issue.

1. The *Los Angeles Times* on the ABM

Southern California is the heartland of the military-industrial-space complex. Each year firms in the area receive more than 4 billion dollars worth of defense-space contracts. The *Los Angeles Times*, the only Los Angeles morning daily, strongly supported the ABM system proposed by the military-industrial complex and the Nixon Administration. During a six-month period in 1969, when the issue was being debated, there were at least 11 different news items available that would tend to cast doubt on the *Times'* editorial position. The *Los Angeles Times* did not print any of them. Readers and journalists might readily see that these items were news-worthy.

Item 1. UPI. The Federation of American Scientists opened a campaign against the ABM and MIRV, claiming these systems would lead to further arms escalation and could cost $50 billion in ten years.[23]

Item 2, UPI. Senator J. Ellender urged President Nixon both to abandon the ABM program and not to extend the NATO alliance. Ellender, a frequent visitor to Russia, claimed that "the Russian people are very desirous of peace," and noted that "during the last 20 years our country has spent in excess of $130 billion to isolate Russia" with a ring of overseas bases and defense spending.[24]

Item 3, UPI. McGeorge Bundy, President of the Ford Foundation and a staff officer on foreign and defense policy for Presidents Kennedy and Johnson, said that the ABM is not needed and that the case being made for its use against future Red Chinese missiles "is so far from made that it is much better to wait."[25]

Item 4, AP. Senator Stuart Symington, member of the Armed Services Committee, claimed that a study made by the Brookings Institute indicated that an ABM system thick enough to stop a Soviet attack would cost $400 billion.[26]

Item 5, AP. An open letter, signed by 3200 scientists and scholars asking President Nixon to stop the ABM system urged "that the proposed deployment of the antiballistic missile system be cancelled and that negotiations with the Soviet Union be initiated as quick as possible to reverse the sterile, wasteful, and dangerous competition in armaments."[27]

Item 6, UPI. Senators Stuart Symington, Albert Gore and William Fulbright challenged the Pentagon's reasoning on the ABM system.[28]

Item 7, AP. The Massachusetts Senate by a vote of 23 to 6 adopted a resolution asking President Nixon to drop the ABM system.[29]

Item 8, UPI. A poll of 1216 physicists in the American Physical Society showed 76 percent were against the ABM system calling it "wasteful and futile."[30]

Item 9, UPI. The Federation of American Scientists, representing 2500 scientists, urged President Nixon to defer deployment of the ABM and stop further development of the MIRV pending disarmament talks. They said:

At this time both we and the Soviet Union have acknowledged

'sufficiency' in nuclear-armed missiles and each is confident of its strength.

. . . with the missile talks imminent, this country should not move ahead with the very two weapon systems we want to prohibit.

Former Vice President Humphrey said in London that going ahead with the ABM would "trigger a whole new level of arms competition and will begin a new armaments spiral."[31]

Item 10. Nine Senators and 36 Representatives issued a joint report warning against the "increasing militarization of American Society."[32]

Item 11. *A wire service account of a St. Louis Dispatch wire service release.* Thirteen Nobel prize winners formed a scientific group to oppose the deployment of the ABM system. They expressed doubts that the system would work. They saw it as probably lessening rather than increasing American security. The group included Herbert F. York, Department of Defense science adviser in the Eisenhower administration; Donald Hornug, former White House science advisor; Harold Urey and Hans Bethe, famous nuclear physcists whose research contributed to the development of the atom bomb. Spiro T. Agnew, talking about ABM critics the day before, claimed that "their criticism is based on a tacit acceptance of ignorance."[33]

Since *Los Angeles Times'* readers were kept from knowing about the above 11 items, it is quite possible they agreed with Spiro Agnew.

2. The *Los Angeles Times* on the Vietnam War

The *Times* has been a supporter of U.S. policy in Vietnam from the beginning. Every day it dutifully records the number of "Reds" killed according to Pentagon accounts. By prominently featuring its Pulitzer Prize awards for coverage of the Vietnam war, the *Times* makes its readers aware of its self-proclaimed excellence in news reporting. But the *Los Angeles Times* has passed up many news items on Vietnam that taken as a group would make any journalist suspect that deliberate suppression was involved. The following news items were not published by the *Times*.

Item 1, AP of February 8, 1967. In an open letter to the President, 400 former Peace Corps members urged the stopping of the bombing of North Vietnam, acceptance of participation of the National Liberation Front in peace talks and the adoption of a policy leading to disengagement.[34]

Item 2, an event in Saigon, May 16, 1967. A 33-year old South Vietnamese teacher, Miss Pham Thi Mai, burned herself to death to protest the United States presence in Vietnam. She left behind letters which were delivered for her to Ambassador Elsworth Bunker for transmission to President Johnson. One of the letters said:

> Most of us hate from the bottom of our hearts the Americans who have brought us the sufferings of this war.
>   . . . the tons of bombs and money you have poured on our people have shattered our bodies and nationalist sentiments.[35]

Item 3, AP of May 13, 1967. Premier Ky said that if he were defeated by a Communist or a Neutralist in the coming elections he would fight the winner militarily. He also stated that press censorship would continue during the election.[36]

Item 4, AP on or near June 5, 1967 by John T. Wheeler. The Viet Cong claims to have seized nearly 2.3 million acres from prosperous landlords and turned them over to the peasants. Premier Ky "turned over only about 20,000 new acres during his nearly two years in office. The evidence is that little has been done about land reform since Diem fell in 1963."[37]

Item 5, a wire service report of March 25, 1968. Lt. Colonel Sidney Roche retired after 27 years experience which included 4 years as a staff officer for the U.S. mission in Vietnam. He expressed doubts about the feasibility of the pacification program, stating: "It hasn't worked for 4 years and it won't work now." He said the South Vietnamese Army "may very well be the worst army in all of Asia." He predicted that the United States could not extricate itself and save South East Asia for the Allied side, "unless we face realities and make some changes. We have 20,000 dead so far and, God forbid, we're going to have another 20,000 dead if we continue as we are." He suggested an all out military effort.[38]

Item 6, AP of June 28, 1968. Colonel McMahon claimed that the body count was possibly a dangerous measurement for determining the enemy's combat potential. He said some units merely report whatever is expected for a particular action regardless of how many enemy soldiers actually were killed.[39]

Item 7, UPI of December 14, 1968. An estimated 30,000 Okinawans demonstrated for the immediate removal of the giant B52 bombers from Okinawa.[40]

Item 8, UPI of April 30, 1969. S. L. A. Marshall, in an assessment made at the request of the Pentagon, said that "40 percent of American caualties in the Vietnam war were due to our own mistakes" such as "too much impetuosity, too much hard charging . . . ."[41]

3. *Los Angeles Times* and the *New York Times* on the Vietnam War

The *New York Times* covered all the above eight news stories that were suppressed by the *Los Angeles Times*. But this does not mean that the *New York Times* has crusaded against the establishment's Vietnam policy. On the contrary, the *New York Times* through the years has used hidden bias to support the American presence in Vietnam. Some of the stories it has passed up indicate deliberate editorial suppression: it passed up the news items listed below. The *Los Angeles Times* also passed up the same items. Since the *New York Times* is considered the most thorough and reliable news agency in the country and the *Los Angeles Times* is ranked among the top 10 out of the more than 1700 dailies, suppression of the same items by both newspapers indicates that a very high percentage of the rest of America's news agencies also passed up these items. The first six items were uncovered and printed by I. F. Stone in his weekly newsletter.

Item 1, AP survey of October 23, 1966, based on the reports of twelve of its correspondents.

> In the South where the enemy deliberately mixes with the population, a massive toll is taken among civilians by artillery and aircraft. There are estimates that up to 5,000 casualties die each month, with 10,000 wounded. . . . The American command estimates that up to 40,000 Viet Cong and North Vietnamese regulars have been slain this year alone. But the figure is known to contain a large number of civilians. After a battle, all the dead other than allied troops are counted as enemy, even women and children.[42]

Item 2, Proclamation delivered at a New York City Press Conference of March 20, 1967. (No U.S. reporters attended even after the press was given advance notice.) In an open letter given to the U.S. student movement for distribution, 70 South Vietnamese students and professors proclaimed:

> We are students and professors in the universities of South Vietnam (Saigon, Hue, Dalat, Can-Tho and Van Hanh) and we thank you for trying to stop this dreadful war in our country. We cannot act officially, as you have done, because the government does not

permit our universities to express themselves freely. We have
launched petitions and appeals, but we cannot allow our names to be
published because we would be arrested and imprisoned. We write
to thank you and to exhort you to continue. We beg you to take into
consideration the following facts:

1. In the South Vietnamese cities, American power in support of
   the Ky government is so great that no one can protest the
   war, without risking his life or liberty. If this were not so,
   millions of people would raise their voices.

2. The Vietnamese people ardently desire the end of the war,
   but they have lost hope. They are not Communists but if the
   war does not end soon they will join the National Liberation
   Front because they see no other way out. . . .

3. **The present government of South Vietnam is not**
   our government and does not represent our people. It has
   been imposed upon us by the U.S. and is run by military men
   who fought for France against Vietnamese before 1954. If we
   were allowed to vote freely, this government could not last a
   single day. We want a government of our own, so we can
   solve the problems of Vietnam ourselves on a basis of national fraternity: negotiate peace with the National Liberation
   Front and North Vietnam, and negotiate the withdrawal of
   American troops with the U.S.

4. Don't believe that the danger of a Communist takeover justi-
   fies continuation of the war. We are convinced that we are
   strong enough to form an independent government. But it is
   for us, not you, to make the decisions because it is our lives
   and our country which are at stake. . . . [43]

Item 3, Report of a news conference on or near March 19, 1967.
Protesting the diversion of welfare funds to the war and supporting U
Thant's three-step plan to end it, 6000 doctors, nurses, health and
social workers declared:

As persons in the health professions, we have been especially
aware of the medical aspects of the war in Vietnam. Observations of
medical facilities estimate six civilian casualties for each military
casualty. The majority are children. Children burned with napalm
will be deformed and crippled for the rest of their lives. Yet a new
and 'more adhesive' napalm is being developed. Herbicidal crop
destruction is spreading disease and death from malnutrition; the
elderly, children and pregnant women are its chief victims. Cholera,

malaria and other diseases have ravaged large numbers of the civilian population. How can we so devastate a people whom we say we are aiding?[44]

Item 4, released to the press May 3, 1967. Twelve Methodist Bishops responding to General Westmoreland's inferences that dissenters were disloyal and unpatriotic, asked the General in an open letter:

> Do you believe national decisions which might lead to a Third World War should not be discussed and debated? . . . Would it be patriotism on the part of those who dissent to say nothing? . . . We are told this is a limited war, yet limit after limit is being exceeded. How can we believe there is any limit beyond which U.S. escalation will not go?[45]

Item 5, AP on or near July 3, 1967. A review of five years of the war by Peter Arnett and Horst Fass.

> In 1962 no one seemed to doubt that the war would be won. It is now five years later. Delusions still crowd realities. In answer to a particularly pessimistic report on pacification, a U.S. official in Saigon is informed by Washington: 'Your report is too leftist and defeatist. Please look for more encouraging aspects.'
>
> In statistical language, there are never any American military defeats in Vietnam. No matter how severe the U.S. casualties, the enemy usually takes far more. If the bodies were not actually left on the battlefield, then they were 'dragged away' or 'killed by air and artillery too deep in the jungle to investigate.' The ability of many 'destroyed' enemy units to return to the fray disputes allied claims. But even now the official impression is given that with 'just a few more troops' the job can be done, say 200,000 more.
>
> . . . A military machine tries to justify its role. Gen. Westmoreland, seeking indices of progress, will cite enemy casualties. Authorities have been stating for years that the guerrillas are demoralized, have been denied recruits and are ineffective. Yet the enemy seems as obstinate and daring as ever. . . . [46]

Item 6, Agence France Presse of December 3, 1967. (Subscribed to by the *New York Times*.)

> Hill 875, which was captured 10 days ago after a 5-day battle that cost 158 American lives has already been abandoned. . . .
>
> Of all the numbered ridges which earned fleeting fame during last month's big battles, only Hill 1338 remains in American or South Vietnamese hands. . . . The territory is vast and the impressive

number of American troops is not sufficient to hold any of it for long.[47]

Item 7, AP of September 18, 1969. At a news conference announcing a November 15 anti-war demonstration expected to bring out 500,000 people, Dr. Benjamin Spock denounced the President Nixon troop withdrawal plan as a "sop" and a "fraud" designed to weaken opposition to the war.[48]

Item 8, Reuters of December 12, 1969. In a speech in Holland a Canadian physician who spent four years in South Vietnam claimed the United States troops regularly committed mass murders. He had related his discoveries in a six-hour interview with Henry Cabot Lodge and was subsequently declared persona non-grata by the State Department. He blamed the U.S. press for not publicizing such atrocities.[49]

Item 9, Reuters of December 19, 1969. A former Sergeant, James Weeks, told of orders that were given to him and other American soldiers during operation "Junction City" in Tay Ninh province in May 1967:

> It was explained to us that anything alive in that area was supposed to be dead. We were told that if we saw a 'gook' or thought we saw one, no matter how big or small, shoot first. No need for permission to fire. It was just an 'open turkey shoot.' . . .
>
> At that time, men, women and children, no matter what their ages all went into the body count. This operation went on for a few weeks. This was a regular 'search and destroy' mission in which we destroyed everything we found.[50]

As mentioned before, the above ten stories were passed up by the *New York Times* and the *Los Angeles Times*. Was it only an oversight or was it deliberate editorial suppression?

4. On The Domestic Scene

The following news items were covered as indicated by the news agencies listed below each item.

Item 1, UPI of October 7, 1969. A member of the President's Commission on Civil Disorders, Victor Palmieri, accused President Richard M. Nixon of playing a dangerous racial "game." He said the President was making

> . . . an explicit appeal to all racial prejudices and resentments of

the white working man. The appeal has many different lyrics—law and order is one—but there is always the same haunting refrain.[51]

New York Times .... no coverage
Los Angeles Times .... no coverage
Honolulu Star-Bulletin .... no coverage

Item 2, AP of July 7, 1969. In an open letter to President Nixon, 550 Roman Catholic nuns who teach Negroes and Indians in 21 states accused the Nixon Administration of retracting school desegregation guidelines. The nuns said that by so doing the President "had given the world another reason to distrust and disrespect the United States."

New York Times .... Page 84, 15 lines
Los Angeles Times .... no coverage
Honolulu Star-Bulletin .... no coverage
*Huntley-Brinkley .... no coverage
*Walter Cronkite .... no coverage

> *Huntley-Brinkley and *Walter Cronkite* newscasts are listed only for coverage of news items occuring from July 1, to September 10, 1969.

Item 3, September 3, 1969. In an open letter, nineteen Congressmen urged Attorney General John Mitchell not to compromise on a suit accusing the nation's automobile industry of conspiring to delay development and installation of smog control equipment on motor vehicles. The Congressmen declared: "If these charges are true, the American people have a right to be fully informed of this outrageous corporate callousness by a full and open trial of the issues involved."

New York Times .... no coverage
Los Angeles Times .... Page One
Honolulu Star-Bulletin .... no coverage
Huntley-Brinkley .... no coverage
Walter Cronkite .... no coverage

Item 4, AP of May 6, 1969. Alsco Inc., the nation's leading supplier of rocket launchers used on aircraft in Vietnam, has admitted illegal war profiteering through inflating the costs of a non-competitive defense contract received in 1966. Earlier, the Associated Press revealed the company had received a $13.9 million contract at the same time the company's dealings were being investigated by a federal grand jury.

New York Times .... no coverage
Los Angeles Times .... III, Page 8, three column inches
Honolulu Star Bulletin .... Page 11, sixteen column inches

Item 5, In a U.S. district court, October 13, 1969. Andrew L. Stone, former president of Alsco Inc., pleaded guilty to conspiracy and making false statements to the U.S. Government. Two other former Alsco Inc. employees pleaded guilty to the charge of conspiracy to use "craft, trickery, deceit," and dishonest means in order to "hamper, hinder, frustrate, defeat, impair and impede" the Renegotiation Board and the Navy.

New York Times .... no coverage
Los Angeles Times .... Page 21, fourteen column inches
Honolulu Star-Bulletin .... Page 7, sixteen column inches

Item 6, UPI of September 10, 1969. Philip Elman of the Federal Trade Commission answered Senator Edward Kennedy's questionnaire about the extent of citizen participation in FTC decision making:

> On balance, the agency (FTC) has not fulfilled the exciting role its creators envisioned for it.
>
> Secrecy . . . has made it impossible for representatives of consumers to appear and defend their interests in proceedings before the agency . . . citizen participation in the agency's processes neither exists nor seems to be desired by the commission. . . .
>
> Investigations ordinarily take years to complete. Almost everything the commission does, and almost every case it decides is based on stale or inadequate information.
>
> At the higher staff levels, longevity, cronyism and political affiliation seem to be preferred over competence and merit.

New York Times .... no coverage
Los Angeles Times .... Page 17, nine-column inches
Honolulu Star-Bulletin .... no coverage
Huntley-Brinkley .... no coverage
Walter Cronkite .... no coverage

Item 7, wire service report of September 17, 1969. Professor Julius Goldberg of Loyola University disclosed that a study of death rates showed that people living in high-air pollution areas of Chicago have significantly higher death rates (1949 per 100,000) than people living in areas with lower pollution (1389 per 100,000).

New York Times....................... no coverage
Los Angeles Times................... Page 2, news roundup
Honolulu Star-Bulletin............. no coverage

Item 8, September 16 through 22, 1969. Between 1965 and 1968, on the Island of Hawaii, 14 miles from the city of Hilo, the U. S. Army secretly conducted open air testing of deadly and incapacitating nerve gas in weapons form. The Army also tested chemical "simulants" and a biological warfare agent called anthrax. The U.S. Army obtained the lease to the land from the state of Hawaii under false pretext of conducting "studies relative to meteorological conditions." To use the land for testing was a definite violation of the lease agreement.

In attempting to keep the people and Congress from becoming aware of this testing, Pentagon officials had to make evasive answers or lie on five different occasions as listed below.

Evasion 1, June 1969. Senator Daniel Inouye hearing of the testing, asked the Pentagon for an explanation. The reply merely stated that the Army was not testing now and had no future plans to do so. The explanation conspicuously failed to mention anything about the previous testing.

Evasion 2, on July 2. A spokesman for the Hawaii Army Headquarters stated: "We have conducted no nerve gas tests in Hawaii whatsoever." He failed to indicate that in using the word "we," he was speaking only for the U.S. Army Hawaii Command, and not for the entire U.S. Army.

Lie 1, July 1969. Honolulu Star-Bulletin reporter Richard Hoyt sent the following question to Defense Secretary Melvin R. Laird after having received no reply from the U.S. Army Hawaii Command:

> Has the Army ever tested either chemical or biological warfare weapons or agents in Hawaii?

The Pentagon replied:

> No. The Army has not tested either chemical or biological munitions in Hawaii.

Lie 2. After testing could no longer be denied, Colonel Raymond T. Reid of the Pentagon's legislative liaison division, in a letter to Representative Patsy Mink, claimed that the nerve gas tests were conducted "with the concurrence and knowledge of the State officials."

Lie 3. On September 18, the Pentagon issued a statement again claiming that the gas testing was not in "weapons form."

On September 22, Army Secretary Stanley Resor admitted that previous Pentagon statements regarding the testing were "inaccurate." This was the Pentagon's way of admitting that the above claims and denials had been lies.

Coverage of these Army testing stories from September 16-22, 1969 was as follows:

New York Times........................ no coverage
Los Angeles Times.................... Page 2, two column inches[52]
Honolulu Star-Bulletin............. Page One coverage

Item 9, wire services, November 24, 1969. At a House Labor subcommittee hearing in San Francisco, Dr. Lee Mizrahi testified that he had discovered—in routine checkups—insecticide poisoning in one-half of 58 children of farm workers. (He added that this in itself was not nearly as alarming as the fact that this was the first medical study done on children of farm workers.)[53]

New York Times........................ no coverage
Los Angeles Times.................... no coverage
Honolulu Star-Bulletin............. no coverage

Item 10, Reuters, December 5, 1969. In a United Nations Report, experts on chemical and biological warfare said that tear gas can cause permanent disability and can even be fatal.[54]

New York Times........................ no coverage
Los Angeles Times.................... no coverage
Honolulu Star-Bulletin............. no coverage

Item 11, Reuters, December 10, 1969. The Main Political Committee of the General Assembly of the United Nations condemned the use of tear gas, defoliants and herbicides by a vote of 58 to 3 with 35 abstentions. Australia and Portugal joined the United States in opposing the resolution.[55]

New York Times........................ Page 13
Los Angeles Times.................... no coverage
Honolulu Star-Bulletin............. Page 9

Item 12, Reuters, December 16, 1969. The United Nations General

Assembly approved by an 80 to 3 vote with 36 abstentions a resolution holding that the use of tear gas, chemical defoliants and herbicides in war was contrary to the generally recognized rules of international law as embodied in the Geneva Protocol of 1925. No votes were cast by the United States, Australia, and Portugal.[56]

New York Times........................no coverage
Los Angeles Times....................Page 21
Honolulu Star-Bulletin..............no coverage

To any objection that "at least these stories got some coverage"— I might respond: News agencies should be expected to cover newsworthy items just as a restaurant should be expected to serve food. The question shouldn't be whether or not the restaurant serves food, but what kind of food, what is its quality, and in what style and atmosphere is it presented.

A pattern is evident in the type of stories suppressed. All of the above items revealed situations, events or incidents which embarrassed the establishment or exposed the truth about some of their policies. There can be little doubt that this is why news editors classified them as not newsworthy, played them down or suppressed them deliberately. These are the type of stories a solid liberal or radical media owner—if there were any—would feature as priority news.

BLATANT CENSORSHIP

Mass media's dedication to the establishment is not always so obvious in their news presentations, but it is clearly manifested by their support and acclaim for the advertising and entertainment characteristics of the commercial communication system. It is here that media owners don't even make any pretense about permitting all viewpoints. The mass media have convinced the American people that since advertising and entertainment don't deal directly with news of the world, it's not important whether or not all viewpoints are presented.

Media owners themselves are fully aware that nothing could be further from the truth. A substantial segment of the population (especially the young) derive their ideas about political, social and economic situations entirely from entertainment and advertising. And of those who do watch a news program or read a newspaper, most still spend much more time tuned into the regular entertainment programing. The average family has the television on six hours per day and the radio on another two to five hours.[57] Advertising itself accounts for at least four times as much program time as news reports. There is little question that the cumulative effect of entertainment and advertising over long periods of time from childhood through old age is as important a factor in developing basic political attitudes as watching news programs. This being the case, it seems essential that there be a vigorous competition among different viewpoints in their depiction of society in humor, drama, song and advertisements.

1. Free Speech in Advertising

The advertising system not only brings media owners up to 100 percent profits; as we shall see, it also serves as a channel for direct and indirect establishment and communication industry propaganda. Groups representing solid liberal or radical viewpoints are almost totally shut out because they do not have the money required to compete. They can't purchase the services of an astronaut ad-man like Scott Carpenter or Wally Schirra, or an entertainer ad-man like Arthur Godfrey, Jack Benny, or Bob Hope. To purchase an eight-page advertising section in *Look* magazine costs about $350,000. To produce a one-minute commercial for television can cost as much as $250,000; to buy the network time to present it on a popular program can cost up to $65,000.[58]

Most advertisements, like most entertainment programs, have a direct or implied political, social or economic message. Full-page network advertisements proclaim how responsible and excellent they are as news agencies. In *Time* magazine, from July through December 1968, there were 14 full-page ads by establishment news agencies depicting their own excellence. One of CBS' ads claimed: "They sort out what's important, or will be, with authority, clarity, responsiblity." There were, of course, no ads during this six month period expressing the viewpoint that CBS' links with the defense establishment, space industry, professional athletics and the commercial communication system lead to distorted, unfair, irresponsible and frivolous newscasting.

Advertising agencies pay thousands of dollars each year for advertisements promoting the concept of advertising. A recent one in *Time* magazine asked:

What is advertising?

Essentially, it's free speech that somebody pays for.

It's a force that supports free choice in the market place of ideas, . . .

There are never any advertisements expressing the viewpoint that selling the opportunity to make free speech effective must make free speech meaningless for the poor.

In one three-week period billionaire Ross Perot was able to present his viewpoints supporting President Nixon's Vietnam policy in 300 newspapers with full-page advertisements and in a half hour television program. His qualifications? He had the $1 million it required. Just because they don't have the $1 million to spend for "free speech," many students, professors, laborers and veterans can not have access to media to claim that President Nixon's policy is a ploy—a way to extend the war through an attempt to have the South Vietnamese Army carry on the fighting. Because media owners agreed with Perot's ideas, they gave him millions of dollars worth of free advertisement by interviewing him for a half hour on a nationwide hookup (CBS), by featuring him on the front cover of their magazines (*Look*) and by including his activities and statements in newscasts.

Through a full-page advertisement paid for by taxpayer's money, the U.S. Army announced to five million *Look* readers: "When a man serves here, [Vietnam] he proves himself a man. To his country. To himself." There are never any ads expressing the viewpoint that a young man serving in Vietnam cannot escape becoming a partner to an unjust, immoral and criminal war initiated and perpetuated by America's establishment.

FMC, Esso Chemicals, Olin, Union Carbide, and Monsanto corporations all proclaim in full-page color ads in *Time* and *Newsweek*, and in television commercials that cost $20,000 apiece, that they are helping the Latin American peasant achieve a better life. There are never any advertisements expressing the very commonly held view that American corporations in Latin America are supporting dictatorial governments, encouraging American military intervention, preventing national economic development, exploiting the natural resources and bringing back most of their profits, and thus are important factors in keeping the peasant from improving his life or achieving political freedom. It is not surprising that Americans are a little shocked when Latin countries nationalize U.S. corporations.

Oil companies advertise their competitive spirit and dedication to

America in wartime. There are never any advertisements revealing that American oil companies' financial ties with Fascist firms in Germany before and during World War II were thought to be so unpatriotic and damaging—as well as patently illegal—that Senator Harry S. Truman branded them as "treason."[59] Oil company ads speak of their dedication to free enterprise and economic competition. There are never any advertisements pointing out the large scale price fixing by oil companies or the huge government subsidies in the form of tax depletion allowances and oil import quotas. Astronaut ad-men and others advertise the anti-pollution efforts of oil companies, but there is no one to advertise how the oil companies are prime polluters of America's ocean shelves, beaches, rivers, as well as air.[60]

General Motors spends millions of dollars on advertisements depicting itself as dedicated to pollution control and auto safety. There are never any advertisements depicting Ralph Nader's and others' views that GM and the other auto manufacturers have engaged in criminal conspiracies to drag their feet on automobile safety engineering and the development and installment of anti-pollution devices for motor vehicles. GM advertises that it is aiding the small businessman; there is no one who has the money to advertise the viewpoint that the huge corporation has swallowed up hundreds of small businesses.

Pharmaceutical companies spend millions each year for advertisements depicting themselves as dedicated to the health and welfare of Americans. There are no competing advertisements pointing out the excessive rigged prices, unethical advertising aimed at both public and physicians, and the contributions of drug companies to the drug problems of youth by their irresponsible selling of millions of amphetamine tablets to phony Tijuana addresses. The public sees no advertisements blaming the drug industry for using its political power to cooperate with the American Medical Association in defeating needed medical legislation during the last thirty years.

Pesticide companies send out their salesmen to sell as much pesticide as they can, often without regard to its effect on animal life, rivers or oceans. Their advertisements only picture the beneficial effects of pesticides, never the negative effect, and there never could be advertisements by those (unorganized individuals) who wish to point out the indiscriminate selling and deleterious effects of pesticides. Even if critics had the money to pay for such ads, they would not be accepted by the media.

Millions of dollars from the nation's household electric bill payments is spent to perpetuate myths fabricated by the private electric companies through their advertising campaigns. The advertisements attack liberalism as communism, consumer-owned electric companies as a dangerous socialistic trend, and government regulation as tyranny. There are very few ads expressing the viewpoint of Senator Aiken that: "The cooperative plan with its dispersal of ownership and control is the truest form of free enterprise."[61]

There are never any ads pointing out that private power companies use their customers' money to support right-wing groups such as the American Economic Foundation and the Foundation for Economic Education.[62] There are no advertisements expressing the viewpoint of Senator Metcalf, who said that private electric companies overcharge Americans billions of dollars every year, and that their advertisements have proven to be false.[63] A viewpoint like Senator Estes Kefauver's is never expressed in full-page color advertisements in mass circulation magazines: "Taxpayers and ratepayers are, indeed, paying for their own brainwashing without having the democratic right to determine whether they wish to do so or not."[64] Most important, there are no advertisements pleading for more effective government regulation so that the great electric monopolies can be properly controlled. There are no ads complaining that the electric companies—which cause pollution—spend less money on anti-pollution research than they do on advertising how they are saving the environment. Senator Metcalf states that the one-sided advertising by the electric companies has been so successful, "the IOU's had convinced a substantial segment of the population that no is yes, that high is low, that of course the world is upside-down!"[65] Defense contractors like Lockheed advertise their dedication and contributions to the nation's defense system. There is no one with equal money to advertise Lockheed's overcharging, cost overruns, excessive wartime profits and patent violations.

Nothing can better show the commercial communications system's complete betrayal of the idea of free speech than a single full-page advertisement that appeared in the *Los Angeles Times* of January 29, 1970. The advertisement was devoted to promulgating some of Carleton Putnam's subtle racist ideas such as his idea that the Northern Europeans are innately superior to the Blacks, Browns, Asians and Southern Europeans. He also sees the mass media as being under the control of liberal oriented minority groups. The black man in Watts is having enough trouble trying to pay for his groceries; he can hardly afford $4000 for a full-page advertisement to reply to this subtle racist message. This brings out an injustice implicit in advertising that is frequently overlooked. Liberal or minority groups either have to remain silent and accept one-sided propaganda attacking them, or spend their money just to have an equal chance to present their view. Their funds can thus be cleverly exhausted by very wealthy radical right groups which support viewpoints like Putnam's. The only conceivable advertising system that could be compatible with the idea of a public right to hear all viewpoints would be one which saw to it that no matter who paid for the space or time to present a political advertisement, the advertisement itself would have to present all viewpoints concurrently.

Mass media owners also manifest their true political stance by their refusal to print certain types of advertisements. When poor, liberal or consumer groups attempt to place advertisements attacking corporate greed, crime or foreign policy, they are often turned down by media owners. the *Columbia Journalism Review* noted that the Writers and Editors War Tax Protest had their advertisement refused by the *New York Times* in 1967 even though the leader of the group, Gerald Walker, was an employee of the *Times*.[66] The *New York Times* refused another advertisement which urged citizens not to support the war through the purchase of war bonds because this money would be used to buy napalm. An executive vice president of the *Times* didn't accept the ad because, in his view, it wasn't in the "best interests of the country." The *Times'* official position as stated on its editorial page is that the columns should remain open to advertisements expressing all points of view. In addition to pointing out this hypocrisy, Malcolm Margolin, formerly with an advertising agency, pointed out that the *New York Times* rejected a *Fact* magazine advertisement that attacked Federal subsidy of the Catholic Church. The advertisement consisted of official government statistics plus a quote by Thomas Jefferson saying: "I am for freedom of religion and against all maneuvers to bring about a legal ascendency of one sect over another."[67] The *New York Times* has always acted as a protector of Church policies; in 1949 they refused a Beacon Press advertisement for Paul Blanchard's book, *American Freedom and Catholic Power*[68] George Seldes also tells of the *Times'* past performance in boycotting Consumers Union advertisements which attempted to expose inferior products and false or misleading advertisements.[69]

The Amalgamated Clothing Workers wanted to buy full-page advertisements in four Chicago dailies explaining why people should buy American made men's wear, and why people "might even resent the retailers who buy foreign made clothing and pocket the higher markups without passing along the savings." All four newspapers refused to carry the advertisement.[70]

All commercial broadcasters in the San Francisco Bay Area refused to run advertisements by three anti-war organizations who wanted to respond to the political viewpoints included in military recruitment advertisements carried free as a public service by broadcasters. KFRC in San Francisco donated 405 minutes in one 5 week period. Post-Newsweek Corporation's WTOP refused to accept advertisements critical of the U.S. participation in the Vietnam war. The announcements, sponsored by Business Executives Move for Vietnam Peace (BEM) were recorded statements of retired Army Brigadier General William Wallace Ford; Rear Admiral Arnold True; Marriner Eccles, former chairman of the Federal Reserve Board and George Wald, Nobel Prize-winning biologist from Harvard. Ross Perot had no such difficulties when it came to finding news agencies willing to accept his money for advertisements supporting the administration's policy in Vietnam.[71]

2. Censorship of Entertainment

Media owners not only have allowed very conservative political viewpoints to completely dominate advertising, they have willingly allowed these same forces to determine what kind of political messages will be allowed in entertainment programs. During the 1950's the media owners were glad to go along with the Senator Joe McCarthy-inspired anti-communists who saw to it that any person in the entertainment business who was in the least bit liberal was blacklisted. The blacklisting was so successfully accomplished by sponsors and advertising agencies that radio and television owners had no need to resort to censorship. Anything that might offend their own moderate or conservative viewpoints was already censored by the agencies and sponsors who depended upon radical right periodicals like *Counterattack* or books like *Red Channels* for guidance in spotting those who knowingly or unknowingly contributed to the leftist line.[72] Murray Schumack, in his book *The Face On The Cutting Room Floor*, notes that in 1955 David Susskind submitted 5000 names for his show

"Appointment with Adventure" to the advertising agency which represented the sponsor, Lorillard Cigarettes. A third of the names were rejected by the agency which said they didn't like blacklisting but couldn't do anything about it. The agency ordered Susskind not to reveal that the entertainers' political viewpoints were the reason for their being blacklisted.[73] Approximately 10 percent of the scripts that were presented for "Alcoa Premier" were cancelled by the sponsor. Procter and Gamble had its own censorship code which stated: "Members of the armed forces must not be cast as villains. If there is any attack on American custom, it must be rebutted completely on the same show."[74] Schumack reveals that writers for television series were handed lists of "don'ts." Writers for "Manhunt" were informed "there must be no derogatory mention of any drugs, foods, [or] automobiles."[75]

While media owners can disclaim direct responsibility for such censorship since they had relinquished the authority, they certainly can be condemned for not offering any opposition. As Erik Barnouw notes in his history of broadcasting, despite the usual rhetoric of devotion to free speech, the networks were obliging and responsive to the establishment blacklisters such as General Motors, DuPont and Metropolitan Life.[76]

In the early 1960's, after a generation had been subjected to heavily censored entertainment, blacklisting began to decrease as networks and syndicates took over more responsibility for program production and fanatical anti-communism lost some of its political power. But censorship still remains—this time the result of the station or network management. Robert Montgomery, producer of many television dramas, claims that today the networks have a different kind of blacklist in order to "cover all those whom the networks dislike for any reason, particularly those who oppose them, by testifying at hearings, making public pronouncements in the press, or writing magazine articles."[77]

A more concrete manifestation of media owner willingness to openly and arrogantly censor entertainment programs is their treatment of even the most mild political dissent. Numerous CBS affiliate managers openly admitted censoring the tapes of the "Smothers Brothers" show ahead of time. If they didn't get the tape in time for this, they blipped out little pieces as it came over the air.[78] They weren't the first ones to have a whack at the "Smothers Brothers."

According to those who should know—the Smothers brothers—75 percent of the shows had sections edited out by CBS network management before they were sent out to affiliates for additional censoring.[79]

A few cases of censorship on the show indicates CBS' underlying attachment to the establishment. After a seventeen-year industry-wide blacklist was lifted, Pete Seeger was allowed by CBS to return to commercial broadcasting on a "Smothers Brothers" show in 1967. But apparently Pete had not got the message of those seventeen years because he wanted to sing his latest song, "Waist Deep in the Big Muddy," a song about a World War II soldier who drowns because his commanding officer made him keep walking on into water over his head:

> Now every time I read the papers,
> that old feelin' comes on
> We're waist deep in the Big
> Muddy and the big fool says push on.

Seeger claims that CBS programming practices asked him to drop this verse from the song and that when he refused they dropped the entire song. When asked if the song is too political for television, Seeger replied:

> I don't think that way about songs. I feel that one song is as political as another, but it is wrong for anyone to censor what I consider my most important statement to date. . . .
> I think the public should know that the airwaves are censored for ideas as well as for sex.[80]

In being taped for another "Smothers Brothers" show, Joan Baez dedicated the song, "Green, Green Grass of Home," to her husband David Harris:

> He is going to prison in June for three years. The reason he is going to prison is that he resisted Selective Service and the draft, and militarism in general. Anybody who lays it out in front like that generally gets busted, especially if you organize, which he did.[81]

This dedication was never heard by the audience. In fact the entire program that included it was not shown on January 5, 1969, the day it was scheduled for: the show was replaced with a re-run. In trying to justify this censorship one top executive stated that the program included "at the very least . . . a monologue which in our opinion would be considered to be irreverent and offensive by a large segment of our audience and therefore unacceptable. . . . "[82]

CBS Vice President Will Tankersley cut out part of David Steinberg's humorous description of Moses' encounter with God in the desert. Steinberg related how Moses was told by the Almighty to take off his shoes and approach a burning bush. Steinberg interjected by suggesting: "We're not sure what he said, but this may have been the first mention of Christ in the Bible." Vice President Tankersley was apparently a little gun shy in protecting religion; four theologians of different faith, when shown the tape, found it fun and not offensive.[83]

CBS eventually solved the problem of the "Smothers Brothers" the old-fashioned way by cancelling the show. The Smothers responded by asking: "Now if we're thrown off this easily, what will happen to someone who has something really important to say?"[84] The Smothers brothers were picked up by another network, but they would probably be among the first to agree that those with "something really important to say" are still on the sidelines because they are too controversial for prime-time programing.

Bobby Darin originally had his song "Long Line Rider" approved for his appearance on the "Jackie Gleason" show, but shortly before the program in April of 1969, he was told the lyrics were "objectionable" and could not be permitted. The lyrics dealt with prison brutality and the official interpretation of alleged atrocities. The lyrics said in part:

> that's the tale the warden tells, as he
> counts his empty shells . . .
> This kina thing can't happen here,
> specially not in an election year.[85]

In December 1969, CBS censored, on two different occasions, appeals asking the audience to send mail for world peace to Mrs. Coretta King. The appeals were made by Carol Burnett and Elke Sommer on different Merv Griffin shows. CBS claimed it was against a network policy that forbids appeals for active support of any cause without prior consultation with the network.[86] Some may wonder if any of Bob Hope's appeals on his *special* hour-long network advertisements for the Vietnam war policy are ever edited out?

The most important censoring leaves no evidence behind; it is censoring through conditioning writers not to submit scripts which may embarrass or expose the status quo in the first place. Rod Serling admits: "We will generally stay away from those things we know either will not be touched or will be so diluted and vitiated that they will bear no resemblance to our original ideas."[87] Another television writer who has spent twenty years in the trade, Oliver Crawford, commented in 1968: "We can't touch Vietnam, abortion, or Presidential heart attacks."[88] When experienced television writers have two out of three of their ideas for scripts rejected, they are bound to stay away from controversial ideas or quit the business.[89] Censorship through conditioning finally surfaced as a political, if not a media-acknowledged, issue when David Rintels testified before a Senate subcommittee. The chairman of the censorship committee of the 3000-member Writers Guild of America stated that broadcast executives:

> allow laughter but not tears, fantasy but not reality, escapism but not truth . . . 75 million people are nightly being fed programs deliberately designed to have no resemblance at all to reality . . . They [writers] have proposed shows about South African apartheid, Vietnam, old folks, mental disease, politics, business, labor, students and minorities, and they have been chased out of the studios . . . These instances are symptomatic of the rigorous and final institutionalization of censorship and thought control on television.[90]

Conclusion

It is clear that the subtle, and not so subtle, censorship of popular entertainment and advertising is merely a more obvious manifestation of the suppression and use of bias in news programs. Despite the interest and concern that censorship of particular items arouse, the power to implant hidden bias in news, advertisements or entertainment over a long period of time is much more important in shaping public attitudes. The primary persuasive factor is not so much the content that ends up as news or entertainment as it is the biased style of presentation, a factor that was ignored by the public until Spiro Agnew made it an issue. Nevertheless, attention to censorship can prove beyond doubt that the controllers of mass media deliberately violate their own professional journalistic standards and the concept of free speech in their attempts to shape public attitudes in ways desired by the establishment. It further shows a blatant arrogance combined with a fear of and contempt for, the common American. It shows that media owners are the last people in the country who want a free and fair dissemination of information from all viewpoints.

22   Can Democracy Survive the Mass Media?

> I predict a difficult future for the United States of America. A great nation cannot survive for long on a shifty and slippery foundation of self-deception and misinformation.
>
> William J. Lederer
> *Nation of Sheep*, 1961

> Our independent American press, with its untrammeled freedom to twist and misrepresent the news, is one of the barriers in the way of the American people achieving their freedom.
>
> Clarence Darrow

Throughout man's existence his eyes and ears on the whole have relayed to his brain a fairly reliable picture of his environment. His responses to this picture have always been good enough to enable him to survive as a species for some two million years. Some animal species have become extinct because they weren't aware of, and thus did not respond to, threats in the environment. Others, while recognizing threats to their survival were not able to do anything about them, because their natural instincts were inadequate to cope with a new and different environment. If man fails, and if humans become extinct, it will not be because of our inability to respond to or cope with danger signals; it will be because we don't recognize these signals in time, or because we overreact to minor dangers.

To recognize the real dangers we need the best communications system possible, one that alerts the people to what lies ahead. This can't be done without giving the people the truest picture of reality possible. The United States has failed, and is failing, to respond adequately to dangers from within because our communication system has not alerted us in time to the real dangers that face our nation and the world. The picture of the world fashioned through media bias, distortions, myths and censorship has been considerably out of touch with reality. The people have responded appropriately to the challenges and dangers communicated to them by the media. They cannot be blamed if some challenges were ghosts and others were distorted. The *blame* for mistaken policies and priorities rests with those who have used the media as a tool to mislead public opinion in ways that benefit their own special interests at the expense of the nation's health and vitality.

There have been cases of improvement in the mass media over the years but only in response to crises, never in time to alert the people to prevent the crises. By the time some crises force the media to pay adequate attention to them it may be too late. Can we wait for a nuclear holocaust or a world destroyed by chemical-biological warfare before we put an end to the arms race? Can we wait until another generation of Americans is propagandized into accepting establishment priorities before our communication system is changed?

The past and present performance of the commercial media demonstrate that we cannot wait for them to lead the way. They respond only to threats of losing money, credibility or prestige. The nation desperately needs a free and open market place of ideas that can only come about when the communication system is designed to serve the public's right to hear all viewpoints fairly presented. The black man or the migrant worker should not be placed at a disadvantage just because he can't afford to own a television station or a newspaper. Dissident voices cannot depend on the wealthy to fairly present their views for them. Nobody is neutral. Objectivity is no answer for it is impossible. Bias cannot be eliminated. Meaningful competition between hostile ideas will only exist when all viewpoints have an equal opportunity to produce their own bias.

The wealthy cannot be blamed for using their communication system and money to persuade people to their point of view. It is inevitable that people use whatever techniques are available to persuade others. Those with the most to hide will naturally strive hardest to monopolize the media, as they know their selfishness would easily be recognized in open competition among ideas. Laws and the politicians that cater to special interests would be exposed for what they are. That the big corporations and their politicians have for decades been able to hide their greed and clothe themselves in an aura of respectability is testimony to mass media's complicity and its effect upon the public.

It is up to Congress and the Courts to insure that the right to equal access and the right to hear all viewpoints are guaranteed, just as it is their job to insure people of equal justice, education and the right to vote. The Courts are coming to interpret free speech as a right which includes the freedom of all views to have some access to the means of communication. Jerome A. Barron, writing in two different law journals, has cited many recent court decisions in making his convincing case for an affirmative interpretation of the first amendment which would not only protect the right to speak, but also guarantee the opportunity to be heard.[1] The Supreme Court in the Red Lion case has rendered a decision which expands the right of free speech to include the audience. Writing for the court in a 7-0 decision upholding the Fairness Doctrine, Justice Bryon R. White stated: "It is the right of the viewers and listeners, not the right of the broadcasters, which is paramount."[2] In expanding the concept of free speech, court decisions can only go so far. Just as additional legislation was needed to put into effect earlier civil rights decisions, the necessary legislation must be enacted to change the communication system so that the right to free speech and all it involves becomes a reality for the mass of men. All the arguments for saving the present commercial communications system—as it is—are no more valid than the arguments to maintain clever forms of racism or a belief in a flat earth. The public must be made to realize that unequal control over access to the technology of persuasion is a condition which inevitably violates free speech and the right to hear all views presented equally. To achieve this may be as difficult as achieving equal justice or educational opportunities for all, but that should not stop us from making the effort. In endeavoring to create the best communication system possible, price should not be a restricting factor anymore than it should be in maintaining an adequate defense. Every penny spent to improve our communication system would be paid back a hundred fold if mistakes like Vietnam and the moon spectacular could be avoided ahead of time. Billions could have been saved by beginning pollution and population control twenty years ago when the danger signals were ignored by our present system.

The purpose of freeing the communication system is to enable the people to have real choices. When they must vote on the basis of distorted views and establishment myths, they are merely expressing the sickness of our communication industry. The polls can only measure the extent to which techniques of persuasion have shaped and programmed public opinion. Until the basic reasoning ability and sense of justice of the people is freed by a fair communication system, the major problems in America will go unsolved. Progress will remain piecemeal and inadequate; there will not be a basic reordering of priorities in time to save the Nation from self destruction.

The battle to establish a vital competition between opposing and hostile viewpoints is a non-partisan battle that every American, reactionary to radical, can join. The battle may not succeed in quickly bringing about a real alternative to the commercial communication system and its inevitable bias, distortion and censorship, but it can succeed in making the people aware of what should be the Nation's most important issue and task.

The effort to improve the quality of life in America has to be first the fight to save America from the distorted view of reality presented by the communication industry. It is a fight to restore the average man's participation in government by really letting him decide important questions. It is the average man, the man who doesn't have large corporate interest to protect, that is the strength of a democracy. His reasoning ability and sense of justice enacted into decisions and poli cies constitute the type of government envisioned by those who wrote America's Declaration of Independence. There has never been a better idea for governing a nation. Our major mistakes have not been the result of democracy, *but of the erosion of democracy made possible by mass media's manipulation of public opinion.* This erosion could only be stopped in the unlikely event that the Courts, the Congress and the American people were to demand that all political viewpoints have equal control over access to a mass communication system that is not for sale to anyone.

Appendix

Books Recommended for Interested Students and Laymen

George Seldes, *Never Tire of Protesting*, Lyle Stuart, N.Y., 1968.

Mark Lane, *A Citizen's Dissent*, Fawcett Publications, Greenwich, Connecticut, 1968.

Nicholas Johnson, *How to Talk Back to Your Television Set*, Little and Brown, N.Y., 1970.

Robert MacNeil, *The People Machine*, Harper & Row, N.Y., 1969.

Robert Montgomery, *A Letter From A Television Viewer*, Heineman, N.Y., 1968.

Robert O'Hara, *Media For the Millions*, Random House, N.Y., 1961.

Harry J. Skornia, *Television and Society*, McGraw-Hill, N.Y., 1965.

William Rivers, *The Opinionmakers*, Beacon Press, Boston, 1967.

Theodore Peterson and others, *The Mass Media and Modern Society*, Holt, Rinehart, and Winston, Inc., N.Y., 1965.

John Hohenberg, *The News Media*, Holt, Rinehart and Winston, Inc., N.Y., 1968.

Herbert Schiller, *Mass Communications and American Empire*, Augustus M. Kelly, N.Y., 1969.

Dale Minor, *The Information War*, Hawthorne Books, Inc., N.Y., 1970.

James Aronson, *The Press and the Cold War*, Bobbs-Merril Inc., Indianapolis, 1970.

Edith Efron, *The News Twisters*, Nash, Los Angeles, 1971

Joseph Keeley, *The Left-Leaning Antenna*, Arlington House, New Rochelle, N.Y. 1971

A. Kent MacDougall, Ed., *The Press: Profiles in Courage and Conviction*, Dow Jones, Homewood, Illinois, 1972

Allan Frederiksen, *Community Access Video*, Book People, Berkeley, 1972

Footnotes

INTRODUCTION – FOOTNOTES

1. U.S. vs. Associated Press, 326 USI, 20, 1945, quoted in William Rivers, *The Mass Media,* Harper & Row, N.Y., 1964.

2. Eric Sevareid reported in a commentary that $500 billion would be the total cost of the Vietnam war according to a group of former monetary officials, *Walter Cronkite,* December 3, 1969; Dr. Eugene Shoemaker, a principal investigator for Apollo, estimated that the scientific achievements of the Apollo program could have been gained with unmanned spacecraft at one-fifth the cost. *Los Angeles Times,* October 9, 1969, p. 3.

3. *A Free and Responsible Press,* University of Chicago Press, 1947, p. 113.

CHAPTER 1 – FOOTNOTES

1. CBS, repeat showing of "Hunger in America."

2. AP, *Stars and Stripes,* Fulda, Germany, May 29, 1969, p. 5.

3. *Congressional Record,* June 13, 1938, p. 2648.

4. Ibid.

5. *Congressional Record,* May 19, 1941, p. 4195.

6. *In Fact,* June 21, 1948.

7. *New York Times,* March 11, 1950, p. 7.

8. Ibid., March 17, 1950, p. 1.

9. Ibid., March 18, 1950, p. 10.

10. Ibid., March 17, 1950, p. 1.

11. Ibid., September 20, 1956, p. 25.

12. Ibid., April 8, 1960, p. 16.

13. A printed record of various network newscasts was compiled by the U.S. Senate Committee on Commerce, 87th Congress, 1st Session: Report 994, part 4, *Freedom of Communications,* subcommittee of the subcommittee on communications, U.S. Government printing office, 1961. Some portions that covered the candidates were not included, so it is possible but not very likely that hunger received some coverage in one of these portions.

14. Ibid., pp. 56, 167.

15. *New York Times,* December 12, 1964, p. 25.

16. Ibid., December 19, 1965, p. 46.

17. Ibid., April 26.

18. Ibid., April 30, 1967.

19. See footnote number 13.

20. Since *Huntley-Brinkley* is seen six days a week, I have included CBS *Saturday Evening News* with *Walter Cronkite* (seen only five times a week) in all analyses in this book so that both NBC and CBS will be represented six days a week.

CHAPTER 2 – FOOTNOTES

1. *Unsafe at Any Speed,* Grossman Publications, N.Y., 1965, p. 329.

2. *Mass Media and Violence,* Vol. IX, Edited by Robert K. Baker and Sandra J. Ball, A Report to the National Commission on the Causes and Prevention of Violence, U.S. Government Printing Office, Washington D.C., 1969, p. 76.

3. "Management of Facial Injuries Caused by Motor Accidents," January 9, 1937, p. 103.

4. January 8, 1937.

5. "Automobile Injuries," September 18, 1937, p. 940.

6. Ibid., p. 944.

7. June 25, 1948.

8. "Medical Criticism of Modern Automotive Engineering," October 30, 1948, p. 627.

9. Ibid.

10. *New York Times,* December 6, 1948, p. 24.

11. Ibid., January 7, 1955, p. 20.

12. Ibid., January 12, 1955.

13. Jeffrey O'Connell and Arthur Myers, Random House, N.Y., 1966, p. 26.

14. Ibid.

15. *New York Times,* August 7, 1957, p. 39, and August 9, 1957, p. 20.

16. O'Connell and Myers, *Safety Last,* p. 29.

17. *New York Times,* March 29, 1961, p. 36.

18. Ibid., October 18, 1961, p. 38.

19. Ibid., April 16, 1966, p. 1.

20. Ibid., November 12, 1957, p. 39.

21. Ibid., March 19, 1962.

22. Ibid., April 1, 1962.

23. April 18.

CHAPTER 3 – FOOTNOTES

1. *New York Times,* May 23, 1969, p. 49; *Los Angeles Times,* September 10, 1970, p. 1.

2. *National Observer,* January 22, 1972, p.7

3. American Cancer Society, 1972

4. *New York Times,* September 4, 1969, p. 21.

5.   Ibid.

6.   Ibid., March 12, 1939, p. 4.

7.   Ibid., February 25, 1938, p. 19.

8.   George Seldes, *Never Tire of Protesting,* Lyle Stuart Inc., N.Y., 1968, p. 63.

9.   Ibid., p. 68, and *In Fact,* August 2, 1948.

10. Dr. J.M. Gehman, *Smoke Over America,* Beoma Publishing House, Paterson, New Jersey, 1943, and Andrew Salter, *Conditional Reflex Therapy,* Creative Age, N.Y., 1949.

11. *New York Times,* March 12, 1939, p. 4.

12. December 23, 1944, p. 11.

13. March 27, 1948.

14. October 24, 1949.

15. July 18, 1950.

16. *New York Times,* July 16, 1952.

17. Ibid., December 12, 1952.

18. Ibid., December 9, 1953.

19. December 21, 1953.

20. "Smoking and News," *Columbia Journalism Review,* Summer 1963, p. 6.

21. Ibid.

22. *New York Times,* October 13, 1960, p. 38.

23. Ibid., October 26, 1960, p. 41.

24. Ibid., October 30, 1960, p. 84.

25. Rowse, *Columbia Journalism Review,* Summer 1963, p. 6.

26. Westinghouse Broadcasting Company, KFWB, Los Angeles, December 16, 1969.

CHAPTER 5 — FOOTNOTES

1.   Ballantine Books, N.Y., 1968, p. 17.

2.   Egeberg, *Los Angeles Times,* September 22, 1969, p. 11; Du Bridge, *Los Angeles Times,* November 24, 1969, p. II:2, and December 21, 1969, p. 1.

3.   Population Reference Bureau, cited in Department of State Bulletin, July 1, 1968.

4.   Ehrlich, *Population Bomb,* Ballantine Books, N.Y., 1968, p. 18.

5.   *Guardian Weekly* (London), September 19, 1968, p. 7.

6.   William L. Rivers, *The Mass Media,* Harper and Row, N.Y., 1964, p. 21.

7.   Small face photographs were not included.

8.   It is possible that some items concerning these issues could have escaped notice since the printed transcripts as assembled by the Senate Committee on Commerce, Report 994, excluded some portions of the newscasts relating to the presidential campaign. However, it is unlikely that any such news items were covered in the sections omitted because neither candidate made hunger, pollution, or population control an important issue in the campaign.

9.   This does not take into account Morgan's daily commentary following his newscast as it wasn't included in the Report. More than any other journalist in broadcasting during the early Sixties, he addressed himself to the problems others ignored.

10. This analysis excludes NBC newscast of July 22 and August 10 because the broadcasts were preempted from their regular time. Request for a transcript of these newscasts was ignored by NBC. I was unable to include CBS on July 30. Upon request for a transcript, CBS replied that it did not provide such a service.

11. This category excludes news items on hunger in Biafra since the hunger situation there was primarily due to the civil war and would not otherwise have been covered as an aspect of world hunger resulting from overpopulation.

12. This category does not include coverage of response to the war in the United States.

13. CBS *Saturday Evening News* is a CBS News presentation, but utilizes different personnel than *Walter Cronkite* weekday newscasts.

14. *New York Times,* November 13, 1968, p. 33.

15. August 25 and 26 were 8:30 a.m. newscasts from KRKD's newsroom using Mutual sources.

16. See footnote 11.

17. See footnote 12.

CHAPTER 6 — FOOTNOTES

1.   Marvin Barrett, ed., *Survey of Broadcast Journalism,* 1968-69, Grosset and Dunlap, Inc., N.Y., 1969; wire service reviews sent out November 10, 1969, NBC and ABC omitted it November 10 and 11, 1969.

2.   *New York Times,* City Edition, November 11, 1969.

3.   *Survey of Broadcast Journalism,* 1968-69, p. 4.

4.   Ibid., p. 7.

5.   Ibid., p. 70.

6.   Ibid., p. 20.

7.   Ibid., p. 4.

8.   *Los Angeles Times,* November 11, 1969, p. IV:22.

9. *Final Report: President's Task Force on Communications Policy.* Superintendent of Documents, Washington D.C., December 7, 1968.

10. *New York Times,* May 21, 1969.

11. *Los Angeles Times,* May 22, 1969.

12. *A Free and Responsible Press,* p. 16.

13. Ibid., book jacket.

14. Ibid., p. 65.

15. March 27, 1947.

16. *New York Times,* November 20, 1948, p. 10.

17. 76th Congress, 3rd Session, Senate Committee Print, Temporary National Economic Committee, Mono. No. 26, "Economic Power and Political Pressures," 1941, pp. 6,9.

18. Ibid., p. 8.

19. Ibid., p. 10.

20. 76th Congress, 1st Session, Senate Report No. 6, Part 6, *Violations of Free Speech and Rights of Labor.* The Committee on Education and Labor, 1939, p. 172.

21. Ibid., p. 218.

22. Ibid., p. 162.

23. Ibid., p. 219.

24. Ibid., p. 219.

25. *Time,* January 3, 1938, p. 9.

26. Committee on Education and Labor, *Violations of . . .,* No. 6, part 6, p. 221.

27. "Mass Communication and Socio-Cultural Integration," *Social Forces,* December 1958, pp. 109-116.

28. *Congressional Record,* March 20, 1950, pp. 3685-91.

29. Ibid.

30. Senate Committee on Commerce Report 994, *Freedom of Communication,* p. 1030.

31. *Newsweek,* September 14, 1959, p. 94, and *Time,* September 14, 1959, p. 94.

32. *New York Times* had an article about Guterma on the 3rd, but it was concerning a different crime.

33. Ibid., February 1, 1967.

34. Ibid., April 8, 1969.

35. *New York Times,* July 24, p. 75.

36. KPFK newscast, Los Angeles, July 24, 1969.

37. *New York Times,* July 23, 1969, p. 95.

38. Cecil Smith, *Los Angeles Times,* July 25, 1969, p. IV:19.

39. Andrew Terrence, *National Enquirer,* June 8, 1969, p. 18.

CHAPTER 7 — FOOTNOTES

1. Macmillan and Company, N.Y., 1969, p. 160.

2. *New York Times,* October 11, 1969, p. 39.

3. Ibid., October 19, 1969, p. 8.

4. World Publishing Company, Cleveland, Ohio, 1968, p. 223.

5. Ibid.

6. Ibid., p. 209.

7. May 31.

8. "The Rich, Risky Business of TV News," *Fortune,* May 1, 1969, p. 95.

9. Ibid., p. 97.

10. Robert MacNeil, *The People Machine,* Harper & Row, N.Y., 1968, p. 78.

11. See table III.

12. John Hohenberg, *The News Media,* Holt, Rinehart and Winston Inc., N.Y., 1968, p. 228.

13. The Commission . . ., *A Free and Responsible Press,* p. 58.

14. Baqdikian, "Death in Silence," *Columbia Journalism Review,* Winter 1964, pp. 35-37.

15. Bryce Rucker, *The First Freedom,* Southern Illinois University Press, 1968, p. 226.

16. CBS, *Walter Cronkite,* November 28, 1969; *Columbia Journalism Review,* Summer 1970, p. 5

17. Rucker, *The First Freedom,* p. 226.

18. Ibid.

19. Ibid.

20. *Fortune,* May 1, 1969, p. 92.

21. Fred Friendly, *Due to Circumstances Beyond Our Control,* Vintage, N.Y., 1967, p. 170.

22. Ibid., p. 183.

23. Friendly, Due To ..., p. 265.

CHAPTER 8 — FOOTNOTES

1. UPI, *Stars and Stripes,* Fulda, Germany, January 1, 1969, p. 5.

2. "The American Media Baronies," *Atlantic,* July, 1969, p. 83.

3. *The First Freedom,* pp. 21-22.

4. *Atlantic,* July 1969, pp. 90-94: *Columbia Journalism Review,* Winter 1969-70, p. 19.

5. Rucker, *The First Freedom,* p. 8.

6. Ibid., p. 24.

7. Ibid., p. 191.

8. Ibid., p. 197.

9.   Ibid., p. 45.

10. Ibid., p. 89.

11. Ibid., p. 193.

12. Ibid., pp. 196-7.

13. McGraw-Hill Book Company, N.Y., 1965, pp. 11, 18.

14. Augustus M. Kelley, N.Y., 1969, pp. 79-87.

15. Ibid., pp. 147-8.

16. *Atlantic,* July 1969, pp. 88-94.

17. Robert Shayon, *Saturday Review,* September 25, 1971, p. 18 tember 25, 1971, p.18

18. April 15, 1967, p. 14.

19. Random House, N.Y., 1964, p. 273.

20. Ibid., p. 279.

21. *Overcharge,* p. 165.

22. *Newsweek,* July 4, 1966, p. 80.

23. *Honolulu Advertiser,* April 18, 1970, p. 10.

24. "Survey of Extremism," *Homefront,* July-August 1969, pp. 49-52.

CHAPTER 9 — FOOTNOTES

1.   *Boston Sunday Globe,* February 18, 1968, p. 2A.

2.   Jack Lyle, *The News in Megalopolis,* Chandler Publishing Company, San Francisco, 1967, p. 106.

3.   Ross, *The Image Merchants,* p. 78.

4.   Ben Bagdikian, "Behold the Grass-Roots Press, Alas!" *Harpers,* December 1964, p. 102.

5.   *Congressional Record,* May 26, 1950, pp. A4041-3, as quoted in *In Fact,* June 12, 1950.

6.   *Editor and Publisher,* October of every Presidential election year.

7.   "How Newspapers Use Columnists,"*Columbia Journalism Review,* Fall 1964, p. 20.

8.   Quoted in Eric Barnouw, *The Golden Webb,* Oxford University Press, 1968, p. 136, from Radio Daily, September 16, 1943.

9.   *Newsweek,* March 25, 1968, p. 97.

10. ABC Evening News, November 6, 1969.

11. Ibid., November 11, 1969.

12. Ibid., November 24, 1969.

13. Ibid., October 10, 1969.

14. *Los Angeles Times,* December 12, 1969, p. IV:32.

15. CBS, *Walter Cronkite,* 1969.

16. Ibid., November 4, 1969.

17. Barnouw,*The Golden Web,* pp. 222-24.

18. Ibid., p. 254.

19. Ibid., p. 119.

20. Ben Bagdikian, "Case History: Wilmington's 'independent' newspapers," *Columbia Journalism Review,* Summer 1964, p. 13.

21. Interviewed on KPFK, September 26, 1969, 11:00 AM.

22. David M. Rubin and William M. Rivers, "The Chronicle, schizophrenia by the Bay" *Columbia Journalism Review,* Fall 1969, p. 44.

23. "Where Does Friction Develop for TV News Directors," *Journalism Quarterly,* Summer 1957, p. 355.

24. *New York Times,* March 24, 1947, p. 19.

25. Edward W. Chester, *Radio, Television and American Politics,* Sheed and Ward, N.Y., 1969, p. 175.

26. *In Fact,* October 13, 1947.

27. Dozier Cade, *Journalism Quarterly,* Fall 1952, p. 404.

28. Friendly, *Due to ...,* p. 127.

29. *New York Times,* May 1, 1967, p. 29.

30. J.R. Freeman, *Columbia Journalism Review,* Summer 1969, p. 45; printed in *Harper's,* August, 1968; Chris Welles, *Columbia Journalism Review,* Fall 1969, p. 51.

31. *Chicago Journalism Review,* December 6, 1969, and March 1969, p. 7.

32. Alfred Balk, "Beyond Agnewism," *Columbia Journalism Review,* Winter 1969-70, p. 16.

33. Paul Eberle, *Los Angeles Free Press,* September 14, 20, and 27, 1968.

34. Hohenberg, *The News Media,* p. 143.

35. *Survey of Broadcast Journalism,* 1968-69, p. 15.

36. Hohenberg, *The News Media,* p. 73.

37. "Local 'Blackouts' on Public Affairs Television," *Columbia Journalism Review,* Spring 1962, p. 40.

38. *Survey of Broadcast Journalism,* 1968-69, p. 15.

39. ABC radio, Edward P. Morgan, October 10, 1960.

40. *New York Times,* May 25, 1960, p. 1.

41. *New York Times,* April 27, 1962, p. 71.

42. Friendly, *Due to . . .,* p. 135.

43. *Los Angeles Times,* Calendar, January 4, 1970, p. 1.

44. June 21, 1969, p. 1.

45. Dwight Whitney, *TV Guide,* July 4, 1970, p. 5.

46. Professor Glimcher as reported by Bernard H. Gould, *National Enquirer,* June 21, 1970, p. 12, confirmed by Glimcher in letter to author.

47. *Survey of Broadcast Journalism,* 1968-69, p. 12.

48. Ibid., p. 10.

49. Ibid., p. 68.

50. *Newsweek,* January 15, 1968, p. 46.

51. July 16, 1967.

52. *Chicago Journalism Review,* November 1969, p. 4.

53. Ibid.

54. See Chapter 21, Number 4, *On the Domestic Scene,* items 10, 11, and 12.

55. KPFK newscast.

56. Ibid., June 26, 1969.

CHAPTER 10 — FOOTNOTES

1. *Image Merchants,* Doubleday and Company, Inc., Garden City, N.Y., 1959, p 236.

2. *Columbia Journalism Review,* Summer 1968, p. 3.

3. Hohenberg, *The News Media,* p. 182.

4. Ibid., p. 185.

5. Peter Bart, "How to Read Financial Pages Without Going Broke," *Harpers,* August, 1963, pp. 31-35.

6. *Columbia Journalism Review,* Summer 1967, p. 36.

7. Ross, *Image Merchants,* p. 237.

8. Ben Bagdikian, "Journalist Meets Propagandist, *Columbia Journalism Review,* Fall 1963, pp. 29-35, 9, William Rivers, *Opinionmakers,* Beacon Press, Boston, 1965, p. 176.

10. Ernest Gruening, *The Public Pays,* Vanguard Press, Inc., N.Y., 1964, p. 81.

11. Ibid., p. 174.

12. Senator Lee Metcalf and Vic Reinemer, *Overcharge,* David McKay Company, Inc., N.Y., 1967, p. 139.

13. *Columbia Journalism Review,* Fall 1967, p. 56.

14. *Columbia Journalism Review,* Summer 1967, p. 36.

15. *Columbia Journalism Review,* Fall 1967, p. 67.

16. KPFK newscast, August 11, 1969, and *New York Times,* August 11, 1969.

17. *New York Times,* August 14, 1962, p. 5.

18. *New York Times,* May 10, 1969.

19. KPFK newscast, July 15, 1969.

20. KPFK newscast, July 17, 1969.

21. July 18, 1969.

22. *New York Times,* May 1, 1970, p. 21.

23. *New York Times,* September 10, 1964, p. 37.

24. *Fact,* November-December, 1966, pp. 18-27.

25. *Stars and Stripes,* Fulda, Germany, May 8, 1969, p. 7.

26. May 6, 1969.

27. September 13, 1969.

28. Nat Hentoff, *Columbia Journalism Review,* Fall 1969, p. 47.

29. KPFK newscast, July 28, 1969, *New York Times,* July 29, p. 1.

30. *Los Angeles Times,* July 28, 1969, p. 5.

31. Ibid.

32. *Survey of Broadcast Journalism,* 1968-69, p. 58.

33. *Hard Times,* September 19, 1969; *Life,* October 3, 1969, p. 62.

34. *International Herald Tribune,* April 19-20, 1969, p. 7.

35. *New York Times,* West Coast Edition, March 27, p. 7.

36. Dr. Edward Glick, "Health News," *Columbia Journalism Review,* Spring 1964, p. 29.

37. Ibid.

38. *Columbia Journalism Review,* Summer 1967, p. 36.

39. Metcalf, *Overcharge,* pp. 2-3.

40. Ibid., p. 260, and *Congressional Record,* April 7, 1965, p. 7285.

41. "Free Press and Fancy Packages," pp. 621-23.

42. *I. F. Stone's Weekly,* October 10, 1966, p. 4.

CHAPTER 11 — FOOTNOTES

1. Ross, *Image Merchants,* p. 177.

2. Sam Zagoria, "Equal Breaks for Labor News," *Columbia Journalism Review,* Fall 1967, p. 43.

3. Senate Committee on Commerce, Report 994, *Freedom of Information,* p. 534.

4. *Honolulu Star-Bulletin,* March 31, 1969.

5. MacNeil, *The People Machine,* p. 80.

6. George Seldes, *The Catholic Crisis,* Julian Messner, Inc., N.Y., 1939, passim.

7. Hohenberg, p. 168.

8. *Newsweek,* September 14, 1959, p. 94,

9. *Columbia Journalism Review,* Fall 1963, p. 30.

10. *I.F. Stone's Weekly,* May 24, 1967, p. 3.

11. *I.F. Stone's Weekly,* February 19, 1968, p. 4.

12. Ibid.

13. December 5, 1968, p. 2.

14. *New York Times,* November 30, 1968.

15. Armed Forces Newscast, Frankfurt, November 29, 1968.

16. April 10, 1969, and June 11, 1970.

17. *South Bay Daily Breeze,* January 13, 1970, p. 11.

18. NET, "Black Journal," August 30, 1969.

19. *Congressional Record,* October 15, E8502; quoted in *I.F. Stone's Weekly,* November 3, 1969.

20. "South Africa on Madison Ave.," October 1969, pp. 30-32.

21. KPFK newscast, July 28, 1969.

22. Ibid., July 30, 1969.

23. Ibid., August 12, 1969.

24. Ibid., August 4, 1969.

25. *New York Times,* July 11, 1969.

CHAPTER 12 – FOOTNOTES

1. Erwin Knoll, "The Coming Struggle for National Health Insurance," *Progressive,* December 1969, p. 30.

2. Sam Shapiro and others, *Infant, Prenatal, Maternal, and Childhood Mortality in the United States,* Harvard University Press, Cambridge, Mass., 1968, p. 162.

3. Ibid., p. 137.

4. Ben Bagdikian, "It Has Come to This," *Saturday Evening Post,* August 10, 1968, p. 21; the Department of Labor estimates the physician shortage to be 100,000, "Your Dollar's Worth," NET, Honolulu, April 29, 1970.

5. *Congressional Record,* July 13, 1950, p. 10117.

6. *New York Times,* August 17, 1950, p. 11.

7. Ibid., August 20, 1950, p. 11.

8. *Congressional Record,* August 30, 1950, p. 13911.

9. Ibid., p. 13904.

10. Ibid., p. 13912.

11. Ibid., pp. 13904-19.

12. *New York Times,* May 8, 1969.

13. *Los Angeles Times,* July 6, 1969.

14. *New York Times,* July 14, 1969, p. 1.

15. October 20, 1969.

16. Senate Committee on Commerce, Report 994, *Freedom of Communication,* p. 440.

17. *Los Angeles Times,* February 19, p. 2.

18. February 17, 1968

19. *National Enquirer,* October 27, 1968,

20. Taylor, *Biological Time Bomb,* p. 212.

21. Bernard D. Nossiter, *The Mythmakers,* Beacon Press, 1967, pp. 142-3.

22. *Los Angeles Times,* November 14, 1969, p. 1.

23. Ibid., November 19, 1969, p. 2.

24. *New York Times,* June 22, 1955, p. 30.

25. *International Herald Tribune,* March 7, 1969, p. 5.

26. Ruth Brindze, *Not To Be Broadcast,* Vanguard Press, Inc., New York, 1937, pp. 187-8.

27. Patricia and Ron Deutsch, "The Truth Can Stop VD," *Parents* magazine, January 1967, p. 57.

28. *New York Times,* October 29, p. 71.

29. Westinghouse Broadcasting Company, documentary series on venereal disease, 1966.

30. *New York Times,* September 9, 1962.

31. Ibid., August 5, 1965, p. 17.

32. Ibid., December 4, 1968, p. 35.

33. *New York Times,* April 11, 1961, p. 31.

34. Deutsch, *Parents,* January 1967, p. 59.

35. *New York Times,* December 13, 1964.

36. Dr. William F. Schwartz, WBC series on venereal disease, 1966.

37. Ibid.

38. Bill Davidson, "The Worst Jail I've Ever Seen," *Saturday Evening Post,* July 13, 1968, p. 17.

39. *International Herald Tribune,* March 7, 1969, p. 5.

40. *Time,* September 20, 1968.

41. *International Herald Tribune,* March 7, 1969, p. 5.

42. *New York Times,* March 6, p. 27.

43. *New York Times* magazine, May 11, 1952, p. 10.

44. *New York Times,* February 23, 1953, p. 31.

45. Ibid., March 3, p. 85.

46. *Los Angeles Times,* November 11, 1969, p. 6.

47. Ibid., November 14, 1969, p. 8.

48. *New York Times,* March 5, 1969, p. 23.

49. *Los Angeles Times,* January 2, 1970, p. 2.

50. *New York Times,* January 2, 1970, p. 17.

51. UPI, *Stars and Stripes,* Fulda, Germany, May 27, 1969, p. 5.

52. Ibid., June 8, 1969, p. 28.

53. Marvin Wagner, Nassau County traffic official, on CBS News, 8:00 a.m., PST, October 20, 1969.

CHAPTER 13 — FOOTNOTES

1. T. Peterson, J. Jenson, W. Rivers, *The Mass Media and Modern Society,* Holt, Rinehart and Winston, N.Y., 1965, p. 232.

2. Jacques Ellul, *Propaganda,* Alfred A. Knopf, N.Y., 1965, p. 46.

3. Viking Press, N.Y., 1948, p. 670.

4. *The Great Fear,* Collier Books, N.Y., 1965, p. 43.

5. Ibid., p. 183.

6. Drew Pearson and Jack Anderson, *The Case Against Congress,* Simon Schuster, N.Y., 1968, p. 431.

7. Ibid.

8. January 8, 1968.

9. *Journalism Quarterly,* Winter 1966, p. 627.

10. William McGaffin and Erwin Knoll, *Anything But the Truth,* G.P. Putnam's Sons, N.Y., p. 25.

11. *New York Times,* April 4, 1967, p. 87, cited in Hohenberg, *The News Media,* p. 9.

12. See Table VI.

13. MacNeil, *The People Machine,* p. 54.

14. July 9.

15. See Table VII.

16. Lyle, *The News in Megalopolis,* p. 87.

17. See Tables II and III.

18. George Turnbull Jr. "Reporting the War in Indo-China: A Critique," *Journalism Quarterly,* Winter 1957, p. 87.

19. September 26 to November 7, 1960.

20. "What the Readers See," *Columbia Journalism Review,* Spring 1962, p. 21.

21. "Health News," *Columbia Journalism Review,* Spring 1964, p. 29.

22. *Survey of Broadcast Journalism,* 1968-69, pp. 25-26.

23. *Columbia Journalism Review,* Winter 1967-68, p. 7.

24. *Los Angeles Times,* November 24, 1969, p. 4.

25. May 6, 1969.

26. *New York Times,* December 1, 1969.

27. *Survey of Broadcast Journalism,* 1968-69, pp. 17-18.

28. December 1, 1969.

29. *Los Angeles Times,* July 1, 1969, p. 6.

30. *New York Times,* July 1, 1969, p. 1.

31. Robert Lasch, "I See By the Papers," *Progressive,* November 1953, p. 18.

32. *Columbia Journalism Review,* Fall 1968, p. 30.

33. Senate Committee on Commerce, Report 994, *Freedom of Communication,* p. 402.

34. Ibid., p. 420.

35. November 4, 1969.

36. November 4, 1969.

37. October 30, 1960.

38. January 19, 1970.

39. Straus Editor's Report, June 13, 1969, as cited by Dale Minor, *The Information War,* Hawthorne Books, Inc., N.Y., 1970, p. 147.

40. July 8, 1969.

41. KPFK newscast, July 31, 1969.

42. KPFK newscast, July 31, 1969; *Los Angeles Times* and *New York Times,* August 1, 1969.

43. KPFK newscast, July 11, 1969.

44. KPFK newscast, December 9, 1969.

45. December 10, 1969.

46. *Providence Journal and Evening Bulletin,* October 6-8 and 13-16, 1958, reprinted in Reo M. Christenson and Robert O. McWilliams, eds., *Readings In Public Opinion and Propaganda,* McGraw Hill Co., Inc., N.Y., 1962, p. 149.

47. Ibid., p. 153.

48. Quoted in Paul L. Fisher and Ralph L. Lowenstein, eds., *Race and News Media,* Frederick A. Praeger, N.Y., 1967, p. 146.

49. June 25, 1969.

50. June 25, 1969.

51. November 11, 1969.

52. Howard K. Smith, "The Deadly Balance," *Columbia Journalism Review,* Fall 1965, p. 13.

53. "A Study of the 'Orthodox' Press," November 11, 1968, p. 2.

54. Bill Henry, *Honolulu Star Bulletin,* December 31, 1967.

55. Westinghouse Broadcasting Company, six-part radio documentary on venereal disease, 1966.

56. Friendly, Due to ..., p. 75.

57. Ibid.

58. MacNeil, *The People Machine,* p. 256.

59. Fisher and Lowenstein, *Race and News Media*, p. 66.

60. *New York Times*, December 17, 1967.

61. Nathan Blumberg, "A Study of the 'Orthodox' Press," *Montana Journalism Review*, No. 11, 1968, p. 2.

62. *New York Times*, November 2, 1968, p. 18.

63. September 20, 1968.

64. *New York Times*, September 20, 1968.

65. September 23, 1968, p. 6.

66. September 16, 1968, p. 15.

67. Percy H. Tannenbaum and Jean S. Kerrick, "Effect of Newscast Item Leads upon Listener Interpretation," *Journalism Quarterly*, Winter 1954, p. 37, and "The Effect of Headlines on the Interpretation of News Stories," *Journalism Quarterly*, Spring 1953, p. 189.

68. *New York Times*, June 19, 1952, p. 1.

69. *Columbia Journalism Review*, Winter 1967-68, p. 10.

70. Hohenberg, *The News Media*, p. 92; *New York Times*, August 10, 1966, p. 4.

71. September 21; *Progressive*, Nov. 1968.

72. *Los Angeles Times*, November 30, 1969, p. B:8.

73. NBC, *Huntley-Brinkley*, February 2, 1970.

74. Ehrlich, KPFK, January 4, 1970; Nelson, "The 'New Citizenship' for Survival," *Progressive*, April 1970, p. 53.

75. KHVH, February 24, 1968.

76. June 1, 1968, p. D:5.

77. June 25, 1968, p. 1.

78. August 12, 1969, p. 14.

79. March 23, 1969, p. 5.

80. December 12, 1969, p. IV:32.

81. *Media for the Millions*, Random House, N.Y., 1961, pp. 239-40.

82. Senate Committee on Commerce, Report 994, *Freedom of Information*, p. 47.

83. Ibid., p. 126.

84. Ibid., p. 124.

85. KGU, Honolulu, December 28, 1967.

86. "The News from Latin America," *Columbia Journalism Review*, Fall 1962, p. 49.

87. July 14, 1969.

88. Armed Forces Network, Frankfurt, October 29, 1968.

89. Ibid., June 6, 1969.

90. See Footnote 46.

91. "How *Time* Stereotyped Three U.S. Presidents," *Journalism Quarterly*, Autumn 1965, p. 563.

92. June 26, 1968.

93. Sandy Goldman, "Can *Newsweek* Really Separate Fact From Opinion?" *Columbia Journalism Review*, Summer 1968, p. 26.

94. Four U.S. correspondents, NET, January 8, 1968.

95. NBC, *Huntley-Brinkley*, January 6, 1970.

96. *Newsweek*, May 6, 1968, p. 104.

97. Senate Committee on Commerce, Report 994, *Freedom of Communication*, September 28, 1960, p. 78.

98. August 2, 1969.

99. *Time*, October 25, 1968, p. 56.

100. See Footnote 46, Chapter 10.

101. *Montana Journalism Review*, Number 11, 1968, p. 2.

102. November 11, 1969.

103. Quadrangle Books, Chicago, 1968, pp. 46-58.

104. *UCLA Alumni Magazine*, Fall 1968, p. 11.

105. T. Peterson and others, *Mass Media and Modern Society*, p. 210.

106. See Footnote 46, Chapter 10.

107. Rowse, *Slanted News*, p. 127.

108. September 15, 1967, pp. 22-26.

109. Hohenberg, *The News Media*, p. 127.

110. P. 66; *Newsweek*, December 25, 1967, p. 75.

111. Jean Kerrick, "The Influence of Captions On Picture Interpretation," *Journalism Quarterly*, Spring 1955, p. 177, and Reuben Mehling, "Attitude Changing Effect of News and Photo Combinations," *Journalism Quarterly*, Spring 1959, p. 189.

112. W.W. Norton and Company, Inc., N.Y., 1961, p. 50.

113. Goldman, *Columbia Journalism Review*, Summer 1968, p. 28; *Newsweek*, February 26, 1968.

114. September 27, 1968, p. 20.

115. September 23, 1968.

116. January 26, 1970.

117. October 25, 1968, p. 50.

118. January 19, 1968, p. 13.

119. February 23, 1968, p. 9.

120. "One Man's Meat: Chet Huntley's Special Interest," September, 1968, pp. 19-20.

121. "You Still May Be Eating Diseased and Dirty Meat," *Pageant* magazine, May 1968, p. 46.

122. *Los Angeles Times,* January 10, 1970, p. 8.

123. Gerassi, *The Great Fear,* p. 265.

124. July 3, 1968,

125. January 12, 1968.

126. Ibid.

127. May 18, 1968.

128. December 28, 1967.

129. January 11, 1968.

130. O'Hara, *Media for the Millions,* p. 230.

131. Senate Committee on Commerce, Report 994, *Freedom of Communication,* October 25, 1960.

132. Ibid., October 27, 1960, p. 877.

133. Ibid., October 26, 1960, p. 842.

134. Ibid., November 3, 1969.

135. Ibid., June 28, 1969.

136. CBS, *Walter Cronkite,* September 5, 1969.

137. Armed Forces Network, Newscast, Frankfurt, May 9, 1969.

138. NBC, *Huntley-Brinkley,* October 30, 1969.

139. June 2, 1968.

140. *Los Angeles Times,* November 30, 1969, p. B:8.

CHAPTER 14 — FOOTNOTES

1. Nathan Blumberg, *One Party Press*, University of Nebraska Press, 1954, p. 11.

2. *New York Times,* November 10, 1944, pp. 1, 11.

3. UPI, *Stars and Stripes,* Fulda, Germany, February 3, 1969, p. 8.

4. *Los Angeles Times,* January 15, 1970, p. 2, and October 28, 1970, p. 2.

5. MacNeil, *The People Machine,* p. 209.

6. Ross, *Image Merchants,* p. 265.

7. Public Affairs Press, 1965, Chapter 12.

8. *The Great Audience,* Viking Press, N.Y., 1950, p. 139.

9. Penguin Books, Baltimore, Maryland, 1963, p. 222.

10. Joseph Klapper, *The Effects of Mass Communications,* Free Press, N.Y., 1960, p. 95.

11. Ellul, *Propaganda,* p. 112.

CHAPTER 15 — FOOTNOTES

1. Ferdinand Lundberg, *The Rich and the Super Rich,* Lyle Stuart, 1968, pp. 144-63.

2. Ibid., p. 19.

3. Ibid., p. 21.

4. Ibid., p. 23.

5. Ibid., p. 24.

6. Ibid., p. 313.

7. *St. Louis Post Dispatch,* March 23, 1969, p. C:1, and March 24, 1969, p. B:14.

8. Prentice Hall, Inc., Englewood Cliffs, N.J., 1967, p. 94.

9. Ibid., p. 85.

10. Beacon Press, 1964, p. 40.

11. Domhoff, *Who Rules America?* p. 97.

12. Ibid., p. 99.

13. Ibid., pp. 127-8.

14. David Wise and Thomas Ross, *The Invisible Government,* Random House, 1964, p. 279, from "Issues and Answers," ABC, June 30, 1963.

15. Pyramid Books, N.Y., 1965, pp. 124-5.

16. Ibid., pp. 220-21.

17. *Los Angeles Times,* October 23, 1969, p. 5.

18. Pearson, *The Case Against Congress,* p. 95.

19. *Progressive,* February 1969, p. 6.

20. *I.F. Stone's Weekly,* December 30, 1968, p. 1.

21. UPI, *Stars and Stripes,* Fulda, Germany, January 21, 1969, p. 4.

22. NBC, "Face the Nation," July 7, 1969; *Congressional Record,* October 28, 1964, p. S13364.

23. ABC, "Issues and Answers," February 16, 1969.

24. Drew Pearson, *Los Angeles Times,* April 3, 1969, p. II:7.

CHAPTER 16 — FOOTNOTES

1. NBC, *Huntley-Brinkley,* July 9, 1969.

2. *Los Angeles Times* and *New York Times,* February 11, 1967.

3. "A Test of the News," *New Republic,* August 4, 1920, pp. 1-40.

4. "Soviet News in the *New York Times,"* *Public Opinion Quarterly,* Winter 1946-7, p. 540-61.

5. "All the News That's Fit to Print," *Commentary,* September 1965, p.33.

6. "The Influence of Media-Industry Ownership on the Performance of the Press: A Case Study," Unpublished Masters Thesis, Southern Illinois University, Carbondale, Illinois, 1967; summary in *Journalism Abstracts,* 1967-68, p. 141.

7. Robert Okey Young, "The Stassen Incident of the 1956 Campaign, A Case Study in Newspaper Political Tactics," Masters Thesis, UCLA, June 1958.

8. "Newspaper Gatekeepers and Forces in the News Channel," *Public Opinion Quarterly,* Spring, 1967, pp. 61-69.

9. Malcolm W. Klein and Nathan Maccoby, "Newspaper Objectivity in the 1952 Campaign," *Journalism Quarterly,* Summer 1954, p. 285.

10. *One Party Press,* 1953, pp. 45-46.

11. *Slanted News,* p. 127.

12. Bryce W. Rucker, "News Services Crowd Reporting in the 1956 Presidential Campaign," *Journalism Quarterly,* Spring 1960, pp. 195-198.

13. *Newsweek,* September 16, 1968, p. 67.

14. *Newsweek,* January 6, 1969, p. 43.

15. Ibid.

16. Simon and Schuster, N.Y., 1968, p. 162.

17. *New Republic,* November 22, 1969; *Progressive,* March 1970, p. 18.

18. "How Network Policy Imposes a TV Dim-Out on Democratic Leaders," *Democratic Digest,* May 1954, p. 21.

19. CBS, August 29, 1968.

20. *Survey of Broadcast Journalism,* 1968-69, p. 25; *Columbia Journalism Review,* Winter 1968-69, p. 3.

21. Neil Hickey, *TV Guide,* April 15, 1967.

22. *Columbia Journalism Review,* Fall 1965, p. 13.

23. MacNeil, *The People Machine,* p. 271.

24. William Bober, M.D., "We Should Legalize Abortion," *Saturday Evening Post,* October 8, 1966, p. 14, and Patricia Lockridge, "Abortion Is An Ugly Word," *Woman's Home Companion,* March 1947, p. 31.

25. Lawrence Lader, *Abortion,* Bobbs—Merrill, Co., Inc., N.Y., 1966, p. 3; Dr. Alan Guttmacher, M.D., *The Case for Legalized Abortion,* Diablo Press, Berkeley, Calif., 1967, p. 121.

26. Christopher Tietze, "Abortion as a Cause of Death," *American Journal of Public Health,* Vol. 38, No. 2 (October 1938), p. 1434; and Edwin M. Gold et al; "Therapeutic Abortions in New York City: A Twenty- year Review,"

Journal of Public Health, Vol. 55, No. 7 (July 1965), p. 964, as cited by Lader, *Abortion.* One New York study found that 90 per-cent of those dying from abortion were black or Puerto Rican, *New York Times,* December 8, 1969, p. 1.

27. *Time,* October 13, 1967, p. 22.

28. *National Enquirer,* January 25, 1970, p. 27.

29. An item which included an argument for legalization appeared on November 18, 1962, but was not included in the *Time's* yearly *Index,* so it is not included.

30. August 30, 1964.

31. *New York Times,* October 30, 1951, p. 18.

32. P. 68.

33. Guttmacher, *The Case for Legalized Abortion,* p. 35.

34. *Honolulu Advertiser,* March 9, 1972, P. C:1

35. Dale Minor, *The Information War,* Hawthorne Books, Inc., 1970, p. 118.

36. *New York Times,* February 12, 1949, p. 1.

37. Based on an estimate by Ernest Fitzgerald, ABC *Evening News,* November 5, 1969, and KPFK newscast, January 27, 1970; Senator William Proxmire estimates a minimum of $10 billion a year is being wasted.

38. See Footnote 11, Chapter 6.

39. See Footnote 30, Chapter 10.

40. John W. Finney, *International Herald Tribune,* April 12-13, 1969, p. 1.

41. NET, PBL, Honolulu, February 28, 1968.

42. Speech given October 23, 1969 to the United Aerospace Workers in Los Angeles, carried live on KPFK radio.

43. Skornia, *Television and Society,* pp. 95-97.

44. Eugene Paul, *The Hungry Eye,* Balantine Books, N.Y., 1962, p. 183.

CHAPTER 17 — FOOTNOTES

1. John Bainbridge, *New Yorker,* December 1, 1945, p. 40.

2. *Time,* February 2, 1967, p. 47, and Reo M. Christenson, "Report on the Reader's Digest," *Columbia Journalism Review,* Winter 1965, pp. 31-36.

3. P. 144.

4. *New York Times,* June 12, 1969, p. 1.

5. Ibid.

6. Favorable articles include those depicting U.S. missionaries and large Latin American corporations.

7. Quoted in Metcalf, *Overcharge,* p. 148.

8. Edison Electric Institute Bulletin, June 1961, pp. 184, 246-8, as quoted in Metcalf, *Overcharge,* p. 149.

9. Christenson, *Columbia Journalism Review,* Winter 1965, p. 33.

10. Bainbridge, *New Yorker,* December 1, 1945, p. 44.

11. *New York Times,* January 27, 1965, p. 1.

12. Warren Boroson, "The Pleasantville Monster," *Fact,* March-April 1966, p. 7.

13. *Columbia Journalism Review,* Winter 1967-68, p. 24.

14. Robert Shayon, *Saturday Review,* November 1969, pp. 48-49, and *Columbia Journalism Review,* Summer 1968, p. 3.

15. February 18, 1950, p. 157; *Reader's Digest,* February 1950, p. 1.

16. Boroson, *Fact,* March-April 1966, p. 26.

17. *Reader's Digest,* October, 1964; Christenson, *Columbia Journalism Review,* Winter 1965, pp. 31-32.

18. Boroson, *Fact,* March-April 1966, p. 3.

19. *Newsweek,* December 4, 1944, p 84

20. November 24, 1944.

21. Seldes, *Never Tire of Protesting,* pp. 82-92.

22. March 16, 1947.

CHAPTER 18 — FOOTNOTES

1. Bernard D. Nossiter, *The Mythmakers,* Beacon Press, Boston, 1967, p. 84.

2. H.L. Nieburg, *In the Name of Science,* Quadrangle, Chicago, 1966.

3. Ibid., p. 301.

4. Ibid., p. 301.

5. Ibid.

6. Lundberg, *The Rich and the Super Rich,* p. 377.

7. Ben Bagdikian, "Houston's Shackled Press," *Atlantic,* August 1966, p. 87.

8. Harper and Row, 1969, p. 96.

9. Ibid., p. 98.

10. Ibid., p. 66.

11. Ibid., p. 249.

12. Rucker, *First Freedom,* p. 125.

13. *Survey of Broadcast Journalism 1968-69,* p. 86.

14. *New York Times,* April 7, 1968, p. 68.

15. *Columbia Journalism Review,* Fall 1965, p. 34.

16. *TV Guide,* January 24, 1970.

17. *Survey of Broadcast Journalism 1968-69,* p. 30.

18. Donald R. Cressey, *Theft of A Nation,* Harper & Row, N.Y., 1969, p. 3.

19. Ibid., p. 253.

20. Ibid., p. XI.

21. Ibid., p. 3.

22. Pearson, *The Case Against Congress,* p. 427.

23. Barnouw, *Golden Web,* p. 175.

24. Senate Finance Committee, "Political Campaign Financing Proposals," 1967, p. 178, quoted in John Whale, *The Half Shut Eye,* Macmillan, St. Martins Press, 1969, p. 111.

25. *Los Angeles Times,* June 3, 1970, p. 24.

26. "Nixon, How the Press Suppressed the News." *New Republic,* October 6, 1952, p. 11.

27. *Slanted News.*

28. Pearson, *The Case Against Congress,* pp. 429-31.

29. Senate Committee on Commerce Report 994, *Freedom of Communication.*

30. "Further Notes on Dodd," *Columbia Journalism Review,* Summer 1967, p. 51.

31. "The Dodd Case, Loose Ends," *Columbia Journalism Review,* Summer 1968, pp. 55-57.

32. *Chicago Journalism Review,* June 1969, p. 3.

33. Sidney E. Zion, "Interest Conflict Laid to Jurist," *Scanlan's,* May 1970, pp. 10-16.

34. *New York Times,* May 18, p. 29.

35. Pearson, *The Case Against Congress,* p. 120.

36. Ibid., p. 123.

37. *Stars and Stripes,* Fulda, Germany, February 28, 1969, p. 24.

38. Excludes weekends and holidays.

CHAPTER 19 — FOOTNOTES

1. *Los Angeles Times,* December 28, 1968, p. 7.

2. Report of the Commission on National Goals, issued November 28, 1960.

3. Dwight Eisenhower, "Are We Headed in the Wrong Direction?," *Saturday Evening Post,* August 11, 1965, p. 24.

4. Seymour Melman, *Our Depleted Society,* Holt, Rinehart and Winston, N.Y., 1965, p. 96.

5. Nieburg, *In the Name of Science,* p. 179.

6. Bruce Ladd, *Crisis in Credibility,* New American Library, N.Y., 1968, p. 117.

7. P. 96.

8. Ladd, *Crisis in Credibility,* p. 117.

9. Statement made at North American Rockwell Corporation, October 1, 1969.

10. NBC, "Meet the Press," May 18.

11. KNBC-TV, Los Angeles, "Newsmakers," August 3, 1969.

12. Ladd, *Crisis in Credibility*, p. 121.

13. *Los Angeles Times*, October 9, 1969, p. 3.

14. Quoted by Lawrence Galton, "Will Space Research Pay Off on Earth?" *New York Times* magazine, May 26, 1963, p. 29; quoted in Nieburg, *In the Name of Science*, p. 76.

15. KNBC-TV Los Angeles, "Newsmakers," November 15, 1969.

16. Ladd, *Crisis in Credibility*, p. 125.

17. NBC, "Meet the Press," December 29, 1968.

18. Armed Forces Network Newscast, Frankfurt, February 24, 1969.

19. Ibid., July 21, 1969.

20. *Los Angeles Times*, July 22, 1969, p. 2.

21. August 4, 1969.

22. KPFK newscast, August 8, 1969.

23. July 21, 1969, p. 8.

24. August 13, 1969.

25. September 25, 1967.

26. July 16, 1969.

27. October 7, 1969.

28. KNX radio, Los Angeles, October 30, 1969.

CHAPTER 20 – FOOTNOTES

1. *New York Times*, December 30, 1968.

2. Ibid., May 14, 1967.

3. *Los Angeles Times*, June 10, 1969.

4. Richard Severo, *New Republic*, March 12, 1966, p. 29.

5. Quoted in *Population Bulletin*, December, 1969, p. 133, from *Science* magazine.

6. *Los Angeles Times*, February 3, 1970, p. 5.

7. *Population Bulletin*, December 1969, p. 134.

8. Editorial, May 6, 1969.

9. *Population Bulletin*, December 1969, p. 134.

10. Selection No. 31, January 1970.

11. October 7, 1969.

12. *San Francisco Chronicle*, October 7, 1969, p. 2.

13. November 8, 1969.

14. November 9, 1969.

15. See Footnote 26, Chapter 16.

16. George Seldes, *Catholic Crises*, Julian Messner, Inc., N.Y., 1939, p. 240.

17. Stanley Lowell, *The Hidden Wealth*, Americans United, Washington D.C., p. 3; from *Des Moines Sunday Register*, March 6, 1966, and *Our Sunday Visitor*, May 22, 1960.

18. *Vatican Empire*, Trident Press, N.Y., 1969, p. 135.

19. *New York Times*, July 13, 1968, p. 3.

20. *Honolulu Star-Bulletin*, July 21, 1970, p. 2.

21. Martin Larson and Stanley Lowell, *Praise the Lord for Tax Exemption*, Robert Luce Inc., Washington, D.C., 1969, pp. 187, 244.

22. *Der Spiegel*, April 30 and August 13, 1958 as cited in Martin Larson, *Church Wealth and Business Income*, Philosophical Library, N.Y., 1965, pp. 75-77.

CHAPTER 21 – FOOTNOTES

1. January 11, 1967, and February 7, 1968.

2. *The Village of Ben Suc*, Knopf, N.Y., 1967, and *The Military Half*, Knopf, N.Y., 1968.

3. *Los Angeles Times*, May 29, 1966, p. Outlook: 3.

4. *St. Louis Post Dispatch*, March 23, 1969, p. 2; later reports published by the *Los Angeles Times*, December 12, 1969, p. 6, and December 13, p. 26.

5. *New York Times*, May 11, 1966, p. 6, November 25, p. 42, and December 2, p. 3.

6. *New York Times*, January 27, 1970, p. 1; *Newsweek*, December 1, 1969, pp. 35-46.

7. *Columbia Journalism Review*, Winter 1969-70, p. 3; and Jon Unger, "The Press," *Scanlan's*, May 1970, p. 73.

8. Quoted by Richard L. Strout, *Christian Science Monitor*, November 24, 1969, p. 1, and Kenneth Reich, *Los Angeles Times*, November 26, 1969, p. 11.

9. Quoted in the *Washington Post*, as noted in a UPI release, *Los Angeles Times*, December 11, 1969, p. IX:8.

10. *The Artillery of the Press*, Harper & Row, N.Y., 1967, p. 108.

11. Quoted by Neal D. Houghton, "The Cuban Invasion and the Press," *Journalism Quarterly*, Spring 1965, p. 427.

12. *New York Times*, June 2, 1969, p. 14.

13. April 7, 1961, p. 2.

14. Ladd, *Crisis in Credibility,* p. 34.

15. McGaffin, *Anything But the Truth,* p. 179.

16. *New York Times,* June 2, 1969, p. 14.

17. *A Citizen's Dissent,* Fawcett Publications, Greenwich, Conn., 1966, p. 18.

18. Ibid., p. 19.

19. Ibid., p. 42.

20. Ibid., p. 48.

21. *Los Angeles Free Press,* July 12, 1968. (The *New York Times* published its review shortly after on July 14, 1968.)

22. Ibid.

23. *New York Times,* February 7, p. 2.

24. February 7, 1969, in *Stars and Stripes,* Fulda, Germany, February 9, 1969, p 24.

25. February 22, 1969, in *Stars and Stripes,* Fulda, Germany, February 23, 1969, p. 5.

26. March 4, 1969, in Ibid., March 6, 1969, p. 6.

27. March 23, 1969, in Ibid., March 24, 1969, p. 4.

28. March 26, 1969, in Ibid., March 28, 1969, p. 2, *Los Angeles Times* had a two-inch article about Senator Fulbright's argument, but did not mention Symington or Gore.

29. April 4, 1969, in Ibid., April 6, 1969, p. 6.

30. April 30, 1969, in *New York Times,* May 1, 1969, p. 21.

31. May 1, 1969, in *Stars and Stripes,* Fulda, Germany, May 3, 1969, p. 7.

32. *Washington Post,* June 1, 1969, p. 1.

33. June 9, 1969, Armed Forces Network Newscast of June 11, 1969.

34. Ibid., February 9, 1967, p. 4.

35. Ibid., May 17, 1967, p. 3.

36. Ibid., May 14, 1967, p. 9.

37. *I.F. Stone's Weekly,* June 19, 1967.

38. *New York Times,* March 26, 1968, p. 1.

39. Ibid., June 29, p. 3.

40. *Stars and Stripes,* Fulda, Germany, December 16, 1968, p. 3.

41. *New York Times,* May 1, 1969, p. 16.

42. *I.F. Stone's Weekly,* May 1, 1967.

43. Ibid., April 3, 1967, from *Le Monde,* March 23.

44. Ibid., April 3, 1967.

45. Ibid., May 15, 1967.

46. Ibid., July 17, 1967, p. 3, from the York Pennsylvania *Gazette and Daily.*

47. Ibid., December 18, from the *London Times,* December 4, 1967.

48. *Honolulu Star-Bulletin,* September 18, 1969, p. 14.

49. KPFK newscast, December 12, 1969.

50. Ibid., December 19, 1969, quotes taken from Wilfred Burchett's coverage of the same news conference in Paris, *Guardian,* February 7, 1970, p. 13.

51. *San Francisco Chronicle,* October 8, 1969, p. 16.

52. *Los Angeles Times,* September 18.

53. KNX newscast, November 24, 1969.

54. KPFK newscast.

55. Ibid.

56. Ibid.

57. *Survey of Broadcast Journalism,* 1968-69, p. 3.

58. *Newsweek,* December 6, 1965, p. 90.

59. *New York Times,* March 27, 1942, p. 1; March 28, 1942, p. 1; June 1, 1942, p. 1.

60. *Los Angeles Times,* December 21, 1969, p. III:9, February 19, 1970, p. 19, and March 13, 1970, p. 1.

61. *New York Times,* April 11, 1949, p. 4.

62. Metcalf, *Overcharge,* pp. 111, 178.

63. Ibid., pp. 3, 138.

64. Ibid., p. 104, also quoted in the *Congressional Record,* August 6, 1958, pp. A7047-8.

65. Ibid., p. 100.

66. *Columbia Journalism Review,* Winter 1967-68, p. 10.

67. "Censorship of Advertising," *Fact,* July-August 1967.

68. *In Fact,* July 4, 1949.

69. *Never Tire of Protesting,* p. 27, and *In Fact,* July 9, 1945.

70. *Chicago Journalism Review,* November 1969, p. 7.

71. Don Irwin, *Los Angeles Times,* February 23, 1970.

72. Barnouw, *The Golden Web,* pp. 254-272.

73. William Morrow and Co., N.Y., 1964, p. 238.

74. Ibid., pp. 244, 246.

75. Ibid., p. 250.

76. Barnouw, *The Golden Web,* pp. 279, 256.

77. *Open Letter From a Television Viewer,* Heineman Paperback, 1968, p. 104.

78. *Los Angeles Times,* February 17, 1969, p. IV:26.

79. UPI, *Stars and Stripes,* Fulda, Germany, June 12, 1969, and *Look,* June 24, 1969.

80. *Honolulu Star-Bulletin,* September 14, 1967.

81. *Los Angeles Free Press,* March 21, 1969, p. 14.

82. AP, *Stars and Stripes,* Fulda, Germany, April 6, 1969, p. 7.

83. *Censorship Today,* February-March 1969, p. 50.

84. UPI, *Stars and Stripes,* Fulda, Germany, June 12, 1969, and *Look,* June 24, 1969.

85. *Censorship Today,* October-November 1969, p. 63.

86. *Los Angeles Times,* December 31, 1969, p. 10.

87. O'Hara, *Media for the Millions, p. 85.*

88. *Newsweek,* July 22, 1968, p. 52.

89. Ibid.

CHAPTER 22 — FOOTNOTES

1. "Access to the Press — A New First Amendment Right," *Harvard Law Review,* June 1967, p. 1641, and "An Emerging First Amendment Right of Access to the Media?" *George Washington Law Review,* March 1969, p. 487.

2. *New York Times,* June 10, 1969, p. 1.

SOURCES FOR QUOTES IN CHAPTER HEADINGS

Introduction. Peterson and others, *The Mass Media and Modern Society,* p. 346.

1. *A Free and Responsible Press,* p. 3.

2. ABC newscast, June 16, 1967, quoted in *Columbia Journalism Review,* Summer 1967, p. 25.

90. *Los Angeles Times,* February 9, 1972, p. 5

3. Frank L. Mott, *Jefferson and the Press,* Louisiana State University Press, 1964, p. 55.

4. Irving and Harriet Deer, eds., *Languages of Mass Media,* Heath, Lexington, Mass., 1965, p. 8.

5. Quoted in Barron, "Right of Access to the Media," *George Washington Law Review,* March 1969, p. 11.

6. *Los Angeles Times,* November 21, 1969, p. 8.

7. *War and Peace in the Global Village,* Bantam, 1968, p. 18.

8. Charles R. McCabe, ed., *Damned Old Crank,* Harper & Brothers, N.Y., 1951, p. 146.

9. No. 12, 1969, p. 57.

10. Friendly; *Due to . . .,* p. 267.

11. *The Popular Arts,* Hutchinson, London, 1964, p. 365.

12. Peterson, *The Mass Media and Modern Society,* p. 239.

13. *ASNE Bulletin,* April 1962, p. 3.

14. Peterson: *The Mass Media . . .,* pp. 24-5; Shirer: *Los Angeles Times,: March 13, 1970, p. II:1.*

15. George Seldes, *The Great Quotations,* Lyle Stuart, 1958, p. 222.

16. *Harper's,* April 1965, p. 49.

17. Ruth S. Knowles, *Reader's Digest,* February 1969, inside cover.

18. *Chicago Journalism Review,* March 1969, p. 8.

19. *New York Times,* July 16, 1969.

21. Ladd, *The Crisis in Credibility,* p. 218.

22. Lederer: *Nation of Sheep,* p. 52; Darrow: Harold A. Innis, *The Bias of Communication,* 2nd ed., University of Toronto Press, 1964, p. 187.

About the Author

Robert Cirino was born in San Fernando, California. Prior to teaching in secondary schools, he worked as a truck driver and merchant seaman. In 1962 he received a Bachelor of Arts degree in social sciences with emphasis in anthropology and history from San Fernando Valley State College. He received a teaching credential from San Diego State College in 1965, and a Master of Secondary Education degree from the University of Hawaii in 1968.